PROFILES IN POWER

FOCUS ON AMERICAN HISTORY SERIES

EDITED BY DON CARLETON

PROFILES IN POWER

TWENTIETH-CENTURY TEXANS
IN WASHINGTON
New Edition

Edited by

KENNETH E. HENDRICKSON JR.

MICHAEL L. COLLINS

PATRICK COX

University of Texas Press

AUSTIN

LIBRARY OF CONGRESS CATALOGING-IN-PUBLICATION DATA

Profiles in power : twentieth-century Texans in Washington / edited by Kenneth E.
Hendrickson, Jr., Michael L. Collins, Patrick Cox.—New ed.
    p.   cm. — (Focus on American history series)
Includes bibliographical references and index.
    ISBN 0-292-70240-X (pbk. : alk. paper)
    1. Legislators—Texas—Biography.   2. Politicians—Texas—Biography.
3. United States—Politics and government—20th century.   I. Hendrickson,
Kenneth E.   II. Collins, Michael L., 1950–   III. Cox, Patrick, 1952–
IV. Series.
    F385.P76   2004
    973.91′092′2764—dc22

                                                          2003020822

CONTENTS

INTRODUCTION

BY MICHAEL L. COLLINS

Texans have long wielded a disproportionate influence in national and international affairs. It is an undeniable fact. From the days of President Woodrow Wilson and World War I, when a "new world order" was taking shape, to the administration of President George W. Bush and the War on Terror, leaders from the Lone Star State have played prominent roles in affecting the course of modern American history, both at home and on the world stage.

As early as 1913, a Texas power elite emerged in the nation's capital, with Colonel Edward House, once labeled the "little gray man" from Austin, establishing himself as President Wilson's most intimate adviser, and three Texan members of House's inner circle accepting appointments to the cabinet—Secretary of Agriculture David Houston, Postmaster General Albert Sidney Burleson, and Attorney General Thomas Watt Gregory. Following World War I, the Texas congressional delegation slowly emerged as arguably the most powerful on Capitol Hill. In time, owing to both the seniority system and the patience and persistence of the irascible Speaker of the House and later vice president John Nance Garner (he said once that the vice presidency was not "worth a quart of warm piss"), an entire generation of Texas politicians rose through the ranks of the House of Representatives. By 1933, no less than eight representatives from Texas chaired major standing committees in the House, thus allowing the Lone Star bloc to handle and therefore influence virtually every piece of President Franklin Delano Roosevelt's New Deal legislation. During the desperate years of the Great Depression, Vice President Garner ("Cactus Jack") surfaced as one of FDR's most stubborn critics, while Garner's pupil, Representative Sam Rayburn, ascended as one of Roosevelt's most loyal and effective lieutenants in the Congress, first as House majority leader, then as Speaker of the House. At the same time, another Texan, Houston financier Jesse H. Jones, the powerful head of the Reconstruction Finance Corporation, towered over the federal establishment as one of the czars of the New Deal. So influential was the RFC chairman in directing billions of dollars of federal funds that Secretary of Agriculture Henry Wallace once called him "the second most powerful man in Washington." On the eve of World War II, as issues of world peace and national defense intensified in significance, the state's two senators chaired two of the most important committees in the upper house—Tom Connally (Foreign Relations) and Morris Sheppard (Armed Services).

Following World War II, Texans continued to exercise an enormous influence in the back rooms and corridors of Congress. While the shrewd and sagacious Rayburn—a masterful parliamentarian and a brilliant cloakroom diplomat—ruled the House as Speaker longer than anyone in U.S. history, his ambitious protégé, Lyndon Baines Johnson, was rising to the position of Senate majority leader, all the while learning well from "Mr. Sam" both the written and the unwritten rules of legislative strategy. During the Cold War decade of the 1950s, the personal and political partnership between the two Texans produced one of the most powerful and fruitful alliances in the history of the U.S. Congress. Together, Rayburn and Johnson reigned like lords on Capitol Hill during the presidency of Dwight Eisenhower.

Of course, the domination of these two giants from Texas over the institutions of Congress was no simple accident of the seniority system. The tremendous clout that they wielded was a reflection of the growth and maturity of Texas as a major economic force within the United States. With the emergence of the powerful oil and natural gas interests, the increasing importance of Texas-based commercial and industrial aviation, and the growing influence of defense industries in Texas, the economic well being of the Lone Star State became inexorably linked with the prosperity and security of the entire nation.

Perhaps it was altogether fitting that the brash and grasping figure of Lyndon Johnson came to symbolize, indeed to personify the rich and powerful state he represented. For in many ways his ascendance to the presidency typified Texas's rise to "superstate" status. No one, not even those who despised LBJ, could deny that he embodied the same characteristics that made so many Americans admire and so many others loathe Texas. Nor could anyone deny that the Great Society programs marked, for better or for worse, a major milestone in the making of modern America. Even today, the long shadow of Lyndon Johnson still looms over Texas politics and over those who represent Texans in Washington. His legacy—both the War on Poverty and the wrenching conflict in Vietnam—still profoundly affects our national life.

It may be true that as Texas's economic clout diminished in the 1980s so too did the influence of the state in national affairs. The Senate rejection of President George Bush's nomination of John Tower for secretary of defense; the resignation of Speaker of the House Jim Wright amid a firestorm of allegations regarding alleged violations of House ethics rules; the free fall and defeat of George Bush following the Persian Gulf War; the termination of defense contracts so vital to Texas; the closing of military installations, such as Carswell Air Force Base in Fort Worth—all seemingly reinforced the argument that Texans no longer represented the epicenter of national power.

But it was likely that these developments were simply the result of national and even global trends. Whether it was the swift and unexpected conclusion of the Cold War, the alarming decline in America's industrial base, the dizzying escalation of the national debt and the resulting reassessment of all federal spending, or the acrid, stridently partisan political climate that contributed to the loss of public confidence in "the system," the Texas experience seemed to parallel the national experience.

The events of the past two years have proved that those pundits who predicted the demise of Texas's influence in the national arena were at best premature in their forecast. With Governor George W. Bush's election to the presidency in 2000, albeit in a bitterly disputed contest that concluded with the now-infamous Florida recount, yet another Texan assumed the nation's highest office. But the case could be made that the incoming Bush team, which included longtime personal friend and confidant Don Evans in the office of secretary of commerce, resembled past Republican administrations more than a Lone Star cast of players.

In 1961 author John Bainbridge commented that, in many respects, "the epitome of America is Texas." He even observed that the Lone Star State is a "little civilization—the United States in microcosm." Although his study, entitled *The Super-Americans,* focused mainly on Texas millionaires, moguls, wildcatters, and wheeler-dealers, the book's thesis deserves to be restated here. To be sure, while in some ways Texas is unique among all the states (some might even use the word "peculiar") in that it is both southern and western in character, it is in many respects a mirror, albeit an oftentimes exaggerated image, of the larger American Republic.

In the following fourteen biographical essays the reader will glimpse the central themes running through twentieth-century America: the trials and lessons of two world wars; the "noble experiment" of prohibition (Senator Sheppard authored the Eighteenth Amendment); the ordeal of the Great Depression, and the New Deal, which changed America forever; the transition from a rural to an urban society; the chilling tensions of the Cold War; the national soul-searching experience of the war in Vietnam; the agonizing struggle for racial justice and human dignity during the civil rights movement; the trauma of Watergate (who could ever forget the inspirational words of Houston congresswoman Barbara Jordan, who spoke so eloquently about a "government of laws, not of men"?).

The following portraits of Texans in Washington also reflect major currents in modern Texas history. The rise and recent decline of the powerful petrochemical industry; the brawling and oftentimes gaudy nature of Texas politics; the emergence of a two-party state (in 1961 John Tower became the first Republican to be elected to a statewide office since Reconstruction); an agrarian society giving way to the white-collar culture of today; the tug-of-war between the state's populist and progressive political traditions on the one hand and what some like to define as Texas's "conservative" heritage on the other (the career of Ralph Yarborough underscores this ongoing battle for the political soul of Texas): these threads are woven into the fabric of Texas and into the lives and careers of the fourteen leaders from the Lone Star State represented in this book.

For some inexplicable reason, people from throughout the United States have always exhibited a particular fascination with Texas. Maybe the almost mythical qualities of the state explain that powerful allure. Perhaps it is the vast and diverse land, the rich and magnificent heritage, and the seemingly larger-than-life individuals who have produced so many popular legends. Novelist John Steinbeck said it best:

> I have said that Texas is a state of mind, but I think that it is more than that. It is a mystique closely approximating a religion. And it is true to the extent that people either passionately love Texas or passionately hate it and, as in other religions, few people dare to inspect it for fear of losing their bearings in mystery or paradox.

This book was designed to supplement any Texas or U.S. history text and to provide an excellent core or corollary text in specialized courses in political science. Furthermore, this book was produced to appeal to general readers in the Lone Star State and the United States. So whether you love Texas "with a passion," or just "love to hate it," the following essays will illuminate the Texas experience and cast additional light upon the story of twentieth-century America.

Despite George Bush's defeat in the 1992 presidential election, Texans continued to play vitally important roles in shaping national policy in the administration of President Bill Clinton. Former Chairman of the National Democratic Party Robert Strauss of Dallas served as ambassador to the former Soviet republics; longtime federal Judge William Sessions of San Antonio continued for a time as director of the Federal Bureau of Investigation; Senator Lloyd M. Bentsen Jr., arguably one of the most respected elder statesmen on Capitol Hill, assumed the post of secretary of the treasury; and former San Antonio mayor Henry Cisneros headed the Department of Housing and Urban Development, at least until personal and public scandal ended his political career. It could even be argued persuasively that the meteoric rise of Dallas billionaire Ross Perot as a formidable independent candidate in the 1992 presidential campaign contributed to a Clinton victory (Perot garnered 19 percent of the popular vote, and many of his supporters were purported to be independents, "Reagan Democrats," or disillusioned Republicans who defected from the Bush camp).

Eight years later, when George W. Bush prevailed in the contested "overtime" recount in Florida by some 900 votes, and in the largely partisan legal battle waged in the United States Supreme Court by a mere two votes, he became the first governor of Texas to attain the presidency. Thus, following one of the most dramatic electoral "cliffhangers" in United States history, he entered the presidency under less than auspicious circumstances. But not even his harshest Democratic detractors (who refer to him as "George II" and "Dubya") can deny that the horrific attacks of September 11, 2001, and the ensuing War on Terror have placed the Midland native in the center of one the greatest national crises in modern American history. Only time will provide testimony to his achievements, or lack of success, in meeting the challenges of the new millennium. The opportunities for greatness and the prospects for failure both lie before him and the country. And contemporary opinion matters little when viewed through the long-range lens of history.

In sum, if the American odyssey is, in the words of FDR, a "story without an end," so too is the story of Texans in Washington. Readers might question why this collection of essays did not include former secretary of state James Baker, former ambassador Robert Strauss, or former senator Phil Gramm. Or for that matter, former secretary of the navy, secretary of the treasury, and governor John B. Connally, a genuine Texas legend in his own right; or long-standing chairman of the House Banking Committee, the combative Wright Patman. We make no claim that the fourteen individuals included in this book compose a definitive list of the "most important" Texans who have served in Washington in the twentieth century. What we do contend, however, is that, in each case, they made major and sometimes colossal contributions to the development of the United States. Their stories presented here, it should be remembered, are selective biographical profiles — profiles in power.

this guy has to be from Texas!

PROFILES IN POWER

EDWARD M. HOUSE

Fig. 1.1. Colonel Edward House, who rose to national influence as political power broker and chief adviser to Texas governors and ultimately to President Woodrow Wilson. Prints and Photographs Collection, Center for American History, UT-Austin (CN 01036).

EDWARD M. HOUSE

BY ROBERT C. HILDERBRAND

Colonel Edward M. House (the title "Colonel" was not military but honorific) holds an unusual place in American political history. Although he served in no official capacity except as one of the United States commissioners to the Paris Peace Conference of 1919, his influence in Texas, national, and international politics is as widely recognized by historians as it was in his own time. In simplest terms he was an "adviser," the amateur prototype of the political professionals who came to dominate American politics during the second half of the twentieth century. In developing this role he displayed skill as a political and diplomatic strategist that impressed the national and world leaders of his time. On a deeper level, House's influence grew out of his talent for friendship, for granting and receiving confidences, for making the voices of sympathy and wisdom sound harmonious in his advice. He was a friend to four Texas governors, and his close personal relations with President Woodrow Wilson developed into the most famous friendship in the history of American politics.

House was born in Houston in 1858, the seventh son of a wealthy cotton planter and exporter. Although of dubious value as recollection, the memoirs he wrote of his childhood and youth sketch out the forces that shaped his developing personality.

One such force was a sense of place, of a Texas large with opportunity, which produced in House a desire for a personal greatness and the power to control the land's vast potential. Yet for House this ambition seemed always undermined by the burden of the greatness of his father's generation. It was not just their deeds, their successful forging of a republic, their victories over nature, Indians, and Mexicans that overwhelmed the young House, but the force and power of their personalities. House naturally focused on his father T. W., his "masterful father," as he described him in his "Memories" of 1929, and felt keenly the impossibility of matching up to the elder House and his generation of Texans. These conflicting feelings of ambition and inadequacy may have caused House to seek the influence he desired outside of public office, perhaps fearing that the limelight, in which his father's generation had basked easily, would reveal his own weakness and unworthiness for power.[1]

For whatever reason, the young House turned his attention away from mastery and toward manipulation, particularly as it involved the control of other men. During House's childhood, and continuing through his collegiate years at Cornell University, this interest often took the form of practical jokes, sometimes subtle and elaborate in nature, through which House was able to control the emotions and behavior of his classmates without exercising the more orthodox forms of leadership. Not surprisingly, considering his developing personality, House was drawn to politics as an avocation. He described in his "Reminiscences" of 1916 how political interest had taken over his life as a result of his fascination with the manipulations surrounding the disputed Hayes-Tilden election of 1876. Although House's account of this "calling" seems dramatized and ascribes to himself more clarity of vision than was likely in an eighteen-year-old boy, it reveals a good deal about his motives for pursuing the role of adviser and working behind the scenes in politics. "I had no ambition to hold office," he wrote, "nor had I any ambition to speak because I felt in both instances that I would fall short of the first place, and nothing less than that would satisfy me."[2]

Before House could embark on any sort of political career, however, he was rocked by the illness and death of his father. House left Cornell in the fall of 1879 to help care for the ailing T. W. and was emotionally unable to return following his father's death in 1880. Fifty years later House recalled that "his death left me adrift." It was in this period of grief and indecision that House met Loulie Hunter, the beautiful daughter of a wealthy and respected Texas family. They were married in August 1881. During the next few years House and his new wife settled into Houston society, while House managed the widespread landholdings left by his father's estate. In 1885 they moved to Austin, apparently for business reasons. Although he had expressed no interest in local or state politics before, House became engrossed in the political life of the capital. He gradually found outlets there for the personal and political skills he had been cultivating and began to create a life for himself beyond the long shadow cast by his father. "It may be," House wrote in 1929, "that my entire life was changed by this move."[3]

House entered politics in a serious way as a result of his friendship with Governor James Stephen Hogg. In 1892 Hogg, who was facing a stiff fight within the Democratic Party for renomination and reelection, convinced House to serve as his unofficial campaign manager. The success of this campaign drew House deeply into Texas politics for a decade. After Hogg retired from political life in 1895, House managed the campaigns of and formed political friendships with the next three Democratic governors — Charles A. Culberson, Joseph D. Sayers, and Samuel W. T. Lanham. At this time House's interest seems to have been focused more on the mechanics than on the substance of politics. He was a traditional gold-standard Democrat, not an early Texas progressive, and although he supported the reforms of the Hogg administration, he did not have an agenda for change of his own. Six years later, in constructing the successful campaign of Joseph Sayers, he helped to defeat the gubernatorial candidacy of the legitimate heir to the Hogg reform tradition, who had, to his misfortune, neglected to ask the Colonel for help. The evidence suggests that House took his pleasure from the contest and from the sense of power that came with victory, rather than from the opportunity to embody any political program.[4]

House's fascination with the processes of Texas politics helped him to develop into a master of manipulation. Working mostly behind the scenes, he maneuvered among the diverse factions of the Democratic Party, used his charm to create a group of loyal supporters, and, most important, learned how to manipulate the state's peculiar primary system to his candidate's advantage. Although House later tried to picture himself in his Texas years as a political reformer who operated in accordance with progressive, good-government principles, there was something of the Boss in the way he worked his political machine. He allied himself with those who controlled the votes of notoriously corrupt counties in South Texas, played fast and loose with the workings of the wide-open Democratic primary, and even bought votes—all, to be sure, in a soft-spoken, genteel manner.[5]

Eventually, House grew restless in state politics. "I had," he wrote, "grown thoroughly tired of the position I occupied in Texas." He was also being urged to run for the governorship in 1902, something that he would not consent to do. By then, House was spending more of his time away from Austin, summering in Massachusetts and establishing another residence near the nation's cultural center, New York City. He dreamed of finding a way to employ his political talents on a national level, to play the role he had developed in Texas in the wider arena of national politics. But he was frustrated by the Democratic Party's preoccupation with William Jennings Bryan and the issues he raised. In 1908, when Bryan brought the Democrats their fourth consecutive defeat in a presidential election, House was fifty years old and felt himself a failure. Despite his wealth and his place in Texas politics, the reality of his life failed to match his boyhood dreams of power and influence. He thus began, as he put it, "to look about" for a candidate to befriend and influence and accompany to a position of national prominence.[6]

On November 24, 1911, House met Woodrow Wilson for the first time.

By then, House had decided that Wilson was the Democratic candidate most likely to succeed in winning the presidency for his party in 1912 and wanted to make a personal assessment. After an hour and a half of conversation, House knew that he had found his candidate. He wrote to his *letter* brother-in-law, Sidney E. Mezes, with whom he shared his political fantasies, that "it is just such a chance as I have always wanted for never before have I found both the man and the opportunity." Although House and Wilson felt a sort of magnetic attraction to each other, their friendship would take a year to develop. Shortly after their initial meeting, House returned to Texas, where he lobbied for Wilson's candidacy but played no significant role in his eventual nomination. When the Wilson movement faltered in the early summer of 1912, House sought to distance himself from the possibility of defeat, and on June 25, the first day of the Baltimore convention, where his candidate would need all the support he could muster, he left for a two-month tour of Europe, ostensibly for his health. *first we hear of it*

House's preoccupation with his health frequently affected his behavior, especially at critical moments in his life. It was the reason he gave for refusing to run for governor of Texas in 1902. It would also, in the years that followed his absence at the moment of decision in the summer of 1912, frequently keep him away from Wilson during periods of tension and crisis. House attempted in his "Memories" to explain the origin of the problem. At age eleven or twelve, he wrote, he had fallen from a swing, injured his head, contracted malaria, and nearly died. The experience left him lacking in stamina and unable to tolerate strains, particularly when accompanied by the summer heat of Austin, or later, Washington, D.C. House's concern with his health, although authentic enough, was exaggerated by a neurotic fear of death. It also gave him a physical reason to back up his emotional inability to risk himself openly in the political arena by playing any role other than that of adviser. House thus constructed and employed a myth of frailty to free himself from the burden of the kind of responsibility that he believed his personality was too brittle to bear. He also used it, more directly, to avoid scenes and situations he knew he would not enjoy or could not control, such as the Baltimore convention, and to earn sympathy from those with whom he shared the details of his malady.[8]

House's description of his physical condition had an effect on Wilson, who had health concerns of his own, with the result that one basis for their friendship was a kind of shared hypochondria. There were other, more important, bases as well, which emerged as their relationship developed in the months following Wilson's election. House was, to say the least, ingratiating: he flattered Wilson, echoed his sentiments, never openly disagreed, and asked nothing for himself. His gentleness of manner, amounting to almost a complete lack of masculine assertiveness, also appealed to Wilson, as it did to many others who sought the Colonel's advice and friendship. Politically, House's talents complemented Wilson's perfectly. The president's greatest skills were rhetorical, House's were political; the president was happiest alone and thinking, House was happiest in conference, talking. House willingly shouldered the burdens of the presidency that Wilson found most odious, making himself into a much-needed buffer between the president and the everyday world of politics. Above all, House was trustworthy; the value of both his advice and his friendship depended upon his complete lack of self-interest, which inspired Wilson's confidence and liberated his facility for emotional attachment.[9]

During the campaign of 1912 House published *Philip Dru: Administrator,* a utopian novel that revealed both his high ambition and his aversion to electoral politics and officeholding. Philip Dru, the book's main character, serves as a sort of literary alter ego for House. After preparing for a military career, Dru suffers an eye injury that turns him in the direction of a life of service to others. As leader of an insurrection, he is proclaimed "Administrator of the Republic" and uses his unanimous popularity to reform the nation's economic and political life. Then, at the peak of his personal power, he leaves the country to travel anonymously (but not before successfully proposing marriage to the woman he loves). Throughout the book, Dru's career is an idealized version of House's, and Dru himself ultimately exercises the kind of power without accountability to which House aspired.[10]

More complex, but no less revealing, is the character of Senator Selwyn, the novel's evil genius who also resembles House in important ways. They share the same sort of political ambitions, and Selwyn succeeds, at least for a time, in fulfilling House's dream of electing a president that he can control from behind the scenes. That Selwyn is destroyed by his success might tell us something about House's inner doubts about himself, especially considering that the cause of Selwyn's destruction is his use of the same sort of tactics that House had employed in Texas. There is, in addition, considerable admiration in House's description of Selwyn's handling of the campaign that brings his candidate to the presidency. To focus his party's efforts, Selwyn divides the electorate into manageable districts and concentrates attention on states in which the outcome is most uncertain — exactly the strategy that House would urge on Wilson in 1916. House's two visions of his own political personality are unified later in the novel when Dru, already in power, discovers that he likes Selwyn and explains his misbehavior as the product of the corrupt political system that spawned him.[11]

Philip Dru: Administrator also expressed House's desire for a moral regeneration to provide a new basis for American life. Economically, this regeneration would result in a kind of socialism that recognized the shared humanity of all, including the workers and the poor; politically, it would produce a renewed interest in public service and good government. In *Philip Dru*, House displayed no particular fondness for democracy or electoral politics, which he characterized as too easily manipulated by unscrupulous politicians and businessmen. Nor did he think much of the separation of powers, which in his view was used to thwart the will of the people. House was no Madisonian who thought that the powers of government must be divided and controlled; he preferred to put his faith in a spiritual transformation that would make such limitations unnecessary.[12]

House and Wilson drew closer together after the latter's election to the presidency in November 1912. Although he had played only a minor role in the presidential campaign, House quickly emerged as a key figure in Wilson's circle of advisers. As House's intimacy with Wilson grew, so did his influence, particularly in matters that involved judgment of a political nature. The first among these was selecting a cabinet, in which House figured prominently. In the weeks following the election, House became a clearinghouse for information about prospective appointees, gathering names and references, analyzing credentials, and evaluating political assets and liabilities. He helped Wilson deal with such potentially explosive questions as how to let William F. McCombs, the out-of-favor head of the national Democratic Party, down as easily as possible and what to do with Bryan, who had to be tamed and rewarded at the same time. Ultimately, House's efforts helped create a cabinet that had a Texas and progressive cast, and one that contained several of his personal friends.[13]

Wilson indicated how much he valued House's advice by offering him a cabinet post of his own. The Colonel could have, Wilson told him, his choice of any department except state, which had been reserved for the domestication of Bryan. Although, as he recorded in his diary, House regarded this offer as a high honor, he quickly turned it down. "My reasons," he wrote, "are that I am not strong enough to tie myself down to a Cabinet department and, in addition, my general disinclination to hold office." House's final remark was most revealing: "I very much prefer to free lance, and to advise with him regarding matters in general, and to have a roving commission to serve wherever and whenever possible." As House understood, his personal ambitions went beyond those that any cabinet position could possibly satisfy. He also seems to have known intuitively that the formal responsibilities of office, which involved more than pretended agreement with the detailed policies of his superior, could undermine his chosen role as a sympathetic general adviser.[14]

House also attempted to influence the tone of Wilson's administration. In 1913 House's main interests, like Wilson's, were domestic and progressive. He hoped, as he made clear in *Philip Dru: Administrator,* for a spiritual reformation that could end class conflict and create a national harmony of interests. House did not believe that this result could be accomplished by laws—indeed in *Philip Dru* he depicted it coming about, contrary to usual progressive ideology, through the "holocaust" of a second civil war. In Wilson, House found a president whose oratory and leadership could, as he put it, "raise the moral stamina of the Nation" enough to transform society. He praised the spirituality and the uplifting tone of Wilson's inaugural address and urged the president to stress the issues of social justice and shared humanity as often as possible, until Americans of all classes came to see that the "strong should help the weak, that the fortunate should aid the unfortunate, and that business should be conducted upon a higher and more humane plane." That Wilson shared these goals, as well as the spiritual values behind them, added cement to his friendship with House.[15]

While operating on this lofty level, as what Wilson called his "second personality" or his "independent self," House expanded on his role as a clearinghouse for the administration. He also moved out of position-filling and into the arena of policymaking. The Houses' apartment in New York City became a sort of adjunct office of the White House, with its own direct telephone line to the president. House talked to and corresponded with practically everyone of importance in political and business circles, and decided which of their plans and ideas were worthy of Wilson's attention. Such a role was bound to attract notice, no matter how discreet the Colonel attempted to be. The word got around, first among office-seekers, who must always require a sharp eye for influence, and then more generally, that House was a conduit to the president. Within a month after the inauguration *Harper's Weekly* was calling him Assistant President House, and *Collier's* found the title that would stick when it referred to him as the "Silent Partner."[16]

House was involved in planning and implementing each of the New Freedom's reforms—tariff revision, the creation of the Federal Reserve System, the introduction of an income tax, the control of the trusts, and the regulation of industrial relations. His chief interest was the banking and currency question. As a cotton planter and broker in Texas, House had seen firsthand the need for a more elastic currency system, and as a progressive, he distrusted the power of private finance. A system of federal control could solve both problems, House thought, and he used all of his personal and political influence to ensure that one was created. He took upon himself the task of gathering information, collecting the banking laws of every nation in Europe, reports and abstracts from college professors of economics and banking, and suggestions from conferences with bankers and financiers. His purpose seems to have been to guide Wilson's thinking away from extreme opinions on the subject, such as those held by conservative bankers and radicals led by Bryan. In the end, the preponderance of mainstream opinion that House presented helped build support for the middle ground occupied by the moderate Glass-Owen bill, which was approved by Congress in December 1913 and provided for the creation of the Federal Reserve System.[17]

House worked long hours during the winter of 1912–1913, maintaining a schedule that belied his claims of frail health. When not holding "court" in New York, he was visiting the president in Washington, where he stayed invariably as a guest at the White House. The Colonel was strengthened, even rejuvenated, by his role in the Wilson administration, by his daily sense that he was influencing the outcome of important events. But as spring approached, portending warmer weather, House felt his stamina ebbing and began to make plans for his annual trip to Europe. He clearly felt guilty about his flight from heat and responsibility, expressing concern that he was deserting the president, but rationalized that he had no real choice in the matter and that he was only conserving his strength for renewed service upon his return. He also justified the trip as an opportunity to advance his idea, still vague and unformed, of creating a "sympathetic understanding" for the maintenance of world peace between Great Britain, Germany, Japan, and the United States. Although House made no real progress in this endeavor beyond making the acquaintance of the British foreign minister, Sir Edward Grey, he apparently found it satisfying to dabble, however amateurishly, in a field even larger than national affairs.[18]

House's trip to Europe caught his imagination and led him to begin shifting his interest from domestic to world affairs. As House busied himself during the winter of 1913–1914 with finding the best candidates for the new Federal Reserve Board, he formulated plans for another, somewhat more specific, mission to Europe. Beyond his general purpose of promoting understanding, the Colonel's main goal this time was to foster disarmament, which he thought would lower the tension, then alarmingly high, between Britain and Germany. This course of action had an obvious appeal for House, considering his need for annual European vacations, and he asked the president's blessing following his return from a winter's visit to Austin. Wilson approved, despite his regret that his friend intended to abandon him again in the summer of 1914, and presented House with a general letter of introduction. Thus armed, House departed for Germany on May 16, 1914, a private citizen with no title other than "personal friend of the president," to undertake what he called "the great adventure." [19]

House traveled for two months in Europe, visiting Berlin, London, and Paris. He was, at the outset, deeply troubled by what he found on the Continent. "The situation is extraordinary. It is jingoism run stark mad," he warned Wilson on May 29, just three days after his arrival in Berlin. Without an American-inspired understanding, he predicted "an awful cataclysm" because no one in Europe could change the dangerous situation developing there. "There is too much hatred, too many jealousies," he concluded. In a series of meetings with government leaders in Berlin, House pushed for disarmament and a relaxation of Anglo-German tensions. The highlight of his stay in Germany was a private conference at Potsdam with Emperor William II. They talked about Anglo-Saxon unity, the Russian problem, and Germany's naval-building race with Great Britain, with House describing for the Emperor what he saw as the American role in bringing about greater understanding among the European powers. [20]

William seemed to accept House's reasoning, and the Colonel, obviously flattered by the Emperor's attention, left Germany in high spirits. After a week in Paris, he headed for London, where he thought he had "ample material to open negotiations [*sic*]." Although congenial in tone, House's conversations with Foreign Minister Grey, Prime Minister Herbert Asquith, and other British leaders proved inconclusive. The British seemed to share the Colonel's objectives — as had the Germans — but were unwilling to be pinned down to any specific plan of action. Grey staved off House's proposal for a meeting with the Emperor during the regatta at Kiel in late June, effectively killing the idea. Still, House could barely contain his enthusiasm over what he believed he had accomplished, writing in his diary that "it is difficult for me to realize that the dream I had last year is beginning to come true." It should have been more difficult; neither side had so much as hinted at a willingness to compromise on the serious issues that divided them. Not for the last time in his efforts as a mediator in European affairs, House had mistaken expressions of friendship for agreement in negotiations and had succumbed to the use by others of his own technique of flattery. On June 28, the day after House had written so glowingly of his hopes for success, a Bosnian nationalist assassinated the heir to the throne of the Austro-Hungarian Empire and set in motion the chain of events that would lead to the European war that the Colonel had been trying to avoid. The "great adventure" had ended in failure. [21]

When House landed in Boston on July 29, the beginning of the World War was only days away. House did not head for Washington to report on his mission to the president but, following his custom, prepared to wait out the summer on the North Shore of Massachusetts. "If I thought I could live through the heat, I would go to Washington to see you," he wrote to Wilson, "but I am afraid if I reached there I would be utterly helpless." The outbreak of the war in Europe did not cause House to change his plans; he could do no better than to offer Wilson advice about the proper American response by mail. In particular, he advised Wilson against any immediate attempt at mediation, which might lessen the president's influence "when the proper moment arrives." Nor did House go to Washington when Ellen Axson Wilson died on August 6, although he was clearly heartbroken at the president's loss of his wife. He wrote Wilson that "her death leaves me unnerved and stunned," but made no move to see his stricken friend until the end of the month when Wilson was resting in Cornish, New Hampshire.[22]

As Europe settled into war in the fall of 1914, House focused his attention increasingly on foreign affairs. He found both party politics and domestic issues had paled beside the opportunities presented by the war, which in his view offered Wilson the chance for wider influence and even greatness. House began to discuss the possibility of a U.S. mediation, envisioning himself in the role of Wilson's traveling emissary to Europe. He also developed a plan for a Pan-American pact, which he first presented to Wilson on November 25, 1914. House hoped that his plan to weld together the nations of the Western Hemisphere would also "serve as a model for the European nations when peace is at last brought about." Wilson, excited by House's idea, wrote out the first draft of the plan himself. It bound the signatories to guarantee each other's territorial integrity and political independence, to settle disputes peacefully, and to refrain from furnishing aid to the enemies of any other member nation. Although the plan would eventually founder over Latin American fears of dominance by the United States, some of its provisions would later reappear in Wilson's thinking about the League of Nations.[23]

In the meantime House was making preparations for another visit to Europe. This time he would not wait for his journey to coincide with his annual summer tour; he obviously saw his mission as too important to put off. House's plan, which was both vague and grandiose, was to search, through what would later be called "shuttle diplomacy," for terms upon which the war might be ended. He was not attempting formal mediation, although before he left Washington he optimistically asked Wilson "if it would be possible for him to come over to Europe in the event a peace conference could be arranged and in the event he was invited to preside over the conference." If, considering the state of affairs in Europe, House was losing some of his grip on reality, he was carrying Wilson with him. The president, who had originally expressed skepticism about the Colonel's idea, shared House's enthusiasm by the time of his departure. This was the period of House's strongest influence on Wilson, as the bereaved president leaned heavily on the Colonel for emotional support. Thus, rather too easily, House's dreams of greatness became Wilson's as well.[24]

House left New York on January 30, 1915, aboard the ill-fated *Lusitania*, which would cross the Atlantic only a few more times before its rendezvous with a German torpedo in May. In London, House revived his friendship with Sir Edward Grey, who spent long hours discussing the war and the possibilities for a lasting peace with his American visitor. Grey's treatment of House suggests that he saw in him the same qualities of sympathetic understanding that had attracted Wilson to the Colonel— and that he recognized the value of flattering the American with his time and attention. As House's visit lengthened, he identified increasingly with the Allied cause in the war, becoming as much a collaborator as a neutral in his outlook. He stayed, on Grey's advice, in London for a month and a half, despite Wilson's warning that he should not "go too far in allowing the English Government to determine when it is best to go to Germany." On the Continent, House stopped first in Paris, where he saw no indication of a willingness to negotiate for peace. Grey had prepared him for this result and provided him with the basis for an explanation by asserting that the Allies could only make a just and lasting peace when their military position gave them the strength to do so. By the time House moved on to Germany, he recognized that his mission could not possibly succeed in bringing about negotiations, a judgment that he needed only ten days in Berlin to confirm before returning to London.[25]

Although it betrayed many of his shortcomings as a diplomat, House's visit to Europe in early 1915 was not without value. Sir Edward Grey, for instance, made use of this opportunity to begin his campaign for a postwar agreement to guarantee world peace. Although House thought Grey's proposal too ambitious for American involvement and, to use his word, "evaded" it by proposing instead an eventual agreement on the principles of civilized warfare, their conversation marked the beginning of a collaboration that would lead ultimately to the creation of the League of Nations. House's letters to Wilson also contained a great deal of valuable information on the situation in Europe, a service that was rendered more important by the generally second-rate nature of the president's duly appointed ambassadors there. Whatever mischief House's amateur diplomacy might cause in the future, it had not caused any yet, and the failure of his mission to bring about negotiations was an outcome that no diplomat, no matter how seasoned, could have exceeded in the spring of 1915.[26]

House returned to the United States on June 13. He had planned to stay *where's his wife?* longer in London, even renting a small house there, but had changed his mind when the sinking of the *Lusitania* convinced him that war between the United States and Germany was inevitable. Again, he did not rush to see Wilson in Washington, despite the crisis over unrestricted submarine warfare and the resulting resignation of Secretary of State Bryan. House, who had heard of Bryan's resignation while still aboard ship on the Atlantic, was the logical choice to become his successor, but the Colonel dismissed the idea publicly as soon as he landed in New York. Then, despite Wilson's repeated urging that he come to the capital, he remained on Long Island and the North Shore until the president finally came up to see him on June 24.[27]

The summer of 1915 was a trying time for House. His fear of the heat, and whatever deeper fears lay behind it, kept him away from Wilson at a critical time in the war — and in the president's personal life. Wilson's position on the sinking of the *Lusitania,* although strong enough to drive Bryan out of the cabinet, was not forceful enough to satisfy House, who now thought that war with Germany could only be avoided by compelling the Imperial Government to renounce submarine attacks against neutral shipping and all passenger liners. This was the aim of the first two *Lusitania* notes, of which the increasingly pro-Allied House heartily approved. But in mid-July, after the crisis had been bogged down in diplomacy for more than two months, Wilson seemed to waver in his determination to bring Germany to heel. His third *Lusitania* note, which clearly reflected the president's desire not to go to war over a technicality, implied that submarine warfare could be carried out legally under cruiser rules and accepted German good behavior on the high seas as sufficient without a formal renunciation of the principle that had led to the attack on the *Lusitania.* Frustrated by this weakening of Wilson's position, House attempted to stiffen the president's resolve. "I have talked with a great many people," he wrote on July 15, "and, without exception, they have expressed a wish that a firm answer be sent. When pressed further, they have told me that in their opinion the country was willing to accept the consequences." When this letter failed to have the desired effect, House, who understood that his success as an adviser depended upon his never trying to persuade Wilson to do something that he did not want to do, found reasons to grant his approval to the new policy.[28]

The sinking of the British liner *Arabic* on August 19 revived the issue of submarine warfare. It also gave House an excuse to resume his efforts on behalf of a stronger American position. In response to Wilson's call for advice, House wrote that "our people do not want war, but even less do they want to recede from the position you have taken. Neither do they want to shirk the responsibility which should be ours." House also demonstrated his understanding of what influenced the president, informing him that his first *Lusitania* note had made him "not only the first citizen of America, but the first citizen of the world." Implying that Wilson's later, more moderate, efforts at diplomacy had diminished his authority, House concluded that "further notes would disappoint our own people and would cause something of derision abroad." Consequently, he recommended that the administration break diplomatic relations with the German government. The Colonel understood that this action would lead to war, which he saw as the logical outcome of Wilson's original position on the illegality of submarine warfare, and was irritated by the president's continuing search for a peaceful solution. "I am surprised by the attitude he takes," House confided to his diary. "He evidently will go to great lengths to avoid war. He should have determined his policy when he wrote his notes of February, May, June, and July." Wilson's attitude was less yielding than House thought, however, and after a tense month of negotiations, he succeeded in forcing the German government to renounce the use of submarines against passenger liners. Although satisfied with this outcome, House emerged from the crisis with no trust in the intentions of Germany and certain that the United States must eventually enter the war on the side of the Allies.[29]

Wilson also asked for House's advice on an "intimate personal matter." During House's stay in Europe, the president had met Edith Bolling Galt and had proposed marriage. What, he wanted to know, did House think of the idea of his remarrying? Would it lessen his influence with the American people? House gave his approval to the marriage, although the depth of his doubt about it is revealed in the argument he invented to justify his approval. If Wilson did not remarry, House wrote, his health would fail and he would become incapacitated or die, thus depriving the world of the one statesman who might bring the European war to an end. It would also deprive House of his access to greatness — as indeed, as House surely understood, would have his raising of any serious opposition to the president's marriage plans. But House could not escape so easily the problems posed for him by Mrs. Galt. She now fulfilled some of the emotional needs, especially for uncritical support and admiration, for which Wilson had previously turned to House. She also replaced House as the president's confidante. The result would be a loosening of the ties that bound the two men together and a weakening of House's influence on the president.[30]

By the autumn of 1915 House was concerned over what he saw as a drift in Wilson's European policy. The Colonel viewed war between the United States and Germany as inevitable, a conclusion that he thought the president was too preoccupied, with hopes for peace and thoughts of marriage, to grasp. Letting his vanity and even his feelings of superiority to Wilson have free rein, House began to hatch a plan that would either end the war through mediation or draw the United States into it on the side of the Allies at the right time and for the right reasons. The Colonel thought that the usefulness of the submarine issue as a cause for war had come and gone with the *Lusitania* and *Arabic* crises; to go to war now over these or similar incidents would seem only a dry and technical defense of neutral rights. Thus House decided to push for an American demarche that would either end the war or clarify the reasons for American entry.[31]

House seized the opening for his plan, which eventually came to be embodied in the so-called House-Grey Memorandum, from two letters he received from Sir Edward Grey in August and September 1915. Grey hinted, in general terms, that the Allies might accept an offer of mediation that included an American guarantee to enter a postwar league of nations and to defend a new world order based on disarmament on land and sea. Although this idea was not specific enough for House's purposes, by October 8 he had formed it into a proposal that he could present to the president. What House envisioned was an American demand for mediation, approved in advance by the Allies, which the German government would either accept, thus ending the war, or reject, bringing the United States into it. The president was, House thought, "startled by this plan," but "seemed to acquiesce by silence."[32]

Wilson had good reason to find House's proposal startling. It was the Colonel at his worst: amateurish, too clever by half, and far too convinced of his superior skills as a diplomat. Whatever perils existed in continued American neutrality were only amplified by House's scheme. The astonishing thing is that the president proved so willing to give House almost complete freedom to act on his idea. It is tempting to explain his behavior in House's own terms and conclude that Wilson was distracted by his wedding plans. But it seems more likely that he saw the proposal in a different light, that he emphasized, in the excitement of Grey's apparently reasonable response to House's first overture, the possibility for a successful mediation to end the war and not, as the Colonel sometimes seemed to do, the construction of a *casus belli*. Still, Wilson approved House's October 17 letter to Grey, which was conspiratorial in tone and gave the clear indication that it might be possible to spring a trap on the unsuspecting Germans. House may have been misleading Wilson about his own intentions, but it is difficult to see how the president could have missed the dangers in permitting the Colonel to maneuver everyone, including himself, into a position where war might become unavoidable. That House understood his freedom of action, if not the dangers in it, seems apparent in his diary entry for October 14. "I now have the matter," he wrote with all too obvious satisfaction, "in my own hands, and it will probably be left to my judgment as to when and how to act."[33]

House acted by laying plans for another mission to Europe, despite attempts by Grey, who feared that the Allies might not be willing to make peace on terms that would seem reasonable to the Americans, to dampen the Colonel's enthusiasm. House responded with irritation, commenting that "the British are in many ways dull." After all, they did not appreciate his efforts to help them. Following preliminary conversations with British and German officials in New York, House sailed for England on December 28. He landed at Falmouth on January 5, 1916, and spent the next two weeks in conversations with nearly everyone of political importance in England. He then departed for Germany, where he stayed three days, long enough to reinforce his opinion that the military extremists there would make war between the United States and Germany inevitable in the near future. House followed this visit with a week in Paris, during which he shocked French officials with his candor about the likelihood that his scheme would draw the United States into the war. Back in London on February 9, House began a round of talks that would conclude with the initialing of the House-Grey Memorandum two weeks later.[34]

At best House's behavior in these talks could be described as duplicitous; at worst he was dishonest in his dealings with both the British and Wilson. While House was reporting to the president that the Allies were sincerely interested in mediation, he was presenting his plan to the British as little more than a pretext for entering the war against Germany. In both cases, the information was false, or at least exaggerated, and House was intentionally misleading everyone. He justified this dual deception by the importance of his mission of bringing the war to a close, although it is not clear whether this was to be accomplished in the end through mediation or American belligerency. It is also not clear whether the Colonel actually fooled anyone. Although, on February 22, 1916, Grey and House put their initials to a memorandum embodying the American's plan of enforced mediation, neither of their governments pursued it with any interest. In London, the War Cabinet could see no reason to trust House or his predictions of American behavior and decided that there was no point even in discussing the matter with Britain's allies. In Washington, Wilson praised his friend warmly for his achievement, but weakened the effect of the memorandum by inserting the word "probably" into the sentence stating that the United States would leave a peace conference as a belligerent on the side of the Allies if Germany proved unreasonable. Possibly the only one deceived was House himself. He returned from Europe convinced that Allied war aims were limited and could be satisfied by the kind of peace possible through mediation. This far from realistic appraisal would eventually lead to more mischief than any of the immediate effects of the House-Grey Memorandum.[35]

After returning home, House continued to be troubled by Wilson's unwillingness to plunge the United States into the war. When he learned that another British liner, the *Sussex*, had been torpedoed late in March, he rushed to Washington in the belief that only his strong advice could stiffen the president's will. "I am afraid he will delay and write further notes," House recorded, "when action is what we need." The Colonel's efforts may have had some effect on Wilson. On March 30, following a meeting of the sort that House called "executive session"—that is, the two men alone—the president moved steadily toward threatening a break in diplomatic relations if the German government continued to employ submarine warfare against passenger liners and merchant vessels. Although House wanted to go further, and to break relations immediately to frighten the Germans into accepting American mediation, he applauded Wilson's strong stand. He also entered into secret negotiations with the German ambassador, Johann von Bernstorff, to prevent the rupture threatened by Wilson's note. This mission seems to have cooled House's ardor for war by involving his ego in the hope for a peace settlement, so that he eventually advised Wilson to accept the German promise, in the so-called *Sussex* Pledge of May 4, 1916, not to employ submarines in the future in a manner that violated international law. Although this German response was not the unambiguous settlement that Wilson and House had hoped for, and really only postponed a reckoning on the submarine issue, it seemed at the time to be a significant victory for Wilsonian principles.[36]

With the *Sussex* crisis apparently settled, House attempted to revive the demarche represented by the House-Grey Memorandum. He knew perhaps better than anyone in America that the submarine issue would arise again, and sooner rather than later if the United States did not put pressure on the British to relax the blockade of Germany. The only solution seemed to be mediation, which House believed the Allies, if not the Germans, would be willing to accept. Although, as House wanted the British at least to believe, the outcome of this exercise was likely to be war, there remained the possibility that mediation for peace might succeed. Such, anyway, was Wilson's hope and the reason why he gave the Colonel permission to raise the issue again with the British foreign minister. Grey's response proved distinctly disappointing to House: "he halts, stammers, and questions," the Colonel wrote in his diary. House still did not see that the Allies had doubts of their own about the value of mediation and mistook their polite encouragement, which was designed not to offend the politically useful Americans, for actual enthusiasm. As much as anything else, House's continued efforts on behalf of his mediation plan indicated how far he was from understanding the true nature of the European war.[37]

During the summer and fall of 1916, House turned his attention to domestic political concerns. It was an election year, and Wilson's return to the White House was anything but certain. After deflecting Wilson's suggestion that he should take over as chairman of the Democratic National Committee, House served as an unofficial adviser to the president's campaign. He devised a strategy that concentrated on districts of no more than one hundred thousand voters in states that were of prime importance — a plan that is strikingly similar to the one he had created fictionally in *Philip Dru* five years earlier. House offered Wilson sound political advice throughout the campaign, which was waged on the twin themes of progressivism and peace, although it does not appear that he played a much larger role in the president's reelection than he had played in his earlier success in 1912.[38]

Wilson's victory at the polls returned the war to the center of America's interest. The president was now determined that the European conflict must be brought to an end, at least partly because he had adopted House's view that its continuation would lead eventually to American intervention over the submarine issue. He thus proposed a new, independent mediation, which he intended to begin by asking the belligerents to state the terms they would be willing to accept as a basis for peace. House objected to this plan for reasons that suggest the differences between his perception of the war and Wilson's. The president envisioned himself in the role of an honest broker bringing the two sides together for negotiations, an outcome that he had hoped for even while approving the devious House-Grey Memorandum several months before. House, however, was too pro-Allied to approve of Wilson's more even-handed approach, which threatened, in the circumstances of the war at the end of 1916, to reverse the intent of the House-Grey Memorandum by drawing the United States closer to Germany. When Wilson persevered with his plan, House attempted to control the possible damage by arguing for moderate language. He also drew closer, perhaps too close, to his personal English contact in the United States, Sir William Wiseman, who took advantage of House's fondness for intrigue as well as his desire to maintain good Anglo-American relations to provide the British government with vital information. That no real damage was done, except perhaps to the mutual confidence between Wilson and House, was due primarily to the fact that the president's plan was always doomed to failure by the unwillingness of the belligerents to search for a compromise peace.[39]

The failure of Wilson's mediation plan was followed by the German government's announcement on January 31, 1917, that it would resume unrestricted submarine warfare the following day. House received the news directly in a letter from Ambassador Bernstorff, then rushed to Washington to lobby the president for a firm response. He found that Wilson still hoped to avoid war despite his decision to break diplomatic relations with Germany. What followed would depend on the actions of German submarine commanders, and not on the arguments that House or any other presidential adviser might make. House, who sensed this reality and always remembered that his influence with Wilson depended on never attempting to persuade him to do something that he did not want to do, kept his distance, first emotionally by refusing to argue and later physically by remaining in New York for most of the period between February 1 and April 2, 1917, when the president asked Congress to declare war. Only after Wilson had called Congress into special session, presumably to deal with the war issue, did House risk another trip to Washington to offer his advice. By then, Wilson had made up his mind for war and House could safely discuss the matter with him. Still, the tone of the Colonel's diary suggests that the two friends knew they were embarking on this difficult voyage with very different levels of enthusiasm.[40]

In a sense, American entry into the war drew Wilson and House more closely together again; at least they were no longer divided by the neutrality that the president had attempted to retain long after House had decided that war with Germany was not only just but inevitable. Thus, although the two men continued to differ over how fully it might be possible to trust or cooperate with the Allies, Wilson employed House as his liaison to the Entente powers, especially to the British and the French. House attempted to enhance his influence, as well as inter-Allied cooperation, by arranging for Foreign Secretary Balfour to visit the United States in April 1917 to discuss Allied requirements and the American contribution to the war. But the Colonel's effort may have backfired as a result of the revelation at that time of the Allies' secret treaties. When the complications of coalition warfare finally required a U.S. representative on inter-Allied committees meeting in Europe, House was the logical choice for the job. It seems clear that the Colonel did not want to go. The position was too narrowly administrative and would seriously limit his influence with Wilson on the larger questions of the war and its settlement, a consideration that may in fact have led to his being promoted for the job by Mrs. Wilson, among others. In the end House agreed to be appointed head of the American War

Mission to Europe, at least in part because Wilson defined his status in the same kind of extraofficial—and flattering—terms he had used before, and the Colonel departed for England in late October 1917.[41]

American entry into the war also complicated the issue of House's influence with Wilson concerning the eventual peace settlement, most especially the question of a postwar world organization. House's interest in shaping the terms of the peace had developed long before Wilson's, and the Colonel had been influential in guiding the president's attention to the subject while providing him with his earliest ideas on the nature of a postwar world. After April 2, however, Wilson's own mind engaged the issues of peacemaking more fully, and House's influence necessarily waned, even if the Colonel continued to be the only adviser with whom the president would discuss his developing plan for a league of nations. House responded to this loss of personal influence by attempting to establish an institutional one. In August 1917 House proposed the creation of a commission, later named the Inquiry, to study the questions of peace and peacemaking. When Wilson approved of the idea and asked House to undertake the Inquiry's organization, the Colonel responded, with uncharacteristic humility, "I do not quite know how I shall do this." He began by appointing his brother-in-law, Sidney E. Mezes, then president of City College of New York, to the post of director, thus ensuring through nepotism his own influence in the new commission. The eventual organization would have a progressive and academic cast, would reflect House's general views on important subjects, and would play a key role in defining America's positions at the Paris Peace Conference of 1919.[42]

In Europe House led a team of Americans that participated in conferences to coordinate the military and economic efforts of the Allied and Associated Powers. It turned out to be a difficult and disappointing task. After attending a session of the Supreme War Council in Paris, during which many topics were addressed but none brought to conclusion, House commented that "I can understand quite readily why Germany has been able to withstand the Allies so successfully. . . . Nothing is ever buttoned up with the Allies; it is all talk and no concerted action." By the time House returned to the United States on December 15, 1917, he was sufficiently discouraged to doubt the ability of the Allies to win the war without significant military and diplomatic assistance from the United States. He thus pressed for rushing American troops into action on the Western Front and advised Wilson of the need for a statement of war aims that led eventually to the drafting of the Fourteen Points.[43]

The Fourteen Points, which the president presented in an address to Congress on January 8, 1918, were a combination of sophisticated propaganda, high-minded principles, and clearly stated if ambiguous war aims that Wilson and House hoped might form the basis for a negotiated settlement of the war. By autumn they seemed about to do just that, as the German government asked Wilson to arrange an armistice followed by peace negotiations based on the president's well-known terms. The possibility of peace sent House to Europe again in mid-October, this time bearing credentials as a Special Representative of the Government of the United States as well as a letter designating him as Wilson's "personal representative" to the Allied governments. This redundancy of status reflected the importance and difficulty of the Colonel's mission, which was to negotiate terms for an armistice that would satisfy both Wilsonian principles for a just peace and the Allies' desire for unmitigated victory. As usual, House carried no formal instructions; his mind and the president's, he wrote, were "generally parallel," and Wilson thought that he would "know what to do" on his own.[44]

Beginning on October 29, House met with the prime ministers of Great Britain, France, and Italy to discuss the terms of an armistice. The Colonel quickly discovered, if he did not already know, that his and Wilson's idea of suitable cease-fire conditions were very different from those of their European counterparts. The Allies wanted an armistice that would ensure themselves a victors' peace by making it impossible for the Germans to resume the war and fight on for better terms. At the same time, they did not want to commit themselves to Wilsonian principles that might limit their freedom of action in the treatment of a defeated Germany. House was outnumbered and overmatched. As he yielded on the technical questions of German troop withdrawal and armament reduction, which effectively turned the cease-fire into a surrender, the Colonel took consolation in the belief that the Allies had at least accepted most of the Fourteen Points as the basis for the eventual peace settlement. House described the outcome of his efforts to Wilson as "a great diplomatic victory" and assured the president that the Allies were now more committed to the American peace program than they "quite realize." In fact, however, they were less committed than House realized—or wanted to admit. The Europeans had maintained reservations on the important questions of the freedom of the seas and reparations, against which the Germans would now be powerless to put up much of a defense. Although it would be an exaggeration to say that the battle for the peace was lost in these prearmistice negotiations, or to assume that much better terms were possible from the Allies anyway, House the diplomat must still be criticized for failing to grasp the full connection between the conditions of the armistice and the shape of the ultimate peace settlement, with results that would soon be apparent.[45]

When was he made Colonel?

After the armistice went into effect on November 11, House remained in Europe to make arrangements for the upcoming peace conference. It was an altogether disappointing time for the Colonel, who seems to have felt his influence with Wilson shrinking just as his own ambitions grew. House frequently complained that he did not know the president's plans, due partly to mutual difficulties with deciphering the code they used, and that Wilson seemed less willing than usual to follow his advice. At the same time, House was undergoing a metamorphosis in his perception of his relationship with Wilson and of his own role in handling the affairs of state. The Colonel had, during the armistice negotiations, developed a taste for the kind of power that can only come from actually making decisions and was no longer satisfied with working behind the scenes as an adviser. This change had surfaced as early as November 14, when House had tried to persuade Wilson to limit his activities in Europe to the making of a preliminary peace treaty, leaving House, presumably, to lead the American delegation to the peace conference itself. When Wilson rejected this proposal with obvious consternation, the Colonel was left with the option of continuing to function primarily as the president's adviser or of making a place for himself as the leader of the rest of the American commission. He chose the latter in what amounted to a major departure from his usual practice. By January 1919, moreover, House had developed a new, grander ambition for himself of manipulating the entire peace conference, a goal that would eventually call into question even his loyalty to Wilson.[46]

After House began to give up his advisory, behind-the-scenes role in favor of a more independent position, his health became precarious, perhaps in response to the stress and anxiety brought on by the important step he was taking. In December he was ill, apparently with influenza, for about ten days. Then, from January 8 to 21, he was stricken with an attack of gallstones sufficiently severe to prevent him from participating in the organizational meetings of the peace conference—and to cause reports of his death to be circulated. This second illness cost House a seat on the Council of Ten, which went to his rival, Secretary of State Lansing, instead. Despite these setbacks, the Colonel managed to establish himself, after Wilson, as clearly the most influential—indeed, as the only influential—American peace commissioner. He was the only one who had friendships with the European prime ministers and who had independent access to the president, the real source of authority within the American delegation.[47]

From almost the beginning, the peace conference went badly for the Americans. Wilson, and to a somewhat lesser degree House, had fundamental differences with the Allies on issues of prime importance to the shaping of the settlement, including territorial adjustments in Europe, the distribution of Germany's colonies, and reparations. Most important, the Americans were determined to create a league of nations as an integral part of the peace treaty, a goal that could only be achieved if all of the other difficulties were ironed out. The situation put obvious pressure on the U.S. commissioners to compromise on everything else to save the League. Through the first month of the conference, down to Wilson's return visit to the United States beginning February 14, the president held firm to his principles and, on his last day in Paris, seemed vindicated by the adoption of the League covenant by a plenary session of the peace conference. As Wilson saw it, the all-important League of Nations had been secured; the other issues could be resolved after he came back to Paris in March.[48]

The state of affairs seemed much more perilous to House, whom Wilson had asked "to take his place" while he was away. At the moment of Wilson's victory on February 14, the Colonel had tried to warn him that he must not expect the same results on all issues, that he would have to compromise, not on "principle" but on "detail," as he had done before, to get things through. House may have been right, but he had reasons of his own for choosing this moment to try to soften Wilson's unyielding position. The Colonel was about to be finally in charge of the American delegation, and his ability to play the role that he had dreamed of and negotiate the peace settlement himself would depend upon his freedom to make compromises. House nearly betrayed his ambition when he told the president that he thought he could "button up" everything during Wilson's month-long absence. Wilson's response—"startled and even alarmed," according to House—caused the Colonel to correct himself quickly and explain that he meant that matters could be brought near to a conclusion for the president to finish off after his return. As House must have seen it, his years of loyal service to Wilson had finally brought him to the point of power; it was now up to him to break the deadlock, preserve the treaty, and save the world.[49]

While Wilson was away the French launched a diplomatic offensive to win acceptance of their territorial demands, especially in the Rhineland, which the president had firmly rejected. Their vehicle for doing this was to propose, along with the British, a preliminary peace treaty that would embody the Allies' conditions concerning Germany's postwar military strength, frontiers, and responsibility for reparations. Agreement on such a treaty would speed up the process of peacemaking, a consideration that House had always thought desirable and did even more so now that he was temporarily in charge of the U.S. delegation. But it would also mean surrendering, or at least compromising, the American position on each of the three issues involved and would reverse Wilson's victory of February 14 on inclusion of the League of Nations as an integral part of the treaty—all in the president's absence. Not surprisingly, Wilson radioed House specific instructions to resist this proposal and to "hold steady" until his return in March. House may not have quite understood because of problems with garbled decoding, but influenced by his own ambition and by the flattery of French premier Georges Clemenceau, he acquiesced personally in the creation of a Republic of the Rhineland separate from Germany and the exclusion of the League from a preliminary treaty.[50]

Wilson landed at Brest on March 13. House came out to meet him in foul weather, the first of many cold days to come in the Colonel's relationship with the president. As they boarded the train to Paris, Wilson was already irritated with House over the unsatisfactory outcome of a meeting that the Colonel had persuaded him to hold with senators to discuss the League. "Your dinner with the Senate Foreign Relations Committee was a failure," the president said, according to House's diary. Then the Colonel broke the news about the compromises discussed in Wilson's absence and indicated his own approval of them. House did not record the president's reaction, but Mrs. Wilson and Wilson's doctor, Cary Grayson, the two individuals closest to Wilson at the time, described him as shocked by what the Colonel had done. Mrs. Wilson, writing twenty years later, remembered that after the meeting the president smiled bitterly and said, "House has given away everything that I had won before we left Paris. He has compromised on every side, and so I have to start all over again and this time it will be harder, as he has given the impression that my delegates are not in sympathy with me." This conversation marked the beginning of the break in House's friendship with Wilson; he had lost the president's confidence and would never be trusted again.[51]

There were complicated emotional reasons for the break between Wilson and House, which have been examined by no less an authority on psychology than Sigmund Freud. But in essence, House fell victim to a logical inconsistency in his own ambition. He had, for many years, based his ability to influence Wilson upon maintaining the appearance, at least, of selflessness, of pursuing no personal goals beyond service to the president and his purposes. Eventually, the satisfaction that House found in this relationship wore thin, and he began to desire authority, even power, independent of Wilson, which he could not achieve without undermining the foundation of his previous influence with the president. The Colonel had periodically tested the strength of his leash since at least the summer of 1915; now he had finally struck out on his own, lost his connection with Wilson, and fallen from grace. House would never be able to see that he was guilty of disloyalty to the president, but considering the terms on which their friendship had been based, Wilson could see it no other way.[52]

Wilson acted quickly in Paris to mend what he perceived as the damage that House had done. He informed the British and French that he would never accept a preliminary treaty that did not include a league of nations, and ordered a press release denying that such a treaty was even being contemplated. House, humiliated, made no comment, thus avoiding an open break and preserving whatever influence he had left with the president. Perhaps not surprisingly considering the low esteem in which Wilson held the other U.S. commissioners, the president continued to assign important responsibilities to the Colonel. House remained the most important American delegate after Wilson himself and, due largely to his continuing influence with Clemenceau, played a prominent role in determining the outcomes of some of the key questions of the peace conference. But the coolness that had descended on all of his dealings with Wilson ended their special relationship, their friendship, forever. After completing work on the peace treaty, the two men parted company at Paris on June 28, 1919, never to meet again.[53]

House apparently never understood the reason for his break with Wilson, which he described later as a "tragic mystery." With the end of the peace conference, he moved on to London, where he participated in conferences that shaped the League's mandate system. This was his last service to Wilson, who rejected with silence the Colonel's letters offering advice on the fight for the treaty in the Senate. In his later years, House wrote frequently about international relations, in particular about the freedom of the seas, for both popular and scholarly journals. He flirted with a return to Democratic Party politics during the campaign for the nomination of Franklin D. Roosevelt in 1932, but despite the obvious warmth of his relationship with FDR, their friendship failed to ripen into the kind of intimacy that might have made a return possible for House. In 1938 he died, after an attack of pleurisy, in his home in New York City.[54]

MORRIS SHEPPARD

Fig. 2.1. Morris Sheppard, father of the Prohibition Amendment,
provided important leadership for defense spending prior to World War II.
Prints and Photographs Collection, Center for American History,
UT-Austin (CN 10269).

MORRIS SHEPPARD

BY RICHARD BAILEY

When Morris Sheppard took his oath of office in the House of Representatives in 1902, at first the other members mistook him for a page. Standing only five feet, four inches tall, he was nondescript in many ways. With such an inauspicious beginning, few observers would have predicted that Sheppard would go on to have such an illustrious career. Fewer still could have imagined that this would be the man who would successfully fight the "whiskey lords" and the "beer barons."[1]

Yet this diminutive lawyer from Northeast Texas participated in most of the major national political reforms in the United States from 1902 to 1941. A Democrat, Sheppard supported President Woodrow Wilson in both foreign and domestic matters. In the 1920s he worked in Congress opposing the Republican policies of "normalcy," and during the New Deal he loyally backed President Franklin D. Roosevelt, even in the controversial "court-packing" case. Not only did he support the main progressive and New Deal laws, he also authored a long list of important legislation; among others, Sheppard personally wrote: the Eighteenth Amendment to the Constitution, the Sheppard-Towner Federal Maternal and Infancy Act, the Federal Credit Union Act, the Selective Service Act, and the Lend-Lease Act.

Sheppard's tenacious personality was one possible reason for his success and power. He balanced his tenacity in working for the causes he cherished with wit, charm, and a relaxed sense of humor. One vignette from 1938 reveals these qualities in Sheppard. At a party in Washington, D.C., Representative Sol Bloom of New York created an awkward moment when he jokingly handed Sheppard, the father of national Prohibition and a man known as the "driest of the drys," a cocktail. Not to be outdone, Sheppard smiled and then picked up a ham sandwich and offered it to the Jewish representative. Though he had the determination of a reformer, he did not take himself too seriously; nor did he lose his perspective.[2]

Born in 1875 in Morris County, Sheppard received an excellent preparatory education in both public and private schools. He then worked his way through the University of Texas, receiving a bachelor's degree in 1895 and a law degree in 1897. He next attended Yale University and earned a master's degree in 1898. Throughout this period he developed his talents as an orator and a debater. While at Yale he was honored for his thesis and asked to deliver the "Masters Oration." He then went into private practice in his father's law firm in Pittsburg, Texas. In 1899 the firm moved to Texarkana. In 1902, after the death of his father, who had been elected to the U.S. House of Representatives, Sheppard ran for and won the seat his father had held.[3]

In December 1902, he began the next and possibly the most difficult step in his education — the humiliation of being a congressional freshman in the minority party; from this he learned what it meant to have no power. At that time his nemesis was Speaker of the House Joseph "Uncle Joe" Cannon, a notoriously dictatorial House leader. Sheppard worked with enthusiasm on meaningless committees and useless bills and would fume because Cannon often refused to recognize him. Bitterly, Sheppard once commented that the situation would "grind into his very soul." Out of frustration he stooped to baiting the Speaker or berating the Republican Party during speeches. But the hotter Sheppard boiled, the less respect he received from Cannon. Not until the insurgents' revolt of 1910, when progressive Republicans and Democrats restricted the powers of the Speaker, did Sheppard beat Cannon on a crucial issue.[4]

Despite his frustrations, Sheppard advanced professionally during the first decade of the twentieth century. He gained a measure of fame as an orator, not just in Congress but nationwide, as he spoke for other Democratic candidates and raised money for the national party. He also earned a reputation as an expert on tariffs. Even though he did not see a significant downward revision of import duties until 1913, Sheppard artfully and articulately championed the cause of tariff reform. Nearly a quarter of a century before the passage of the Federal Deposit Insurance Corporation Act, he introduced a bill that would have insured small bank deposits. He also was a pioneer in favoring the use of airplanes to deliver the mail, and he played a key role in the building of a new and safe repository for all important national documents, the National Archives.[5]

In 1913 Sheppard had even more reason to be encouraged. In that year, as he entered the United States Senate, the Democrats had gained control of both houses of Congress for the first time since antebellum days. At the same time they welcomed the inauguration of Woodrow Wilson, only the second president from their party since the Civil War. The new president was partial to southerners and especially Texans. Three cabinet members and the enigmatic Colonel Edward M. House, the president's closest adviser, all hailed from the Lone Star State.[6]

Perceiving that he now had greater influence, Sheppard determined to affect, if not fashion, events in Congress. He supported and helped to pass the Underwood-Simmons Tariff, the first significant downward revision of import duties since before the Civil War. Then he labored successfully for the extension of rural credit. In 1914 he supported women's suffrage as one of only three southern senators to vote for a proposed constitutional amendment. He also worked to calm border conflicts between the United States and Mexico, even though it meant clashing with political foes in his home state, such as the conservative Texas governor Oscar B. Colquitt and the flamboyant governor-elect James E. Ferguson. Both Colquitt and Ferguson were antiprohibitionist and opposed Sheppard on that issue. They also saw their own political advantage in blaming border troubles on a lack of help from the federal government. Sheppard, however, emphasized the broader interests of the United States and consequently supported the foreign policy of the Wilson administration toward Mexico and the work of Secretary of State William Jennings Bryan. Similarly, he urged preparedness for a possible conflict involving the United States in Europe.[7]

Increasingly Sheppard focused his efforts on one issue—prohibition. The reasons for his interest in temperance were established in his youth. He had first given up strong drink along with smoking while attending Yale Law School, thereby hoping to avoid any distraction or expense that might prevent his academic success. In 1896 he joined the Methodist Church, which was in the forefront of the temperance movement. One source alleged that he became a "dry" after seeing a picture of an alcoholic's stomach in a biology textbook. Still another possible motivation for his antiliquor sentiment was that he saw firsthand the damage that alcohol had done to families when he spoke at the gravesides of deceased members of his fraternal insurance organization, the Woodmen of the World. From his point of view, his determination to lead a clean, morally upright life, together with his striving to be effective in his work, dictated that he be a prohibitionist.[8]

But for Sheppard the allure of prohibition politics was more than personal. It also became a pivotal issue in Texas state politics. For many Texans opposition to liquor was the single issue that attracted them to organized politics. Its strong appeal became, for many, a bridge from a laissez-faire attitude to a belief in a more active role for the federal government. An Anglo-Protestant Texan could easily take the short step from eliminating the evils of the saloon to stopping the wrongs of child labor; he could also see that opposition to the "beer barons" was not drastically different from curbing the exploitative practices of steel, railroad, or banking magnates. But fundamentally, emotionally, and religiously, Anglo-Protestant Texans like Sheppard opposed strong drink in general and the saloon in particular. Realizing this, Sheppard rode that emotional wave to victory in a bid for his second term in the U.S. Senate in 1918 and, eventually, to the passage of the Eighteenth Amendment to the Constitution.

Victory on the issue of prohibition, however, did not come easily. On the contrary, the Eighteenth Amendment's ultimate success in 1919 came only after a series of failures. Antiliquor forces in Texas had been defeated in 1887 and again in 1911, when they had attempted to impose statewide prohibition legislatively. Sheppard himself had met defeat in the House on several liquor-related bills from 1902 to 1912, including one that would have banned the shipment of alcohol into dry areas. Then, while a freshman senator in the 1913–1914 session, he tried unsuccessfully to introduce a constitutional amendment on prohibition. Later, in the 1915–1916 session, he failed to pass a bill that forbade the sale of liquor in the District of Columbia.[9]

Dry forces, however, gained strength in the election of 1916, primarily through the work of the Anti-Saloon League. With more troops on the lines, Sheppard began winning a series of tactical battles in the Senate and ultimately the war against the saloon. On January 9, 1917, Sheppard finally did secure passage of his bill to outlaw drink in the District of Columbia. Then, on August 1, 1917, Sheppard, after several months of maneuvering and compromise, orchestrated the passage of SJ 17, the Eighteenth Amendment. After passage in the House and ratification by the states, prohibition went into effect nationwide on January 16, 1920.[10]

An event occurred eight months later that critics of Sheppard believed to be humorously appropriate, but supporters considered merely an unfair happenstance. Federal officials found a rather substantial moonshine operation on land owned by Sheppard. They uncovered 400 gallons of bottled homemade whiskey, barrels, corn, mash, and a still capable of producing 130 gallons per batch of "white lightning." While the discovery received much coverage in the press, further investigation revealed that the operation belonged to a cousin of the senator. Morris Sheppard was still the "driest of the drys."[11]

More seriously, the passage of the Eighteenth Amendment led to praise and approval for Sheppard. He was honored when the leaders of the fight for the women's vote asked him for help in passing the Nineteenth Amendment. He also received several offers of support for the vice presidential nomination and, from some radical drys, for the top spot on the Democratic ticket in 1920. But the narrow base of this enthusiasm did not gain either nomination for the senator.[12]

Sheppard's victory became a high tide of accomplishment rather than a portent of future success. Perhaps tired of war and Wilsonian idealism, the

American people elected Warren G. Harding to the presidency in 1920. In the following year the Republican congressional majority considered Harding's election to be a repudiation of the goals of Sheppard's party. First, they reversed America's tariff policy by passing the Fordney-McCumber Act, raising import duties on farm products and other commodities to all-time highs. Then they lowered taxes significantly, especially for the very wealthy. They also abandoned notions of government central planning and ownership of public services, returning railroads and the merchant marine to private hands and abandoning plans to fund the development of hydroelectric power. Similarly, in foreign affairs most Republicans rejected any notion of supporting or joining the League of Nations. Generally these policy changes disappointed Sheppard.[13]

The Texas senator was, however, not without influence. He used party loyalty and bipartisan organizations to limit the negative effects of "normalcy" during the Harding and Coolidge administrations, and he even helped to pass some social reforms. The best example of his power throughout the decade of the 1920s was the significant, if little known, Sheppard-Towner Act. Sometimes called the Federal Maternal and Infancy Act, this legislation was enacted in response to the problem of high maternal and infant mortality in the United States. Although the bill was fought by such groups as the American Medical Association and organizations opposed to women's suffrage, Sheppard maneuvered it through the Senate. Partly a testimony to the power of the newly enfranchised women, and partly evidence of the legislative skills of Sheppard, the bill passed the Senate 63 to 7. From 1921 to 1927, the act established clinics, generated literature, and paid health workers for the purpose of educating mothers and prospective mothers about the needs and dangers of pregnancy and childbirth. In 1927 lawmakers extended these provisions for two years, but in 1929 the program lapsed when Congress did not appropriate funding. The idea was, however, reenacted into law as a part of the Social Security Act in 1935.[14]

Still another example of Sheppard's growing influence through bipartisanship was his membership in the blocs that formed to protect certain interests in the 1920s. Postwar agricultural depression brought about the organization of the Farm Bloc. This group, of which Sheppard was a charter member, numbered about twenty-two senators and about one hundred members of the House. Some considered the Farm Bloc to be radical, but Sheppard argued that its organizers "were animated not only by a desire to secure fair play for agriculture but also by the idea that the salvation of the farm meant the salvation of the nation." Subsequently, Sheppard also joined the Progressive or La Follette Bloc, which favored more and better agricultural credit, earlier (January) inauguration of the president, direct primaries, and the abolition of the electoral college system. Again, defending against charges of radicalism, Sheppard proclaimed that they only wanted to "devise legislation of a non-partisan character against privilege and greed."[15]

Paradoxically, these bipartisan efforts did not diminish Sheppard's standing with party leaders. In fact, he gained a reputation as one of the most loyal Democrats. This prestige led Democrats to select him as a member of the Steering Committee in his second term as senator. Hence he had authority in choosing committee assignments and planning Democratic floor strategy in the Senate.[16]

Sheppard's effectiveness as a legislator continued in 1926 when he pushed through Congress the Sheppard-Hudspeth Act. As he perceived the problem, the United States was dependent on France and Germany for mineral potash, an important fertilizer. During World War I the U.S. supply was severely limited. He therefore wanted to develop domestic commercial potash capability. Earlier, geologists had determined that large quantities of the substance existed in West Texas and New Mexico. Sheppard tried in the 1924–1925 session to pass legislation to support and subsidize the exploitation of these deposits, but President Coolidge and the Bureau of the Budget were opposed, so the bills died in committee. But Sheppard did not relent, and after much persuasion and hard work, he succeeded in passing the bill. On June 27, 1926, President Coolidge signed the Sheppard-Hudspeth Potash Act into law.[17]

After this success, Sheppard faced a serious decision in 1928. In that year the Democrats nominated Al Smith of New York for president. Supporting the party's nominee had ordinarily been no problem for Sheppard. In 1904 he had supported Judge Alton B. Parker of New York, despite philosophical differences with the candidate. Again in 1920 and 1924 Sheppard supported James Cox and John W. Davis, respectively, although neither was his first choice. But Smith presented more of a problem. Smith openly and aggressively favored the repeal of the Eighteenth Amendment. Beyond the fact that Sheppard was the architect of Prohibition, his name was so strongly associated with the Eighteenth Amendment that it probably was one of the keys to his support in Texas. But party loyalty, which had always been an important feature of Sheppard's political life, won out, so in spite of a seemingly insurmountable conflict, he decided to support Smith, unlike many Democrats in Texas.[18]

This loyalty to the Democratic Party, Sheppard's seniority in the Senate, and a phenomenal attendance record paid dividends to the senator. In 1929 the Democratic Steering Committee appointed him Democratic whip, the second most powerful post in the Senate. Democratic leaders pointed out that Sheppard deserved the job since he was the "father of National Prohibition." Then in 1930 the voters of Texas returned Sheppard to the Senate for a fourth term. In this election Sheppard won without even returning to the state to campaign.[19]

The most important issue on the minds of the American people that year was the economy. Oddly enough, the worldwide depression aided Sheppard. Most significantly it reversed the power of the two parties. The majority of voters reasoned that since the Republicans had taken credit for the prosperity of the 1920s, they must take the blame for the subsequent economic stagnation. Often Sheppard would criticize the Hoover administration for the failure of its depression policies. He also rode the wave of Democratic victories in 1932 to positions of power. In the Seventy-third Congress, organized in 1933, he became chairman of the prestigious Military Affairs Committee, remained on the Steering Committee, and was the senior Democratic member of three other committees—Commerce, Irrigation and Reclamation, and Manufactures.[20]

Sheppard acquired additional influence because of the tremendous power exercised by the new president, Franklin D. Roosevelt, whose power, in turn, derived from several sources. First, Roosevelt had an overwhelming mandate from the electorate. He had defeated the Republican candidate, President Herbert Hoover, by a landslide. In addition, both houses of Congress were in the hands of the Democrats and extremely willing to follow their popular president. Lastly, a feeling prevailed that the nation faced an emergency: unemployment and the bank crisis urgently needed solutions.

Therefore, Sheppard's willingness to support Roosevelt was one of his sources of strength. In fact, he could support the president honestly and sincerely on nearly every issue except prohibition. On most of the New Deal legislation he worked diligently and with conviction. He was in the vanguard of the New Deal, having favored so much progressive legislation since 1902.

He also contributed to the New Deal legislative proposals of his own. One of the most important of the laws sponsored by Sheppard during the early New Deal period was the Federal Credit Union Act. He claimed that it was the only act passed by the Seventy-third Congress's Second Session that had originated in the legislative branch. In spite of opposition from the Treasury Department, the Federal Reserve Board, and the Post Office, the bill passed the upper house without debate and became law in 1934. The act extended the availability of credit to people at reasonable interest rates. The Morris Sheppard Federal Credit Union of Texarkana, Texas, received the first charter under the new law.[21]

Truly your friend,

Morris Sheppard

Fig. 2.2. Vice President John Nance Garner (left) with senators Tom Connally (center) and Morris Sheppard (right) gave Texas unprecedented influence during President Franklin Roosevelt's first two terms. Adams (Walker Dickson) Photographs, Center for American History, UT-Austin (CN 00338).

In the spring of 1934 Sheppard received another title, although largely an honorary one. At the comparatively young age of fifty-eight, having served for thirty-two years, he became the dean of the Congress. But two years later Sheppard had to return to Texas to face a reelection campaign in the Democratic primary. Despite his power and prestige, reelection could have been a problem. Early speculation was that Governor James V. Allred of Wichita Falls wanted Sheppard's Senate seat, but that rumor proved false when the popular governor announced for reelection as the state's chief executive. Then Sheppard received word that Representative Martin Dies of Orange would challenge him. That rumor also proved inaccurate. When the primary was held, Sheppard faced five opponents, but none posed a real threat. Defeating them all easily, he gathered nearly 65 percent of the vote.[22]

However, Sheppard could not relax and enjoy the pleasures of his victory. In 1937 he faced a challenge to Roosevelt and the New Deal, and, consequently, to his own influence. Earlier, in 1935, in the *Schecter Poultry* case, the U.S. Supreme Court had declared that the National Industrial Recovery Act, a cornerstone of the early New Deal, was unconstitutional. In a five-to-four decision, the majority stated that the law granted essentially legislative powers to the executive branch of government. Then in early 1936, in another five-to-four decision, the Court declared the Agricultural Adjustment Act (AAA) invalid because it taxed one sector of the economy to aid another.[23]

Following the Court's ruling on the AAA, Sheppard aggressively attacked these two decisions in particular and the Court in general. Echoing similar comments by the president and fearing that the Court posed a serious threat to other New Deal legislation, Sheppard called the majority opinions ridiculous, preposterous, and the "epitome of obsolescence." He stated that the decisions were those of "a closed mind . . . of a mind that has ceased to live, and that can ruminate only on a dimly recalled past."[24]

Seeking to change the position of the Court, on February 5, 1937, President Roosevelt sent a proposal to Congress in which he suggested that the president should be empowered to appoint a new justice for each one who was over seventy years old and who refused to retire. Since six members of the Court were septuagenarians, the plan would enable the president to increase the number of justices of the federal tribunal to as many as fifteen. The following day Sheppard announced his approval of the plan, even though most southern Democrats opposed it. The Texas state legislature encouraged the Texas delegation to oppose the bill. Junior senator Tom Connally of Texas alleged that the idea was unconstitutional. The "court-packing" scheme was generally unpopular, and that unpopularity grew as the Senate Judiciary Committee debated the issue for five months. During that time, however, events seemed to bypass the need for the bill, as the Court began to uphold several New Deal laws. Furthermore, one of the anti-Roosevelt justices resigned. Thus, when the Senate voted to recommit the bill to committee, the plan died. Reflective of Sheppard's sense of urgency and yet the futility of fighting on for the bill was an undelivered speech in Sheppard's papers entitled "Shall the New Deal Survive?" The death of the "court-packing" bill was the first major defeat for Roosevelt and was the beginning of the end of the New Deal.[25]

The recession of 1938 further damaged the New Deal's fortunes. But Sheppard faced a difficult dilemma and played a role in still another blow to Roosevelt's domestic reforms. First an allegation surfaced that the administration had used undue political influence to affect the outcome of the 1938 general election. In June, Sheppard took the chairmanship of an ad hoc Special Committee to Investigate Senatorial Campaign Expenditures. During the conduct of the committee's investigation, he faced several conflicts. In pursuance of his duties he clashed with a close friend of Roosevelt, Secretary of the Treasury Henry Morgenthau, and a popular new program, the Works Progress Administration. So even though New Deal critics had predicted that Sheppard would not conduct a vigorous investigation, most editorial comment proclaimed that his work had been thorough and unbiased. Sheppard's committee did find evidence of the use of federal workers in political campaigns. After the committee made its final report in January 1939, Sheppard coauthored a bill known as the Hatch Act, which governed the political activities of elected and appointed officials. Partly because of the controversy over the president's attempt to purge the Democratic Party of anti-New Dealers, domestic reform practically ended. When the president spoke on behalf of New Dealers in Democratic primaries in the South, many southern voters resented this outside influence, and it was mostly ineffective.[26]

In his last term in the Senate, Sheppard's greatest influence was in the area of preparedness and peacetime defense. His effectiveness resulted primarily from his role as chairman of the Military Affairs Committee. Through this position he supported a variety of legislation to promote the cause of a strong national defense. He worked diligently in support of a veterans' committee in the Senate and for the various veterans' bonus bills, including the Patman Bonus Bill, which was designed to grant veterans of World War I an earned bonus earlier than originally promised. In the case of the Patman bill he even voted to override President Roosevelt's veto, stating that "this time I think he's wrong." He also negotiated between various veterans' groups and the White House. Furthermore, Sheppard labored for legislation to establish veterans' hospitals in Texas and to fund trips to battlefields for Gold Star Mothers and the widows of men killed in battle. He also introduced and helped pass a more efficient promotion system for the United States military. In an effort to increase awareness of the value of the military, he helped pass a resolution designating April 6 as "Army Day." Then, at President Roosevelt's request, Sheppard offered a bill to increase the number of cadets at the West Point Military Academy by five hundred.[27] As a result of Sheppard's work toward bolstering national defense, he received a letter from General Douglas MacArthur thanking him for his work. According to the general, Sheppard had shown a "comprehensive and sympathetic understanding of the problems of the army and of national defense." To him MacArthur wrote, "No man now in Congress, has done quite as much for the security of the United States of America as you have."[28]

From the strong and influential position as chairman of the Military Affairs Committee, Sheppard continued to advocate more money for defense. Appropriations that passed in the spring of 1938 with Sheppard's help included increases in military spending. Then in 1939 he asked for still more outlays for defense, especially for air defense. In arguing for this legislation, he emphasized the need to defend the Panama Canal and, in so doing, uphold the Monroe Doctrine. Against some vocal opposition he guided the defense appropriations bill through the Senate. On March 7, 1939, that body voted 77 to 8 to spend $358 million to bolster the nation's defenses.[29]

Approximately one week later Adolf Hitler annexed the Sudetenland, creating a crisis in Europe. Even though there was no immediate declaration of war, many Americans believed that conflict was certain. This belief led to a reconsideration of the Neutrality Act of 1937, which had effectively imposed an arms embargo on U.S. munitions makers. President Roosevelt stated that the act had been a "terrible blunder." He especially wanted the right to sell arms to the Allied belligerents in case of war in Europe. All such problems seemed no more than academic in the spring and summer of 1939, but on September 1 the argument became more than just rhetorical. On that day Hitler unleashed the "Blitzkrieg" on Poland. When Congress met in special session on September 21, Sheppard argued emphatically for the repeal of the Neutrality Act. Fellow Texan Tom Connally led the fight in the Senate to repeal the arms embargo portion of the law and replace it with a "cash-and-carry" provision, which authorized arms sales to belligerents but prohibited delivery in U.S. ships, and Sheppard supported the bill eagerly. On November 4 this bill became law.[30]

Soon after the passage of the "cash-and-carry" bill, Sheppard told the press that preparedness and national defense would be the most important issues of 1940. He was correct. In January he worked on the details of government contracts offered to defense industries, many of which were in Texas. In the spring he held hearings on a variety of weapons, including a "super-weapon" called the Barlow bomb, which did not prove feasible. In June he supported the nomination of Republican Henry L. Stimson to the position of secretary of war. This bipartisanship showed the world that American citizens were united on matters of national defense.[31]

But the measure that caused the most bitterness and conflict was the selective service bill. While others wanted to avoid taking any position on a bill that might be unpopular with their constituents, the aging Sheppard took an early and courageous stand by supporting the bill. Robert A. Taft of Ohio and Burton K. Wheeler of Montana headed the powerful isolationist bloc in the Senate. In the debate over the issue Sheppard alluded to a possible German attack on the United States and a potential Japanese threat to U.S. possessions in the Pacific. With the Texas senator's artful leadership, the vote was taken on August 28 and the nation's first peace-time draft passed 58 to 31. On September 14 the conference committee, which Sheppard chaired, reported out the Selective Service Act. It quickly passed both houses and was signed by President Roosevelt on September 16. Sheppard also participated in the drawing of draft numbers on October 28.[32]

The heavy workload required to ensure passage of the draft bill affected Sheppard's health. He tried to rest before the next session of Congress, but speaking engagements kept him busy. When Congress reconvened in January 1941, he was at his post, but friends urged him to rest. A news correspondent reported that Sheppard "would rather die on duty than leave the front at this critical time." Sheppard immediately began the work for a measure requested by the president known as "lend-lease." Through this proposal the United States would become the "arsenal of democracy," by giving our allies "ships, planes, tanks, and guns." On February 27 he addressed the Senate about this bill, which passed on March 8, and was signed into law three days later: that speech was Sheppard's last. On April 4 he suffered a brain hemorrhage from which he died on April 9, 1941.[33]

Praise for the life and mourning for the passing of Senator Morris Sheppard of Texas came from many in high places. President Roosevelt said that he was "courteous, kindly," and a "gentleman." "He was my friend through many years." Later General MacArthur told Lucille Sheppard, the senator's widow, that Morris Sheppard had been the first American casualty of World War II. The Army broke precedent by naming an airfield after a nonflier when they christened the new base at Wichita Falls, Texas, as Sheppard Field.[34]

In the years following his death, neither historians nor the public have had a particularly high opinion of Morris Sheppard. Even though a simple listing of his accomplishments ought to convince anyone of his importance in influencing the course of U.S. history, two elements have obscured both the popular image and the professional views of this unique Texas politician.

First, he was so closely linked to prohibition that the misfortunes of that experiment have hurt his reputation. Even though a new generation of revisionist historians has shown that reforming the evils of the open saloon was a progressive, urban, middle-class movement, the popular notion remains that prohibitionists were ax-wielding fanatics, rural bumpkins, or uneducated fundamentalist preachers. Reducing Sheppard's career to simply being a prohibitionist, and then drawing a caricature of those who supported the Eighteenth Amendment, is, of course, unfair.

Second, Morris Sheppard does not fit the mold, or at least the popular image, of the powerful Texas politician. As a quiet, unassuming man, with little or no braggadocio, he was clearly not a "wheeler-dealer." A charming man, he was typically liked by all, even his political foes. He succeeded through hard work, sincerity, and persuasive logic rather than by building a powerful political machine. Ten times he ran for public office and ten times his constituents elected him. His career was never tainted by any serious accusation of scandal. The prohibitionists rebuked him for supporting Al Smith in 1928; others questioned his support of senatorial candidate Earle B. Mayfield, an alleged Klansman, in 1922. In both of these instances Sheppard was open and honest about his position, and although his logic can be questioned, he reasoned that he was a Democrat and should, therefore, support the nominees of his party.

As the post-Vietnam era continues to become poisoned with reports of common political and business scandal, the story of the honesty and hard work of Morris Sheppard in public service can be a refreshing antidote. Though not a typical political manipulator, he clearly was one of the Texas power elite of the twentieth century.

JOHN NANCE GARNER

Fig. 3.1. Vice President John Nance Garner teamed with President Franklin Roosevelt to pass the "New Deal" during the early 1930s. Garner (John Nance) Papers, Center for American History, UT-Austin (CN 11164).

JOHN NANCE GARNER

BY PATRICK COX

John Nance Garner, the first Texan to serve as Speaker of the House and as vice president of the United States, became one of the most influential political leaders from the Lone Star State in the twentieth century. Elected to Congress in 1902, Garner gained increasing influence and prestige until he became Speaker in 1931 when the Democrats regained power in the early years of the Great Depression. After an unsuccessful run for the presidential nomination in 1932, Garner became Franklin D. Roosevelt's running mate. As a stalwart Democrat, Garner distrusted Wall Street, and he championed New Deal legislation aimed at correcting the nation's financial woes. He helped to steer through Congress most of the New Deal programs that forever reshaped the role of the federal government, becoming arguably the second most powerful man in the nation behind FDR. In July 1940, however, as a result of political disputes with Roosevelt and his opposition to a third term for the president, Garner left Washington, D.C., and the life he had known for nearly forty years. Garner and his wife Ettie lived the remainder of their years in their hometown of Uvalde.

Born on November 22, 1868, in post–Civil War Texas, John Nance Garner grew up in a log cabin at Blossom Prairie in Red River County in Northeast Texas. His father, John Nance Garner III, came to Texas from Tennessee, served in the Confederate army, and settled after the war in Red River County. The elder Garner became a successful cotton farmer and local politician in his home county. Garner's mother, Rebecca Walpole Garner, the daughter of a banker, encouraged her son's education. The young Garner attended small rural schools at Bogata and Blossom Prairie. At eighteen he went to Vanderbilt University in Nashville, Tennessee, where he stayed only one semester, possibly because of ill health or the rudimentary education provided by his inadequate rural school preparation. He returned to Clarksville, Texas, read law, and was admitted to the bar in 1890. Although he displayed some talent at baseball when he played shortstop for the "Blossom-Coon Soup Hollow" team, Garner wisely saw the benefits of the law office and courtroom over the dusty diamonds and cotton fields of Northeast Texas.[1]

In 1892 Garner moved to Uvalde, where he quickly developed his legal and business career. He joined the firm of Judge John H. Clark as circuit-

Sourcing close by paragraph

riding attorney for South Texas counties. His cases were diverse, ranging from land title disputes to horse and cattle theft. At one point, he owned the Uvalde newspaper as a result of a legal settlement. He also acquired a title company and renamed it the Garner Abstract & Land Company. The company's bylaws allowed the owner to purchase and sell property in addition to providing land titles. Garner located the office on the town square and later moved it to the second floor of the town's Grand Opera House.[2]

Uvalde at the turn of the century was a rough-and-tumble community with a large number of saloons. Located sixty miles due west of San Antonio, the town emerged as a center of ranching, shipping on the Texas and Pacific Railroad, banking, and gambling. During the early years in Uvalde, as he built his law practice and expanded his real estate business, Garner developed a reputation as a hard drinker and sharp poker player, an image he maintained for the rest of his life. When a vacancy opened in the county judge's office, Garner made his first political run in the Democratic primary.[3]

After a brief courtship Garner married Mariette "Ettie" Rheiner on November 25, 1895, at the Christian Church in Sabinal. Ettie was the daughter of Peter Rheiner, a Swiss immigrant who spoke five languages, joined in the California gold rush, served in the Confederate army, and then moved to Texas. Her mother died when Ettie was very young. She was educated at boarding school and ironically met Garner after he heard about her opposition to his candidacy for Uvalde county judge. In an age when few women expressed their political opinions, Ettie opposed his candidacy because of his reputation for drinking and poker-playing. The couple had one son, Tully, born September 24, 1896.[4]

Garner made a successful run for state representative in 1898. During his two terms in Austin he authored only a few bills and spent most of his time learning the procedures of the Texas House. While in Austin, Garner earned his nickname "Cactus Jack" after he unsuccessfully proposed the cactus as the state flower. The bluebonnet prevailed, but the moniker "Cactus Jack" lasted a lifetime for the ambitious politician. As a state representative, Garner also filed legislation to divide Texas into five states to offset the congressional influence of New England. He worked on land legislation favored by large ranchers in South Texas that defended patents issued by Spain and Mexico. He voted for antitrust legislation, insurance regulation, and other reform measures. When the 1900 census results indicated that Texas would gain three new congressional seats, Garner secured the chairmanship of the House Committee on Congressional Districts. He worked to keep San Antonio out of the new Fifteenth District as it covered all of South Texas from Corpus Christi on the Gulf of Mexico to Brownsville and west to Del Rio on the Rio Grande. Garner later termed the district simply as "the biggest in Texas."[5]

In the 1902 congressional election, Garner bested several experienced opponents. Senator Joe Bailey and former governor Jim Hogg supported Garner over State Senator Joseph Dibrell of Guadalupe County. More importantly, Garner secured the endorsement of South Texas political boss Jim Wells. The most influential political voice in South Texas, Wells worked with Garner on state legislative issues critical to the interests of the large landowners below the Nueces. Wells wanted a reliable successor to Congressman Rudolph Kleberg. The Wells machine, combined with Garner's political skills and energetic campaign, proved to be too much for Dibrell in the Democratic primary. The following November, Garner defeated his Republican challenger, Nueces County lawyer John C. Scott. On Garner's 1902 campaign, the *Seguin Enterprise* reported that "his advocacy of the income tax (which is a new feature in the campaign) struck a popular chord." The newspaper noted also that Garner solicited support from African American voters, who still voted in significant numbers for Republican candidates. "Speaking of the negro in politics he showed them their complete elimination from Republicanism in Texas . . . and urged them to stay with those who were their real friends in real times of trouble," the *Enterprise* reported. After all, Garner "appreciated and understood them thoroughly," the paper asserted. However, Garner adhered to the beliefs held by most Democrats of this era—specifically the belief in white racial superiority as justification for Jim Crow segregation.[6]

When the Garners moved to Washington, members of Congress had no offices. The couple moved to Mrs. List's boarding house at 1311 K Street, where they worked on congressional and constituent issues, with Ettie Garner serving as secretary for the Fifteenth Congressional District. "While I typed the letters, Mr. Garner took care of his departmental work on his way to the capitol." Ettie stated. She also fulfilled the many social obligations of a congressman's spouse. When "calling" at the White House, she noted the more pleasant aspects as well as the difficulties of being the wife of an elected official: "The tea table, over which the social secretary presided, was pretty; the president's wife chatted with you; you had your cup of tea and a cake that tasted particularly good because it was baked in the White House, and left, feeling warm and pleasant. You had become an entity to the first lady of the land. . . . I used to enjoy the social life but after about ten years it began to be rather monotonous." Although she tired of the social scene, Ettie remained a vital force and a capable administrator throughout her husband's long political career.[7]

The incoming congressional class of 1902 included a number of men who influenced the nation's history including William Randolph Hearst, Joe Cannon, Claude Kitchin, Jim Byrnes, Joe Robinson, and Carter Glass. Garner centered his early congressional career on the difficult economic and political issues of the era: tariffs, income tax, isolationism, and U.S. neutrality following the start of World War I in Europe. Because of his link to Jim Wells, Garner concentrated on bringing needed public improvements to Texas and federal expenditures to his district. The balance sheet showed considerable success: an intracoastal canal from Galveston to Corpus Christi, deepwater ports at Brownsville and Aransas Pass; an international bridge and weather station at Brownsville; new post offices and a federal soil survey for South Texas; and increased military funding for Fort Brown. Garner succinctly described his philosophy for acquiring federal dollars for his district when he declared, "Every time one of those Yankees gets a ham, I am going to do my best to get a hog." [8]

After the Democratic victory of 1910 placed the party in control of Congress, Garner's colleagues elected him to the position of Democratic Party whip, the third-ranking House member. In 1913 Garner moved to the Ways and Means Committee from Foreign Affairs, where he had served with Kitchin, Cordell Hull, Henry Rainey, and A. Mitchell Palmer. As a member of Ways and Means, Garner proposed a graduated income tax provision with increased levies on upper-income individuals. He included the provision as an attempt to offset lost revenues resulting from Democratic legislation to lower tariffs. Garner successfully pushed for passage and ratification of the Sixteenth Amendment to the Constitution in 1913, which established the income tax. "I felt that the income tax ought to be based on the theory of paying according to ability, and that is the theory that finally was written into the law." Garner kept a portrait of Andrew Jackson in his office, prompting many comparisons to "Old Hickory" and his philosophy. He enjoyed the comparisons to the nineteenth-century leader who was often popularly viewed in the early decades of the twentieth century as a defender of individual freedoms and a foe of entrenched eastern financial interests. [9]

Another landmark bill in 1913 reformed the nation's banking system. Garner steered President Wilson's controversial Federal Reserve Act through Congress, overcoming traditional opposition from agrarian and southern Democratic congressmen who were historically aligned in opposition to eastern banks and investors. The compromise legislation distributed power between board members appointed by the president and a regional banking system with boards of private bankers. When President Wilson signed the bill, the legislative victory established Garner as a congressional authority on finance and taxation, a reputation that he relished and enhanced for the remainder of his career in Washington, D.C.[10]

While Garner took a leadership role in some progressive economic reforms, he steadfastly opposed the efforts of prohibitionists to restrict alcohol sales and distribution. A lifelong "wet" who made no secret of his fondness for liquor, he united with other wet Democrats to oppose women's suffrage, another progressive issue closely aligned with the temperance movement. Garner undoubtedly reflected the views of the majority of his South Texas district. Yet he faced opposition for his stance against prohibition and relied on the South Texas political bosses and liquor interests to maintain his position in public office. Otto Wahrmund, San Antonio Brewers Association president, urged Brownsville residents not to join a reform coalition against Garner as it "would mean a vote against not only all of the local Democratic nominees, but our friend, the Hon. John N. Garner, as well!" Garner strongly opposed fellow Texan and U. S. senator Morris Sheppard's prohibition legislation that led to the Eighteenth Amendment in 1919. He saw little value in efforts by "drys" to restrict alcohol or to blame liquor for a myriad of social problems.[11]

During the debate over the Underwood Tariff bill in 1913, Garner's witty comments made him popular with the capital press corps. The Democratic bill lowered tariffs on most imported goods, but Garner worked to maintain the duty on wool and mohair, a primary agricultural industry in his district. Republican representative J. Hampton Moore, former Philadelphia mayor, taunted Garner in the debate over the bill in a poem that became known as "Garner's Goat."

> Of all the creatures in the land
> Of pedigrees supremely grand,
> There's none that do respect command,
> Like Garner's goat of Texas

The House rocked with laughter during an otherwise dull debate as Moore completed eight verses, but Garner quickly replied:

> Hampy Moore is a helluva poet;
> He can't tell a sheep from a go-at.

Afterward, in a mock ceremony on the Capitol steps, reporters crowned Garner the king of the one-liner and installed him as the "Patron Saint of Angora." The press members gave Garner a flag with a banner that read: "The Triumphant Goat." *Harper's Magazine* stated that, with Garner's reply, even the "bravest legislators would risk devastation" if they dared to engage the Texan in debate.[12]

Foreign affairs also occupied much of Garner's tenure in Congress, especially during Wilson's terms. The violence of the Mexican Revolution began in 1910 to spill over into Garner's South Texas district. Garner appealed to Wilson to strengthen the U.S. military presence on the Rio Grande and said the army's failure to assign more troops along the border constituted "criminal negligence." Although both Texans and Mexicans shared responsibility for years of cross-border bloodshed, Garner blamed the Mexican government for being "responsible for the bandit outrages in the Brownsville section of Texas." With the local economy suffering from the civil unrest, local officials, ranchers, and border merchants wrote to Garner demanding federal protection. Jim Wells complained to Garner in 1915 about the small number of troops assigned to Brownsville, which he termed "the only important point upon the Rio Grande border this side of El Paso." With the revelation of the Plan of San Diego in August 1915, which called for an armed uprising that would free Mexican Americans from "Yankee tyranny," Garner led the chorus from Texas for immediate federal protection. The U.S. troop escalation began in earnest as the Wilson administration responded to the pleas of Garner and other Texas officials. The local economy began to surge with the influx of soldiers along with the necessary federal expenditures to keep them in the field. Garner's actions during the border crisis enhanced his position with his constituents and with the Wilson administration.[13]

Dull sentence

President Wilson turned to Garner when other Democrats, notably senior Democrat Claude Kitchin, opposed the administration's program for military preparedness. Although many Democrats and isolationist Republicans opposed the president's efforts to build up the nation's armed forces after war had begun in Europe in 1914, Garner consistently favored Wilson's escalation policy. He voted for the U.S. declaration of war against Germany in 1917. Garner became President Wilson's chief liaison with Congress once the United States entered World War I. He spent many long hours in closed-door meetings with President Wilson and his aide Joseph E. Tumulty to plan legislative strategy for the war effort. His personal work with the White House further enhanced the Texas influence in the Wilson administration. And his work with the White House and in the Congress demonstrated the ascendancy of Texas in the national Democratic Party and in the corridors of power in Washington.[14]

Garner considered retiring from Congress when the Republican Party won the White House and recaptured both houses of Congress in 1920. But the political tide had already begun to turn several years earlier, before the end of the war. In the midterm congressional elections of 1918 President Wilson actively campaigned for Democratic candidates, ignoring Garner's advice to stay out of the congressional elections. Republicans gained slim majorities in both houses after Wilson argued that a Republican Congress would harm his efforts to secure peace; then in 1920 the GOP returned to its earlier dominance with landslide victories. South Texas political bosses Jim Wells and Archie Parr then persuaded Garner to remain in Congress and utilize his extensive knowledge of Washington politics to protect his position along with their interests. Some supporters urged Garner to run for the Senate against long-term incumbent Senator Charles Culberson in 1922. But Garner told his friend Jim Wells that, in spite of the Democratic setbacks of 1920, "I believe that if the Democrats carry the House next year and I am reelected to Congress, I will be elected Speaker." However, the Democratic leadership quickly returned Garner to reality when the ailing Claude Kitchin selected Finnis J. Garret of Tennessee as the minority leader. Kitchin resented Garner's close relationship with President Wilson during the war and had fought with Garner over a number of legislative issues.[15]

Garner had other obstacles in the form of Democratic opposition at home. In the most serious challenge since his first election to Congress, Garner faced an opponent backed by the Ku Klux Klan in the 1922 Democratic primary. Endorsing the Invisible Empire's racist, nativist, and law-and-order platform, Klan-backed candidates challenged anti-Klan Democrats in Texas from city hall to the U.S. Senate. Unlike some incumbent Democrats who embraced the Klan's agenda, Garner accused the Klan of being foreign to the American way of life. In retaliation, the Klan burned a cross in a rally at Uvalde and vowed to defeat him. Garner won the bitter primary election, but lost many counties, including his home county of Uvalde. Bascom Timmons, a friend of Garner's and his "official" biographer, concluded that Garner based his decision to remain in Congress on the Klan challenge. Garner detested the Klan's methods and structure. He also undoubtedly desired to become Speaker of the House.[16]

Upon winning reelection, Garner returned to fight new battles as a spokesman for the House Democratic minority. With Republicans in firm control of the White House and Congress, Garner carefully selected his issues. During two consecutive legislative sessions, he led the Democratic charge against Treasury Secretary Andrew Mellon's proposed income tax reduction for the wealthiest Americans. Garner successfully pushed a measure through Congress giving smaller incomes a tax rate reduction of 60 percent and larger incomes a smaller cut. His proposal and persuasive influence maintained Democratic unity and drew many Republicans to his side. When President Calvin Coolidge signed the Garner substitute tax bill in 1924, Garner believed the measure established a graduated tax system that "will be little changed regardless of which party may be in power at any time." This victory further enhanced Garner's reputation as an expert on fiscal affairs while also appealing to a broad base of middle-income Americans. Garner also capitalized on the loyalty of House Democrats who increasingly trusted his leadership on both domestic and foreign policy issues. By the mid-1920s, therefore, Garner had earned a reputation as the "best politician on either side." [17]

House Democrats finally selected Garner as the minority leader after the Republican sweep in the 1928 elections. Garner's friend from the other side of the isle, Nicholas Longworth, served as Speaker. The pair had entered Congress at the same time and had served together on the Foreign Affairs Committee. The erudite urban Pennsylvania Republican and the laconic rural Texas Democrat were as unlikely a combination as any pair in Congress. In the spirit of bipartisanship, Longworth and Garner met regularly with a select group of Republican and Democratic members in a small back room in the capitol. Bascom Timmons claimed that Representative John McDuffie of Alabama christened the Longworth-Garner sessions the "Board of Education." Although the "Board" originally convened while the Eighteenth Amendment remained in effect, a bookcase with glass doors and green curtains held the "refreshments" that helped lubricate the private discussions on legislation and procedure. After having drinks and completing business, Garner frequently adjourned the sessions with a toast associated with him for the remainder of his life: "Now we'll strike a blow for liberty." [18]

After the Wall Street crash in October 1929, Garner recognized that the American economic system was in need of basic structural reform. He unsuccessfully fought President Herbert Hoover and his administration for lower tariffs, expanded public works, and an early bonus for World War I veterans. In a rare public address, he spoke to the nation in a coast-to-coast radio broadcast in opposition to the Smoot-Hawley Tariff. He aimed his talk directly at average American consumers. Garner convincingly explained how much the tariff would raise the cost of every item from soap to tombstones at a time when the depression was strengthening its grip on the population. [19]

The congressional elections of 1930 reflected the nation's concern with the Great Depression, as Republicans lost their 104-seat majority, but the House remained almost evenly divided. Nearly a year passed after the election before Congress reconvened, and during that time several members had passed away, giving the Democrats a bare majority. After the death of Longworth, Garner finally realized his lifelong ambition to serve as Speaker of the House. "He is as explosive as dynamite, as booming as a bass drum, as active as a cricket," *The New York Times* said a few days prior to Garner's bid for Speaker. On December 7, 1931, Garner became the thirty-ninth Speaker by a margin of only three votes. He thus became the first Democrat to hold the position in a decade. In his acceptance speech to the House of Representatives, Garner stated, "I made no promises as a candidate for this office, and I make none now." [20]

Garner's fame and image grew as Speaker. He became a nationally known figure as the press labeled him the "Texas Tiger," "Texas Jack," and "Chaparral Jack." Editorial cartoonists often pictured him in western garb with an oversize Stetson or sombrero, puffing on a stubby cigar and confronting his antagonists. Now that he was Speaker, his name appeared regularly as a heavyweight contender for the Democratic presidential nomination. He downplayed his own popularity and stated that Governor Franklin Roosevelt of New York "looks like the man for us in 1932." [21]

Over President Herbert Hoover's objections, Garner pushed a $1 billion public works program through Congress. He also worked for passage of the Reconstruction Finance Corporation (RFC), the new agency to provide loans for public improvements. The RFC represented the federal government's largest peacetime effort to influence the economy. The speaker also secured the appointment of fellow Texan Jesse H. Jones of Houston to the RFC board. Although President Hoover and other critics viewed these programs as unnecessary government intervention in the business and personal affairs of Americans, Garner and his congressional supporters saw the necessity of increasing government expenditures to meet the crisis. More than 5,000 banks failed nationwide between 1930 and 1932. On March 29, 1932, Garner delivered a defining speech before the House on the need for increasing taxes to expand the federal government's expenditures to fight the depression. One student of Garner's career characterized the statements as the "most celebrated speech he [Garner] ever made in Congress." *The New York Times* reported that "rarely in the annals of parliaments has the intervention of one member in a crisis dispelled it so promptly and so effectively as did Speaker John Garner's address to the House." [22]

As the most visible national Democrat in 1931, Garner's success spawned growing speculation about a potential presidential bid. Although Garner continued to maintain that New York governor Franklin Roosevelt appeared to have the inside track to the nomination, many of the Speaker's friends and supporters pushed him for the Democratic nomination. Garner-for-President clubs formed in Texas in December 1931. Controversial newspaper publisher William Randolph Hearst promoted Garner in a nationwide radio address on January 11, 1932. After the broadcast, the Hearst newspaper chain followed with a lengthy series entitled "The Romantic Story of John Nance Garner." San Antonio hosted a statewide "Garner for President Rally," where a formal campaign committee organized on his behalf.[23]

Garner attracted southern and western Democrats who identified with his pragmatic approach to confronting the depression while maintaining the political and social status quo. Garner sewed up the Texas delegation and won the California Democratic primary, but he trailed Roosevelt and former New York governor Al Smith when Democrats convened to nominate a president in Chicago in late June, 1932. At this point, Garner probably foresaw the probable outcome of the process and hoped for a strong Democratic ticket that would increase his power as House Speaker. Nevertheless, Texas senator Tom Connally nominated Garner at the Democratic convention as a "Democrat without prefix, suffix or qualifying phrases. The supreme hour calls for a man." Sam Rayburn served as Garner's floor manager at the convention as Garner listened to the proceedings on the radio from his Washington apartment. Franklin Roosevelt led after the first three ballots but could not secure the necessary two-thirds majority from the delegates to win the nomination. Garner, wishing to avoid a debacle that would deadlock the convention, instructed Rayburn to release his delegates. California and Texas then switched to Roosevelt, giving him the nomination on the fourth ballot. Sam Rayburn observed that "Garner was willing and really wanted the California-Texas delegations to be released and had expressed the hope that they would vote for Mr. Roosevelt."[24]

Following FDR's nomination, Democratic delegates then unanimously picked Garner for vice president. Roosevelt's forces promoted the idea of a Roosevelt-Garner ticket when they worked to bring in the final votes for the presidential nomination. Roosevelt called Garner prior to his nomination and offered him a place on the ticket. After he learned of his nomination for vice president, Garner responded with an acceptance letter, stating that "outside influences over which we have no control are not wholly accountable for the depression." The major causes, Garner declared, rested with the national legislation and policies "for which the Republican leaders are wholly responsible." Garner stated that he was in "awe that in our hands is about to be placed the destinies of our country." While Garner appeared to embrace his place as the vice presidential nominee, he later explained to Bascom Timmons that he had given up his life-long dream of being the Speaker of the house. Garner said, "I believe the country needs the Democrats in power at this time." However, Garner added, "when I give up the Speakership I will give up a place wanted." [25]

Roosevelt and Garner won a landslide victory in November 1932 over a beleaguered President Hoover. The Democratic ticket carried forty-two of the forty-eight states. The national economy was as frigid as the outside temperature when Roosevelt and Garner took office on a cold March 4, 1933. Garner, who had also been reelected to his House seat, gave a farewell speech to his colleagues in the Congress. The House members then escorted him through the Capitol to the Senate chamber, where he took the oath of office for vice president, the first and only man to ever hold both the House Speakership and vice presidency on the same day.

The Senate and the office of the vice president still resembled nineteenth-century institutions in 1932. The Senate was entrenched in a system of rigid adherence to seniority and senatorial privilege that dated back more than a century. The Senate still conducted its business according to Thomas Jefferson's *Manual of Parliamentary Procedure.* The vice president, the constitutionally designated presiding officer of the Senate, was seldom seen or heard unless a tie vote occurred. At that point, the vice president could cast the deciding vote. Garner proclaimed that the vice presidency was "the spare tire on the automobile of government" and "a no man's land somewhere between the legislative and the executive branch." Throughout the history of the nation, the vice presidency remained a mostly symbolic, legislative position. The usefulness of the vice president usually ended with the national election. Only a handful of vice presidents exercised their duty as the presiding officer of the Senate. An even smaller number became involved in executive and cabinet-level discussions. In fact, with the exception of Martin Van Buren in 1836, no vice president had managed to be elected president in his own right; vice presidents had become president only when the chief executive died in office. Garner would alter the vice presidency in an unprecedented manner. Never the "spare tire" on Roosevelt's team, he attended and actively participated in Roosevelt's cabinet meetings on national policy and legislative strategy. He thus effectively transformed the largely ceremonial office into an influential executive and legislative position. [26]

Garner quickly became, after the president, the single most important man in the government and, arguably, the nation. Within days of the November election, Roosevelt began consulting Garner on the administration's legislative agenda. Garner's political knowledge along with his respect and great persuasive powers proved to be invaluable, especially during Roosevelt's first one hundred days. The new vice president's whiskey-drinking, poker-playing style was an additional asset that helped lubricate the legislative process for the New Deal. Garner presided over the Senate, where more than a fifth of its members had served with him in the House. These included Democratic senators Joe Robinson of Arkansas, Alben Barkley of Kentucky, Carter Glass of Virginia, and James Byrnes of South Carolina. The influence of the Texas congressional delegation and especially Garner's protégé Sam Rayburn also provided vital support to the New Deal programs. From 1933 to 1938 no fewer than eight Texans held regular committee chairmanships and headed two special committees. Rayburn became a key leader and House majority leader in 1937. Other influential Texans included Marvin Jones, James Buchanan, Hatton Sumners, and Joseph Mansfield. Because Garner knew the strengths and weaknesses of both houses, he was able either to push bills through or bury them. He was, as one writer stated, "a mole rather than an eagle." A master at working individual senators on the floor, he was the "wise old man of Congress." On most evenings after a legislative session, Garner convened his "Board of Education," holding court over bourbon and branch water.

Garner's tactics made him the most powerful vice president in history. Although he was not always in accord with administration programs, especially those requiring deficit spending, he continued to support the New Deal until the spring of 1937. "He is conducting the office he occupies in a way which, compared with that favored by his immediate predecessors, amounts almost to a revolution," *The New York Times* noted on Garner's popularity with the Congress. "He has a way with 'the boys' that takes him safely past many of those prides and jealousies that flourish in all legislative atmospheres. He likes them, and they like him, and that means a great deal." Many other publications recognized Garner's stature and influence. "In truth, he is the first Vice President to emerge as a real legislative force since the early days when the Senate President worked with the White House occupant," the *Literary Digest* observed. "Not everything New Dealish does he approve but once approved by the High Command (President Roosevelt), it meets with his unquestioned approval." [27]

Garner steered a dazzling number of important bills through the Congress in the crisis atmosphere of FDR's first one hundred days. These New Deal programs included the Emergency Banking Relief Act, the Federal Emergency Relief Act, the Federal Deposit Insurance Corporation (FDIC), the Federal Securities Act, the Civilian Conservation Corps (CCC), the National Industrial Recovery Act (NIRA), and the Public Works Administration (PWA). Garner won a notable victory when he convinced a reluctant President Roosevelt that minimal insurance for bank depositors constituted an essential part of banking and economic recovery. As he tended to New Deal legislative priorities, he shunned public appearances and ceremonial affairs. As *Time* magazine noted, "Jack Garner, with his love for poker and baseball, his fondness for a good highball with good friends, his habit of going to bed every night at 9 o'clock sharp, did not fit the public concept of an able politician, much less of a great statesman." Garner remained a key source to friendly reporters, but he declined to make public speeches or radio addresses. As he informed one reporter, "I'm a member of a firm—the junior member. Go to headquarters for the news." [28]

Garner kept a steady communication with Jesse H. Jones at the RFC. Jones informed Garner of the agency's loans and policy changes, but also kept him apprised of backroom discussions among the Roosevelt inner circle. Whenever Garner or Jones left the capital, they stayed in close contact with each other. Even when he left Washington for Uvalde, Garner communicated with Jones and relied on him for information. In the summer of 1934, Ettie Garner told Jones that her husband wanted news, even during his hunting and fishing trips at home. "PLEASE make him feel good by giving him all the 'low down,' I believe it is called," Ettie wrote to Jones. "He always says he is not interested in all such, but I notice he laps it up like a thirsty dog does water." [29]

The 1934 national elections increased the Democratic majority as many northern and western Republican incumbent senators fell to challengers. In the following congressional session, another round of New Deal programs, sometimes called the "Second New Deal," swept through both houses. The Civil Works Administration (CWA) and the Works Progress Administration (WPA) created millions of jobs as new schools, airports, roads, and other construction projects shot up across the nation. Expanded from its initial 1933 program, the Agricultural Adjustment Act (AAA) of 1935 provided assistance to farmers and ranchers with crop subsidies, production controls, and conservation programs. Garner likewise made his presence known on new legislation to regulate the nation's largest businesses. Along with Sam Rayburn as House sponsor, he pushed passage of the Securities Act of 1934, which brought Wall Street brokerage firms under the regulatory control of the Securities and Exchange Commission. The Utilities Holding Company Act, sponsored by Garner protégé Sam Rayburn, brought the large utility monopolies under federal supervision. Rayburn and Garner often rode together to the Capitol so as to discuss legislation and strategy. Garner also backed Rayburn's Rural Electrification Act (REA). Farm homes and rural towns that private utility companies passed over for electric service began to receive power from REA-funded electrical cooperatives in the late 1930s. Garner, known for

Fig. 3.2. Ettie Garner, wife of Vice President John Nance Garner, worked as Garner's assistant and carried out official duties during the couple's four decades in Washington, D.C. Garner (John Nance) Papers, Center for American History, UT-Austin (CN 10957).

his conservative, traditional beliefs in <u>limited federal government services</u>, was less enthusiastic about later New Deal programs. In spite of his misgivings about the National Recovery Act and the National Labor Relations Act (known as the Wagner Act), <u>he kept his counsel and advice behind closed doors</u>.[30]

Garner was the first vice president to make official overseas trips for an administration. Although he was averse to ceremonial affairs in Washington, both John and Ettie Garner attended functions and ceremonies in Europe, Mexico, and the Philippines. Viewed more as an isolationist and parochial Democrat in his earlier years, he assumed a broader role as an administration spokesman as he substituted for a president with serious physical limitations. He refused to change in other areas, however, continuing to avoid public statements, decline invitations to most Washington galas, and reject appeals to speak on national radio. Jealously guarding his privacy and time with Ettie, Garner refused security coverage by the Secret Service. "There is nobody crazy enough to shoot a Vice President," he speculated.[31]

Democrats enthusiastically renominated Roosevelt and Garner at their 1936 national convention in Philadelphia. Many newspapers and political writers predicted a close presidential election that year, but they underestimated the New Deal's appeal and the strength of the Roosevelt-Garner coalition. In Del Rio, Texas, in his old congressional district, one critic repeatedly interrupted a Garner speech by asking, "Is it true you play poker and cards?" Garner ignored the man, but after many interruptions, Garner finally replied, "Yes, Room 5, Starr Hotel, right after this meeting."

The incumbents swept the election in the greatest presidential landslide in modern U.S. history. The Roosevelt-Garner ticket won every state except Vermont and Maine and carried over 60 percent of the popular vote. Furthermore, the Democrats maintained a 75 percent majority in both the House and the Senate. While prospects appeared bright for the administration, dark clouds quickly formed ahead of a major political storm that blew into Washington in early 1937.[32]

Once Roosevelt and Garner took their oaths of office in January 1937, the vice president expressed concern with the expansive Democratic majorities in the House and Senate. To solidify his influence in the House, Garner actively worked for Sam Rayburn's election as majority leader, the second-ranking member of the House of Representatives, and a pathway to Rayburn's election as Speaker in 1940. Garner also maintained concerns about a number of the New Deal's expanded federal expenditures and the government's growing presence in American society. As the months passed, Garner's philosophy came into conflict with "the boss," President Roosevelt. When the vice president's hope for paring programs and balancing the budget faded, he began to refer to some federally funded efforts as "plain damn foolishness." The sit-down strikes in early 1937 that closed automobile plants in Michigan marked a breaking point in the Garner-Roosevelt relationship. Garner thought the strikers violated property rights, and he criticized the disruptions by union workers. "In Texas we would call that stealing," he stated to the president and other administration officials during one heated exchange in a cabinet meeting. He believed that Roosevelt agreed with him that the sit down strikes were illegal, but he knew that FDR and most of his cabinet favored tacit support for the unions. Conservative Texas Democratic congressman Martin Dies, with Garner's blessing, called for a legislative investigation of the sit-down strikes.[33]

President Roosevelt then shocked Garner and congressional Democrats with his plan to expand the federal judiciary, including the addition of up to six new members to the Supreme Court. The president's "court-packing" plan of 1937 widened the rift between Garner and FDR. Garner and his allies in Congress believed that the plan gave the president unprecedented powers in the selection of Supreme Court justices. Although he remained publicly silent on the proposal, Garner said privately that "it will be many, many moons before the boss signs that bill." Garner's friend House Judiciary Committee chairman Hatton Sumners of Dallas announced his opposition to the proposal in a speech to the Texas Bar Association. Garner let his opinion be known when he openly gave a thumb's down as the bill was first read to the Senate. As Democrats in Congress divided over the contested legislation, a prolonged battle between Roosevelt supporters and their opponents erupted over the plan's Supreme Court provisions.[34]

In the midst of the struggle over the court-packing bill, Garner went on vacation to Uvalde, an unprecedented departure for him during a legislative session and an act that publicized the rift between him and the president. Following Garner's lead, many southern senators broke ranks with the administration. The death of Senate Majority Leader Joe T. Robinson in July 1937 doomed what little chance the judiciary reform plan had in the Senate. A greatly changed bill that barely resembled the original proposal finally passed Congress. To add to FDR's problems with Garner and the Senate, the administration intervened in the selection of the successor to Senator Robinson. Kentucky Democrat and New Dealer Alben Barkley won by a single vote, and Garner blamed Roosevelt for interfering in the internal affairs of the Senate. Adding more fuel to the fire, southern senators defeated an antilynching bill passed by the House the following year. Thus, by 1938 Garner opposed most of Roosevelt's proposals, especially those involving government spending. The new coalition of Garner Democrats, combined with Republican opposition, completely altered the administration's agenda as spending bills, tax revision, and other of FDR's priorities stagnated in the backwater of congressional committees. Secretary of the Interior Harold Ickes said that Garner was "sticking his knife into the President's back."[35]

The fateful blow to the Garner-Roosevelt alliance occurred when the president attempted to purge opposition Democratic members of Congress in the 1938 elections. Garner made sure the opposition bloc in Congress voted against almost every domestic program spending increase the president desired. He then used all his influence to defend his congressional friends against Roosevelt's efforts to unseat them. The vice president delivered a pointed commentary prior to the 1938 elections: "The President of the United States ought not to take part in congressional fights." Although Roosevelt toured the nation in an attempt to unseat a number of Democratic critics, his efforts were mostly unsuccessful. Only one Democratic congressman on FDR's purge list lost a primary election. One noteworthy election came following the death of Garner ally and House Appropriations Committee chairman James Buchanan of Austin. New Deal advocate Lyndon Johnson, the Texas director of the National Youth Administration, won the special election running as an FDR supporter. However, the Johnson victory was an exception to the losses the president suffered elsewhere. The Republicans also gained eight Senate seats and eighty-one House members, thus giving more strength to the administration's opponents. The president remained powerful, but he had misjudged the depth of constituent loyalty to senators and representatives.[36]

As the dust settled from the 1938 elections, Garner saw no reason to thaw his frosty relations with the White House. By this time, Garner adhered to his strict view of the separation of powers and genuinely feared that Roosevelt's popularity threatened to usurp the traditional role of Congress. He also feared that Congress was losing to the president its prerogative to debate and refine legislation. Garner observed that FDR frequently used the media to communicate his objectives and bypassed the vice president and the congressional leadership.

Garner's public opposition undoubtedly stoked the flames of Roosevelt's opponents. New Deal critics had formed the Jeffersonian Democrats in 1936. This probusiness group, which included a number of wealthy Texans, became the nucleus of a vocal campaign against FDR and the New Deal. They made personal attacks on the president and his family and attempted to identify them with communism. However, the Jeffersonians received little popular support in 1936. Their numbers grew in the late 1930s after the Supreme Court battle and with Garner's staunch opposition to FDR's domestic agenda. The organization evolved into the Texas Regulars in the 1940s and contained many of Garner's friends and supporters. Although he agreed with many of their positions, Garner never openly participated in or supported the activities of the Jeffersonian Democrats or the Texas Regulars.

Speculation arose about a possible third term for Roosevelt soon after the 1936 election. The debate intensified after the 1938 House and Senate elections, in which the president's agenda met with across-the-board losses. While Roosevelt maintained silence on an unprecedented third term, thus increasing the hopes of Democratic aspirants, Garner emerged as the front-runner in national polls as the leading Democratic successor to Roosevelt. Garner's ability to attract press coverage undoubtedly contributed to his rise in the polls. His forthright image, no-nonsense style, and many years of service combined to make him a strong candidate — so long as FDR chose not to run again. A March 1939 Gallup poll placed Garner well ahead of other potential Democratic nominees, without Roosevelt in the race. As Postmaster General Jim Farley stated, the president resented the attention on Garner as Roosevelt "did not like to see the trees grow too tall around him." Farley revealed that in a private meeting with Roosevelt in July 1939 when the discussion came to Garner and the 1940 election, FDR revealed his assessment of his vice president: "there's Garner. He's just impossible." [37]

After he retired to Uvalde, Garner maintained that in 1939 he had urged a Jesse Jones presidential candidacy. "Jesse Jones I put at the top of the list of all administrative officials during my time in Washington. More than anyone I have known he rises above red tape. Yet he does things according to law." Garner also said he thought that his old friend Jones "would poll more independent votes than any other candidate we could nominate." But Garner held the respect of many Democrats, especially those who opposed a third term for FDR. [38]

Garner's criticism of the sit-down strikes incurred the wrath of one of the most prominent union chiefs. John L. Lewis, head of the CIO, told the House Labor Committee in July 1939 that Garner was a "labor-baiting, whisky-drinking, poker-playing, evil old man."

The press had a field day with the remarks, as Garner and Lewis appeared in newspaper editorial cartoons throughout the nation. In response to Lewis's remarks, at their 1939 annual convention in Dallas, Texas newspaper editors posed as "Milk-Drinking, Rag-Chewing, Fun-Poking Evil Old Editors" in defense of Garner. The incident merely increased speculation that Garner would be the next Democratic presidential nominee. Although Cordell Hull, Jim Farley, Harry Hopkins, and Jesse Jones each harbored presidential aspirations, Garner emerged as the leading candidate and the center of the "Stop Roosevelt" Democrats. In a March, 1939 article that detailed the "Garner Rebellion," the vice president told *Time* magazine that he would not prevent a campaign on his behalf. He finally admitted the following December that he would accept the nomination. "I would be against a third term on principle even if I approved every act of Roosevelt's two terms," Garner stated to Bascom Timmons. "I would oppose my own brother for a third term." [39]

A story in the *New York Herald Tribune* noted the open break between FDR and Garner over the presidential race in 1940: "The man whom he had previously referred to affectionately as 'The Cap'n,' or 'Boss,' and who had spoken affectionately aforetime of him as 'Old Man Common Sense,' have reached a historic parting of the ways." The article also recognized Ettie Garner's contributions to her husband's efforts. "Mrs. Garner has had more than a wife's usual share in bringing her husband to the top. She is his secretary, in fact as well as by title, and she works eight to ten hours a day in the vice-president's office looking after his mail, his 'fences' and his political future just as she has done since 1902."[40]

Many Democrats found themselves in the same difficult position as Sam Rayburn, the influential Texas congressman. Loyal to both the president and his mentor John Nance Garner, Rayburn found himself in the middle of the storm. "There is not a question in the world that if President Roosevelt should decide not to run, Garner is much the strongest candidate and if things go on as they are now, he stands a very fine chance of getting the nomination," he said in early 1940. "I also believe he can be elected, if nominated."[41]

Events overseas soon eclipsed domestic affairs, and specifically the debate over a third term. When Hitler's armies invaded Poland in September 1939, World War II began in Europe. Later that year, the German army quickly occupied the Netherlands and Belgium. France fell in June 1940, leaving Great Britain standing alone to face Nazi Germany. In late 1939, Congress had rescinded the Neutrality Act and increased arms sales to Britain and France on a "cash and carry" basis. The Selective Service Act of 1940 created the first peacetime army. Although isolationist sentiment remained strong in middle America, Garner and other southern Democratic critics of the Roosevelt administration rallied around the president's foreign policy. FDR aggressively attempted to move American public opinion toward the Allies, who confronted the Axis of Germany, Italy, and Japan. Concerns for national defense, increased sales of southern commodities, and a military buildup pleased Garner and his congressional friends. The crisis in Europe stimulated the "Draft Roosevelt" effort to secure a third Democratic nomination for the president.

In spite of these developments, Garner challenged Roosevelt in a series of early primaries in 1940. But Roosevelt won handily in New Hampshire, Wisconsin, Illinois, Oregon, and California before officially declaring his intent to run for a third term. With war clouds on the horizon and the magic of the Roosevelt name, rank-and-file Democrats wanted to send a clear message that they trusted their president in times of despair and challenge, even if it meant breaking the long-standing taboo of a president running for a third term. In addition, Roosevelt clearly united the disparate Democratic base in what became known as the Roosevelt coalition. Roosevelt and the New Deal had thus transformed the Democratic Party with an alliance that extended far beyond the traditional conservative, southern bloc that supported Garner.

As the Democrats gathered at their national convention in Chicago, Garner knew that Roosevelt would be the nominee. He instructed his friend Bascom Timmons to serve as his spokesman at the convention. Roosevelt received the nomination on July 17 and selected Henry Wallace as his vice presidential running mate. By choosing Wallace, FDR picked the polar opposite of the feisty Garner. Wallace, a cabinet member and loyal supporter of the New Deal, lacked legislative experience. Many congressional Democrats intensely disliked Wallace. Speaker of the House William Bankhead of Alabama unsuccessfully contested the Wallace nomination, an indication of the opposition to Wallace and the lingering resentment many congressional Democrats held against both Wallace and FDR. Southern congressional leaders knew that without Garner they would lose a great force and presence in working with the administration. Timmons never placed Garner's name in consideration for renomination. He said that Garner had left Washington on July 22, 1940, after beginning to clear out his office for his permanent return to Uvalde.[42]

Garner stayed home on election day, the only time in his life he failed to vote during a presidential election, although Ettie Garner voted in Uvalde. "The opposition vote was very large but so was the affirmative vote," Jesse Jones noted to Garner shortly after the Roosevelt-Wallace victory in November 1940. "A good deal was said about your not voting, but that was to be expected," Jones said. Garner replied, "I didn't vote, but you can imagine the reason. I never was much of a hand to profess one thing and do another."[43]

Garner made his last appearance in Washington at the 1941 inauguration of President Roosevelt and Vice President Wallace. Garner let "tears course down his ruddy cheeks as he kissed 'the boss'—President Roosevelt—good-by," the *Washington Post* reported. "You just can't help tears from coming when you part with old friends," Garner stated as he concluded thirty-eight years of public service in the nation's capital. He administered the oath of office to Wallace and left at the conclusion of the ceremony for his Washington apartment. The Senate and House passed resolutions commending his service. Garner told visiting press members that he planned to return to Uvalde, live to the age of ninety-three, "ride horseback, go fishing and tend to my business. I always live for the future." A half dozen reporters saw the veteran politician depart from Washington's Union Station on January 21, 1941. Garner carried his suitcases aboard the train and never crossed the Potomac again for the remainder of his life. He refused to criticize the administration and said he planned to become a "personal isolationist" at his Texas home. Garner privately predicted that Roosevelt would run for a fourth term. "He will never leave the White House except in death or defeat," he told Bascom Timmons.[44]

Although Garner never returned to Washington, Uvalde was not the end of the line for the venerable Texan. True to his word, he spent many long hours hunting and fishing with his friends along the shady banks of the Frio River. He read newspapers and the *Congressional Record* on a daily basis. He entertained many friends and associates in his two story brick home set among towering pecan trees at 333 Park Street in Uvalde. He filled the house with collectibles and other memorabilia of his years of public service. He followed events in the capital and managed his widespread investments in real estate, banks, and ranches. However, he rejected offers to write his memoirs and even burned boxes of letters and memoranda that covered his entire public career.[45]

The hospitable Garner frequently entertained visitors to his home, both acquaintances and others who simply wanted to come by to greet and shake the hand of Cactus Jack. President Roosevelt came in 1942, and President Truman arrived during his successful reelection campaign in 1948. By the 1950s, Garner's November 22 birthday became an annual celebration with national and state Democrats in attendance. Among his visitors were Senators Lyndon Johnson and Ralph Yarborough, Texas governor Price Daniel, future Texas governor Dolph Briscoe, House Speaker Sam Rayburn, and scores of other state and local officials. He continued to endorse Democratic presidential candidates Harry Truman, Adlai Stevenson, John Kennedy, and Lyndon Johnson. On his birthday in 1963, Garner received birthday greetings from President Kennedy, apparently the last phone call placed by the president before his assassination in Dallas later that day.

The Garners celebrated their golden wedding anniversary on November 27, 1945. Ettie Garner passed away at the age of seventy-eight in 1948 after a lengthy illness. She, along with Eleanor Roosevelt, redefined the roles for spouses of administration officials with their active involvement in policy and in the decision-making process. Ettie Garner provided continuous support and administrative assistance from the time that her husband entered Congress until he boarded his last train home in 1941. A few years after Ettie's death, Garner donated the family home to the City of Uvalde for a museum and memorial to his late wife. Still acknowledged as an elder statesman, he moved to a small cottage behind the main house and continued to live an uncomplicated life interrupted by famous and not-so-famous visitors. At age ninety, Garner swore off drinking and smoking. "The docs say whiskey and cigars are going to shorten my life span," he laughed. Garner commented that people continually came to visit him "to see what a Vice President looks like. They expect to see some big imposing man, and it's me. I'm just a little old Democrat."[46]

Garner died at his Uvalde home on Tuesday, November 7, 1967, only fifteen days shy of his ninety-ninth birthday. His friend Dolph Briscoe Jr. served as the main speaker at the simple memorial service. Uvalde residents, Washington officials, and Vice President Hubert Humphrey attended the funeral services in tribute to "Mr. Garner." He was buried alongside Ettie on a rocky hill dotted with prickly pear cactus at the Uvalde Cemetery.[47]

Because of the dominating legacy of Franklin Delano Roosevelt, John Nance Garner receded in the public memory after his death in 1967. Many historians and Roosevelt biographers, caught up in the monumental issues of the Great Depression and World War II, also overlooked Garner's role in expanding and shaping the modern executive branch. In his history of the vice presidency, Mark O. Hatfield argues that "the vice presidency of John Nance Garner stands as a watershed in the evolution of the office." Garner literally transformed the office that he had so often derided into one of administrative authority and influence. Few vice presidents have had Garner's legislative knowledge and ability to influence and actively work for passage of important legislation. He also became the first vice president to travel abroad as the official representative of the president and the nation, setting a trend that every one of his successors followed. Moreover, with his opposition to the popular Roosevelt at the end of the 1930s, Garner represented a traditional voice within the Democratic Party. As FDR expanded the base of the Democratic Party throughout the nation, Garner solidified the southern wing's domination of congressional politics for another generation.[48]

Garner expressed sincere reservations over the growing power and influence of the presidency, especially at the expense of the Congress. Although his style often appeared antagonistic and his philosophy often seemed better suited to the horse-and-buggy era, Garner served as a voice for an ongoing evaluation of the balance between the executive and legislative branches of government. He seemed to personify the old school of American politics, but he ultimately defined the modern vice presidency. In sum, he laid the foundation for his successors to serve as administrative spokesmen, foreign emissaries, and policy strategists. During his four decades of public service, therefore, John Nance Garner made his mark upon the national scene.

JESSE JONES

Fig. 4.1. Jesse H. Jones, Houston business leader and publisher, served as chairman of the Roosevelt administration's Reconstruction Finance Corporation, which provided millions of dollars in loans to rebuild America during the depression. Jones (Jesse Holman) Papers, Center for American History, UT-Austin (CN 08130).

JESSE JONES

BY WALTER L. BUENGER

Between 1917 and 1945 Jesse H. Jones spent more time in Washington, D.C., than in Houston, Texas, the city he called home. He worked for the Red Cross during World War I. He played a prominent role in the national leadership of the Democratic Party in the 1920s. As head of the Reconstruction Finance Corporation in the 1930s and secretary of commerce and federal loan administrator during World War II he exercised a measure of control over the U.S. economy second only to President Franklin D. Roosevelt. After so many years outside of Texas, years of close contact with nonsoutherners, did it really matter that Jesse Jones was from Texas? Yes, more than it would today, but not in the sense that he was the "epitome of the Texas millionaire." [1]

The fact that Jones was from Texas helps explain the source of his power and his use of that power. Jones, like many other Texans and other southerners, was "born a Democrat." His enchantment with a fellow southerner, Woodrow Wilson, long kept him a Democrat. Further, Jones shared with other southerners an increasingly distinctive worldview. His traditional community still mattered to him in a direct and meaningful way. The roots of his status and prosperity and the threads of his most intense loyalties stretched to his family and his old-fashioned community of Houston, not some new nationwide community of fellow bankers. Party and worldview united him with other southerners in Washington during the New Deal. His power base in the federal bureaucracy rested not just on the support of his president, Franklin D. Roosevelt, but on staunch support in Congress, support anchored by the Texas delegation and other southerners. Jones dealt with this group much as he had with the elite of Houston: personal loyalty flowed from friendship, kinship, and common values. Because of his party, worldview, and the nature of his political power, Jones favored economic policies and regulations that preserved local control and promoted decentralized growth. He directed resources to Texas that otherwise might not have come to the state. [2]

Jesse Jones was no Jett Rink—the fictional protagonist of the film *Giant*, a poor outcast, unaided by family, who rose to wealth from poverty by risking all on a series of gambles. Rich or poor, Rink remained a temperamental loner and a coarse-mannered maverick. Historians have cast Jones as a

"Texas millionaire" in the mold of Jett Rink. Rather, Jones grew up in an elite world shaped by traditional communal values and relationships, and he never completely abandoned that world.[3]

Jesse Holman Jones was born in Robertson County, Tennessee, on April 5, 1874. He was the fourth of five children born to William Hasque Jones and Anne Holman Jones. His mother died when Jesse was six, so much of his early care came from his widowed aunt, Nancy Hurt. Jones's father was a prosperous farmer and tobacco merchant who worked out of Nashville, to the south of his farm. In 1883 William Jones sold his farm and moved the family to Dallas, Texas, where he helped his brother, Martin Tilford Jones, manage a rapidly growing lumber business. In 1886 William purchased six hundred fertile acres astride the Kentucky-Tennessee border, a few miles north of his previous farm. A ten-room brick house, described by one of Jones's biographers as "the finest outside of Nashville," became the new family home.[4] Jesse Jones never knew the life of a "Tennessee dirt farmer."[5]

Those who insist that Jones rose from rags to riches cite as evidence his having only completed the ninth grade. In a long letter to a former teacher, the usually terse Jones offered this insight on his limited education: "As you already know, I did not learn easily at school, and although my father was financially able to send me to college, quoting Laurette Taylor in 'Peg o' My Heart,' I saw no reason to learn the height of mountains I never intended to climb. Having no intention of adopting any profession, I was impatient to get to work." After age fifteen, his only formal education was a brief stint at a business college.[6]

His extended family, however, schooled Jones in the art of business. From age thirteen to seventeen he aided his father and his mother's kin in growing and marketing tobacco on a relatively large scale. After that he returned to Texas and worked for his uncle M. T. Jones. When Jesse's father died in 1893, Uncle M. T. took on some of the roles of a parent to Jesse and proved a hard taskmaster when it came to teaching Jones about the lumber business. In 1898 when M. T. died, however, his will named Jesse Jones general manager of a business empire valued at more than $1 million. By the age of twenty-four, Jones had made it far up the managerial ranks and learned from his family the art of making a deal and running a business.[7]

Jones's family also introduced him to sources of credit and taught him how to use it. When Jesse was fourteen years old his father took him to the bank and opened an account so that his son could purchase tobacco. Later, through his father and uncle, Jones formed close personal relationships with two of the most prominent bankers in Texas: Royal A. Ferris, president of one of the forerunners of First National Bank of Dallas, and

T. W. House Jr., president of T. W. House and Company, the largest bank in Houston. His father left him only modest wealth, but his family opened the door to credit and gave Jones a powerful managerial position. They endowed Jones with access to lucrative business opportunities and nourished in him the vision and creativity needed to take full advantage of those opportunities.[8]

Essentially, Jones began his business career as part of a traditional elite class with its own values that included a strong sense of obligation to the rest of the community. Nowhere was this clearer than in his attitudes toward blacks, for Jones displayed the classic paternalism of the "better folk" of the South. In a memorandum to his designated biographer he set down this revealing passage about his early childhood: "My best friends were two Negro boys, just about grown, who lived in a cabin in the corner of our yard and I was happiest with them. Their names were Neil and Albert. I do not remember their surname." In Jesse Jones's world blacks lived close by and depended on his father. They were friends but did not command enough respect to make their last names significant. Doubtless, familiarity and the expectation of deference increased when Jones supervised African Americans in the family fields and tobacco factories.[9]

As an adult Jones aided and protected blacks, but he expected them to keep their place. By 1917 Jones owned a half interest in the *Houston Chronicle* and enjoyed local prominence. When discrimination led to the riot of a battalion of black soldiers stationed outside of Houston, the *Chronicle* defended stationing black troops in the South. Later the *Chronicle* led the assault on the Ku Klux Klan in Houston. However, the editors of the *Chronicle,* who never made major policy statements without checking with Jesse Jones, were at times as willing as other southerners to use violence to keep African Americans in their place and never challenged segregation. In addition, opposition to blatant bigotry was in Jesse Jones's self-interest: the Ku Klux Klan's negative image hurt the effort to attract northern capital to Houston; and soldiers of any color stationed nearby only increased the economic vigor of the city. Yet Jones retained a paternalistic sense of obligation toward blacks. As he grew wealthier, he made a point of encouraging and recognizing African American upward mobility. Viewing education as the path to progress, Jones endowed scholarships at several black colleges in the South. Jones epitomized the combination of paternalism and progressivism that fixed blacks in a separate and inferior sphere but allowed continued contact with whites and a measure of self-determination.[10]

Jones's approach to race offers a paradigm for his relationship to his community and a special insight into his source of power and its use. Jones was not a "new" man. Nor did he remain traditional. He was a transitional figure. He stood between the traditional paternalism of his class and the sanitary separation of the races advocated by progressives. He acted out of a traditional sense of obligation and a conviction that increased wealth demanded new methods. In business and politics he stood between community and corporation, protecting his city from domination by large national corporations and the centralizing tendencies of federal regulators. But he also did more than virtually any other Houstonian to improve transportation and attract large-scale industry, thus moving Houston further away from traditional communal life. He not only represented characteristics of old and new; he engineered the transition from old to new. Contemporaries asked to reflect on Jones consistently emphasized his obsessive desire to make a profit. Close behind came descriptions of his gigantic ego and his insistence on having his own way, on maintaining control. These sometimes conflicting traits along with the importance of traditional communal behavior in his rise to power and wealth probably explain why Jones only went halfway toward corporate America. Corporate America brought profit but also a loss of control and commitment to the traditional community.[11]

After arriving in Houston in 1898 to take charge of M. T.'s estate, Jones turned his attention to his own affairs. By 1905 he had his own lumber business and was expanding his interest in banks and trust companies. Lumber fit well with financial services because, before the 1930s, lumberyards often offered credit to builders and homeowners and then packaged the mortgages together for purchase by banks or trust companies. In Jones's case the lumber dealer also became a builder.

Credit for further business expansion and information on opportunities came from others of Jones's class. For example, in 1910 Captain James A. Baker facilitated the lease by Jones of a prime piece of downtown real estate from the Rice Institute Board of Trustees, which Baker chaired. On that site Jones constructed the Rice Hotel. Financing for the project came from the endowment left by William Marsh Rice to found Rice Institute. Earlier, in 1905, T. W. House, his brother Edward M. House, and the nephews of William Marsh Rice joined Jones in organizing Union Bank and Trust. The considerable political influence of E. M. House ensured favorable state regulation of that bank. Baker, the House brothers, and the Rice brothers were all from wealthy, well-established, second-generation Houston families that enjoyed political, economic, and social influence. Members of this Houston elite originally trusted Jones because of birth into their class and kinship to their colleague M. T. Jones. They consistently aided him because he had clearly demonstrated a talent for making money.

Avarice drove Jones to take more chances than most of his class. Shrewdness ensured that these chances were not as risky as they seemed. When the Panic of 1907 hit Houston hard, causing the failure of T. W. House and Company, Jones was prepared. All of his businesses were cash rich, and he had arranged to borrow from several banks. He quickly secured financing, and when others in Houston sold at bargain-basement prices, Jones bought them out. He purchased bank stock, real estate, and a part interest in the *Chronicle*. Attracting new tenants to Houston such as the Texas Company (which later became Texaco) and helping sell Houston Ship Channel bonds to local banks heightened the value of these investments. The opening of the Houston Ship Channel in 1914 vastly improved his city's link to the sea and its potential for economic development. Demands for the various commodities routed through Houston increased after the U.S. entry into World War I, and the expanded volume of trade and location of petroleum-related industries along the ship channel created an economic boom that continued into the 1920s.[12]

By the 1920s it was clear that Jones pursued wealth with an unusual passion and that he possessed equally unusual shrewdness and technical skill in arranging financing. Once when he paused to look back on his life he wrote: "I have always been restless and in a hurry, for what I do not know, because I have been fortunate and reasonably happy."[13] To some degree his obsessions and skills separated him from the Houston elite. Some members of that elite, especially those whose roots in Houston reached back to before the Civil War, disdainfully referred to him in his first years in Houston as a "wheeler-dealer." He married late, had a reputation as a skilled gambler, never built a fancy mansion, sometimes crossed the boundary between hard bargains and shady deals, and took less time out for leisure than most members of his class. Still, at one time or another he held most of the offices reserved for the elite, such as king of the annual cotton pageant, he participated in elite social events, and he took the required European vacations. Over the years members of Jones's extended family gravitated to Houston. He served as chief of the clan, offering its members advice and career opportunities. After 1927, Jones and his wife Mary Gibbs Jones lived in a fine apartment atop the Jones-owned and -built Lamar Hotel. Many members of his extended family lived in other apartments in the same building. His attorneys and other close advisers were Jones's kin or formed close personal bonds to him. Like others of his class, in this tight-knit, highly personal world he did business in much the same manner as had his father and uncles. The family, or as Jones called it, the "business family," not the corporation, was the primary business organization. Jones was more a patriarch than a CEO.[14]

What most united Jones with others of his class, however, was a penchant for service to the community. Perhaps he hoped that the status that came with service would ease his puzzling restlessness. Perhaps he was simply fulfilling the obligations that had been bred into him. Of course, he also recognized that service ensured profit. Thus, he helped rescue failing banks at the time of the Panic of 1907 to preserve the health of the entire Houston banking community. No depositors lost money, and the value of bank stock remained stable. Assisting in the financing of the ship channel added jobs to the Houston area and drove up the value of real estate, including that of his personal holdings. Similarly, giving money and time to charities helped the needy and demonstrated his status. Participation in local and state politics was both expected of those of his class and, as in the case of the creation of a state banking system, profitable.[15]

For many years Jones confined his efforts to Houston and Texas, but Woodrow Wilson ushered him into a broader arena. Jones and his newspaper had supported Wilson in 1912. Through Wilson's brother-in-law Stockton Axson, a friend of Jones's, and through E. M. House, Jones drew closer to Wilson. The election in 1912 of Jones's brother-in-law, Daniel E. Garrett, to the U.S. Congress from Texas also heightened the Houstonian's interest in national affairs and his access to national leaders. From the beginning Jones's rise in public service mirrored his rise in business. Family and friends opened the right doors. Energy, talent, and new friends carried him forward. In the summer of 1917, with the United States now involved in fighting World War I, Jones accepted Wilson's appointment as Director General of Military Relief for the American Red Cross.[16]

Jones spent two years in Washington, D.C., in the service of the Red Cross. During that time he set up and staffed almost one hundred hospitals. He organized the transportation of the wounded and built convalescent homes for them. He supervised the distribution of thousands of articles of clothing—socks, sweaters, and mufflers by the ton. Jones also became the chief liaison between the Red Cross and President Wilson. The president distrusted many of the representatives of big business who dominated the Red Cross organization, but he trusted Jones, who often found himself pleading the organization's case when it needed a public show of support by the president. Jones emerged from his Red Cross years with a far wider set of intimate friends and acquaintances. He had lived beside former and future Republican Presidents William Howard Taft and Warren G. Harding. Fondness for Woodrow Wilson and service to the Red Cross gave rise to a lasting tie between Jones and Herbert Hoover and his wife, Lou Henry Hoover. The three shared a respect for Wilson's ideals and a dedication to public service that transcended partisan boundaries. Jones also met prominent Democrats, such as Cleveland H. Dodge,

John W. Davis, Joseph P. Tumulty, Bernard Baruch, and Franklin D. Roosevelt. At the end of his stint with the Red Cross, he accompanied Wilson, Baruch, and Colonel House to the Paris Peace Conference. While there, he met the leaders of most of the world powers, and, as he liked to regale his fellow Houstonians, warmed his stocking feet before the fireplace in Buckingham Palace. He was not a high-level diplomat, but in addition to continuing his work for the Red Cross he seems to have been a useful aide to Wilson, Baruch, and House, who kept him moving between London, Paris, and Geneva.[17]

His World War I experience and close association with Woodrow Wilson changed Jones, but not completely. He would always retain a worshipful, if realistic attitude toward Wilson. Yet in some ways Wilson simply confirmed an attachment to the Democratic Party and an anti–Wall Street bias that had existed in Jones long before 1912. He would move in broader and broader circles and become increasingly active in politics, but in doing so he would use the same highly personal relationships that allowed his rise to great wealth before 1912. His concept of service extended beyond his city, and at times he appeared willing to sacrifice personal gain. In February 1919 he told his most trusted associate, Fred Heyne, that he could not leave Europe for Houston "merely to look after my own private affairs." More bluntly, he cabled N. E. Meador, another close associate: "am not willing to leave what I am doing here for money considerations." In March 1919 he sailed for home. Houston and self-interest had pulled him back.[18]

During the 1920s the evolving character of Jesse Jones comes into clearer focus. He married in 1920. He continued to take an interest in the ship channel and participated in a heated public disagreement about its future. Active in other popular issues of the day, he increasingly turned to the *Chronicle* to express his point of view, and in 1926 he acquired total ownership of the paper. Ever-expanding access to credit allowed him to build more and larger buildings. He carefully planned and constructed large structures in Dallas, Fort Worth, Washington, D.C., and New York City as well as Houston. He found tenants to fill these buildings, and his profits mounted. Satisfying his penchant for total control of all his endeavors, he increased his holdings in National Bank of Commerce until he owned a majority of the stock. As the decade closed Jones was richer and more prominent than ever.

Jones also remained active in national politics in the 1920s. He chaired the national finance committee and became the chief fund-raiser for the Democratic Party in 1924. While raising money for that year's election Jones renewed ties with prominent Democrats such as Franklin D. Roosevelt. Although Calvin Coolidge trounced his friend, John W. Davis, Jones performed admirably. Davis insisted that Jones could not "have done more" and that no one else "would have attacked the task with as much unselfish earnestness." [19]

As recompense for his effort the Democrats decided to hold their 1928 presidential convention in Houston. It also helped that Jones had pledged $200,000 if the party did indeed meet in Houston. The frugal Jones gave his own check to the party but quickly ensured that he did not have to pay the full bill. Senator Tom Connally noted that Jones "scurried about Texas raising money in order to reimburse himself." [20] Out of gratitude for bringing the convention to Texas and to avoid splitting the party by supporting Alfred E. Smith, the Texas delegation nominated Jones for president. They did so over the strenuous objections of William C. Hogg, fellow Houstonian and son of former Texas governor James S. Hogg. Having observed Jones's sharp business deals for some time, Hogg pleaded with Texas governor Dan Moody, in a widely distributed letter, not to nominate Jones. The plainspoken Hogg said of Jones: "He is always using the other fellow's chips to his own advantage—if that qualifies him to be President of this country, say so, but for your own sake don't stand on the platform of our first Southern session of the National Democracy since secession and make yourself and your friends ridiculous by referring to Jesse Jones' great heart, his great humanity, his great accomplishments, and his great spirit." [21]

The 1928 Democratic National Convention proved to be a bonanza for Houston. Local merchants made less money than they had hoped, but the convention put the city in the national eye and resulted in generally favorable press coverage. The convention story also illustrated how Jones acted for his city. In January 1928 Jones contracted to have the convention come to Houston with no formal commitment from the city's government. Instead he presented it to the mayor as an accomplished fact and quickly asked other members of the local elite such as future Texas governor Ross Sterling to arrange for the convention scheduled for the following June. The Houstonians built a convention hall, found lodging for the delegates, and took care of all the other details in just a few months. The elite, who still controlled the most significant institutions within the local economy and who certainly controlled local politics, volunteered their time and their money for the good of the city and their own eventual profit. [22]

On the eve of his departure for an extended stay in Washington, Jones once again orchestrated an impressive display of elite cooperation. In October 1931, two Houston banks were on the verge of failure. After two days of meetings in Jones's offices in the Gulf Building, the bankers, oilmen, cotton dealers, and attorneys who composed the city's business aristocracy pooled several million dollars to guarantee problem loans at the two banks. National Bank of Commerce absorbed one bank. A wealthy local family purchased the other bank, which was owned by the current governor of Texas, Ross Sterling. No bank failed. The governor's friends protected his reputation. Unlike depositors at other failed banks in the days before the federal government insured deposits, the banks' customers suffered no loss. With confidence in the Houston region's banking system shored up, the value of bank stock and other local investments remained stable. As Jones told his board of directors, "whatever the cost to prevent disaster, it would be cheaper than not to prevent it."[23]

Such an argument did not work in most other cities facing similar problems. Nor did it work for President Herbert Hoover when he tried to organize the National Credit Corporation to "voluntarily" manage the growing economic woes of the country as it slid into the depression. It would be simple and simplistic to say that it did not work in New York and Detroit and for President Hoover because Jesse Jones was not directing the show. Jones brought strength of purpose and decades of skillful leadership to the crisis of 1931. At a deeper and more significant level, however, voluntary cooperation worked in Houston because of the nature of the local community and because the ownership and control of local businesses remained more traditional than modern. Humble Oil, for example, was a subsidiary of a giant corporation, but its local managers, who were also large stockholders in the corporation, were long-standing members of the Houston elite. That company, led by Ross Sterling's former partners, made a significant contribution to the bank bailout. Like Jesse Jones, they remained part of the local community and its tight-knit elite.[24]

Like Humble Oil, Jones emerged from the 1920s in transition to a modern form. He understood the corporate point of view. He realized that the owners no longer managed large corporations and that this made taking even a short-term loss more difficult. He knew managers thought nationally not locally and were loyal to their professional managerial class not their city. Jones's political and business experiences moved him beyond the worldview of the Houston elite. Yet he still valued the type of voluntary cooperation possible only in places like Houston, and he always expected representatives of big business such as J. P. Morgan Jr. to act like the Houston elite. Jones once asked Morgan to save a bank in New York City, citing his own actions in Houston as an example of what could and should be done. Morgan refused.[25]

Unlike Herbert Hoover and other advocates of voluntarism, Jones either already knew, or quickly learned from men like J. P. Morgan, the limits placed on cooperation by the rise of corporate America. He also possessed a different ideology. In a 1949 letter to Cordell Hull, Jones had this to say about his political ideology: "I have always regarded myself a liberal, and, except for voting for McKinley against Bryan, I have voted the Democratic ticket. Although 19 when my father died, I never knew what his politics were. He never discussed politics in the home. From my knowledge of him I am sure, however, that he was a Democrat. While I was only 22 when Mr. Bryan first ran, and had no property of any kind, I could not understand what he meant by free silver, and voted accordingly." For the tight-fisted Jones no money was free, yet he was able to vote for Bryan on later occasions, and he stayed in the Roosevelt administration long after friends such as John Nance Garner had left. He stayed because he and his family were Democrats. As David Sarasohn has argued, that meant that to at least some degree he accepted the necessity of reform and of a more active federal government.[26]

Family tradition combined with admiration for Woodrow Wilson to bind Jones to the Democrats, reform, and active government. Jones supported the dying ex-president financially in the final years of his life. Wilson's vision and his courage remained with Jones long afterward and made Jones want to regard himself as a liberal. Jovial fellows like Warren G. Harding might be conservatives and Republicans, but truly good men were liberals and Democrats.[27]

Yet the firmest adhesive that kept Jones a Democrat despite often moving in Republican social and business circles in Washington and New York was his home and his community of Houston. As he demonstrated in the 1931 Houston bank bailout, it was a world in which self-interest and community interest intertwined. This world had a pronounced sense of anticolonialism, of resentment of domination of the local economy by non-local masters of capital and corporations. Jones articulated this anticolonialism when asked about the creation of the Reconstruction Finance Corporation and the makeup of its board of directors: "If such a government agency is to be created, the directors should realize that most of the country lies west of the Hudson River, and none of it east of the Atlantic Ocean." He put his anticolonialism into action later when he insisted that "no New York banker" would control significant RFC agencies.[28]

Jones understood that to let the economy sort itself out on its own and then rebuild would, in the long run, concentrate ownership and control of all major economic institutions in the hands of those with the deepest pockets, the financiers of New York and other money centers. Economic control would inevitably be centralized in the private hands of Wall Street. Better an active government that sought to maintain some measure of decentralized growth and control.[29]

Only the Democrats promised a government active enough to shore up local communities and force corporate cooperation. Such was the ideology Jones possessed in 1932, an ideology based on the Democratic Party, Woodrow Wilson, and traditional community values flavored by Texas anticolonialism. Yet positioning between the corporate and the communal world limited and made flexible Jones's ideology. One perceptive analyst has recently written, "Hoover had a hard time seeing reality." Seeing combines what is before the eye with what is behind the eye. Jones's ideological blinders and life history differed from Hoover's and allowed the Texan to deal much more effectively with the problems of the Great Depression.[30]

In September 1933, Jones bluntly told those attending the annual meeting of the American Bankers Association, "Be smart for once. Take the government into partnership with you." None in the room applauded. When called upon to speak again later that evening Jones was brief and to the point, "Half the banks represented in this room are insolvent; and those of you representing these banks know it better than anyone else." Only a Democrat from a place like Houston would have said that. Only a successful businessman with long-standing credit relationships with many in the room could have been given any credibility by the audience. With a foot in two worlds he could speak to both and be listened to by both. That was to be the source of both Jones's strength and the tension between him and other New Dealers.[31]

When President Herbert Hoover appointed Jones to the board of the RFC in January 1932, writers for the *Washington Post* declared that the job and the huge amount of money involved would not frighten Jones, and they gave this description of him: "He is tall, gray haired and distinguished in appearance. He is retiring, has no hobbies save work, unless the Democratic Party and charity work might be hobbies, speaks publicly but infrequently, dresses conservatively and without regard for the mode."[32]

Jones later coyly denied having angled for a position on the RFC, but he did visit key Democrats in Congress such as John Nance Garner, Carter Glass, and Joseph Robinson days before his appointment and discussed with them the newly created agency. When the depression worsened and attempts at voluntarism such as the National Credit Corporation failed, Hoover finally acquiesced to a more active role for the federal government. He conceived of the RFC as a lending agency to prop up key elements of the economy, and the initial agency created by Congress had a capital stock of $500 million and power to borrow $3 billion more. By its original statute the life of the corporation was to be one year with loans limited to banks, insurance companies and other financial institutions, and railroads. To encourage Democratic support and prevent any hint of partisanship in the distribution of loans, Hoover agreed to appoint three Democrats to the original seven-member board. Garner and Glass both recommended Jones.[33]

Requests for loans quickly inundated the RFC; most came from large railroads and banks. Charles G. Dawes, a former Republican vice president and ambassador to Great Britain and a Chicago banker, together with Jones fine-tuned the details of the RFC's first loan, $15 million to A. P. Giannini's Bank of America. Within a month the agency processed a thousand loans. The number of loans increased rapidly over the next few months. The most controversial, and the one involving Jones most directly, was the loan to Dawes's Central Republic National Bank in Chicago. Dawes resigned from the RFC Board in June 1932; three weeks later at the urging of Jesse Jones and with the support of President Hoover the RFC lent Dawes's bank $90 million. Jones, who was on the scene in Chicago preparing for the Democratic National Convention, did a quick inspection of Chicago's banking situation and became a vocal advocate of the Dawes loan. Jones called it "probably the most constructive of any loan the RFC made." He insisted that the loan prevented the closing of a large money-center bank, restored confidence in the entire banking system, and retarded a further slowdown of the Chicago area economy. Jones's political party certainly found the loan "constructive" when they charged the RFC and Hoover with favoritism toward Republicans and big business.[34]

Disputes about the RFC's proper function quickly took on a partisan tone and reflected a split between Wall Street and Main Street. When the RFC came up for legislative renewal in the summer of 1932, Speaker of the House Garner wanted to expand its lending capabilities, by allowing direct loans to individuals, and increase its accountability to the average citizen, by making public all loans. Jones agreed with Garner, who was quickly becoming his closest ally in Washington. Rather than prevent the collapse of key economic institutions, Jones hoped to stimulate the economy by expanding the availability of credit. Hoover vetoed Garner's version of the RFC, and the bill that finally emerged allowed only a modest expansion of lending capabilities. It did, however, remove all ex officio members except the secretary of the treasury and allow loans to state governments and for public construction projects. Removal of ex officio members eliminated Eugene Meyer, the head of the Federal Reserve Board and RFC chair. Meyer had been one of Jones's primary adversaries on the RFC

board, so in the months between the summer of 1932 and the inauguration
of the new president the next March, the RFC drifted toward the type of
agency desired by Garner and Jones.[35]

President Franklin D. Roosevelt quickly appointed Jones the new chair
of the RFC, a job he clearly wanted and expected. Indeed Hoover's failure
to appoint him chair the previous summer had irritated Jones. Once chair,
Jones presided over a rapid and extraordinary expansion of the power of
the RFC.[36]

In his study of the RFC, James Olson points to several reasons for its
longevity and power. The RFC's structure made it politically convenient
to use for a variety of tasks. It had been set up as an independent agency,
and from time to time Congress added to its capital. It virtually became a
government bank that made loans, earned interest, and received repayment of loans. By January 1936 the RFC had lent $8 billion, been repaid
$3.2 billion, and earned $294 million. This money was a congressman's
dream. Congress could create an agency and direct that it be financed by
the RFC without making a specific appropriation. Indeed, the RFC supplied capital for most of the prominent New Deal agencies, including
the Federal Emergency Relief Administration, Public Works Administration, Works Progress Administration, Civil Works Administration,
Federal Home Loan Banks, Tennessee Valley Authority, Electric Home
and Farm Authority, Disaster Loan Corporation, Farm Credit Administration, Federal National Mortgage Association, Federal Land Bank, and
Commodity Credit Corporation.[37]

Because the role of the RFC was so pervasive and the domination of the
RFC by Jones so complete, members of Congress came to depend on
Jones for taking care of pet projects. In turn Jones depended on them for
support of his version of the RFC. Jones proved to be an astute politician
well skilled in lobbying members of Congress.[38]

Jones's congressional support and the wary respect of FDR ultimately
depended on the Texas delegation. Probably no state enjoyed more influence in Washington. This was particularly true in the House, where
Texans chaired numerous important committees. If the Texas delegation
formed a united front it was unlikely that any item of business could make
it through the House. Jones's ties to this group ran deep. His brother-in-
law, Daniel Garrett, served in the House on and off from 1913 until his
death in 1932. Garner and Jones became very close friends, and even after
leaving the House, Garner remained influential with his fellow Texans.
Sam Rayburn and Marvin Jones, probably the two most significant members of the delegation, were not as personally close to Jones, but they did
cooperate with him on many occasions. So did energetic new members of

the delegation like Wright Patman. Support of the Texas delegation gave Jones raw political power denied other heads of federal bureaucracies. President Roosevelt and other prominent government officials acknowledged his power and did not lightly cross him.[39]

At the risk of belaboring a point, Jones's strong ties to the Texas delegation obviously depended on more than mutual interest. Wright Patman, who called himself the last populist, and Jesse Jones, who voted against Bryan in 1896, stood at opposite ends of a common range. The Democratic Party, traditional community life, preference for highly personal politics, and resentment of Wall Street bound them together. Jones better tolerated Wall Street and big business. Patman more completely supported the Democratic Party and better understood the small businessman. Yet they and the rest of the Texas delegation had much more in common than they had with any nonsouthern Democrat such as FDR.[40]

Roosevelt's support, however, was crucial to Jones and the RFC. Certainly some of that support derived from Jones's political power and skill. Jones and the RFC also proved useful to FDR, but beyond that, Jones became a type of anchor for Roosevelt—not to the right as some have said, but to the middle. Roosevelt and his advisers pursued many cures for the depression. Initially they sought to expand credit. Then in 1936–1937 they sought to balance the budget. After 1938, by design and as an outgrowth of defense spending, they sought to expand consumer spending. Jones, no doubt influenced by Garner, advocated earlier than FDR the expansion of credit, and he certainly better understood the mechanisms needed to both expand credit and improve the stability of the money markets. Jones even opposed a balanced budget at the expense of the expansion of credit. He also supported improving consumer spending if done in a businesslike way. With time FDR came to respect Jones's ability to keep his administration in the middle of the road, and he quickly learned to rely on Jones's technical competence.[41]

Jones was an early and vocal advocate of deposit insurance and helped win FDR's reluctant support. He also helped win the support of his friend Carter Glass, the key member of the Senate Banking Committee. Jones had supported state deposit insurance in Texas. And even though the state system had run into problems in the 1920s, he saw deposit insurance as critical to restoring depositor confidence. After the bank holiday of 1933 the RFC helped certify the soundness of banks and in the process pushed the wisdom of the Federal Deposit Insurance Corporation (FDIC) with bankers and politicians. In both its passage and promotion Jones played an influential role in the FDIC, an enduring feature of New Deal reform.

Despite early reservations, by inauguration day Jones fully supported the purchase of preferred stock by the RFC and later came to see it as critical to recovery. Buying preferred stock took the majority of his time in 1933–1934. As he said in his memoirs: "In one stroke Congress had turned the tide toward recovery. But it took many months of hard work and much persuasion for us to convince the banking fraternity that this was so." [42] The RFC purchased preferred stock in a bank or several other types of financial institutions equal to the amount of common stock. This improved the capitalization of banks, and, since lending limits increased with capitalization, in theory it permitted an expansion of lending. Banks on the verge of failure such as Houston's First National used the purchase of preferred stock and the restructuring of assets to avoid insolvency. The problem was that many bankers thought it would demonstrate weakness to the public if they sold the RFC preferred stock. Jones bore the brunt of teaching them otherwise and by 1935 had achieved considerable success.

Between 1932 and 1935 the RFC gradually evolved from making indirect attempts to expand credit, by providing more money to banks and insurance companies to improve their capitalization, to direct lending to local, state, and federal governmental agencies and, eventually, to direct lending to individual companies. Jones was somewhat reluctant to lend directly to businesses other than railroads because he did not want the government to compete with banks, but when the banks did not do the job he expected of them Jones became an advocate of direct loans to sound businesses.

From the first Jones had wanted the RFC to be more aggressive than had its original creators. He cheerfully lent to other governmental agencies and helped finance such projects as a 244-mile aqueduct from the Colorado River to Los Angeles. Under his leadership the RFC also purchased bonds for various PWA and WPA projects. Typically Jones set up semi-independent agencies to deal with particular credit problems and funded them through the RFC. The Commodity Credit Corporation (CCC) was probably the most important of these and certainly the most important to Texas farmers. The CCC purchased farm loans from banks, but it also lent directly to farmers. The CCC lent money with farm commodities as collateral, and it typically lent at a level higher than the market price. For example, if the price of cotton was nine cents a pound the CCC lent at ten cents a pound. If the price of cotton went above ten cents per pound, farmers sold their cotton and repaid the loan. If it stayed below ten cents per pound farmers turned over their collateral to the CCC. This raised the price of cotton or at least kept it stable. Like the FDIC, government price supports have been an enduring feature of the American economy since the New Deal. [43]

When even the purchase of preferred stock failed to expand the supply of credit, Jones came to believe that bankers were simply refusing to make loans. That left him with no choice but to advocate direct lending by the RFC, something that many critics saw as socialism. Although encouraged by the success of the CCC in direct lending, Jones still insisted that the RFC exercise caution in evaluating loan prospects outside of agriculture. After a lifetime of watching the bottom line, he always demanded that the RFC not take a long-term loss. This obsession with long-term profit permeated every action of the RFC. Yet Jones convinced Congress to expand the terms of direct lending from five to ten years and, eventually, to drop all time limits on repayment. He also slowly streamlined lending procedures and increased the number of RFC loans. This was particularly true after early 1938 when Roosevelt became a convert to increasing consumer spending. Loans to small businesses never reached the levels some called for because Jones regarded those loans as having the greatest chance of failure. Even these loans, however, slowly grew in number in the late 1930s and early 1940s. The efforts of the RFC to increase the amount of mortgage money available for home construction also bore increased fruit late in the 1930s. By the close of the decade the government played a larger role in every aspect of credit. In most cases the chosen instruments of the increased reach of government were Jesse Jones and the RFC.

Jesse Jones and the RFC were almost one and the same. Just as he acted as the patriarch of his "business family" in Houston, he became the patriarch of his "RFC family" in Washington. While at first careful to select members of the RFC board and RFC employees with an eye to politics, Jones gradually assembled a group of men who were intensely loyal to him. Even after FDR kicked Jones upstairs to the office of federal loan administrator, Jones continued to exercise day-to-day control of the RFC through Emil Schram, the new chair and a loyal member of Jones's "family." From 1933 to 1945 no loan was approved, no procedure adopted without Jones's oversight and blessing.[44]

For a time in the fall of 1937 it seemed that Jones's total control of the RFC, indeed the RFC itself, was about to come to an end. Persuaded primarily by Henry Morgenthau, Roosevelt's close friend and Hudson River valley neighbor, that a balanced budget would restore confidence in the economy and free up capital going to finance the national debt, FDR reduced spending and ordered the RFC to reduce loans. Since the departure of Meyer, Morgenthau had become Jones's most persistent adversary. Morgenthau was far more conservative than Jones in his approach to the role of government in the economy. Perhaps because of jealousy as well as ideology, he sought at every turn to rein in the actions of the RFC. An improved economy in 1936 gave Roosevelt enough confidence to go along with the policies of his friend. The results were the disastrous recession of 1937–1938 and new life for the RFC. Because of its flexibility FDR turned to the RFC and Jones to expand government spending. Jones readily complied, probably with delight at Morgenthau's failure, but he did not go as far or as fast as small businessmen and Keynesian economists would have liked.

After becoming federal loan administrator in 1939, Jones presided over the RFC, Export-Import Bank, Federal Housing Authority, Home Owners' Loan Corporation, and several other federal lending agencies. Key Jones disciples headed up each of these entities. FDR offered Jones several cabinet positions, but he did not want to leave his area of expertise and his base of power. Despite the break between Garner and FDR over the latter's determination to seek a third term as president, Jones supported Roosevelt's reelection. The German invasion of France in May 1940 and the weakness of the Republican candidate convinced Jones that the two-term precedent should be broken. He was rewarded by appointment as secretary of commerce, which he agreed to take if he also could remain as federal loan administrator. A unanimous House and Senate voted that Jones should hold both offices.

World War II turned Jones into one of the biggest spenders in the history of the federal government. After May 1940, Jones and others in government worried far less about running the RFC like a business. Interest rates on loans plunged down. Loans that might previously have been turned down gained quick approval. Agencies that encouraged consumption, such as the Electric Housing and Farm Authority, or diverted resources, such as the RFC Mortgage Company, were shut down. New RFC agencies designed to stimulate production of materials necessary for war took their place. For example, in the summer of 1940 the Rubber Reserve Company began to buy up stocks of rubber. After Japanese victories in early 1942 shut off most sources of natural rubber, the RFC financed the production of synthetic rubber. RFC funds procured metals required for the war, built defense plants, and financed the homes of defense plant workers. From 1932 to mid-1940 the RFC had lent about $10 billion; from that point to 1945 it lent four times that amount. RFC money built plants around the country and later turned them over at bargain-basement prices to private industry. Money flowed wherever needed. Federal spending, more specifically RFC spending, ended the depression and helped win the war.

Clearly Jones took with him to Washington in 1932 an ideology and a style of doing business that strongly influenced his later actions. He also took with him the desire to lift up his home city and the state of Texas. When he died in 1956 the directors of National Bank of Commerce said of him: "Throughout his entire career, in times of prosperity and expansion, war and depression, he was ever mindful of the safety of this Bank and gratified at its success. From this he was never diverted by public preferment or acclaim and of all his varied enterprises his thoughts turned first to this Bank of which he was deeply proud."[45]

The National Bank of Commerce was a metaphor for his city and state. Other investments brought him a higher return, but the development of the bank best symbolized the development of the region. He nurtured both with an eye to profit and pride. Jones's most visible assistance to the state came during its centennial. He ensured that federal funds would build the San Jacinto Monument and that due national recognition would come to the state in 1936. Beneath that highly visible crust lay a maze of federal investments in Texas businesses. Perhaps they got no more than their share, but Jones made sure they got that share. First National Bank in Houston received a much needed infusion of capital through the purchase of preferred stock by the RFC. Cameron Iron Works obtained a large defense contract and at war's end an inexpensive plant through the RFC. Jones's anti–Wall Street ideology and common vision with Texans meant that he could never agree to concentrating federal expenditures in any particular region. Together with the Texas delegation he turned on the spigot of federal funds from 1932 to 1945, and that infusion of capital transformed the state from a rural agrarian to an urban industrial society.

Jones never intended this transformation to upend the established social order. While he often insisted that businesses to which the RFC lent funds change their management, he did so for what he considered sound business reasons and he tried to preserve local control. He often insisted, for example, that local investors match the investment of the RFC in their area's banks and other businesses. He opposed the extension of government control of business except when necessary. Likewise he had no desire to upend the local class structure or alter relations between blacks and whites. While agreeable to government help for the truly needy, he had little sympathy for radical or visionary dreams of remaking the social order: this lay at the heart of his simmering dispute with Henry A. Wallace, a friend of Roosevelt's and vice president during his third term.[46]

Unlike some fellow Houstonians, Jones was not a doctrinaire defender of unfettered competition and never viewed Roosevelt as a dangerous demagogue out to destroy private property.[47] He wanted to conserve what he could of elite control and traditional community life, but his contributions to the New Deal were possible only because he had grown to under stand that government must play an active role in modern life. As he told an interviewer for *The New York Times* in 1939: "The day has gone forever when business men can expect to go merrily on their way, conducting their affairs as they see fit, without any interference from government. The public has such a big stake in the continuing functioning of the economic machine and is so greatly affected by a breakdown that its government must apply the brakes when the speed limits are exceeded."[48]

In 1945 Roosevelt asked Jones to step aside and let Henry Wallace take over as secretary of commerce. FDR offered Jones a variety of other appointments, but Jones refused and angrily resigned from all his government positions. After years of feuding with Wallace, he could not abide being replaced by him, and he took out his acrimony on the Democratic Party the rest of his life.

Soon after leaving government service Jones returned to Houston. He built a few more buildings and resumed an active role in community affairs. Gradually his body wore out and he died on June 1, 1956.[49]

Self-interest—narrowly defined as pocketbook incentives—offer an appealing explanation of human motivation. The appeal becomes particularly great for a man of "stalwart avarice and piratical trading spirit" as Will Hogg described Jones.[50] Undoubtedly avarice was an engine of change for Jones and his city. He pushed himself and Houston toward greater wealth and in the process transformed himself and Texas into a clearer image of corporate America. Yet the transformation was incomplete, for vestiges of party and place remained. Imagine a Jesse Jones brought up outside of ties to the Democratic Party and without the nurturing role of his family and a traditional communal elite. His innate energy and skill would have carried him far, would have made him perhaps a replica of Herbert Hoover. But the South and Texas, with their less mature economic and social forms of human interaction, where the "best men" were Democrats, made a critical difference in the life of Jesse Jones.

TOM CONNALLY

Fig. 5.1. Tom Connally, longtime U.S. senator who never lost an election, was a stalwart supporter of President Franklin D. Roosevelt. Connally was a key player in the creation of the United Nations and the North Atlantic Treaty Organization (NATO). Prints and Photographs Collection, Center for American History, UT-Austin (CN 10270).

TOM CONNALLY

BY JANET SCHMELZER

In 1953 Tom Connally retired from the United States Senate. During those last days in office he reminisced about all the struggles and accomplishments of his long political career. While packing into boxes the papers, books, and memorabilia that represented fifty years of service to the nation and Texas, he thought back to those times that held the most meaning for him. "One was the successful fight against President Roosevelt's proposal to enlarge the Supreme Court back in 1937," he recalled with fondness and satisfaction. "The other is the work I did at San Francisco in the creation of the United Nations." He was most proud of these two accomplishments, and remembering such achievements would make his somewhat reluctant retirement more palatable.[1]

Such memories brought Connally much pleasure in 1953, for he could sit back and let his thoughts "race backward" to an earlier time some seventy-six years before. Born on August 19, 1877, in McLennan County, Texas, Thomas Terry Connally was the son of Jones and Mary Ellen Terry Connally. Surrounded by seven sisters and considered to be the "favorite" of his mother, he was fortunate to be part of a close and loving family, held together and guided by devoted parents. In 1882, by which time Connally was old enough to take on chores and other responsibilities, the family had moved to a larger farm near Eddy, in Falls County, Texas. There he had the typical childhood of a farmer's son on the Texas prairie, where days were spent doing "regular farm work." But since his father placed a high value on an education, Connally was sent to school in Eddy, until he graduated at the age of fourteen.[2]

In 1892 the Connallys decided to enroll Tom at Baylor University. While studying a strict curriculum of Greek, Latin, history, mathematics, and philosophy, he acquired positions of responsibility and prestige, becoming editor of both the Baylor *Annual* and magazine, *The Literary*. He also was a first lieutenant in the college military organization and a member of the Erisophian debating society. In June 1896, he graduated with three degrees—bachelor of arts, bachelor of oratory, and a diploma in military science.[3]

Shortly after graduation, Connally decided that his ultimate goal was a career in politics and that the best route to achieve this objective was to become a lawyer. With this in mind, in fall 1896 he enrolled at the University of Texas Law School, where he was an ardent student. Finishing his degree was not an easy task. In April 1898, when the United States declared war against Spain, Connally "lost all appetite" for his law books and joined the Second Texas Infantry Regiment. Almost immediately he received the rank of sergeant major, but he would not see any action. Meanwhile, considering the extenuating circumstances that had prevented Connally from finishing the last two months of classes, the law school had generously granted him a diploma in absentia. Elated by this news, he quickly returned to Texas upon his discharge from the army in November 1898 and rushed to Austin in order to pick up his license to practice law.[4]

Connally was filled with optimism and energy as he began his legal career. Moving first to Waco and then to Marlin in 1899, he concluded that in a smaller town "it would be easier to get recognition." Within a short time he discovered that attracting cases even in Marlin was a strain on his patience. He attended picnics, public meetings, and any gathering that might put him into contact with a potential client, but these efforts did not pay off. Only after he had defended successfully two murder suspects and moved to an office in a new local bank did more townspeople begin to seek his counsel.[5]

To fulfill his real dream of entering the political arena, Connally seized the opportunity to run for the District Seventy-two seat (which included Falls, Williamson, and Milam Counties) in the Texas House of Representatives in 1900. Because he was the only Democrat and the only candidate in the race, he won easily. Attending the first session of the Twenty-seventh Legislature on January 8, 1901, he worried that at twenty-three his youthfulness would not present the proper image of an "elder-statesman." He therefore began wearing a Prince Albert coat, which he hoped would add "years and sagacity" to his appearance. With blue eyes and wavy brown hair, he was a handsome, six-foot, two-hundred-pound young man in his long, double-breasted frock coat. But to his dismay this attire did not suddenly make him a seasoned politician. In fact, Connally felt uncomfortable looking "like a dude" and decided to dress "more comfortably." "Showing off" at this stage in his political career, he concluded, was "too much just yet."[6]

His first years in the statehouse proved to be an educational initiation into politics, providing lessons that would serve him well in the future. His committee assignments of Judiciary, Military Affairs, State Affairs, as well as Counties and County Boundaries trained him in the internal mechanisms of the legislature. Appointed to several special committees, Connally studied the political strategy of other members, such as John Nance

Garner of Uvalde who served with Connally on the Congressional Districts Committee. Initially hoping to push through a series of bills during his first term, Connally gladly settled for the singular success of his Falls County road system bill and for the skills that he had acquired in the process.[7]

How to get a bill passed was not the only political lesson that he learned in 1901. What occasioned a dilemma for Connally was the impending U.S. Senate election of Joseph Weldon Bailey of Gainesville, whose candidacy was clouded by a questionable involvement with the Waters-Pierce Oil Company, a subsidiary of Standard Oil Company of New York. To resolve this political controversy, Texas House Speaker R. E. Prince of Navarro County established a special investigating committee. Although the entire committee agreed that the evidence exonerated Bailey, a minority report, with which Connally agreed, adamantly refused to condemn those members who had brought the incriminating charges. As a consequence, Bailey visited with those members whom he might convince to vote against the minority report. Face to face with Bailey, Connally steadfastly refused to change his stance, thus earning him the haunting status of being "a recognized enemy of the state's most powerful politician." Even after Bailey was elected U.S. senator in January 1901, Connally was "not impressed by the great man." He was willing to pay politically for this decision in order to have a clear conscience. "The position I regarded with awe," he recalled, "but the man I did not."[8]

Elected to a second term, Connally felt very comfortable as a seasoned legislator and readily accepted his new responsibilities. During the early proceedings of the Twenty-eighth Legislature, he had the honor of placing the name of Pat M. Neff of McLennan County into nomination for Speaker of the House. Once the election was over and Neff became Speaker, Connally served on several committees and chaired the Judiciary Committee, which considered more than one hundred bills. Having already established his reputation for supporting antimonopoly legislation, he quickly authored the antitrust bill that became known as the Connally-Meachum Act of 1903. Proud of this achievement, he wanted to redefine the prohibitions against any actions in "restraint of trade," strengthen penalties, and align Texas law with federal antitrust guidelines.[9]

Although legislative business kept Connally busy much of the time, a romantic interest also vied for his attention. In 1899 he met Louise Clarkson of Marlin and fell desperately in love with this beautiful young woman with the "lovely voice," dark brown hair, and "excellent figure." As the courtship became more serious, Connally pursued Louise "with great ardor." For five years he wooed Louise until she accepted his proposal. Finally, on November 16, 1904, they were married in Marlin.[10]

After the adjournment of the legislature in 1903 Connally was preoccupied with his law practice and with establishing a home for Louise. He had enjoyed his political experiences in the Texas House but felt uncomfortable about running for a third term. He was not, however, the kind of man who could stay away from politics for very long because he thrived on the excitement and challenges that elections and public office provided. By 1906 he had decided, therefore, to seek the next available office, which turned out to be the county attorney. Easily elected, he was responsible for prosecuting both misdemeanors and felonies committed in Falls County. Following two terms as county attorney, he resumed his private practice in order to support his family, which now included a son, Ben Clarkson, but he never stopped thinking about future offices, especially Congress. When the right opportunity occurred, he would act.[11]

In 1916 the Eleventh Congressional District seat, representing McLennan, Bell, Falls, Coryell, and Hamilton counties was vacant, and Connally recognized that winning this election was a distinct possibility. In addition to Connally, two formidable challengers, Judge Tom L. McCullough of Waco and Judge John D. Robinson of Belton, had declared their candidacy. To defeat them Connally would have to come up with some dazzling campaign strategies. After opening his campaign and presenting his platform in Eddy on April 14, he decided to acquire the "best advertising" that he could. He purchased a new "shiny black" six-cylinder Buick roadster with "the brightest red wheels you ever saw." As Connally traveled through the five counties in his district, the car attracted crowds and "naturally some of that attention rubbed off" on him. Such gimmicks may have helped to make him better known with the voters, but he was still far from being the front-runner. When the opportunity arose, therefore, he agreed to a series of debates with McCullough. Being a skillful and composed orator, Connally was confident that such speaking engagements would enable him to chip away at McCullough's lead. Since Robinson had assumed the posture of the "sure winner" and was thus hardly campaigning at all, Connally had every chance of winning if he could just keep up his furious campaign schedule. He did and when the Democratic primary was held on July 22, Connally was victorious. Because the November general election would be a mere formality, Connally celebrated his victory immediately—"I was now a member of the United States House of Representatives."[12]

Washington, D.C., was not a calm place in March 1917. Connally was coming to Congress at a time when many people were sadly convinced that the period of U.S. neutrality was over. In Congress the usual activities proceeded but were dampened by the realization that a serious foreign policy crisis loomed. Connally was fortunate in that John Nance Garner was responsible for placing Texans on committees. Since they were already acquainted and had worked together in the Texas Legislature, Connally was comfortable with Garner's decision to place him on the Committee to Investigate Expenditures in the Department of Labor and the Committee on Privileges and Elections. But more important was Connally's seat on the Committee on Foreign Affairs, which could be an extremely influential position in the event of war.[13]

On April 2, 1917, President Woodrow Wilson appeared before a special session of the Sixty-fifth Congress to ask for a declaration of war against Germany. Connally was deeply moved by the gravity of the situation. Like his colleagues, he was tense and solemn as he listened intently to the president's message. When the speech was over, he was "wrung out emotionally" and "huddled" with fellow Texans who sought solace together. Such comfort was momentary, for Connally, a member of the Foreign Affairs Committee, was soon in attendance at "explosively emotional" committee meetings debating the joint war resolution. At the final committee balloting when his name was called, Connally, having prayed "for Divine guidance," voted in favor of the resolution—recalling later that "a cold chill ran through me."[14]

Once the joint resolution was approved by both houses and had the president's signature on April 6, 1917, the United States was at war. Immediately the House had to deal with war preparations. One of the more volatile issues, which caused a sharp division among the members, was conscription. Although House Speaker Champ Clark was an advocate of a volunteer army and had persuaded many members to that point of view, Swager Sherley of Kentucky countered with "compelling" arguments for conscription. Connally, too, supported the draft because this system would guarantee an "orderly military buildup" instead of an "ineffectual voluntary force." When the vote was taken, the House had approved conscription.[15]

With so much activity in the House, Connally used every opportunity to hone his political skills. Observant of the unwritten rule that first-term members of Congress should be silent, Connally was very judicious in choosing when to speak. Deliberately avoiding any participation in some of the more controversial war bills, he finally chose to sponsor an increase in passport fees from one to ten dollars, which would help pay for the cost of the foreign service. Gradually he felt more comfortable giving speeches on the House floor. While his first address was in favor of agricultural inspectors having the power to examine farm products, he considered his "maiden speech" to be his "long talk on the war" on September 1, 1918.[16]

No matter what he did as a congressman, Connally could not escape the nagging thought that his real responsibility to his country was to enlist in the army. This he did on September 12, 1918. He received the rank of captain and adjutant of the Twenty-second Infantry Brigade, Eleventh Division, stationed at Camp Meade, Maryland. As much as he may have wanted to get into the fighting overseas, the war was over before he could see any action. He felt a "trifle embarrassed" because he had been "in more wars and fought less than any living man." [17]

In December 1918 Connally returned to the House of Representatives. The issues soon confronting Connally and other members of Congress were the Versailles Treaty and the League of Nations. Cognizant that the House did not have a role in the ratification of treaties, he could do nothing to determine the fate of the Versailles Treaty, but he sat in the Senate gallery and watched the treaty fail to receive Senate approval. [18]

The presidential election of 1920 signaled a change in the political climate. The decade of the 1920s was characterized by conservatism and isolation under the guidance of the Republican Party and Presidents Warren G. Harding and Calvin Coolidge. An opponent of Republican policies, Connally would pursue, as much as possible, his legislative agenda in both foreign and domestic areas. A veteran of World War I and a spokesman for ex-servicemen, he sponsored bills that raised the age of army volunteers from eighteen to twenty-one and that called for the creation of a House Veterans Committee. Appalled by the corruption in the Harding administration, he urged the House to investigate the Veterans Bureau, the Alien Property Custodian, and the United States Shipping Board. He was also very outspoken on the equity of revenue taxes and tariffs. [19]

During the 1920s Connally earned recognition as an able spokesman on foreign affairs. He was often called upon to give the Democratic response to Republican policies. He encouraged the government to seek peaceful methods to avoid future wars and was an advocate of international cooperation in disarmament. In 1921 he offered an amendment to the Naval Appropriations Bill that would require a multinational conference on arms limitation. Although his amendment was defeated, he would attend, as an observer, the Washington Conference in 1921 at which capital-ship construction was limited for the United States, Britain, Japan, Italy, and France. In a more official capacity in 1924 and 1925, he was a delegate to the Interparliamentary Union, an organization dedicated to the reduction of weapons and to resolving disputes peacefully. [20]

In 1928 Connally saw the U.S. Senate as his next political goal. On April 17 he declared his candidacy and opened his campaign. Although the odds were against him, he was prepared for a difficult fight. The incumbent senator was Earle B. Mayfield, reportedly a member of the Ku

Klux Klan. From the beginning Connally realized that he would not win the primary but that he must finish second to be in the runoff. He therefore focused his campaign on defeating his two "most dangerous" rivals— Colonel Alvin M. Owsley of Dallas and Congressman Tom Blanton of Abilene. Not until the votes were counted from the primary on July 28 did Connally feel somewhat more confident about winning. Mayfield had not received a majority, and Connally had indeed come in second. Now the race became dirty and personal. Mayfield attacked Connally by hinting that he was incompetent, antifarmer, and a secret member of the Klan. Connally ruthlessly accused Mayfield of selling out to public utility companies in return for large campaign contributions. On election day in August, Connally had won, beating Mayfield by almost sixty thousand votes.[21]

In 1929 Connally joined the United States Senate. Although starting out exuberant and optimistic, he soon became frustrated and annoyed. Because the Republicans dominated the executive and legislative branches, he encountered roadblocks and obstacles whenever Democratic proposals were put forward. When Congress began considering an agricultural marketing bill, he tried unsuccessfully to pass amendments that would increase the income of farmers. Although labeling the Smoot-Hawley Tariff Act as a "monstrous piece of deception," he could do nothing to prevent its passage.[22]

What angered Connally the most was that time and again President Hoover and his administration would cripple Democratic efforts to fight the depression. In response to demands that drought-stricken farmers needed immediate financial help, Congress set up a $20 million loan fund. Yet Connally had to battle with Secretary of Agriculture Arthur M. Hyde to expedite getting this money into the hands of farmers. When Democrats put together a $1 billion public works program, Hoover vetoed it and forced a substitute compromise bill. Concerned over the plight of veterans, Connally submitted a pension bill covering the Spanish-American War, only to have Hoover respond with another veto. Then a proposal was made that would allow veterans to obtain a loan of up to 50 percent of the value of their World War I adjusted service certificates. As usual, Hoover handed down a veto, but this time Connally and others were able to find enough votes for an override.[23]

Slowly the political pendulum began swinging in favor of the Democratic Party. In 1931, with the inception of the Seventy-second Congress, Democrats finally controlled the House and sliced the Republican majority in the Senate to one. Connally too benefited from the shift. He finally gained a much desired seat on the Senate Foreign Relations Committee, resigning from the Banking and Currency Committee and remaining on Privileges and Elections as well as Public Buildings and Grounds.[24]

In 1932 the Democrats had every possibility of winning the presidency. Nominating the right man was essential, and Connally was very much a part of this process. From the beginning he was a leader of the Garner campaign, making sure that the Texas delegation was pledged to him. At the Democratic National Convention he placed Garner's name into nomination. By far the most powerful challenger was Franklin D. Roosevelt, governor of New York, whose campaign organization recognized Connally's influence within the Texas delegation. Following all the nomination speeches, the balloting began in the early morning hours of July 1—Roosevelt was leading the field but was short of the necessary two-thirds majority. During the second ballot, Arthur F. Mullen of Nebraska, Roosevelt's convention floor leader, sought out Connally in order to strike a deal. Would Garner withdraw if the vice presidency were offered? Connally promised to relay this invitation to the right people. Meanwhile the third ballot was taken, and Roosevelt was still short of votes. Finally, late in the afternoon, Garner decided not "to be responsible for a shattering" of Democratic Party unity and therefore released his delegates and somewhat reluctantly accepted the vice presidential nomination. In November 1932 Roosevelt and Garner were elected.[25]

After the election Connally was in a much more powerful position in the Democratic-dominated Senate. Although still in his first term, he had acquired seniority on both the Finance and Foreign Relations Committees and had earned the chairmanship of the Public Buildings and Grounds Committee. Often fondly referred to as "Old Tawm," he was recognized as a skilled debater who was able to speak candidly and honestly, often disarming an opponent with his quick wit and tall tales. On the other hand, when pushed to the point that his temper flared, he would berate his antagonist unmercifully. Even his appearance gave him a certain stature among his fellow senators. Tall, and still weighing about two hundred pounds, he dressed very much like another admired orator—William Jennings Bryan. Underneath a long, black frock coat Connally wore a stiff white shirt that was adorned with gold studs and was accented with a black bow tie and a black ribbon holding a pince-nez. With his wavy locks gently falling across the back of a white detachable collar, he appeared the handsome "southern gentleman."[26]

Encouraged by the Democratic victory, Connally supported the New Deal philosophy. He therefore approved of such measures as the banking holiday decree, unemployment relief, the Emergency Banking Act, the Agricultural Adjustment Act, and creation of the Home Owners Loan

Corporation. An advocate of reducing the gold content of the dollar, he encouraged Roosevelt to adopt this policy as a means of inflating prices. When the Social Security bill came to the Finance Committee, Connally agreed to the necessity of aiding the elderly, but he argued that the proposed allotment of $30 per month was inadequate. He tried to no avail to raise the amount.[27]

Dedicated to improving the level of income and profits for rural Americans, especially Texans, Connally lobbied for amendments to the Agricultural Adjustment Act of 1933. Since an extended drought and low market prices had created a crisis in the cattle industry, he and Congressman Marvin Jones of Texas sponsored the Jones-Connally Cattle Relief Act of 1934, which classified cattle as a commodity and allowed ranchers to apply for federal aid. In 1935 they secured for cotton farmers the right to receive from the Department of Agriculture a bounty for exporting their crops overseas.[28]

In jeopardy as well was the oil industry, which "lay in a state of collapse." Because of increased production, oil was flooding the market and prices were spiraling downward. Aware that oil was an integral part of the Texas economy, Connally was determined not to allow this industry to disintegrate during the depression. After much wrangling in Congress, he gathered enough votes to insert into the National Industrial Recovery Act of 1933 the Connally "Hot Oil" Amendment, which would prohibit the interstate shipment of oil in excess of set production limits.[29] But when in 1935 the Supreme Court declared the "hot oil" provision unconstitutional, Connally had to start over. Finally he came up with the acceptable Connally "Hot Oil" Act of 1935, which restored the principles of the original amendment and satisfied the constitutional requirements of the Court.[30]

In August 1935, in the midst of tedious committee work, Connally suffered the loss of his wife, Louise. He was "depressed and morose." For thirty-one years they had been extremely happy. She was his greatest admirer; he thought of her as a "wonderful woman with great personal charm and a devoted wife and mother."[31]

But Connally could not grieve forever. He had to continue his work in the Congress. Though considered a "party loyalist," he "wandered occasionally from the [New Deal] fold." He certainly was not a "yes man" during the Roosevelt administration and at various times was in direct conflict with the New Deal. Without question, the most serious disagreement that Connally had with Roosevelt was over the proposed reorganization of the Supreme Court in 1937. Against the president's court-reform proposal, or "court-packing" plan, from the beginning, Connally clearly expressed his position in a speech before the Texas Legislature. In spite of being a "devoted, personal friend of the President," he declared that the reorganization plan "would violate my superior obligation to the Constitution of the United States." The plan would, he continued, "absolutely undermine and destroy the independence of the court" and set a dangerous precedent for future presidents who might manipulate the composition of the Court for their own political purposes.[32]

Connally was drawn directly into the fight when he was appointed to the Senate Judiciary Committee. Part of the opposition's strategy was to draw out the hearings before the Judiciary Committee, and in this Connally was an adroit player, using his debating and courtroom skills to badger witnesses who backed the president's proposal. Besides initiating long argumentative exchanges with witnesses, Connally employed the delay tactic of inviting numerous lawyers to speak to the committee. He gathered his forces from Texas—fifty-five people in all—some of whom presented lengthy speeches to the committee. Finally, after two long months of slow-moving hearings, committee members, upon learning that a Supreme Court vacancy had been created by the resignation of Associate Justice Willis Van Devanter, voted 10 to 8 against the bill.[33]

But the issue was not dead. Roosevelt doggedly pursued a court-reorganization plan. He pushed Senator Joseph T. Robinson of Arkansas, who was the majority leader and the president's chief spokesman, to introduce a compromise. Then, when Robinson suddenly died, the contest was over. As Connally recalled later, "the court fight was Roosevelt's first major defeat as President. He never forgot it."[34]

Connally was right. During the 1938 midterm elections Roosevelt sought to "purge" the Congress of his opponents. Although not up for reelection until 1940, Connally recognized that "the President was determined to shame me, too." At least two times he was clearly snubbed by Roosevelt. On one occasion, during a campaign trip through Texas, Roosevelt announced the nomination of Texas governor James Allred to a federal judgeship while Connally, who had recommended another candidate, stood on the same train platform with the president. Moreover, at several stops, Roosevelt referred to his "good friends" from Texas, such as Sam Rayburn and Maury Maverick, but never mentioned Connally. While angry and irritated, Connally did not feel threatened, his tenure in the Senate being unaffected and his relationship with the president remaining cordial but cool from then on.[35]

While New Dealers focused on economic relief, recovery, and reform, dramatic world events were changing the direction of American foreign policy. Since the end of World War I several world powers—Ger-

many, Italy, Japan, and Russia—had fallen under totalitarian governments. These critical political developments had pushed more and more
Americans into the isolationist camp. Opposed to the isolationists from
the days of Woodrow Wilson, Connally, already noted for his razor-sharp
retorts, was merciless in his attacks against senators with what he viewed
as shortsighted views on the United States' role in world affairs. He had
bitter, vehement arguments with Arthur H. Vandenberg of Michigan, his
adversary for many years. Connally ridiculed him as a "hard-boiled isolationist even as a youth," who "made an obvious show of stamping out of
the chamber into the cloakroom" whenever Connally spoke.[36]

The major issue that divided the isolationists from the internationalists
was neutrality. In 1935 a neutrality bill to limit the export of munitions to
any belligerent when a state of war had been declared by the president
came to the Senate floor. This bill put Connally in a serious predicament
politically. In the beginning Connally attacked this isolationist measure
because it would "tie the President's hands," would be a "serious invasion
of the President's powers to initiate and direct our foreign policy," and
would send a signal to the world that "we will fight under no circumstances at all." Unable to persuade enough senators to kill this bill, he re-
sorted to negotiating a compromise that would limit the life of the act to
February 1936. Connally hoped that in the next session of Congress the
Neutrality Act would expire quietly. He was wrong. Because of his preoccupation with Roosevelt's court-packing plan, he was not in a position to
prevent the act from being extended until May 1937. In fact, in the spring
of 1937, he voted with the majority of the Senate to make the act permanent. Recognizing the inevitable, he had sided with the neutrality advocates, even if it meant surrendering to a policy with which he disagreed.
Even when Roosevelt admitted that signing the Neutrality Act was a "terrible blunder," Congress would not reconsider.[37]

On September 1, 1939, Hitler invaded Poland. Two days later Britain
and France declared war. World War II had begun. If left untouched, the
shortsighted neutrality policies of the Congress would mortally wound
the enemies of Hitler. Something had to be done—and quickly—to
change the direction of U.S. foreign policy. On September 21, Roosevelt
called Congress into special session hoping to secure the repeal of the arms
embargo. Because Key Pittman, chairman of the Senate Foreign Relations
Committee, was ill, Connally was given the responsibility of drafting the
administration's repeal bill, which would allow the sale of arms to belligerents on a "cash and carry" basis, and of leading the fight both in the Foreign Relations Committee and on the floor of the Senate. He was indeed
ready for the task. Like the German tanks that were rolling across Europe,

Connally ran over the committee, pushing the bill through by a sixteen to seven vote. On the Senate floor the isolationists tried to defend the arms embargo but to no avail. Connally, assisted by Alben Barkley of Kentucky, Claude Pepper of Florida, and Elbert Thomas of Utah, maneuvered to undermine the opposition. In a two-hour speech, Connally refuted the isolationist arguments. After a month of debate a vote was taken — sixty-three to thirty. Connally had succeeded in getting the new Neutrality Act of 1939 passed. Now countries like Britain and France would have a fair chance of defeating Hitler.[38]

In the midst of all this prewar congressional activity, major changes occurred in two Senate chairmanships. On June 22, 1941, Finance Committee chair Pat Harrison of Mississippi died. As it happened, Walter George of Georgia chaired Foreign Relations and was the ranking Democrat on Finance. He therefore chose the chairmanship of Finance. As a consequence, the one man who had gained stature and respect as an expert on foreign affairs would at last obtain the important chairmanship of the Foreign Relations Committee. On July 31, 1941, Connally received the appointment.[39]

As the first months of his chairmanship passed, Connally was kept advised of the threatening postures of Germany and Japan. In response to the escalating tensions, Connally told the press on December 5, 1941, that Japan was "the latest threat to our security." Apprehensive that the United States might lose access to "strategic raw materials" from the Dutch East Indies, he cautioned that the "national defense effort would be fatally handicapped." If the United States should ever be faced with such a crisis, Americans, he warned, should be "prepared to defend our established rights by arms if necessary."[40]

Connally's concerns were soon to be justified. On Sunday, December 7, 1941, he had lunch with Harold Ickes. Besides discussing the "critical situation with Japan," they also enjoyed some lighthearted moments; Ickes wrote that Connally had "a fund of funny stories." Afterward, Connally decided to go for a "relaxing drive" and casually turned on the radio. The news was blasting that the Japanese had bombed Pearl Harbor. Stunned, he raced home, where a message from the president awaited him. He was to come to the Oval Office at 9:00 P.M. "The air hung heavy with gloom," he recalled, as the meeting began. Listening to the president and cabinet members run through the progression of events, he "began to boil." He "sharply questioned" Secretary of the Navy Frank Knox about why American warships "were caught like tame ducks" at Pearl Harbor. The answers were not satisfactory. The next day Roosevelt asked Congress to declare war against Japan. Connally brought to the Senate floor the war resolution—at 4:10 P.M. On December 8, when Roosevelt signed the resolution, the United States was at war. Three days later Congress declared war on Germany and Italy as well.[41]

The war did not change Connally's responsibilities in the Senate. For example, in an effort to head off a possible wave of labor strikes that could cripple production in critical war industries, Connally authored an anti-strike bill in 1943. Following a conference committee compromise, the Congress passed the War Labor Disputes Act (Smith-Connally Anti-Strike Bill). Known for his consistent southern-bloc position toward certain measures, he opposed an anti-poll tax bill, citing that only a constitutional amendment could end the practice. After all, he argued, the question was "not one of race or color" but of "upholding the Constitution or defying it."[42]

What did change for Connally during the war was his new role in developing a postwar foreign policy. In December 1941, he was invited to meet British foreign minister Winston Churchill. Together with Roosevelt and Churchill he helped write the Declaration of the United Nations which spelled out the basic war objectives of the twenty-six countries fighting Germany, Italy, and Japan. In January 1942, he decided to invite a State Department official to appear before the committee on a weekly basis, in order to better keep the Foreign Relations Committee abreast of foreign developments. Even Senator Vandenberg admitted the practice was "excellent." Then in May, along with Senator Warren Austin (R-Vt.), Connally accepted an appointment from Secretary of State Cordell Hull to join a bipartisan Advisory Committee on Postwar Foreign Policy that would not only supply the president with information but would also make recommendations. Because of this subcommittee assignment, Connally was able to help design a postwar world organization.[43]

Gradually a bipartisan foreign policy emerged. In 1943, to review the several congressional resolutions that outlined the postwar principles of the United States, Connally appointed a bipartisan Foreign Relations subcommittee. In November the committee agreed to the Connally Resolution (S. Res. 192), a compromise that called for international cooperation to secure peace, international organization to prevent aggression, and the advice and consent of the Senate to any treaty carrying out these provisions. Although his name was on the resolution, Connally acknowledged the contributions of the Republicans, crediting in particular the "valuable" work of his longtime adversary Vandenberg. Then in 1944, at the request of Hull, Connally put together the "Committee of Eight" to draw up plans for an international organization. This Foreign Relations subcommittee of four Republicans and four Democrats, Connally recalled, "inaugurated the 'bipartisan' group of senators on foreign policy." When at Yalta the decision had been made to hold a multinational conference in San Francisco to create a new world organization, Roosevelt announced that a bipartisan delegation from Congress would be a part of the United States contingent—a strong suggestion made by Connally because both Democrats and Republicans in the Senate would have to ratify any United Nations Charter treaty. As a consequence, Connally, Vandenberg, Representative Sol Bloom (D-N.Y.), chair of the House Committee on Foreign Affairs, and Representative Charles Eaton (R-N.J.), the ranking Republican on the House Committee on Foreign Affairs, were appointed to the delegation.[44]

Upon the death of Franklin Roosevelt in April 1945, President Harry S. Truman assured the San Francisco delegation that the United Nations Conference would go on as scheduled. Connally was ready to help create an international organization that he had fully supported since the Treaty of Versailles and the League of Nations. Assigned to Commission Three on the Security Council, Connally and his fellow commissioners were responsible for framing the structure and procedures of the Security Council. On the critical question of allowing a permanent member of the Security Council to have the veto power, Connally, an advocate of the veto, was determined to persuade the others to his point of view. He argued that without the power to veto a proposal in an international dispute the United Nations Charter would be useless. A master of dramatic oratory, he then stood before them and "ripped the charter draft in my hands to shreds and flung the scraps with disgust." His theatrics worked—the veto was approved. Another question before the commission was whether or not a veto could be used to prevent discussions or debate in the Security Council. Connally opposed any restriction on freedom of speech in the Council. Once the Russians were convinced to share this position, this part of the veto controversy too was settled. Finally, after nine weeks the United Nations Conference had completed its task, creating the first world organization since the League of Nations—and a far stronger one at that. With great pride, Connally was the second American to sign the charter after Secretary of State Edward Stettinius, chairman of the American delegation.[45]

Back home in Washington, D.C., Connally orchestrated Senate ratification of the United Nations Charter. To "stress the bipartisan nature of our joint effort," Connally arranged with Vandenberg to arrive at the Senate together. "Arm in arm," they enjoyed an enthusiastic welcome from their colleagues. To dispel any misgivings of fellow Republicans, Vandenberg then generously praised Connally for never displaying the "faintest hint of partisanship" and for allowing all delegates to "play our full role in the deliberations." Confident yet cautious, Connally carefully guided the hearings of the Foreign Relations Committee and succeeded in winning a twenty-one to one vote for the charter. But always nagging at Connally was the vivid memory of 1919 when the Senate defeated the League of Nations in the Treaty of Versailles, a fact that he was determined not to let pass unnoticed by his colleagues. "They know that the League of Nations was slaughtered here in this chamber," he shouted. "Can't you see the blood?—There it is on the wall." After days of debate the Senate in a bipartisan spirit and under the watchful leadership of Connally stood firm by ratifying the UN Charter eighty-nine to two.[46]

The end of World War II and the creation of the United Nations did not push foreign policy into the background for Connally. The postwar world meant increased responsibilities for himself and the Senate Foreign Relations Committee. Once the atomic bombs had been dropped on Hiroshima and Nagasaki, control of such destructive weapons became a matter of paramount importance. In the fall of 1945 the Senate set up a special committee on atomic energy, of which Connally was a member, to study the entire question of atomic weapons and energy. As the committee worked on a plan to implement controls on the use and experimentation of atomic energy, a major division of opinion surfaced—should control be placed in civilian or military hands? Although preferring "civilian control of almost everything," Connally, in this instance, sided with the military because "the bomb was a matter of national defense," and under civilian control "information might leak out." Over several months the debate continued until a compromise bill was hammered out, resulting in the Atomic Energy Act of 1946, which established the Atomic Energy Commission and the Joint Congressional Committee on Atomic Energy and employed both military and civilian agencies in the formation of atomic energy policy.[47]

But other countries that possessed atomic weapons had to become a part of any mechanism to monitor their use and proliferation. Any hope of controlling atomic weapons would now rest with the United Nations, which Connally was anxious to "help launch . . . on a smooth voyage." In January 1946, while working on setting up the mechanics of the United Nations, he was given the responsibility of securing the creation of a United Nations Atomic Energy Commission (UNAEC). After some setbacks, he succeeded in this task when the General Assembly approved the UNAEC without a dissenting vote.[48]

Recognized as both an expert on and a spokesman for Truman's foreign policy, Connally found himself receiving from the administration more and more diplomatic assignments. In 1946 along with Vandenberg he accompanied Secretary of State James Byrnes to the Paris meetings of the Council of Foreign Ministers, which were to prepare drafts of peace treaties with the Axis Powers. Attending the sessions that summer, he found this mission frustrating, especially since the Soviets were constantly creating obstacles with their stubbornness and intransigence. On the committee to work out the Italian peace treaty, he participated in a "grueling, difficult task." While some countries wished to include crippling penalties, he argued for provisions that would allow Italy to "maintain the status of a primary power." In the end he was forced to agree to less generous terms because Secretary Byrnes "was anxious to finish the conference." [49]

Since 1941 Connally had enjoyed an important role in the Senate as chair of the Foreign Relations Committee. But during the 1946 congressional elections the "unthinkable" happened: the Republicans gained control of the Senate and thus Connally lost his chairmanship to Vandenberg. For many years these two men had been opponents, even though both believed in bipartisanship and cooperated "reasonably well," each one recognizing that "nothing would be gained by having a fuss." Always in friendly competition, they referred to each other as "Old Tom" and "Old Van." Aware that he did not possess the "intellectual apparatus of Vandenberg," Connally exhibited some jealousy, which was revealed "in very private, unguarded moments." Yet Vandenberg was always appreciative that Connally had treated the Republicans with respect and allowed them to participate in the formulation of a bipartisan postwar foreign policy. [50]

After what may have seemed like an eternity during his two-year exile as the leader of the Foreign Relations Committee, Connally finally resumed the chairmanship in 1949 when the Democrats regained control of the Senate. And just in time as far as he was concerned, for the Senate was going to be considering the North Atlantic Treaty Organization (NATO) and Connally wanted to be in a position to exert significant influence. Because Secretary of State Dean Acheson had already started the negotiations, Connally was quick to inform the secretary that the Senate would not "accept a finished document stuck under our noses"; therefore, Acheson would find it advisable to "work closely with us." As a result, Connally suggested changes that would mollify any complaints from the isolationists. He was able to control the hearings on the treaty and then secured a unanimous committee vote of approval. [51]

A much more difficult fight arose over the Mutual Assistance Bill of 1949, which was the military assistance program for NATO. Clearly, the concept of bipartisanship was put to the test. Connally would have to work diligently to secure support from the opposition to Truman's foreign policy. Republican senators strenuously objected to those sections of the assistance bill that would give the president a "blank check" to supply other countries with munitions. In the Foreign Relations Committee Connally was forced to accept cuts in the appropriations in order to win Republican support. On the Senate floor he enlisted senators to deliver speeches in an effort "to keep my supporters on their toes." Always counting the votes in his favor, at times losing his temper and becoming irritable, he employed every parliamentary device to pass this bill as quickly as possible. Finally, after "a hard four-day fight," the Mutual Defense Assistance bill of 1949 was passed.[52]

On June 24, 1950, the North Koreans crossed the 38th parallel into South Korea. The Korean crisis, Connally remembered, "signified the end of the bipartisan approach" to American foreign policy. Republicans who had already begun to drift away from bipartisanship now were openly defiant toward President Truman. Connally, the recognized congressional spokesman for Truman's foreign policies, felt obliged to answer the barrage of criticisms concerning the president's handling of the Korean situation. When Truman relieved General Douglas MacArthur as commander of the United Nations forces, however, Connally endorsed the idea that the Foreign Relations Committee and Armed Services Committee should hold joint hearings about the dismissal. In this way the evidence, he believed, would justify the actions of Truman and would help calm the uproar over MacArthur's firing.[53]

Although the Korean conflict was still unresolved, Americans turned their attention to the upcoming elections in 1952. So did Connally. Rumors spread in Texas that either Governor Allan Shivers or Attorney General Price Daniel would challenge Connally in the Democratic primary. No matter which one ran against him, Connally knew that the anti-Truman sentiment would be used to "confuse Texan voters into lashing me to the mast with the President." When Shivers decided to seek reelection as governor, Daniel then announced for the United States Senate. Daniel's slickly run campaign eroded support for Connally by linking him, as expected, with Truman's unpopular foreign policy. He aroused the emotion of state pride and the issue of states' rights by accusing Connally of failing to fight for the right of Texas to own the tidelands. He also drew to his side the oil industry, which by now considered Connally "just an aging, unreliable windbag." Connally was partially responsible for this drift toward Daniel. He had failed over the past few years to keep "his fences mended" with the oil industry. Equally critical was his failure to maintain a stronghold of supporters and a solid campaign organization.

Back home in Texas in April, after reviewing the political situation, Connally concluded that reelection would have "entailed a hard, arduous, back-breaking campaign over the whole state, in an endeavor to overcome the tidal wave of lies . . . it was too great a price to pay." After twenty-four years in the Senate, Connally announced his retirement.[54]

In 1953 Connally could look back on a career dedicated to his state and his country. Unquestionably, during all his years of government service he had tried to represent the political temperament and to protect the economic interests of Texans. Always a stalwart Democrat, he was a conservative on such issues as civil rights and a liberal on such ideas as federal aid to agriculture. By the time of his retirement he was a recognized expert on U.S. foreign policy, having been involved in some of the most momentous decisions of the twentieth century.

But like many other public figures before him, Connally had outlived his time. A rapidly changing world and an ever-evolving political environment were passing him by, leaving this old southern warhorse behind. So he retired after thirty-six years in Congress, having never lost an election. He spent the remainder of his life enjoying his family and friends, occasionally joining in Democratic Party activities. At the age of eighty-six he succumbed to pneumonia and died on October 28, 1963. One of the last "authentic giants of the century" was gone. "Politics is a cussed trade," he once reportedly said, "even when you're good at it." And if anybody knew the truth about politics, it was Tom Connally.[55]

SAM RAYBURN

Fig. 6.1. "Mr. Sam," the nickname given to Sam Rayburn, served as Speaker of the House during the presidencies of Roosevelt, Truman, Eisenhower, and Kennedy. Rayburn (Sam) Papers, Center for American History, UT-Austin.

SAM RAYBURN

BY D. CLAYTON BROWN

When Sam Rayburn died on November 16, 1961, the nation knew it had lost a great leader. "Sam Rayburn . . . was the greatest of the great Speakers of the House of Representatives," wrote Harry Truman. "He was the second most powerful person in the United States Government. It is my opinion that Sam Rayburn was one of the greatest and most respected Statesmen who ever lived." Eleanor Roosevelt wrote: "He was one of the finest Speakers and Representatives. My husband at all times had great respect and affection for him." These eloquent statements refer to the political side of Mr. Sam's life, a life that began in the Texas House of Representatives when he was twenty-five and continued until his death at age seventy-nine. Other statements made at the time of his death had a more personal tone. Senator Mike Mansfield of Montana wrote: "I feel that I have lost both a father and a brother, but I know that the nation's loss is greater still. He is the last of the old frontiersmen." And from former president Dwight Eisenhower came this short and poignant phrase: "As his friend of many years, I mourn his passing." Journalist Eric Sevareid combined the political and personal nature of Rayburn when he said: "He was the salt, soil and substance of our political system and inheritance. We shall not see his like again in the Speaker's chair, for the old ways, the old image of America are going as the old men go." [1]

This last statement referred to the value system that was so much a part of Rayburn's personality. The longest-serving Speaker of the House descended from self-sufficient farmers whose lifeblood was the soil. The Rayburn clan, like generations of pioneers preceding them, lived close to nature and the earth, and as was the case of an America of bygone days, they depended on one another and developed a sense of fair play. These people believed in trust and honesty, explaining the pioneer belief that a man was only "as good as his word."

Rayburn, born in 1882 in Tennessee, moved with his family to the high-yield cotton-growing area of Northeast Texas in 1887 and settled near the town of Flag Springs. Sam was one of eleven children. Though the family scraped for every dollar, it should not be assumed that the Rayburns were poor. In the agrarian environment in which they lived cash was scarce for nearly all. "We were short of money," Rayburn once recalled, "but we had a comfortable home, plenty to eat. My father couldn't put us all through college, but most of us went anyway." As a boy Sam learned to be resourceful, not to settle for less, and to be ready to make the sacrifices required to achieve a goal. His long days spent working the cotton rows alongside his father and brothers, his observance of the rotation of the year's seasons, and seeing new life come forth each spring gave him patience and taught him that hard labor would, over time, bear fruit. But in this context of relative hardship, an environment in which baptisms were conducted in a pond or creek, the young Rayburn learned that money and material wealth were not always labor's reward. Instead one's compensation might be a modest life filled with contentment and satisfaction, or one of public service, as long as it was a life of respect for others and for oneself. Around the rural town squares of Rayburn's youth, men and women who shared this southern agrarian value system were plentiful.[2]

Rayburn's personality at all stages of his career reflected this background. His friends always described him as hardworking, patient, and steadfast to his word. His personal life and business conduct were said to be simple, but he ran the House of Representatives, by everyone's assessment, out of his hip pocket. His refusal to keep notes was famous, and he always explained that when a man was honest he didn't need to worry about what he said. The "Rayburnisms," short quips of personal philosophy, were part of his mode of operation. They included: "Any fellow who will cheat for you will cheat against you"; "Any jackass can kick a barn down, but it takes a carpenter to build it"; and his most repeated Rayburnism, "If a man has good common sense, he has about all the sense there is." Such views of life were once heard throughout rural America, and Rayburn's expressions endeared him to his friends and won him respect around the world. At the peak of his power, when he was regarded as second in power only to the president of the United States, he was admiringly and simply called "Mr. Sam."

Rayburn's adult life prior to becoming a member of Congress had both common and uncommon features. In 1900, when he was eighteen years old, he left home in order to attend Mayo Normal College at Commerce, Texas, where he worked as a janitor and dairy hand and at other odd jobs to pay his tuition. Financial strains forced him to leave Mayo and to teach school for a while, but he finished the curriculum at Mayo in time to graduate with his class. He returned to teaching in small country schools, but in 1906 he left teaching in order to enter politics. The Texas House of Representatives was his first political goal, and that year he was elected to represent Fannin County.

Only twenty-four years old when he took the oath of office as a Texas legislator, Rayburn kept a low profile during his first year. He entered the University of Texas Law School in Austin to take a special three-month review class, which proved to be sufficient preparation for Rayburn to pass the state bar exam. During his second term Rayburn chaired two committees and served on four others. Well liked and highly respected, Rayburn was elected Speaker of the Texas House during his third term, an amazing feat for such a young man. His one term as the Texas Speaker was not particularly eventful, but he was remembered as a party loyalist who still managed to be fair and impartial. Rayburn himself said that he had enjoyed being Texas Speaker more than he had enjoyed holding any other public office.[3]

The young Texan's move to Washington, D.C., occurred in 1912 when he was elected to represent Texas's Fourth Congressional District. In a race of eight candidates, Rayburn won by 493 votes over his closest rival. During his campaign he pointed to his clean record in the Texas House and freedom from special interests. He championed lower tariffs, the need for inheritance and income taxes, electoral reform, and the right of workers to organize. These issues were popular in 1912, as evidenced by their presence in the platform of the Progressive Party, led by Theodore Roosevelt. Rayburn's goal to reach Washington was well known by his friends in Austin, and thus his decision to run came as no surprise.

At the age of thirty-one, unmarried and free of family responsibilities, Rayburn settled down to a career in the U.S. House of Representatives that lasted uninterrupted until his death. He was a strong supporter of President Woodrow Wilson and received an assignment to the Committee on Interstate and Foreign Commerce. He fought for regulation of the railroads and supported the American role in World War I. Rayburn, however, "realized there would be a long, long period of hard work, careful planning, and continual friend-making," wrote one biographer, "before he would be eligible for the final goal: to serve as Speaker of the U.S. House of Representatives." Indeed, such was the case. Rayburn entered into a period of quiet and routine work until events turned to his favor in 1931 when he became chairman of the Committee on Interstate and Foreign Commerce.[4]

This period of calm, however, should not be overlooked or relegated to a minor place in Rayburn's career. To begin with, he maintained his personal ethics and spirit of cooperation, which meant punctual attendance at meetings and acceptance of extra work. His willingness to accept tasks of drudgery gained him favor with senior Democrats who in turn promoted his career. Later, when he was Speaker of the House, Rayburn gave the following advice to first-term legislators: "Get to know your committee chairman, let him know you want to work and help him do a good job of running the committee so it can make a record, and he'll help you with your problems." Particularly helpful to young Rayburn were John Nance Garner of Texas, who acted as House Democratic whip; William C. Adamson, chairman of the Committee on Interstate and Foreign Commerce; and Tennessee congressman Cordell Hull.[5]

Democrats were, of course, out of favor during the Republican Party–dominated 1920s. Young Democrats were therefore relegated to strengthening the party in their home districts, maintaining ties with House leaders, and patiently gaining seniority. Rayburn was unhappy during these years. His party was in the minority, and he had little chance to promote his constituents' interests or his career. He started reading during his spare time and nearly always kept one book in his office and another in his Washington apartment. It was during this Republican era that his parents died and his attempt at marriage to Metze Jones failed. The marriage ended in divorce after about three months, and Rayburn never talked about it, neither to family members nor to political friends. It was a matter that both he and Metze always kept to themselves. Rayburn was greatly disappointed with this failure because he had always wanted a large family and frequently said that he regretted "not having a little towheaded boy to teach how to fish." Therein lay his devotion to the House of Representatives. A long day for Rayburn was standard; he commonly went into his office on Saturdays and always seemed bored on weekends, restlessly awaiting the arrival of a new week of congressional business. The enthusiasm and love that would have gone to a family went instead to the House and to his constituents. His one opportunity to forge a family had come and gone during the quiet Republican years. Any damage that his divorce might have caused with the voters of the Fourth District never materialized.[6]

Until the national public sentiment changed, bringing the election of Democratic majorities in Congress, Rayburn had little opportunity for legislative activity. Like other Democrats, his best friend during these years was time, and hence seniority; therefore, he kept his seat on the Interstate and Foreign Commerce Committee and continued to work alongside Garner and the Democratic leadership. He fended off challengers in the Fourth District, solidified his position at home, and simply endured, becoming well known in the House and well liked by the Democratic elders and the ranking Democrat on his committee.

The Republican era ended dramatically with the Wall Street crash of 1929: the Democrats won control of both houses in 1930. For Rayburn things started moving quickly. He took over as chairman of the Interstate and Foreign Commerce Committee in 1931, and he played an important role in the nomination of Franklin D. Roosevelt for president in 1932.

The 1932 Democratic National Convention could have been disastrous for Rayburn. He was indebted to Garner, who had guided him since as far back as 1913, and felt that he must remain loyal to a fellow Texan as long as he had a chance, albeit slight, to receive the party's nomination. But on the other hand Roosevelt was quite popular, and, given President Herbert Hoover's vast unpopularity, the Democratic nominee was expected to become the next president. Therefore, had Rayburn offended Roosevelt, or had Garner fought hard for the nomination, Rayburn's career might have been endangered. Garner showed statesmanship; he did not want the convention to deadlock as it had in 1924 and therefore released his delegates after the third ballot. Rayburn had hoped this would happen, and as soon as Garner made the decision, Rayburn swung the Texas vote over to Roosevelt, even though some members of the Lone Star delegation wanted to keep fighting for Garner.[7]

When the New Dealers, with a flurry of activity, descended upon Washington after Roosevelt's victory, Rayburn was in a position full of power and opportunity. As chairman of the Interstate and Foreign Commerce Committee, Rayburn played a major role in the preparation of several pieces of reform legislation, some of them with far-reaching impact. In these particular battles, as well as in others, he used his middle-of-the-road, or compromise, philosophy in order to strike a bargain that was fair to all.

After the Wall Street crash and the resulting revelations of considerable fraud in the brokerage industry, "the reputation of Wall Street for financial wisdom, care of other people's money, and common honesty," wrote one historian, "was never lower." Wall Street investors considered themselves to be responsible members of a private elite, but the general public and the Roosevelt administration had a different opinion of them. The original draft of the Securities Act of 1933, put together by the so-called Roosevelt brain trust, went to Rayburn's committee, but Rayburn felt that the original bill would put too much authority into the hands of the Federal Trade Commission (FTC). The commission "would become the Czar of American business," wrote one observer, "because it required all companies to get FTC permission before issuing stock."[8]

Rayburn therefore persuaded the brain trust to write a less authoritarian bill and held hearings on it before his committee. Representatives of Wall Street met with Rayburn and tried to kill the bill. He listened to their objections but left the meeting convinced that the bill was fair and feasible. He took it to the House floor, where he answered all objections and explained the details of the legislation. It passed. The Senate version was not as well written, so ultimately the House bill became law as the Truth-in-Securities Act. A Rayburn characteristic vital to understanding his success was apparent in this episode. He had refused to hold all brokerage firms accountable for the wrong-doing of some and had refused to go along with the New Dealers' attempt to concentrate complete authority in a government body. On the other hand, he did not yield to the objectionable demands of the industry. His sense of fair play had shone through, and while the press and the general public had not noticed it, his evenhandedness had been duly noted by insiders.

The ease with which Rayburn had guided the passage of the Securities bill, however, was not an omen of things to come. Roosevelt wanted to regulate the stock exchanges so as to protect the public interest. Among other provisions, he proposed the establishment of more realistic conditions for buying stocks "on the margin," a practice widely abused and partly responsible for the crash in 1929. Again the measure went to Rayburn's committee, and again it authorized the FTC to regulate the industry. In this instance Wall Street was ready for a fight and "some of the mightiest names of high finance," wrote one observer, "flanked by their legal and financial experts, came swarming into Washington for public hearings before Rayburn's committee." Rayburn faced an array of belligerent witnesses and after several weeks of testimony asked Roosevelt's experts to draft a revision incorporating some of the objections presented to the committee.[9]

Rayburn took it to the floor, where critics described the measure as a communistic idea. The industry had rallied considerable support for its position, and Rayburn faced tough opponents. Fortunately, senior Republican Carl Mapes of Michigan agreed with Rayburn and provided some help. Support for the bill proved to be stronger than it first appeared. It passed 281 to 84. A similar measure passed the Senate, and in the conference committee Rayburn conceded that a special Securities and Exchange Commission should be created to carry out the new law. Rayburn had become identified with one of the most important examples of New Deal legislation, the Securities Exchange Act.

The major battle of Rayburn's career, however, still lay ahead—in the Public Utility Holding Company Act of 1935. The law dealt with the pyramiding of stocks, or the creation of holding companies. By the 1930s the practice of stock pyramiding had become a political issue, and the Roosevelt administration sought to stop it. Rayburn had a particular interest in this subject and served as the House sponsor of the regulatory bill. The bill contained one provision that was particularly offensive to the utility companies—the "death sentence," which called for abolition rather than regulation of holding companies. Wendell Willkie, who would be the Republican candidate for president in 1940, led the effort to oppose the bill and exerted considerable pressure against Congress. Rayburn's committee conducted the House hearings on the bill; so great was the pressure that his committee broke rank and voted to remove the death sentence clause despite Rayburn's attempts to keep the measure intact.

Being floor leader of the bill, Rayburn had to fight hard to defend it, but despite his best efforts, he could not persuade the House to reinstate the death sentence provision that had been removed by his own committee. The House vote marked a severe setback for Roosevelt—and for Rayburn. In the Senate the death sentence had remained intact, but the House conference committee refused to budge, forcing a compromise that killed the death sentence proviso.

Despite Rayburn's loss in fighting for the death sentence provision, his role in the passage of the Public Utility Holding Company Act raised his own stock among members of Congress and the White House. To begin with, he had accepted the responsibility to defend a piece of legislation that was particularly technical and difficult to understand. (He had, of course, relied on White House assistance in this respect.) Nearly everyone was impressed with his knowledge of detail and ability to counter the charges made by opponents who could be quite adept at exposing flaws in the proposal. At the same time Rayburn had resolutely stood firm. He had refused to back down on the death sentence, even to the extent of being overturned by his committee. This was unusual behavior for Rayburn, who preferred to avoid punitive legislation. But his unflinching position in the struggle had endeared him to the president, "a powerful asset," wrote a biographer "when the time came to make his bid for a House leadership position." [10]

Rayburn's legislative style and personal way of dealing with people was best illustrated in the creation of the Rural Electrification Administration (REA) in 1936. By that time most urban residents had electrical service, but only 10 percent of the farms had service, and in many areas the percentage was far lower. Morris Cooke, the "father of the REA," had persuaded Roosevelt to create the agency by executive order in 1935, but its temporary status and lack of dependable funding had thwarted its progress. In 1936 Senator George Norris, "father of the TVA," and Rayburn jointly introduced legislation for a permanent REA. Rayburn's committee held hearings on the measure, and Rayburn led the floor fight for its passage.

In this case Rayburn followed his usual practice of taking the middle ground. Norris wanted to exclude power companies from receiving REA funds, but Rayburn disagreed, saying that they could be of some help. The goal was to extend service to farmers, he would say, not to punish the electrical industry. Rayburn's provision remained intact in the House bill, but Norris had kept the companies out of the Senate bill. Now the two highly respected members of Congress, anxious to see their people in the countryside enjoy modern conveniences, reached an impasse in the conference committee. "We quarreled for a long time," Norris recalled, "but neither side would yield an inch." [11]

Norris left the room, determined to keep the power industry out of the program. Rayburn immediately followed and, catching up to Norris, said: "Now Senator, don't be discouraged . . . just let it rest awhile. Within a few days we will notify you we are ready to have another meeting." [12]

By the next meeting, the House conferees had developed a compromise. Why not let rural electric cooperatives, or public bodies, have first preference in qualifying for REA loans but still keep the door open to any power companies that applied to the REA? Norris conceded. In 1936 the Rural Electrification Administration, with its new statute of authority, embarked on a program to organize cooperatives and extend electrical service throughout rural America. Rayburn was, of course, the cosponsor of the bill, and the REA was one of his proudest achievements. It proved to be one of the most successful and lasting contributions of the New Deal and remains today a fixture in American rural and now suburban life.

By 1936 Rayburn had developed into a legislator who clearly disliked punitive laws and preferred compromise whenever possible; he was well known as a man of conviction willing to fight to the end when a fight was necessary. The Texas lawmaker was also well positioned from a tactical point of view in the House. Roosevelt liked him and regarded him as a firm believer in New Deal reforms. His career was poised for another jump. It came in 1936.

That year, while Roosevelt ran for reelection, House Speaker Joseph W. Byrnes died. Rayburn at the time was in Texas and left to attend Byrnes's funeral in Nashville, Tennessee. The vacancy of the Speakership brought an opportunity for Rayburn to climb higher in the House leadership. Majority Leader William Bankhead quickly replaced Byrnes, leaving open the position of majority leader, which was normally presumed to be next in line to that of Speaker. Rayburn committed himself to run for majority leader against John J. O'Connor of New York, a Tammany Hall Democrat. O'Connor had already announced his candidacy and had obtained pledges of support soon after Byrnes's funeral.

Rayburn let it be known that he was a candidate but took a slower approach, and while O'Connor appeared to be the front-runner, the president had not indicated his choice. Vice President Garner stepped into the race and effectively damaged O'Connor's chances by pointing to his reputation as a mouthpiece for Tammany Hall. The powerful Texas delegation united behind Rayburn. Furthermore, Rayburn held a reputation as a stalwart New Deal supporter. Roosevelt indicated his preference for Rayburn, and two state delegations, Louisiana and Pennsylvania, announced their support for the Texan. Rayburn was gathering momentum, and when Massachusetts representative John McCormack endorsed him, big-city bosses aligned their support as well. Rayburn wound up winning the job of majority leader easily by a vote of 184 to 127 when Congress convened in January 1937. He could now expect to reach the Speaker's chair in a reasonable time unless something went dreadfully wrong. Garner's contribution to Rayburn's success should not be overlooked. As vice president and as an experienced Democratic politician, his anti-O'Connor campaign obviously had an impact on the race.[13]

Compared with his experience during the early years of the New Deal, Rayburn's stint as majority leader was uneventful. However, Speaker Bankhead suffered poor health, requiring Rayburn to preside frequently over the House in the Speaker's chair. This had the effect of conditioning him and his fellow representatives for Rayburn's election to the speakership in 1940. That year Bankhead died, and with no nominee from the Republicans, the House elected Rayburn Speaker. He reached his life's goal, but would always say: "I came within a gnat's heel of remaining a tenant farmer."

As in the case of his ascendance to the chair of the House Commerce Committee, Rayburn's achievement of the speakership came at a time when events seemed to heighten the responsibility of the office. Soon after he took over as presiding officer, the House was embroiled in one of its most dramatic debates, one with serious consequences: the extension of the military draft in September 1941. In the previous year the government had established a peacetime draft as a measure of military preparedness, but the conscripts, according to law, were limited to one year's service. As war raged in Europe, however, Roosevelt wanted the period of service extended on grounds that the United States could not afford to be without enlarged armed services as Nazi Germany had isolated Great Britain and invaded the Soviet Union in June 1941. While popular opinion in the United States favored the Allies, opposition to entering the war was widespread throughout the nation.

The real fight over the draft extension came in the House, where isolationist sentiment was strong. Rayburn took the position that foreign policy should remain largely the prerogative of the president and argued for the extension. Rayburn's biographer stated that the Texan exerted unusual effort to persuade those House colleagues not adamantly opposed to the bill. "I need your vote," he would say. "I wish you would stand by me because it means a lot to me." Members of Congress faced a heart-wrenching decision: a vote against the bill might imperil the country, but a supporting vote would bring the United States closer to war. American sentiment at that point was leaning toward noninvolvement in the European conflict.[14]

When House debate began, it was emotional. As Speaker, Rayburn had to be fair and could not threaten or pressure anyone opposing him. During the vote, however, he used the means of his position to encourage passage. As the clerk called the roll, the count went back and forth, and it was impossible to predict the final tally. As the clerk counted, one member changed his yea to a nay, narrowing the vote to 203 to 202 in favor of passage. At this point Rayburn froze the vote and announced passage of the bill. Some confusion appeared on the floor, as opponents wanted to make a move to recast the vote, but Rayburn informed them that only a person from the winning side could make such a motion. Opponents still objected and wanted to reconsider the vote. Twice Rayburn refused, and he carried the day. His tactics could be interpreted as "strong-arming" the isolationists. However, when the Japanese attacked Pearl Harbor and Germany subsequently declared war on the United States, Rayburn's tactics were seen as life-saving measures, and his prestige grew. He was seen as a leader and not a strong-arm politician. "He had pushed the Speaker's powers to the limit," wrote one observer, "and had triumphed, not only for himself but, as later events proved, for the nation as well."[15]

Once the United States entered the war, a strong sense of unity and purpose swept across the country, and the House reflected that new sense of solidarity. Indeed, a striking example occurred in 1944 when Rayburn became involved with the project to develop the atomic bomb. The Manhattan Project, code-name for the U.S. nuclear weapons development project, had been under way since the nation's entry into World War II, but in 1944 it needed more funding. Until this point the Roosevelt administration had managed to take funds from various agencies in such a way as to avoid a special appropriation. Now, in a dramatic visit to Rayburn's office, Secretary of War Henry Stimson and Army Chief of Staff George C. Marshall asked him to obtain a $2 billion appropriation for the project without letting the House know the purpose of the money — in other words, to approve the appropriation without revealing the project to members of Congress. In both chambers the congressional leadership managed to get the money without disclosing the secret. Rayburn simply asked, and since the House respected him so much, the members agreed. Not until the bomb was used against Japan did Congress realize what had been going on.

As Rayburn was settling in to the congressional routine in the spring of 1945 with a sense of relief after the hectic events of 1944, President Roosevelt died. Although insiders in Washington knew of his growing weakness, Roosevelt's death still came as a surprise to most Americans. Rayburn and Vice President Harry Truman had already become close friends, sharing drinks together in late-afternoon sessions at the Speaker's "Board of Education." While he was having a drink with Speaker Rayburn, Truman received the call to come to the White House to be informed of Roosevelt's death. Like many Americans, Rayburn was shaken by Roosevelt's death. He had felt a sense of closeness to the man who had brought relief directly to his constituents with rural electrification, farm-to-market roads, educational programs in soil conservation, publicly owned electric power, and other sorely needed projects. He did not, however, let his grief slow him down. The war was winding down, but the United States now had a long agenda of unmet needs, both domestic and international, when the war concluded. Rayburn intended to make use of his closeness to the new president—he and Truman were on a first-name basis—to help meet those needs.[16]

However, concerns over the postwar economy and rising international tensions between the United States and the Soviet Union created problems for Truman and the Democrats. The 1946 midterm elections gave the Republicans control of both chambers of Congress, and Rayburn had to step back in the line of ascension to minority leader. He talked about retiring, but Democratic leaders persuaded him to accept the lesser post, arguing that no one else in the House could handle it. He detested having to step aside for a party that he considered unsympathetic to the needs of the common man, but for Rayburn a satisfying victory for his party came in 1948 when Truman ran for president. The Republican presidential candidate, Thomas Dewey, was favored to win, but Truman's "whistle-stop" campaign led to a late surge that overpowered him. Democrats regained control of Congress, and Rayburn returned to the Speaker's chair.

In 1952 the Republicans nominated Dwight Eisenhower for president while the Democrats nominated Adlai Stevenson. Eisenhower was so popular in Texas that many Democrats there endorsed him, refusing to campaign for Stevenson. They were known as "Shivercrats" since Texas governor Allan Shivers led the Democratic defectors. Rayburn remained loyal to his party, which meant an open break for him with the Shivers camp. Eisenhower endorsed state ownership of the Texas tidelands, a dispute involving jurisdiction over offshore oil resources, and his victory in 1952 ended the dispute. Congress passed a bill giving Texas its jurisdiction over the tidelands, and Eisenhower happily signed it. Rayburn opposed the measure but was outgunned, particularly in view of the fact that in 1952 Republicans had again captured the House, relegating him to minority-leader status for the second time. In the Fourth District the question over the tidelands never became an issue for Rayburn, and his fight with some Texas Democrats had no impact on his constituency. His enormous power and prestige in the House were not tarnished, and when in 1954 the Democrats regained control of Congress, he returned to the speakership.

Here he stayed, becoming the longest-serving Speaker in American history. Free of serious challengers at home and recognized worldwide as a statesman, Mr. Sam was becoming well known around the country, owing in part to the television coverage of the 1952 Democratic National Convention and also to his reputation as a fair leader of the House. Rayburn had always treated his opponents with respect and avoided exercising his power excessively. "It is a wise man," he would say, "who realizes that the church is bigger than its pastor." [17]

By the mid-1950s Rayburn had become untouchable. His personality and history of leadership, which stretched back to 1931 when he chaired the Interstate and Foreign Commerce Committee, were well known, and among young members of Congress he was an awesome figure, almost a living legend. For the rest of his career, "the golden years," as described by one biographer, he relied to a considerable extent on his powers of persuasion. A combination of circumstances also strengthened his hand. For one thing, he and Eisenhower had similar personalities and philosophies in spite of some obvious differences that each was always quick to point out. Each had a centrist philosophy and "a strict sense of national duty. Both understood the necessity of compromise. Both were men of goodwill, abhorring venomous personal attacks." And even though they disagreed on specific matters, they created an environment of mutual trust and respect between the House of Representatives and the White House. In evaluating this period of "consensus politics," the emphasis should be placed on Rayburn's and Ike's sameness, their similar approach to duty, and their emphasis on goodwill. To be sure, partisan politics never disappeared, and each on occasion had sharp criticisms of the other. But they were still much alike. The general public recognized the similarity, extending their trust in the two leaders to work out the daily business of governing. Consequently, the consensus of the 1950s, at least between Congress and the White House, originated in part from the relationship between the president and the Speaker.[18]

To some extent Rayburn's influence at this point extended to the Senate, where Lyndon Johnson, a fellow Texan and Rayburn protégé, was majority leader. The Rayburn-Johnson relationship has been the subject of several writers, and in some ways it is a perplexing subject. Johnson had come first to the House in 1937 as a staunch supporter of Roosevelt, and he worked hard to please Rayburn, who was majority leader at the time. Rayburn liked Johnson and through the years had a mentoring relationship with him. When Johnson rose to Senate majority leader, he and Speaker Rayburn maintained their closeness and worked to achieve harmony. Since both branches of the Congress were led by Texas Democrats with similar ideologies who shared a close friendship, the daily business of government flowed smoothly.

Certainly these were Rayburn's best years. His history of service and devotion to civic duty, plus his behind-the-scenes manner of conducting business, explained why *Look* magazine wrote of him: "he is more valuable to have on your side than any other man in Washington, if it's pending legislation you have in mind.[19]

In 1957 Rayburn accomplished a goal that originated in the latter years of his life: he opened the Sam Rayburn Library at Bonham, Texas. The library was built by the Rayburn Foundation solely with private funding, which began with the $10,000 Collier Award that Rayburn had received in 1949 for outstanding legislative service. He wanted the institution to serve as a research center for congressional affairs and named as its director one of his staff members, H. G. Dulaney, who served from 1957 until his retirement in 2002. Rayburn used the building as his office when he was in Bonham, but he encouraged the facility's use by students, including schoolchildren, as a resource center. The library, under the leadership of Mr. Dulaney, has retained the Rayburn personality and style. It is a beautiful marble edifice that houses Rayburn's papers and other documents and includes a replica of his House office. But, most important, the library has a welcoming attitude toward the public, hosts many functions, and maintains a friendly atmosphere.

Rayburn's library seemed to be the final tribute to a distinguished career, the ending point of his political life. But Rayburn still had energy. In 1960 he backed Lyndon Johnson's bid for the Democratic nomination for president. During the early months of the campaigning, Senator John F. Kennedy of Massachusetts worked hard in the state primaries and surged forward after winning the West Virginia primary, while Johnson remained at work in the Senate. Rayburn had originally thought Kennedy was too young and inexperienced to be president, a thought shared by many prominent Democrats such as Eleanor Roosevelt. Kennedy, nonetheless, outmaneuvered Johnson and won the nomination on the first ballot.

Probably the most intriguing part of the 1960 race was Johnson's acceptance of the vice presidency. Rayburn and Johnson were solidly op-

Fig. 6.2. Sam Rayburn clearly expresses his views to President Kennedy and Vice President Johnson. Rayburn (Sam) Papers, Center for American History, UT-Austin (CN 07172).

posed to it, but Kennedy wanted Johnson, realizing that he needed southern support to win the election. Johnson agreed, but warned Kennedy that Rayburn first had to be convinced. Rayburn remained opposed, but after Kennedy personally pleaded his case and Mr. Sam's own advisers worked on him, the Speaker agreed. Rayburn quickly swung behind Kennedy, frequently saying, "That boy grows on you." Kennedy showed the highest respect for Rayburn and agreed with the *New York Times* when it asserted that Rayburn was "Mr. Everything."[20]

Rayburn now approached the final episode of his career: the fight over the House Rules Committee, one of the "worst fights of my life," he said. At the age of seventy-nine, Rayburn, whose only health problem was failing eyesight, wanted to amend the powers of the Rules Committee, which could keep legislation off the floor. The committee was controlled by conservatives who were opposed to the proposals of the Kennedy administration, and Rayburn wanted to keep the Rules Committee from ruining the new president's domestic programs.

He personally took over the battle against Howard Smith, the committee chairman. The Speaker proposed that the committee be enlarged so as to allow the appointment of more liberals to it. In some respects it was a fight over ideology. In an emotional struggle reminiscent of the New Deal battles, Rayburn won by five votes. It was a particularly sweet victory for him, one that put to rest the rumors that he was losing his grip on the House. Again, Rayburn had made the right move. His prestige and command of respect were at that point not exceeded by any public figure. As Rayburn himself put it, "It's easy to be an obstructionist; its hard to be a constructionist."[21]

Time was running out for Rayburn, though. While at home in July 1961, he complained of back pain and went to his local doctor, who found nothing wrong. Back in Washington he started losing weight and strength, but still there was no correct diagnosis of his condition. Convinced that he could overcome the mysterious illness, he went home in September for a prolonged rest. Further tests at Baylor Medical Center in Dallas revealed what Rayburn had dreaded: cancer. The disease had already spread and doctors gave him only about two weeks to live. He lasted for six weeks before dying at the Risser Clinic in Bonham, on November 16, 1961.

There followed one of the greatest outpourings of public grief ever associated with a legislative leader in American history. Rayburn's funeral service, conducted at the First Baptist Church of Bonham, was attended by President Kennedy, former presidents Truman and Eisenhower, and future president Johnson. A crowd of twenty thousand stood outside the church. His biographers, D. B. Hardeman and Don Bacon, concluded that Rayburn's pastor at the Primitive Baptist Church at Tioga best described the Speaker at his funeral: "He has fought a good fight. He has been a fair and loyal man. . . . He has kept faith with the democracy of our country." Thirty years later, H. G. Dulaney, when asked to compare other political leaders with Rayburn, said, "It can't be done. Rayburn is incomparable."[22]

LYNDON BAINES JOHNSON

Fig. 7.1. Lyndon B. Johnson, pictured with his wife Lady Bird, capped a tumultuous political career when he captured the presidency in a landslide election in 1964. Prints and Photographs Collection, Center for American History, UT-Austin (CN 10841).

LYNDON BAINES JOHNSON

BY KENNETH E. HENDRICKSON JR.

In 1948 a relatively obscure, insecure, but effective and highly ambitious Texas congressman ran for the United States Senate. The Democratic primary in this race proved to be one of the most controversial in modern American political history. It was corrupt, of course; that was not unusual in Texas, but what is more important is that the winner was Lyndon Baines Johnson. That election was the beginning of Johnson's rise to national power.

Johnson was born in the Texas Hill Country in 1908 and until his early adulthood spent most of his time in this raw, underdeveloped region. His father was Sam Ealy Johnson Jr., whose family had come to Texas in the 1840s and over the decades had experienced mixed fortunes in farming and cattle ranching. When Sam was born his parents were on hard times, living in the small settlement of Buda. When Sam was ten they moved to a farm on the Pedernales River, where he grew up. He became a teacher, although he never finished high school, and in 1904 he entered politics, running successfully for a seat in the Texas House of Representatives. While serving there, Sam met and married Rebekah Baines in 1907. After that the need to make a living induced him to retire from politics and devote himself to farming.

Rebekah's mother's family had come to Texas in 1851; her father's somewhat earlier. She grew up among people devoted to education and intellectual pursuits as well as farming and ranching, so it is fair to say that her family was somewhat more refined than the Johnson clan. After completing college, Rebekah taught for a while and worked as a journalist in Fredericksburg and Austin. She married Sam after a whirlwind courtship, following which the young couple moved into the Johnson family farm home on the Pedernales.

The marriage of Sam and Rebekah Johnson was stormy, at least part of the time. They had come from diverse backgrounds and really had little in common. Sam was somewhat reckless and playful, enjoying a good time with his male companions and an occasional bottle. Rebekah, on the other hand, valued books, culture, and "higher" interests. She also felt somewhat alienated by the presence of the extended Johnson family—hence the considerable tension in their relationship.

Lyndon came into this union as the firstborn child on August 27, 1908. Later, he was joined by three sisters and a brother. For the first five years of Lyndon's life the family remained on the farm, but in 1913 they moved to the village of Johnson City, where Sam enjoyed a brief era of prosperity selling real estate and managing several investment properties. Meanwhile, Rebekah sought to create an aura of refinement in the home and saw to the children's education and cultural development. In 1917 Sam was once more elected to the state legislature, where he retained his seat until 1924.

Sam Johnson bought out the family farm from other heirs in 1919 in a move that proved to be financially disastrous. When land and crop prices collapsed after World War I, he was left with obligations he could not pay. In 1922 he sold the farm and moved his family back to Johnson City, where they were forced to adopt a lifestyle much less pretentious than they had previously enjoyed. Sam showed signs of stress caused by his financial problems, and there were certainly major tensions within the family. These may have had a psychological effect on Lyndon, which was reflected later in his overwhelming drive, ambition, and greed. In any case, Lyndon finished high school and reached his early maturity during this troubling time. Then there followed a three-year period of aimlessness caused by uncertainty, self-doubt, and the lack of the financial resources required to attend college. Finally, in 1927, the family rallied behind him, and Lyndon was sent off to school at Southwest Texas State Teachers College in San Marcos.[1]

Southwest Texas was a typical teachers' college of that period. It did not offer the prestige of a state university like the University of Texas at Austin (UT), but neither did it make the same demands upon its students. Still, it could offer an adequate education to those students willing to apply themselves diligently. In any case, Lyndon Johnson, who had graduated from an unaccredited high school, would probably never have been admitted to UT. He was even required to pass special entrance examinations for admission at San Marcos. Johnson's academic record at Southwest Texas was mixed. His grades were not spectacular, only slightly above average in fact, but he worked steadily toward his goal, a teaching credential. Then and throughout his lifetime he claimed to love education, although he was by no means an intellectual.

There are many stories about Johnson's college experience that supposedly foretold his later behavior in politics. He exhibited brashness, ambition, and a desire to lead his peers and overwhelm them on the one hand, while flattering and currying favor with his elders and superiors in order to impress them on the other. According to one story, Johnson was outraged when he was not welcomed into the dominant fraternity, the Black Stars, which was controlled by the athletes. In retaliation he joined with another group called the White Stars and maneuvered them into control of campus politics. According to another tale, Johnson exerted enormous influence over the entire campus through his job as assistant to the college president, Dr. Cecil E. Evans. The real truth behind these stories is almost impossible to judge because they are based on the selective memories of Johnson's contemporaries. Documentary evidence is very scarce. Still, there is little doubt about his personality—ambitious and energetic, ruthless and domineering. He was willing to do practically anything to achieve his goals.

Midway through his college career, Johnson paused for a year to teach at the small Hispanic school at Cotulla. He not only taught; he served as principal, coach, and leader of numerous extracurricular activities as well. This experience certainly evidenced his penchant for perfection, and it also affected him personally. Later, he would say that it was the year at Cotulla that drove him to vow that someday he would do everything in his power to help the underprivileged in American society.

After Cotulla, Johnson returned to San Marcos to complete his degree and graduated in 1930. That fall he began a teaching job in Houston, but before the completion of the academic year he resigned to become secretary to the newly elected congressman from Texas's Fourteenth District, Richard Kleberg. Thus, in 1931 Johnson's political career began.[2]

For three years Johnson served Congressman Kleberg in Washington, D.C. During that time he learned a great deal about politics and the workings of the government. Kleberg was interested only in the facade and superficial trappings of his office, so Johnson did most of the work and did so willingly. He repeated the pattern of frenetic behavior he had exhibited in college and at Cotulla, both in his work habits and in his relationships with other people. He dominated the small staff in Kleberg's office, and he also attempted to dominate the so-called "Little Congress," an organization of young staffers. Through these efforts he met and ingratiated himself to many important people. He also learned how to use his personal contacts to get things done.

As far as the New Deal is concerned, Johnson's ideological approach is unclear, but he certainly strove to see that the people of Kleberg's district received their fair share of the bounty. His personal life also took an important turn during this period. In 1934, while visiting his father in Austin, he met and was smitten by a young lady named Claudia Taylor. Very soon Lyndon and Claudia, better known by her nickname "Lady Bird," were married.[3]

In 1936 Johnson promoted himself for the position of Texas state director of the National Youth Administration (NYA). He succeeded in becoming the youngest state director in the country. He and Lady Bird moved back to Texas, where he set up his office in Austin, surrounded himself with cronies, and, with characteristic zeal, set out to make Texas's NYA program the best in the nation. Once again he succeeded. He cultivated all the right people, such as the influential utilities lawyer Alvin J. Wirtz, mastered the crazy quilt of federal rules and regulations governing the NYA, and developed an excellent program of work-study for those youths who were still in school and work-relief for those who were not. He also dealt effectively, if not courageously, with the problem of race. He provided as much assistance as he could for needy blacks while at the same time maintaining segregation. In this way, he was able to satisfy the administration in Washington, which more or less demanded equality, and the people of Texas who were still living in the world of Jim Crow.[4]

In early 1937 Johnson sensed an opportunity to gain national office when he heard of the untimely death of Congressman James P. Buchanan. With the backing of Wirtz he set out to run for Congress. Basing his campaign on unbridled support for President Roosevelt and the New Deal, and by means of exhausting field work, Johnson was elected. The Johnsons then moved back to Washington, which would be Lyndon's base for the next three decades and where, for a time at least, he would become the most powerful man on earth.

As the representative from Texas's Tenth Congressional District, Johnson served his constituents well. He voted for practically all New Deal legislation, although he avoided floor debate and controversy, and he tried to attend to virtually all special requests from his home district. In order to make sure the folks back in Texas did not forget what he was doing for them, he stayed in close touch through skillful use of the franking privilege (free mailings for members of Congress) and issued exaggerated claims about his importance and achievements in numerous press releases.

His first and perhaps most notable success on behalf of a Texas constituent concerned the building of the Marshall Ford Dam by the Lower Colorado River Authority (LCRA). The LCRA was but one of what would eventually be fourteen river authorities in Texas. These were mini-TVAs, given authority under their charters from the state to administer the waters of the various river basins for beneficial uses such as flood control and hydroelectric power. Prior to his death, Representative James Buchanan had been using his influence to secure funding for the LCRA to build a dam on the Colorado River just north of Austin. Because Buchanan was so powerful, construction had begun even before the final approvals were given.

Hence, his unexpected death left the project in limbo. The contractors, Brown and Root Construction Company of Austin, already had a substantial investment in the half-completed dam. The owners, George and Herman Brown, and their attorney, Johnson's friend Wirtz, needed help.

Johnson, using all the influence a freshman representative could muster and drawing upon his acquaintanceship with the president, helped obtain the needed authorizations. According to some biographers, he may have exaggerated his role in the project; but in any case, Brown and Root made millions of dollars from this and subsequent government contracts. Thus was established a mutually beneficial relationship that would last throughout Johnson's life.

Although the dam project enriched its builders, it undoubtedly helped the people of the lower Colorado Valley as well. It curtailed flooding and provided a source of hydroelectric power. Johnson worked hard to see that this electricity became available to the people through the Rural Electrification Administration (REA). Again the benefits cut both ways. Johnson saw to it that an REA cooperative was established, and Brown and Root secured the contracts for the construction of the power-line towers.

While in Congress, Johnson built up a cadre of rich and powerful supporters who financed his political career and advised him along the way — and for whom he did favors whenever he could. Among his benefactors, in addition to the Brown brothers, were Wirtz, Ed Clark, a successful Austin attorney, and Charles E. Marsh, the multimillionaire owner of two Austin newspapers. Marsh had a mistress, Alice Glass, with whom Johnson supposedly had an affair. His critics and unfriendly biographers use their discussion of this affair to illustrate Johnson's lack of character. Whether the affair actually occurred, however, is subject to debate and has not been conclusively shown. Without doubt Johnson and Glass were friends — they maintained a correspondence throughout their lives — but to the more cautious of the Johnson scholars, the affair was an imaginary one concocted later in the fertile minds of some of Johnson's acquaintances.

It is clear that Johnson did not regard his seat in the House of Representatives as the culmination of his political career. He believed the presidency was out of reach, but he certainly wanted to advance to the United States Senate. His first chance for that came in 1941, occasioned by the death of Morris Sheppard. Johnson ran in the special election that followed against George Mann, an able young attorney, and W. Lee O'Daniel, the utterly incompetent biscuit salesman then serving as governor of Texas. Although at first he appeared to have little chance, Johnson was well financed, and he campaigned vigorously. He may even have won had not the returns from several East Texas precincts been altered at the last minute by the O'Daniel forces. Hence, the governor, not Johnson, went to the Senate. Johnson did not demand an inquiry, fearing that it would uncover certain improprieties in the financing of his own campaign by Brown and Root. After all, he expected to have another opportunity to win a Senate seat the very next year.[5]

Johnson's plans were altered by the Japanese attack on Pearl Harbor on December 7, 1941. He had promised his constituents that if war came he would enter the service, and he felt honor-bound to that commitment. Of course, he had no intention of resigning his congressional seat to enlist. Instead, he secured a leave of absence from Congress and took a reserve commission as a lieutenant commander in the U.S. Navy. For a time he served in Washington and then on the West Coast with practically nothing to do. Finally, Johnson maneuvered himself a spot as a member of a three-man team to inspect and report on operations in the Pacific theater. While there, he flew as an observer on one bombing mission against the Japanese, and, since his plane came under attack during the raid, he was awarded the Silver Cross for heroism. A little later, the president ordered all members of Congress serving in the military to either resign their seats and stay in the service for the duration of the war or return to Washington. Johnson took advantage of this order to return (not all members of Congress did), thus ending his military career. However, for the rest of his life he used this brief experience to argue that he knew and understood the needs of members of the armed services.[6]

Johnson continued to support the Roosevelt administration after his return, but he was now thoroughly bored with the House and looked forward to entering a new phase of his career. He even talked of leaving politics. Meanwhile, there were several significant developments in his life. His first child was born in 1944, and he and his wife laid the foundation for their later accumulation of substantial wealth. This was accomplished by means of the purchase of a nearly defunct radio station in Austin, KTBC. This purchase has been the subject of enormous controversy among Johnson's friends and critics as well as among his biographers. Critics charge that Johnson used his influence, and that of his friends, with the FCC to clear the way for the purchase. They also charge that undue influence was exerted in the right places to secure an advantageous frequency for the station and later to provide the Johnsons with a virtual monopoly of the TV market in the Austin area. Johnson's friends argue that all these charges are based on falsehoods and exaggerations and that the Johnsons' success was attributable largely to hard work and astute business decisions. Whatever the case, it is certainly true that the radio station soon became profitable and that Lyndon and Lady Bird used the capital they accumulated from its operations to invest in other businesses, real estate, and eventually the fa-mous Johnson Ranch on the Pedernales.[7]

Johnson's next chance for the Senate came in 1948 when O'Daniel decided to retire. Johnson's controversial campaign against ex-governor Coke Stevenson brought him to the next phase of his career: his time of immense power. There is overwhelming evidence that Johnson won the Democratic primary of 1948 by illegal means. This is really not subject to debate. The question is to what extent Johnson was personally involved in the actions that produced this outcome. Since practically all the evidence is circumstantial or based on hearsay, the truth may never be known. What is known is that Johnson faced the election with great uncertainty. He des-perately wanted to run, but he feared that failure might end his political career. He even talked of retirement, but in the end he entered the race. Once this decision was made, he plunged into the contest with his usual intensity.

Johnson employed technology very effectively in 1948. He was not the first Texas politician to use radio, of course, but he used it more exten-sively and effectively than any candidate before him, including O'Daniel. He also introduced a new technological innovation—the use of the heli-copter as a campaign vehicle. This enabled him to move rapidly about the state and make numerous appearances in far-distant locations in a single day, a great advantage over his opponent, former governor Stevenson, who insisted on motoring leisurely around the state, campaigning mostly in county seats.

Johnson was the underdog to the popular Stevenson at the outset of the race, and in spite of his intense campaigning he never made up enough ground. Stevenson won the first primary by more than seventy thousand votes; however, since he did not have a majority, it became necessary to schedule a runoff. It was in connection with this phase of the election that most of the controversial events took place.

Congressman Johnson had three powerful allies in the runoff: money, deceit, and fraud. The money, or at least the bulk of it, came from George and Herman Brown, who believed that Johnson as a senator would con-tinue to serve their interests just as he had in the past. The deceit was in-troduced by Johnson's consistent efforts to portray Stevenson as prolabor and soft on communism. Neither of these allegations contained even a ker-nel of truth, but they were promoted so intensely, and Stevenson's defense was so ineffective, that some people began to have doubts about the gov-ernor's positions.

Regardless of the significance of the other factors, the outcome of the election was finally determined by fraud. Johnson won in 1948 in much the same way he had lost in 1941. There were, no doubt, irregularities on both sides, but the key to it all lay in the activities of George Parr, the political boss of South Texas, who conspired to manufacture votes for Johnson. In the past Parr had always supported Stevenson, but at one point while he was governor, Stevenson had refused to appoint one of Parr's men as district attorney in Laredo. Parr swore vengeance, and now his chance had come. By manipulating the vote tally in Jim Wells County, Parr ensured Johnson's victory by the scant margin of eighty-seven votes statewide. Stevenson challenged the outcome before the Democratic Party Executive Committee, before the party convention, and in court, but under extremely questionable circumstances, the vote was allowed to stand. Some of Johnson's biographers allege that he was fully aware of the maneuverings on his behalf and may even have participated in them, but in reality the evidence is too skimpy to make an informed judgment. In any case, Lyndon Johnson had now reached what for him, at the time, was his highest political goal. He was a member of the United States Senate.[8]

Now known jokingly by both friends and critics as "Landslide Lyndon," Johnson entered the Senate in January 1949. He already had some contacts and possessed a remarkable understanding of the inner workings of the legislative branch of government, but even so Johnson's rise to power in the Senate was more rapid and spectacular than anyone expected. Using techniques that had worked well for him in the past—the cultivation of powerful colleagues such as Richard Russell of Georgia, deference to the strong, intimidation of the weak, vast knowledge of the system, and inhumanly hard work—Johnson in swift succession became minority whip (1951), minority leader (1953), and by 1955, majority leader. By then he had already become the nation's most powerful senator.

Johnson's goal in the Senate was to serve Texas while at the same time making a name for himself in the national political arena so that he could take advantage of any opportunities that might later arise. To do this he supported issues important to powerful constituencies in Texas, such as the deregulation of natural gas and the high oil depletion allowance, while straddling the fence on certain inflammable issues such as labor, welfare, and race. This allowed him to avoid being labeled a "true believer," either liberal or conservative. He measured success pragmatically in terms of getting bills passed, not ideologically by trumpeting causes, and he established a pattern of seeking compromise and consensus in order to achieve results.

There were three achievements that Johnson regarded as the most significant of his senatorial career. These were his handling of the outrageous behavior of Senator Joseph R. McCarthy of Wisconsin, his contributions to space legislation and the founding of NASA, and the Civil Rights Act of 1957.

Before 1954 Johnson had never openly opposed McCarthy, even though he knew the senator's claims about Communists in the federal government were wild exaggerations. After the Army-McCarthy hearings, however, Johnson supported the Senate's decision to investigate McCarthy's behavior. Johnson's major contribution to the ensuing developments was to convince his fellow Democrats not to make the investigation a party issue, thus denying the Republicans any opportunity to claim that McCarthy was being pilloried. This strategy worked brilliantly, and when McCarthy went down, every senator was able to argue that he voted his conscience and not the party line.

In the final analysis the Civil Rights Act of 1957 was a watered-down version of a much stronger bill that had little effect on race relations in this country. Still, its passage was a remarkable breakthrough—it was the first law of its kind since Reconstruction—and Johnson deserves the lion's share of the credit for its passage. Before 1957 Johnson had always opposed civil rights legislation while at the same time proclaiming that he was not prejudiced. Thus he found himself in an awkward position when the House passed an administration-sponsored civil rights bill early in the summer of 1957. The original bill was powerful. It gave the Justice Department authority to issue injunctions to enforce the equal rights provisions of the Fourteenth Amendment, and it gave the attorney general the power to protect voting rights guaranteed by the Fifteenth Amendment. For certain violations it prescribed trial without jury.

When the bill came to the Senate, Johnson, as majority leader, could not avoid dealing with it, but he had to find a middle ground. To oppose the bill out of hand would ruin him in the North, but to support it in its original form would kill him in the South. He solved this dilemma by using his power and persuasive abilities to produce a new version of the bill, one providing guarantees that could not be enforced. Then by forging a strong coalition of westerners and southerners, he pushed it through the upper house. Since practically all the enforcement powers were removed from the original bill, the final product was little more than a sham. Nevertheless, Johnson was able to take credit for a momentous achievement without offending the South in a manner fatal to his ambitions. Still, his problems with civil rights were not over. Eisenhower administration supporters came back during the following two years with stronger bills, and in 1960 the civil rights revolution began with the North Carolina sit-ins. Sensing that change was in the air, Johnson supported the Civil Rights Act of 1960, which was once again a watered-down version of a stronger bill, but he found himself gravitating almost in spite of himself toward a more liberal position on the issue. By the end of 1960 he was for all practical purposes committed to strong civil rights legislation, but the fruits of his commitment would not come until 1964.

There were fewer headaches for Johnson in the realm of space policy. He was chairman of the Senate Preparedness Subcommittee when the Russians launched *Sputnik* in 1957, and in the aftermath he led the congressional investigation of American science and technology. This investigation led to the revelation of the so-called missile gap and to the passage of the National Aeronautics and Space Act of 1958, without question the most important legislation to bear Johnson's name as sponsor. He emerged as the best-known and best-informed member of Congress on space matters, and some observers suggested that the issue might even launch him into the White House.

But Johnson's prospects for the presidency were not really very bright. Although he retained control of the Senate Democrats during the last two years of the Eisenhower administration, he came under increasing pressure and criticism from the liberals—people like Paul Douglas, Estes Kefauver, Eugene McCarthy, and William Proxmire. Additionally, his southern heritage and his reputation as an opportunist were impediments to presidential ambitions. Moreover, by 1960 he was tired and concerned about his health—he had had his first heart attack in 1955—so once again he contemplated retirement from politics. Hence, his quest for the Democratic nomination for president in 1960 was, while serious, in some ways half-hearted.[9]

Senator Johnson allowed his followers to work on his behalf behind the scenes in 1960, but he did not formally announce as a candidate until early July. Meanwhile, Senator John F. Kennedy of Massachusetts campaigned vigorously and won most of the primaries. This practically assured Kennedy of the nomination although that was not clearly understood by many at the time. At the Democratic National Convention in Los Angeles, Johnson joined in a momentary flurry of "stop Kennedy" activity, but this collapsed early and the Massachusetts senator won easily on the first ballot. What happened after that has long been the subject of much intense speculation.

After his victory, Kennedy offered Johnson second place on the ticket. The twin questions have always been why did Kennedy offer, and why did Johnson accept? The two men were complete opposites in terms of their backgrounds and outlooks. What is more, their rivalry had grown substantially since 1956 when both had sought the vice presidency, they did not get along particularly well, and both were possessed of enormous

Fig. 7.2. Lyndon Johnson as he campaigned by train on the 1960 Democratic ticket with John F. Kennedy. Roberts (Bruce) Photograph Collection, Center for American History, UT-Austin (CN 08833).

egos. However, Kennedy no doubt saw Johnson as a useful complement to his candidacy. As a Protestant southerner he might buffer the obstacles to success posed by Kennedy's eastern, Catholic liberalism. On the other hand, Johnson's decision is somewhat more difficult to understand. In all likelihood, it stemmed from a combination of ego, ambition, the intense obligation he always felt to serve, and the remote possibility that somehow the vice presidency could be a stepping-stone to the Oval Office.

Whatever the explanation, the Kennedy-Johnson ticket was a formidable one, and some observers have argued that Johnson's presence in the campaign was the key to the Democrats' success. The election was, at the time, the closest in the history of the modern presidency. Kennedy and

Johnson defeated Vice President Richard Nixon and Henry Cabot Lodge by little more than one hundred thousand votes.[10]

Even though he was galled by his removal from the limelight and jealous of the adulation enjoyed by Kennedy for the expenditure of so little effort, Johnson served loyally as vice president. His power and influence were practically gone, and although Johnson had begun the enterprise with high hopes, Kennedy, in fact, gave him little of importance to do. Still, he had a few responsibilities that allowed him to make meaningful contributions. As chair of the Space Council he boosted and supported the growing commitment of the federal government to NASA, and his work in this arena led Kennedy to endorse the goal of landing a man on the moon before the end of the 1960s. As roving ambassador, Johnson represented the nation and the president, when and wherever Kennedy could not. He traveled to the Far East, Europe, Africa, and South America, and although little of significance came out of these excursions, Johnson performed his largely ceremonial duties with dignity.

Johnson's most important contribution as vice president stemmed from his chairmanship of the President's Committee on Equal Employment. The purpose of this committee was to monitor the employment practices of government agencies and contractors to ensure that minorities (not yet including women at this date) received fair employment opportunities. Johnson worked hard at this job and established for himself more believable credentials as a civil rights advocate than he had previously enjoyed. He came to be identified as the primary administration spokesperson for black Americans. Although he played no direct role in the legislative consideration of the Civil Rights Bill of 1963, he did give the Kennedy men his invaluable advice on how to maneuver the bill through Congress. Ironically, it would be Johnson, not Kennedy, who would follow that advice in securing passage of the momentous Civil Rights Act of 1964.[11]

By the fall of 1963 the Kennedy administration was in trouble politically in the South and also faced potential problems occasioned by the constant infighting between the conservative and liberal wings of the Democratic Party in Texas. Determined to ease these tensions, President Kennedy planned a fence-mending trip to Texas in November. There, hosted by Vice President Johnson and Governor John Connally, he would attempt to charm the warring factions back together. Kennedy might have succeeded, but in one hideous instant in Dallas his life was snuffed out and everything was changed by the horrific actions of assassins. Kennedy was declared dead at Parkland Hospital at 1:30 P.M. on November 22, 1963. Johnson was sworn in as president at 2:40 P.M. on *Air Force One* by his old friend Judge Sarah T. Hughes.

Johnson had achieved his ultimate ambition by the unthinkable. Like nearly everyone else, he was momentarily taken aback, but he rallied quickly in order to avail himself of the enormous outpouring of sympathy and good feeling for him that followed in the wake of the assassination. There followed a three-year period of almost unparalleled achievement during which Congress, both guided and goaded by a driven president, passed more substantive legislation than during any other brief period in American history.

In 1964 the Republican Party was temporarily overtaken by its ultra-conservative elements who nominated Senator Barry Goldwater of Arizona for president. Goldwater's extremist right-wing rantings soon destroyed any slim chance he might have had, and Johnson rode to victory on a wave of residual sympathy, general commitment to the notion of improving American society, and faith in his promise that there would be no escalation of the conflict in Vietnam.[12]

All the facets of Johnson's complex character and personality and all of his political experience and expertise came into play in his approach to the presidency. He worked with determination and incredible energy. He was, as always, extraordinarily demanding of those who worked for him and deferential toward those who worked with him. He set out an agenda for change in American society that he hoped to achieve without at the same time promoting class conflict. In other words, he set for himself an impossible task.[13]

Johnson's agenda was labeled the Great Society, a term that he uttered frequently after assuming office but that did not come into general usage until after his State of the Union address of 1964. It was in this message also that Johnson announced his "declaration of war on poverty." When the president spoke of a Great Society for America, he meant specifically civil rights for African Americans, an end to poverty, improved educational opportunities for all, improved health care for the poor and the aged, an improved quality of life in the cities, protection for the consumer, conservation, and environmental regulation. In other words, a grand combination of practically all the major reforms proposed in this country since the Populist Revolt of the 1890s.

This was at first glance truly a radical agenda, and to achieve its apparent goals would have required nothing less than massive income redistribution, an approach Johnson had no intention of pursuing. He wanted legislation addressing all these issues, not necessarily a final cure. Therefore, he and his advisers adopted, almost willy-nilly, a strategy of providing more opportunities for individuals to realize the American dream, not one of forcing class realignments. This course did bring some improvement, but inevitably it failed to change the essential nature of American society. Practically all the problems addressed by the Great Society still haunt America, some of them with more intensity than ever. Still, measured in terms of the sheer speed and magnitude of the legislation, the Great Society was impressive, indeed breathtaking. Moreover, there were numerous benefits that cannot be denied even though the program never even approached the achievement of an egalitarian society. The president launched his crusade in early 1964, and even before his momentous victory in the presidential election that year, he experienced three remarkable legislative successes: the Tax Reform Act, the Civil Rights Act, and the creation of the Office of Economic Opportunity.

Kennedy had been working with little success to achieve tax-cut legislation. His economic adviser, Walter Heller, had convinced him that lower taxes, combined with controlled deficit spending, would promote long-term growth. This was the program that Kennedy had called "fine tuning" the economy. Johnson gave his unqualified support to the plan and secured passage of the tax-cut bill in early 1964, thereby triggering an era of prosperity that would last until late in the decade.

The passage of the Economic Opportunity Act (EOA) marked the real beginning of the Great Society. The EOA had no distinct focus but instead authorized a series of related programs that produced a variety of results and a great deal of controversy. Among the most controversial was the Community Action Program (CAP). The CAP required that local anti-poverty projects be developed, conducted, and administered to the greatest extent possible by the people to be served. CAP would then provide grant funding to local Community Action Agencies (CAAs) set up by these people. The result, of course, was to give the poor and the alienated a formal base from which to work against the establishment. Idealistically, that was fine, but in practice many CAAs did relatively little to alleviate poverty and a great deal to heighten tensions between poor communities on the one hand and city administrations, police departments, and school boards on the other. More important from the standpoint of antipoverty goals, however, was the fact that the CAP budget was always relatively small and the funds had to be distributed among literally thousands of local agencies. Hence, the impact was slight and even frustrating.

Also authorized by the EOA were programs like Project Head Start, a preschool program for underprivileged children, Upward Bound, designated to assist poor but talented youth to prepare for college; a Legal Services program; and Neighborhood Health Centers. Far more significant in terms of its intentions and far more controversial in terms of its results than any of these was the Job Corps.

President Johnson was very fond of the Job Corps idea because it re-

minded him of his two favorite New Deal programs, the Civilian Conservation Corps (CCC) and the NYA. The Job Corps provided funds for the
creation of camps for youths between the ages of sixteen and twenty-one
in which they would receive education, vocational training, and work experience. There were a few rural camps in the West set up by the Park Service, the Forest Service, and the Bureau of Land Management that were
reminiscent of the CCC camps of the 1930s, but most of the sites were
in urban areas, usually occupying old military bases. Participants had to
be out of school and unemployed. Hence they tended to come from the
very lowest levels of society and were mostly black and Hispanic. The
idea was to provide them with skills that would be saleable in the market-
place. While in the program participants would receive a $30-per-month
allowance and a $50-per-month credit to be paid upon completion of
the course. Unfortunately, too many of the targeted youth were already

beyond redemption. The Job Corps was characterized by a high drop-
out rate, generally low morale, and internal problems and conflict. Few
who completed the Job Corps program found their lives substantially
improved.

The most important of all the Great Society legislation was that which
dealt with civil rights. The first was the landmark Civil Rights Act of 1964.
Johnson had nothing to do with the contents of this bill; it had been
essentially written earlier during the Kennedy administration. Johnson's
role was to help maneuver the bill through Congress, and this he did with
consummate skill. He courted and wooed and intimidated Republican minority leader Everett Dirksen of Illinois and put him in a position from
which he could either claim credit for the passage of the bill or accept responsibility for its defeat. Dirksen chose the former course because he recognized that the times and public opinion at long last were demanding
action on this vital issue. As a result of Dirksen's efforts, the Senate voted
cloture on a southern filibuster for the first time ever, and the bill passed
with no weakening amendments.

This law provided the toughest federal controls over state voting ever
produced, mandated equal access to all public accommodations and government facilities, empowered the U.S. attorney general to seek injunctive
relief against school districts still practicing segregation, and forbade discrimination in employment for any reason including gender. Tough as it
was, the voting rights provision of this law did not produce speedy results,
so it was followed by the Voting Rights Act of 1965, which allowed the federal government to send examiners to register voters in any county where
there was prima facie evidence of discrimination. This law was effective,

and soon the number of black registered voters in the South began to increase dramatically.

These civil rights acts were vitally important and produced results that
were profoundly significant to the American electoral system and to American society, but they had little effect upon the economic and social conditions experienced by poor minorities. Johnson hoped to address these issues through other facets of the Great Society program.

The desire to improve America's educational system was very close to
Johnson's heart. The effort was embodied in several important pieces of
legislation including the Elementary and Secondary Education Act and
the Higher Education Act of 1965. The former was intended to provide
funds for the improvement of schools in low-income districts, but it was
written in such a way that nearly 90 percent of all school districts qualified.
It also provided for the purchase of library and instructional supplies, special education programs, and educational research and development. The
law was carefully worded so as to avoid any semblance of interference with
local control.

The Higher Education Act funded community service programs, library improvements, professional exchanges, fellowships, and struggling
institutions. However, its main purpose was to broaden educational opportunities for low-income families. Hence, it provided for scholarships,
loans, and recruiting funds. It also expanded the Work-Study Program
which had begun in 1963.

Improved medical care, especially for the aged and poor, was also important to Johnson. As president, his commitment resulted in the creation
of Medicare and Medicaid. The former came in the form of an amendment
to the Social Security Act of 1935. It included a hospitalization plan and a
plan to cover physician's fees, both tied to the Social Security income de-
duction. Medicare was followed by Medicaid, also an addition to the original Social Security Act, which provided grants to the states to partially
subsidize the major medical costs of the poor, who were also frequently
aged. Both of these programs were intended to meet an obvious need, but
like so many other aspects of the Great Society, their impact has been min-
imized over time. Skyrocketing medical costs during the past two decades,
attributed in part by many critics to these very programs, have somewhat
mitigated the benefits of Medicare and Medicaid, so that today there are
still millions of Americans without access to adequate medical care.

Johnson's concern with the quality of urban life in America was reflected
in a plethora of legislative measures aimed at the improvement of practically every city service. Included here were the Urban Mass Transporta-

tion Act, the Solid Waste Disposal Act of 1966, and the Omnibus Crime Control and Safe Streets Act of 1968, all of which offered financial assistance to cities in the form of federal grants. Most important, though, to the urban-improvement phase of the Great Society were the Model Cities Act of 1966 and the Public Housing Act of 1968.

Intended to be administered by the newly created Department of Housing and Urban Development, the Model Cities Act was to improve the quality of urban life by providing what were to become known as "block grants" to cover 80 percent of the cost of approved projects. These projects could be in just about any area of urban life such as employment, education, health care, crime prevention, and recreation. Like CAP, the Model Cities program emphasized local initiation and administration.

The Housing Act of 1968 was the grandest public housing scheme in all of U.S. history. After housing was first recognized as a public responsibility in 1931, Congress had created a temporary program to guarantee mortgages. This approach was expanded by the New Deal in 1937 and again by the controversial Urban Renewal Act of 1949. The new law expanded on its forerunners dramatically. It called for the construction annually of hundreds of thousands of units of subsidized housing, and it provided an expanded mortgage insurance plan. The hope was to overcome the major problems associated with earlier efforts that had tended to bypass the most needy, but unfortunately this program did likewise. The Federal Housing Administration, which cleared all applicants for assistance, tended to approve those closest to the upper limits of eligibility, while participating contractors tended to build cheap and shabby housing. Hence the dream of making livable housing available to all Americans was not realized. Moreover, public housing projects all over the country that were built during this time continue to fester with poverty, crime, and disease.

The Great Society produced a vast array of legislation dealing with conservation, the environment, and consumer protection. Included were the Wilderness Act of 1964; the Water Quality Act and Solid Waste Disposal Act of 1965; the Water Resources Planning Act of 1965; the Clean Water Restoration Act of 1966; and the Air Quality Act of 1967. Johnson also created a large number of new national parks, scenic areas, recreational sites, wildlife refuges, and wilderness areas.

Among the Great Society laws designed to protect the consumer were the Fair Packaging and Labeling Act; the National Traffic and Motor Vehicle Safety Act and the Highway Safety Act of 1966; the Meat Inspection Act of 1967; and the Coal Mine Safety Act of 1968. These and other laws nearly doubled the regulatory responsibilities of the federal government and, in the eyes of supporters, represented the final culmination of the progressive response to industrialism that had commenced in the late 1800s. For critics these efforts represented an unwarranted and unwise intrusion into the private sector that could only result in the growth of a massive bureaucracy, increased costs, and confusion.

Also of interest to consumers were the cultural aspects of the Great Society. These included the National Museum Act, the Public Broadcasting Act of 1967, and the creation of the National Endowments for the Arts and Humanities. These represented only the second effort in national history by the federal government to support the arts — since the temporary Federal Arts Projects of the New Deal and early World War II periods.

Efforts to evaluate the Great Society will no doubt continue for many years and will be consummated only when scholars have the full advantage of greater historical perspective. But no matter what that final result, it is clear even now that this represented the greatest outpouring of social legislation in American history. Yet this unprecedented beneficence on the part of the federal government, avowedly on behalf of all sectors of society, did not solve many of the problems it addressed. In fact, many of them are worse now, thirty-five years after the Great Society attacked them. The question that analysts must address is, Why did the Great Society ultimately fail? Was it because the legislation was ill-conceived or the programs underfunded or badly administered, or because the expansion of the population and the social and economic woes of the country have simply overwhelmed any effort to deal with them? In the end, the answer will probably involve a combination of all these factors. But in any case, it must be remembered that in none of the great surges of reform in American history from the late nineteenth century to the present was serious consideration ever given to the fundamental alteration of traditional values or the economic system. Many observers believe that social and economic reform can never succeed unless accompanied by drastic measures such as income redistribution.

In any case, President Johnson cannot be condemned out of hand for the failure of the Great Society to solve problems effectively and bring an end to social and economic injustice and misery in America, but he is certainly vulnerable to criticism for the hyperbole he uttered while in the process of promoting his reforms. This no doubt contributed to the rise of expectations that could not be fulfilled, and accounts, at least in part, for the frustration and violence that characterized the response of some elements of the populace to the Great Society.

Had it not been for the Vietnam War, Johnson probably would be remembered by future historians as one of the greatest American presidents in spite of the failure of his domestic policy to achieve total success. But he was sucked into the war in Southeast Asia, and it destroyed him.[14]

Johnson's decisions on Vietnam—decisions that drew the nation into a major war with disastrous consequences—resulted from a logical continuation of the Cold War policies of his predecessors. American leaders had opposed a Communist victory in Southeast Asia after World War II and had committed the United States to the support of a noncommunist regime in South Vietnam after 1954. Besides sharing the assumptions of his predecessors, Johnson was surrounded by advisers like Dean Rusk, McGeorge Bundy, and Robert McNamara, many of whom were more hawkish on communism than he was.

When Johnson assumed the presidency the situation in Vietnam was highly unstable. The American-backed government in South Vietnam was shaky and the land was rife with internal subversionists known as the Vietcong; the North Vietnamese had amassed a very real military threat that seemed capable of overrunning the South very soon; and Johnson and his advisers truly believed that if South Vietnam were to fall to the Communists, the result would be disastrous for the South Vietnamese people and would pose serious dangers for American interests across the Far East. In 1964 Johnson made up his mind to act. He began looking for an excuse to escalate the U.S. military involvement in Vietnam while at the same time assuring the American people, as he had all through the presidential campaign, that there would be no expansion of the U.S. commitment. Finally, in August 1964, the Gulf of Tonkin incident provided a solution to his problems. Claiming that American naval forces in international waters had been subjected to an unprovoked attack, he asked Congress for carte blanche authority to defend American interests. The Tonkin Gulf Resolution passed with only two dissenting votes. Whether the incident represented a real or serious threat has always been subject to question. Hence, Johnson was vulnerable to the charge of deceit from the very beginning.

At first the president continued to move cautiously, merely authorizing occasional air strikes to retaliate for Vietcong raids against American installations. However, in March 1965, believing an attack from the north was imminent, Johnson authorized sustained bombing raids above the 17th parallel. This proved to be the critical decision—the beginning of a full-scale American commitment.

The Johnson administration had limited objectives in Vietnam. The president had no offensive designs on North Vietnam; he only wished to defend the South from aggression and internal subversion by the Vietcong. At first, he apparently believed these objectives could be reached in a short time, so he did nothing to prepare the American people for a long and costly war. Nor did he mobilize the economy effectively, in the apparent belief that such action would complicate and weaken his Great Society plans. By the time he realized his mistake it was too late—or was it? That is the question that tore at the essence of American society at the time and has baffled analysts and scholars ever since. Why did Johnson continue to pour men and resources into Vietnam for so long, even after it became clear that the strategy he and his advisers had adopted was not succeeding?

Johnson's strategy was to pressure the North Vietnamese continuously by means of a bombing campaign against their homeland, and to turn back their aggression in the South, by sending there some two hundred thousand American troops. Johnson relied heavily on General William Westmoreland for military advice and analysis even though many White House advisers soon began to doubt Westmoreland's reliability. As it turned out, it took much longer for the American military presence to stem the tide of aggression in South Vietnam than Westmoreland had predicted and Johnson had hoped. Meanwhile, in the United States opposition to the war increased until it became a veritable avalanche of protest.

Johnson's twin strategies of massive yet limited bombing in the North coupled with limited ground action in the South were flawed from the start. The bombing campaign was supposed to avoid civilian targets yet interdict the flow of men and supplies to the South and at the same time encourage the enemy to negotiate. In reality, while the bombing may have hampered the Vietcong's supply lines, it never cut them off; moreover, it was responsible for the deaths of thousands of civilians. As for the morale of the North Vietnamese, the bombing seemed to strengthen rather than weaken their resolve to carry on the struggle. It is true that some analysts argue persuasively that it was bombing that ultimately forced the enemy to the bargaining table, but the process took much longer than Johnson had envisioned.

The ground-fighting phase of the war was a calamity. It proved necessary to commit more than twice as many U.S. servicemen as Westmoreland had anticipated, and even then the enemy could only be checked: the capacity of the Vietcong and North Vietnam to wage war was never destroyed. In the process, some 58,000 Americans were killed and thousands more were injured or psychologically and emotionally scarred. As for the number of Vietnamese killed and wounded, it can only be guessed at, but considering both military personnel and civilians on both sides, it is certainly in the millions. Moreover, this costly ground war was fought mostly by draftees from the lower classes of American society who served one-year tours of duty. Their morale was low and support at home diminished as the war dragged on. The American people watched an edited, tape-delayed version of the war on television, but this was nonetheless a horrible enough image that it contributed to the erosion of U.S. support for the war effort. Because the troops served their tours on a rotating basis, many of those who returned home while the war continued received little or no attention except from their own families. By the time the war finally ended, public opinion had become so alienated that the returning veterans were received not as heroes but often with scorn and indifference. The folks at home were exhausted by the length and horror of the conflict, and besides, there had been no victory.

By the end of 1965, Johnson believed that the United States had gone too far to withdraw. Withdrawal from Vietnam would tarnish American honor and cast doubt upon the nation's willingness and ability to keep its treaty commitments and protect the world from communism. Thus, Johnson's only options were complete victory or negotiated peace. The first of these was really no more feasible than withdrawal since the military strategy employed was not calculated to produce a complete victory. Johnson feared that an all-out war might lead to Chinese or Soviet intervention with disastrous results. So negotiation was the only out, yet Johnson had a weak hand to play in trying to initiate a dialogue. Until 1966, the war was not going well, and the government in South Vietnam was utterly unreliable. Still, the president made some halfhearted and predictably unsuccessful efforts to get talks started. In December 1965, he ordered a bombing halt that lasted until the end of January 1966. During that time several foreign governments began efforts to bring the two sides together, but nothing happened; in fact, the North Vietnamese government's only response was a demand for unconditional American withdrawal.

Another failed effort to open peace talks occurred in late 1966, when Polish diplomats attempted to broker secret negotiations in Warsaw. Januscz Lewendowski devised a ten-point proposal that he hoped would bring the two sides together. Johnson appointed Averell Harriman to represent the United States in the projected talks, but again nothing happened. Inexplicably, the United States intensified the bombing in the Hanoi area at the very time the talks were supposed to begin. The North Vietnamese used this as an excuse to withdraw from the talks; perhaps they had never intended to participate. In any case, this effort failed.

Yet another chance to open peace talks was bungled in 1967. During a brief bombing halt early in that year Prime Minister Harold Wilson of Great Britain and Premier Aleksey Kosygin of the Soviet Union attempted to facilitate negotiations on the basis of a sustained bombing halt in exchange for reduced infiltration by the North. This effort failed when the

Americans, apparently fearful that the North Vietnamese would actually step up their activities during a prolonged halt in the bombing, demanded a promise to deescalate within twenty-four hours.

Johnson's constant assertions of peaceful intentions coupled with escalation and premature claims of success led to the growing impression among the American people that the president was a hypocrite and a liar. Hence, opposition to the war, small at first, grew rapidly in 1966 and 1967. This opposition emanated from three sources: the political left, those who objected on moral grounds, and those who saw opposition as a way to gain some political advantage. The third group was the most dangerous to the administration because it included some, like Robert Kennedy, who had influence and who had previously supported the president.

Throughout 1967, in the face of mounting criticism, Johnson doggedly insisted that the situation in Vietnam was improving. This was an illusion based on inaccurate reports from the field, and the president fell into the trap of proclaiming that the end might be in view. Then came the Tet Offensive of January 31, 1968, a massive coordinated, and unexpected, attack that penetrated well into South Vietnam. Although it was by no means a conclusive military success, this effort by the North Vietnamese and the Vietcong beclouded all of Johnson's claims and expanded the so-called "credibility gap" into a yawning abyss. This in turn led directly to Johnson's decision to leave the White House.[15]

On March 1, 1968, Johnson's old friend Clark Clifford took over as secretary of defense. He had always supported the Vietnam policy of the government, but now, as he studied conditions more thoroughly, he concluded that it could not succeed and he advised Johnson to begin serious efforts to secure a negotiated peace. Almost simultaneously, the military asked Johnson for permission to commit another 106,000 U.S. troops to Southeast Asia, another major escalation. The president was now faced with a critical policy decision.

Meanwhile, Johnson's approval rating plummeted, the major news media demanded change, campus antiwar activities escalated, Eugene McCarthy almost beat the president in the New Hampshire Primary, and Robert Kennedy announced his candidacy for the Democratic presidential nomination. In the face of these pressures Johnson finally gave in. He rejected the request for more troops, and he announced in his momentous speech of March 31, 1968, that the bombing of North Vietnam would be halted. He also stunned the nation by announcing that he would not seek reelection. Many rejoiced. Of course, they could not know that Richard Nixon would win the presidency and that the war would drag on for another five agonizing years.

When Johnson formally left office on January 20, 1969, conditions were unsettled, to say the least. At home the nation had suffered through the excruciating spring and summer of 1968, which witnessed the assassinations of Martin Luther King Jr. and Robert Kennedy, increased riots in many U.S. cities, and more strident and even violent demonstrations on college and university campuses across the nation. August had brought the debacle of the Democratic National Convention in Chicago where, amid near hysteria in the convention hall and chaos outside, Vice President Hubert Humphrey was nominated to be Johnson's successor. Meanwhile, the administration had little success in enticing the enemy to the bargaining table, and Nixon, claiming he had to have a secret plan to secure peace, was elected president.[16]

After the inauguration, Johnson retired to his Hill Country ranch on the Pedernales River. For the first time in more than twenty years he was not a major public figure. He busied himself with his memoirs—assisted by a staff of writers—and his business affairs, and he indulged in heavy smoking and drinking, which jeopardized his health. In 1970 he began to suffer severe chest pains almost every day. In April 1972 he had a major heart attack that almost killed him. He managed to survive for another nine months, but finally, on January 22, 1973, he died. Ironically for a man who loved crowds and public adulation, he was at home alone at the time. His body was taken to Washington, D.C., where it lay in state in the Capitol rotunda for seventeen hours, after which funeral services were performed at the National City Christian Church. Then Johnson was returned to Texas and was buried on the banks of the Pedernales.[17]

RALPH YARBOROUGH

Fig. 8.1. Ralph Yarborough, Texas's dynamic and outspoken U.S. senator during the 1960s, was the only senator from a former Confederate state to vote for all the major civil rights bills from 1957 to 1970. Lee (Russell) Photograph Collection, Center for American History, UT-Austin (CN 10386).

RALPH YARBOROUGH

BY MICHAEL L. COLLINS AND PATRICK COX

Few places are more typical of Texas than Henderson County. Stately pines tower over groves of post oak, hickory, and pecan trees. The growing seasons are long and warm; the brown clay soil and sandy loam yield bountiful harvests of cotton, corn, potatoes, peanuts, and that familiar southern staple, black-eyed peas. Hereford cattle graze in pastures not far from watermelon patches. Nearby, idle oil derricks and rusting pumps stand like silent sentries alongside farm-to-market roads. Across a pastoral setting, scattered dairies dot the countryside. In every corner of the county simple country churches grace the landscape, physical reminders of the people's simple faith in Providence. Friday night football is something of a religion in these parts of East Texas. So is politics. More than a simple pastime, Democratic Party affairs generate a missionary zeal and competitive spirit. Populist traditions likewise continue to shape the attitudes and thus the voting behavior of county residents. Their pantheon of local folk heroes includes some of the titans of Texas history: Oran Roberts, the pipe-smoking "Old Alcalde," who led the secessionist movement in 1861 and who later served as governor of the Lone Star State; John H. Reagan, former Confederate postmaster general and then United States senator, author of the Interstate Commerce Act, and father of the Texas Railroad Commission; James Stephen "Jim" Hogg, the progressive governor, sponsor of the state's first antitrust law, and champion of agrarian interests in the late nineteenth century; and Ralph Yarborough, the messiah of modern-day Texas liberalism.[1]

"The People's Senator," his many admirers called him—and for good reason. During his fourteen-year career in the U.S. Senate, from 1957 to 1971, Yarborough sponsored more legislation than any senator who ever represented Texans in Washington. Virtually every major piece of education, health, and labor legislation passed during the era bore his stamp. So too did most environmental and conservation initiatives.[2]

If demonstrating political courage is the true measure of statesmanship, then Yarborough must rank as one of the outstanding statesmen of his time. He was the only U.S. senator from the South who voted for every major civil rights bill from 1957 to 1970. During his first year in Washington, he stepped forward as one of only five senators from states of the old Confederacy to vote for the Civil Rights Act of 1957. And he stood alone among his colleagues from the South in supporting the sweeping Civil Rights Act of 1964. Then he cast one of only three southern votes in the Senate in favor of the historic Voting Rights Act of 1965, thus ensuring for himself a special place in the history of the "Second Reconstruction" of the 1960s. Always he fought for the causes of the poor, the powerless, the disenfranchised, and the forgotten. Not once did he turn his back on those who sent him to Washington: farmers, blue-collar workers, small business owners, African Americans, Mexican Americans, men and women concerned about their children's future, and anyone who believed that government should represent not just the powerful and the privileged but also the common folks who cannot afford a paid lobbyist. By 1968 he publicly opposed U.S. involvement in the war in Vietnam, and in the end he paid a heavy price for it.[3]

Born on June 8, 1903, in the town of Chandler, located some twelve miles west of Tyler, Ralph Webster Yarborough was the seventh child of Nannie Jane Spear and Charles Richard Yarborough. Growing up in a large family of nine children was not unusual in those days; neither was the strict Baptist upbringing nor the primary education that young Yarborough received in Chandler. As a boy, Ralph engaged in children's games with his brothers, sisters, and schoolmates, and he enjoyed the thrill of hunting in the woods. Predictably, the boy in denim overalls paid little attention to girls, even to his neighbor, Opal Warren, who later recalled of her future husband: "The girls were all interested in Ralph, but he was more interested in history, basketball, and debate." As Opal observed, Ralph learned to love the world of books. A voracious reader and a student of history, he gloried in stories of the Texas frontier and in accounts of the American Civil War, especially the exploits of his childhood heroes, chief among them Robert E. Lee, Thomas J. "Stonewall" Jackson, and the Colossus of Texas, Sam Houston.[4]

Yarborough recollected that he "grew up in the background of the Old South." During these formative years, he prided himself on his southern heritage and, more specifically, his family history. He listened to tales of his paternal grandfather, Captain Harvey Yarborough, a prosperous planter and slaveholder who had migrated from Alabama to the Texas wilderness in the early days of statehood. He heard family members explain how grandfather Yarborough had organized the first company of Confederate volunteers to be mustered into service in neighboring Smith County and of how he had worked in an arms factory in Tyler that manufactured more rifles for the Confederacy than any facility west of the Mississippi. According to family tradition, his maternal grandfather, Jackson Spear, too young to enlist in the regular army of the South, had served as a guerrilla fighter in Mississippi, disrupting Yankee communications and supply lines before working as a plantation overseer during and after the Siege of Vicksburg.[5]

Like any young man raised in a small town in East Texas, Yarborough understood the traditional values and everyday concerns of common, working people. At an early age, therefore, he was imbued with the virtues of self-reliance and instilled with an awareness that social justice can best be achieved through the triumph of popular government. At the same time, he learned from his parents the customs of hospitality and the importance of being a good neighbor. So, in the process of becoming a man, he grew to realize what it meant to be a southerner, a Texan, and a Yarborough.

After graduating in 1918 from the tenth grade in Chandler, Yarborough enrolled for his final year in the Tyler public school. After all, successful completion of the eleventh grade was a requirement for matriculation in any college or university—and the boy from Henderson County had ambitious plans. Being fascinated with military history and with the lore of the War Between the States, as southerners called it, Yarborough dreamed, as many young men of his day did, of the "Long Gray Line" at West Point. While President Woodrow Wilson was proclaiming that the recently concluded Great War in Europe was to be the "war to end all war," and as American "doughboys" were returning from the battlefields of France, Yarborough wrote Congressman Jim Young of Kaufman County and requested an appointment to the United States Military Academy. The day the letter of appointment arrived in the mail, it became official; Richard and Nannie Yarborough's boy was on his way to "the Point."[6]

The United States Military Academy was more than many miles away from Henderson County. At first, the traditions and mystique of West Point were awe-inspiring. Before long, however, that boyish sense of wonder gave way to reality. The spartan discipline of the institution did not bother him; his beginnings in Texas had prepared him well for that. Surely, too, a young man of his values needed no lectures about the ideals of "duty, honor, and country." While he had fully expected that life as a cadet would not be all glamour and glory, the cloistered existence and daily routines at the academy turned out to be more tedious and less adventuresome than expected. The postwar service academy was in a confused and disorderly state and hostile to Douglas MacArthur, its newly appointed superintendent. Moreover, Yarborough soon realized that some of his classmates had already earned college degrees elsewhere, so the competition in the classroom was fierce, more so than he had ever anticipated. Although he excelled in several academic subjects, including history, his scores in mathematics were disappointing, especially so since he wanted to become a field artilleryman. Quickly he learned that only the most outstanding cadets would receive their assignment of choice; as for the rest, they would be commissioned into the infantry. In conversations with sons of career army officers, he became convinced that many assignments, perhaps those that he might likely receive, were anything but desirable. An army career seemed even less attractive when the newly elected president of the United States, Republican Warren G. Harding, announced deep cuts in the War Department budget. As the school year droned on, the seventeen-year-old plebe thought more and more of his home in Texas. Finally, in the spring of 1921 he decided that he did not want to spend most of his life as a junior officer being "shuffled from one army post to another."[7]

Upon returning to Chandler, Yarborough hired on as a teacher in a one-room school in nearby Delta. Still, he had already seen enough of the world to know that his future lay beyond the boundaries of Henderson County. After attending one term at Sam Houston College in Huntsville, he learned of a program sponsored by the Department of War that encouraged American veterans to pursue their education in France. Upon learning that no government financial assistance was available, and being short on cash, he traveled to New Orleans, then worked his way across the Atlantic on the French cattle boat *Missouri,* earning his passage by tending to livestock, each day spreading hay and shoveling manure from their pens while assuring himself that a better future awaited him in Paris.[8]

But the city on the Seine turned out to be only a way station in the education of the young dreamer. Yarborough was not even allowed to apply for admission to the world-famous Sorbonne. "If you couldn't speak French, you couldn't pass through the gates," he later recalled. Worse still, the high cost of living in Paris forced him to room in a cheap and common boardinghouse and to eat at only the least expensive restaurants. While he found time to tour the many museums, cathedrals, and historical and cultural sites of Paris, he soon ran out of money. So when he heard that a young American could live in Germany on as little as $5 a month, he purchased a third-class ticket on the Paris-to-Berlin express.[9]

As the train hurtled him from one European capital toward another, he sensed that, despite their geographic proximity, the two countries were worlds apart. Once he crossed into the Rhineland occupation zone, he realized that he was an *auslander,* not even *angemelted,* or formally registered as an alien. He did not understand the German language, but he understood that the postwar Weimar Republic was a welter of social un-

rest, political agitation, and economic chaos. First at Stendal, where he remained for several months, then during his stay in Berlin, he witnessed the
ravages of inflation and thus the slow undoing of the German middle class.
He encountered the tidal wave of unemployed refugees from neighboring
Poland and Czechoslovakia. He saw riots in the streets orchestrated by the
Spartacus League, allied with the "Reds" of the newly organized communist movement. He experienced firsthand the hunger, the anger, the bitterness, and the feelings of betrayal expressed by the German people.[10]

Little did Yarborough know, or for that matter little did anyone realize
at the time, what these dark forces would someday unleash. If the future of
Germany seemed at best uncertain, so too did that of Ralph Yarborough.
But at least from this new perspective life back in Texas now held more
certainties, or so it seemed. Although Ralph remained a young man in
search of himself, by 1922 he appeared to have lost some of the wanderlust
of youth. After a stopover in London, he signed on as a worker aboard an
America-bound steamer and headed home. As he later recalled, the docks
in England were crowded with young men looking to work their way back
to the States. Then one day when a ship's master with a cargo of thorough-
breds called out, asking if anyone knew how to handle horses, Yarborough
yelled back, "I'm from Texas."[11]

At last, he had come full circle. He had traveled halfway around the
world and back, seeking and sometimes following the advice of others. But
perhaps the best advice he had ever gotten was from a hometown justice
of the peace, his father, Charles Richard Yarborough, who wanted all three
of his sons to become lawyers. After toiling on a threshing crew working
across Oklahoma and Kansas in the harvesting seasons of 1923, Yarborough collected his modest savings and a few belongings, then struck off to
law school at the University of Texas in Austin. During the next three
years he lived, worked, and studied in the shadow of the famous Tower of
Learning. In so doing, he learned more than just a respect for the rule
of law. In his studies he gained a greater appreciation of how the American system of justice could be made to work for the people. Outside the
classroom he again experienced what it meant to work for a living, in the
evenings waiting tables in student boardinghouses and shelving books in
the university law library to help finance his education. Then, in the summer of 1926, he traveled to the Texas Panhandle and labored in the oil
fields near Borger.[12]

In 1927, at the age of twenty-four, Yarborough graduated from the University of Texas School of Law with the highest honors. Soon thereafter he
joined the law firm of Turney, Burgess, Culwell, Holliday, and Pollard, located in El Paso. During the next four years, Yarborough continued to

grow and mature both as a person and as a professional. Soon he established himself as one of the state's leading authorities on land and water rights. He also continued to cultivate his interest in the history and lore of the Lone Star State. In June 1928 Yarborough returned to East Texas and married his childhood playmate and neighbor, Opal Warren, who had been teaching school in Clarksville, Texas, and Pine Bluff, Arkansas. The couple married at a ceremony at the Third Avenue Presbyterian Church in Corsicana on June 30, 1928. Ralph had settled down now. He had entered into a successful law practice and thus appeared to be prepared to support a wife and to raise a family. He even seemed to have given up on the idea of running for county attorney in his native Henderson County, especially since Opal had vowed, "I won't marry a man in politics." [13]

Then came the crash on Wall Street, the Panic of 1929, and the onset of the Great Depression. Early in 1931 Yarborough traveled to Austin to testify before a committee of the state legislature on proposed legislation that involved disputed land titles along the Rio Grande. Sitting in the hearing room was Attorney General James V. Allred, who was so impressed with the witness's knowledge and presence that he turned to an aide and said, "I want that young man Yarborough for an assistant." It was an ironic twist of fate that thrust the man from Chandler into public life. [14]

Before long, Assistant Attorney General Yarborough would be handling important litigation on behalf of the people of Texas. He argued several lawsuits that netted both the Permanent School Fund and the Permanent University Fund literally tens of millions of dollars from oil and natural gas revenues. In the celebrated *Mid-Continent* case he won $1,083,500, which was at the time the second-largest monetary judgment ever recovered by the state of Texas. He represented the state's interest in another suit against Magnolia Petroleum over oil and gas revenues from approximately 3.9 million acres of public lands. In still another memorable case, he authored the first legal opinion regarding state claims to the so-called tidelands, or offshore oil reserves along the Gulf of Mexico. He even drafted the first underground water conservation law ever enacted in Texas history. Few people at the time realized the impact of these legal victories. The Permanent School Fund alone earned hundreds of millions of dollars as the fund exceeded $8 billion by the 1990s. Yarborough thus became literally the first "billion-dollar attorney" in the state. [15]

Little wonder that by the time the dynamic Jimmy Allred was elected governor of Texas in 1934, he had come to recognize and admire the talents of the seemingly indefatigable Ralph Yarborough. When Governor Allred entered office early in 1935, his young protégé opened a law office in Austin and received an appointment as lecturer at the University of

Texas School of Law. Although he was again in private practice, Yarborough continued to be involved in promoting and protecting the public interest. He accepted an appointment to the original board of directors of the Lower Colorado River Authority (LCRA) and helped in the planning of a series of strategically located dams on the Colorado River to provide flood control and cheap electricity for Central Texas. At the same time, he advocated the rapid extension of the newly created federal Rural Electrification Administration (REA), which was fathered by House Majority Leader Sam Rayburn of Texas. These projects brought thousands of jobs and millions of dollars into the depressed economy of Central Texas.[16]

Like millions of his generation, Yarborough was profoundly affected by the Great Depression and by President Franklin Delano Roosevelt's New Deal programs that were designed to bring relief, recovery, and reform to a nation stricken by an unprecedented economic paralysis. As a member of the board of the LCRA and as an outspoken proponent of rural electrification and public works projects in his home state, Yarborough recognized that any efforts to revive both the American economy and spirit depended on a massive mobilization of national resources. After observing the failure of the Hoover administration to deal with the depression, Yarborough was now witnessing the fruitful innovations emanating from Washington: the Public Works Administration, the Works Progress Administration, the Civilian Conservation Corps, the Tennessee Valley Authority, the Agricultural Adjustment Administration, the National Recovery Administration, and more. He was watching as Roosevelt and the Congress reformed the nation's banking and currency systems, the stock exchange, the public utilities industry, and the tax codes, while implementing minimum wage standards, child labor legislation, the legal recognition of labor's collective bargaining rights, pensions for the elderly, and unemployment insurance. As an apostle of FDR, he came to bear testimony to the innovative accomplishments of the New Deal. While the role of the federal government in American society was being redefined during these desperate years, so too was Yarborough's vision of government. In short, the Texan grew in his faith that government could change people's lives for the better.

In all of Texas there was perhaps no greater champion of the New Deal than Governor Allred, who in 1935 appointed his former assistant as judge of the Fifty-third District Court in Travis County. The following year Allred appointed Yarborough as presiding judge of the Third Judicial District, which included thirty counties in Central Texas. He declined offers to run for Congress and supported Lyndon Johnson, who was running to fill the Tenth Congressional District seat vacated by the death of Congressman James Buchanan, the powerful chairman of the House Appropriations Committee. The tall, angular Johnson, who served as head of the National Youth Administration (NYA) in Texas, first encountered Yarborough as an LCRA director while serving as an aide to Congressman Richard Kleberg. Johnson was running hard to emerge from a crowded field of candidates in the special by-election called by Governor Allred. To separate himself from eight other opponents, Johnson announced his support for President Roosevelt's controversial proposal to increase the number of justices on the Supreme Court from nine to fifteen in order to create six new vacancies on the tribunal. As Yarborough later recalled, "Lyndon was supporting the court-packing plan, and I was too." Although Yarborough refused to publicly endorse Johnson's bid, he later remembered, "I made my position known and it cost me pretty heavily among the lawyers" of the Travis County Bar Association, most of whom were bitterly opposed to the Court scheme and thus to Johnson's election.[17]

In 1938 the political arena beckoned Yarborough. Despite few newspaper endorsements, little money, and even less name recognition, Yarborough announced his candidacy for state attorney general. Although he campaigned in the Democratic primary with a characteristic vigor, he lost to Gerry Mann, the diminutive former All-American quarterback from SMU, known widely in Texas as the "Little Red Arrow." But in the process of touring around the Lone Star State by automobile, delivering speeches and shaking hands, Yarborough earned the respect of many fellow Texans who saw him as a man of integrity and commitment. At the same time he learned much about the logistical and financial demands of a political race in a state as vast as Texas.[18]

If Yarborough had any further political plans at the time, World War II changed them. When news of the Japanese attack on Pearl Harbor streaked across the United States like a lightning bolt, Yarborough rushed to the nearest recruiting office and volunteered to serve his country, this despite the fact that he was well beyond the draft age. Because of his year at West Point, his three years in the National Guard, and his legal and judicial experience, he was commissioned a captain in the United States Army Judge Advocate General Corps. Following training in Ann Arbor, Michigan; Camp Swift, Texas; and Fort Leonard Wood, Missouri; Captain Yarborough was assigned to a desk job in the Pentagon.[19]

But shuffling papers in Washington was not for Yarborough — not when there was a war to be won. In a matter of months he requested combat duty and, in 1943, was reassigned to the Ninety-seventh Infantry Division being deployed in Britain as part of the First Army Group in preparation for Operation Overlord. Following the D-Day Invasion in June 1944, the Ninety-seventh was attached to General George Patton's Third Army, which was spearheading the Allied drive across Europe in March and April of 1945. As the Ninety-seventh rolled through northern France and Belgium en route to western Czechoslovakia, Yarborough participated in the liberation of numerous villages. When word came of the fall of Berlin, his unit was occupying the town of Pilsen in the Czech Sudetenland. Following V-E Day, while U.S. forces pulled back across Germany, Yarborough observed the wreckage and rubble left in the path of the war, and he never forgot those charred images of destruction and death, scenes of a civilization in cinders.[20]

Still the conflict raged in the Pacific. Yarborough was with the Ninety-seventh as preparations were being made for an Allied invasion of the Japanese Islands, but such an invasion was never necessary. The division was halfway across the Pacific when Yarborough learned of the United States' atomic bombing of Hiroshima and Nagasaki and of the subsequent unconditional surrender of imperial Japan. Finally the war was over, but the work of rebuilding Japan was only beginning. After a brief tour in the Philippines, Yarborough, now a Lieutenant Colonel, received orders to report to Yokohama, Japan, where he joined American occupational forces under General Douglas MacArthur. Since Yarborough was one of the few who had had any experience governing anything, he was named as military government officer in charge of central Honshu Province. For the next eight months he administered this densely populated region, which includes one-seventh of the land area and population of Japan. Restoring civil authority, establishing an orderly economic and political transition to peacetime conditions, coping with the enormous problems of rehabilitating a war-ravaged nation, and helping repatriate thousands of Korean prisoners, Yarborough contributed to his country's efforts to revive Japan from the ashes of defeat.[21]

Yarborough flew back to Texas in June 1946. Especially gratifying as he stepped off the plane in Austin was the sight of a smiling Opal and their fifteen-year-old son, Richard, who appeared to have grown to manhood during the four years that his father had been away. Readjusting to civilian life was not easy for Ralph—it never is for those who serve in wartime. Everything seemed to have changed—everything, that is, except the support and love of his family and friends.

The postwar years found Ralph Yarborough returning to his law practice in Austin. To maintain a bond with other veterans of similar experiences, he joined the local posts of the American Legion and the Veterans of Foreign Wars. He worked long hours to rebuild his law practice, and he reacquainted himself with old friends.

Once again, Yarborough was in his element. In 1949, when President Harry Truman attempted to assert federal claims to the offshore tidelands, the controversy emerged as perhaps the most critical issue in Texas politics during the next several years. Although Yarborough had written the first legal opinion supporting state claims to the potentially oil-rich tidel lands in 1931, he soon found that others had been given the credit for his earlier contribution. The tidelands issue still dominated the landscape of state politics when, in 1952, Yarborough decided to reenter the arena. At first he considered filing for the post of state attorney general, but then one day in the corridors of the capitol in Austin, Governor Allan Shivers informed him, as a matter of fact, that he and his advisers had already chosen the Democratic nominee for that post. Yarborough was thus discouraged from challenging Shivers's protégé, John Ben Sheppard, who would be running for attorney general with the backing of the party's powerful establishment. So Yarborough decided not to oppose Sheppard. Instead, with the quiet encouragement from a powerful party elder, Speaker of the House Sam Rayburn, Yarborough announced his candidacy for governor of Texas in 1952. He also secured financial backing from independent oil producer J. R. Parten and Dickinson banker Walter Hall, who promised to unite loyal Democrats behind Yarborough.[22]

Yarborough's grassroots campaign bore all of the appearances of an old-style populist crusade. Stumping around the state, delivering as many as ten speeches a day, clasping hands, meeting as many people face-to-face as time would permit, he exuded enormous energy and displayed a natural knack for campaigning. Everywhere he traveled he railed out against the powerful forces of entrenched wealth and privilege, and he berated the political establishment in Austin that had allegedly corrupted the democratic process. But the deck was stacked against him. The well-financed Shivers machine outspent, outadvertised, and in some ways outmaneuvered him. Yarborough learned that, in many instances, county Democratic officials were warned by the governor's operatives not to aid the insurgent campaign against Shivers. There were even reports that some had been threatened with reprisal if they openly supported Yarborough. Newspapers across the state virtually ignored or even dismissed the challenger's charges of graft within the Shivers administration. In the end, Yarborough carried only twenty-one counties in losing to the incumbent. In spite of his failed effort, Yarborough established the base of his political support that would follow him for the remainder of his public career.[23]

Shivers had assured voters in the Democratic primary that he would support the party's presidential nominee in the fall election. But he broke that promise by bolting party ranks that summer, endorsing the Republican standard-bearer, Dwight David Eisenhower, whose opponent, Governor Adlai Stevenson of Illinois, favored federal control of the Texas tidelands. The following year President Eisenhower signed into law a measure that recognized state claims to the offshore oil reserves, thus effectively ending that debate. While the "Shivercrat" rebellion had therefore helped "Ike" carry Texas in 1952, it had also diminished the governor's stature with Democratic regulars around the state.[24]

Yarborough may have lost the election, but in the process he had won more followers across the Lone Star State. By 1954, he stood poised to mount an even greater challenge to Shivers and his organization. Continuing to charge that the Shivers crowd had corrupted the institutions of state government, Yarborough alleged that the governor had allowed "fixers and influence peddlers to operate in Austin." He called for a thorough investigation of the "insurance mess," a reference to the hundreds of wildcat underwriting companies operating in Texas without adequate capitalization. He even questioned a reportedly suspicious real estate deal involving Shivers and South Texas rancher and land developer Lloyd Bentsen Sr., which reportedly had netted the governor a $450,000 return on a $25,000 investment, one that allegedly involved the selling of vast acreage in the Rio Grande Valley, without relinquishing the water rights on those lands, to unwitting buyers. Yarborough hammered Shivers for ignoring an earlier promise not to seek a third term as governor. He claimed Shivers wanted a "self-perpetuating political machine." During the course of the primary campaign, Yarborough endorsed a gas-pipeline tax, in part to provide for needed revenues to support increased appropriations for education. Most observers were stunned when the returns from the July primary showed Yarborough emerging from the field of candidates with 645,994 votes to Shivers's total of 668,913 votes, thus forcing a runoff. As reports of voting irregularities later surfaced, many contended that the primary election had been stolen.[25]

Some journalists predicted that the ensuing battle would be a classic Texas shootout. Instead, it turned out to be a brawling campaign of deliberate deceit and character assassination, brutal even by Texas standards. Now the debate shifted from substantive issues to a series of vicious personal attacks against Yarborough. The Shivers machine spared no tactic in trying to sully Yarborough's character and to ruin his reputation. Waging a smear campaign aimed at destroying Yarborough by appealing to seething racial bigotry and to a frothing fear of communism, the Shivers camp pulled out all the stops. First, in white communities they circulated campaign brochures that labeled Yarborough a "nigra loving" liberal who endorsed desegregation of public schools. They even reportedly hired a black man to ride around East Texas in a new Cadillac, flaunting money and boasting that he was supporting Yarborough for governor. At the same time, in black neighborhoods they distributed a pamphlet entitled *The Big Lie,* distorting Yarborough's record by suggesting that he opposed the Supreme Court's landmark 1954 decision in *Brown* v. *Board of Education of Topeka,* which overturned the "separate but equal" doctrine and ordered the integration of public schools in the United States. Shivers claimed that the NAACP wanted to integrate "every phase of daily living." In reality Yarborough had publicly refused to denounce the decision, yet had also suggested that he opposed "forced" integration. His position created criticism from liberals within his camp, even after several closed-door meetings with his closest advisers.[26]

But the most infamous episode in the 1954 Texas gubernatorial race involved efforts to link Yarborough with a union movement in Port Arthur, Texas, which Attorney General Sheppard alleged was of "proven communist leadership," one inspired by Marx and controlled from Moscow. Shivers spoke only in terms of innuendo, pointing out that the Congress of Industrial Organizations (CIO) had organized hundreds of retail store clerks, waitresses, and maids in Port Arthur, and that the union movement had paralyzed the city and "scuttled" the economy of the entire Gulf Coast, that the union was "communist-dominated," that the leftist American Civil Liberties Union was behind it, and that Yarborough supported it too.[27]

On the eve of the election, supporters of the governor aired a thirty-minute television "documentary" entitled "The Port Arthur Story." The program was politics at its worst, accusing the allegedly communist-infiltrated CIO of overseeing the "death of a city" and of posing a threat to the security of the state and nation. Scenes of deserted city streets, of apparently idle factories with stilled smokestacks, and of seemingly boarded-up businesses were offered as evidence. Of course, viewers never realized that these images had been filmed at 6:00 A.M. on a Sunday morning. Predictably, at the conclusion of the program, Yarborough's photograph appeared on screen, along with shots of surly-looking characters said to be strikers. The film aired in every television market in the state—with the exception of Port Arthur. The Shivers campaign ordered all copies of the film destroyed after the election. The distribution of a booklet, also entitled "The Port Arthur Story," followed. So did statements by Shivers that "Reds, radicals, communists, and labor goon squads" supported his opponent. Shivers contended that he had not approved of either the paid political program or the companion tabloid, but many politicians who used such hit-and-run attacks during the McCarthy era denied so doing.[28]

The deception orchestrated by the Shivers forces was complete, as the public was misled about Yarborough's alleged support for a state sales tax and further frightened by the charge that he would "unionize" the entire state. A quiet campaign of intimidation was also waged, as state employees with Yarborough bumper stickers on their cars were reportedly threatened with dismissal. Such tactics were obviously designed to scare voters. Apparently they worked. Aided by a last-minute media blitz, Shivers defeated his rival, this time by almost 92,000 votes. Shivers also succeeded in aligning Texas with other states in the Deep South as supporters of "massive resistance" to integration defeated moderates and liberals throughout the region.[29]

There was nothing to do now but look ahead to 1956. By then more Texans were beginning to see Yarborough as something of a prophet—and well they should have. The phenomenon of McCarthyism abated by 1955. More important, in Texas the Shivers regime became enveloped by a series of scandals: the collapse of numerous loosely regulated insurance corporations, such as the behemoth known as ICT, headed by the flamboyant and unscrupulous Ben Jack Cage; the resulting loss to the public of millions of dollars in unpaid claims and investments; the unethical and sometimes illegal promotion schemes of several underwriting companies; the acceptance of corporate gifts by members of the State Insurance Commission. All of these revelations underscored Yarborough's earlier call for more stringent state regulations of the insurance industry. As another benefit to Yarborough, the scandals tended to take voters' attention away from the difficult integration issues.

Even more shocking to Texans was the mismanagement of the Veterans Land Board, which had been established in 1950 to supervise a $100 million fund to finance a long-term, low-interest loan program to assist servicemen in acquiring land with little down payment. The web of fraud and graft disclosed by investigations into the General Land Office led not only to the conviction and imprisonment of Land Commissioner Bascom Giles but also to literally hundreds of criminal indictments that stunned and even outraged voters around the state. Although Governor Shivers and Attorney General Sheppard were not directly implicated in the most sensational scandal ever to rock the state capital, the affair effectively ended both of their careers.[30]

The 1956 gubernatorial race promised to be a wide-open scramble. Yarborough looked over the field of candidates, which included author, rancher, and right-wing extremist J. Evetts Haley and the old Hillbilly Flour merchant and former governor and U.S. senator W. Lee "Pappy" O'Daniel. But everyone knew that the man to beat was Senator Price

Daniel, who had been persuaded by Shivers and others to give up his seat in the U.S. Senate to pursue the governor's mansion. With the support of a coalition of organized labor, progressives, intellectuals, and farmers known as the Democrats of Texas, which was something of a party within a party, Yarborough managed to force Daniel into a runoff, even as he maintained a position against "forced integration" in favor of "moderation." Once again, however, Yarborough lost the runoff by the most narrow of margins; only 3,171 votes out of almost 14 million ballots cast separated the two rivals. Just as before, reports of foul play tainted the election results. Yarborough carried more counties and believed that he had won by 30,000 votes, based on questionable returns from a dozen counties. Yet he did not contest the outcome.[31]

The defeat was especially frustrating for Yarborough, who had come so far in the past four years. Yet what seemed at first like a disappointment soon turned out to be an opportunity. When Daniel resigned to assume the office of governor, it opened the way for Yarborough to make a run for the Senate. Although Daniel appointed wealthy Dallas attorney William A. "Dollar Bill" Blakley to fill the vacant seat in 1957, the new governor was also required by state law to call a special election. In the meantime, reactionaries attempted to head off Yarborough yet again: desperately they tried to push a bill through the state legislature proposing to change Texas law by requiring a majority in the special election instead of a simple plurality. This tactic, they hoped, would force Yarborough into still another runoff, in which a conservative could prevail. The "Pool Bill," named for Democrat State Representative Joe Pool of Dallas, had behind-the-scenes support from Senate Majority Leader Johnson and Speaker Rayburn. After what seemed like an endless series of maneuvers, however, the bill failed to pass the Texas Senate. For the fourth time in five years, Yarborough's legions marshaled their forces, manning phone banks, stuffing envelopes, and passing out brochures and bumper stickers.[32]

This time their persistence paid off. On April 7, 1957, Yarborough's supporters turned out to vote, despite torrents of rain and tornado conditions around the state. Many observers agreed that a low turnout would help Yarborough's rivals, notably Congressman Martin Dies of Orange, the conservative Democratic former chairman of the House Un-American Activities Committee who had promoted his own career by destroying other peoples', and attorney Thad Hutchinson of Houston, the only Republican in the race. While early returns showed Yarborough trailing far behind, when all the ballots were tallied late that night Yarborough was declared the winner with 38 percent of the vote, no small accomplishment considering that twenty-two candidates had crowded the ballot. Dies and

Hutchinson split the conservative vote, thus allowing Yarborough to poll a clear plurality. It was the ultimate vindication for Yarborough, his family, and an army of supporters around the state.[33]

That evening the smiling and by now familiar figure of Ralph Yarborough appeared before a crush of admirers who had gathered to celebrate at his headquarters on Austin's Congress Avenue. Opal and Richard flanked him. The next morning a story in the *Austin American* reported the jubilation at Yarborough's victory party, quoting one capitol lobbyist as saying, "It was fantastic. There wasn't a big shot down there. Only people!"[34]

Once Yarborough arrived on Capitol Hill, the first task at hand was to assemble an able staff. The second concern was to try to land the right committee appointments. And for that he needed to depend on the powerful Senate majority leader, Lyndon Baines Johnson. A shrewd and adept player at the game of power politics, LBJ had been anywhere but in Yarborough's camp in recent years. In fact, at every opportunity, he had placed obstacles in Yarborough's path. Although he had remained neutral in the recent Texas runoff, insiders knew full well that Johnson preferred the more conservative Dies to Yarborough. Still, Lyndon stayed out of the fight, perhaps for fear of dividing Democrats and thus inadvertently aiding the lone Republican in the large field. Johnson had much to lose as his position as Senate majority leader hung in the balance.

To the pragmatic Johnson, that Yarborough won instead of Dies mattered little. What mattered most was that Yarborough's triumph in 1957 assured the Democrats of retaining a slim, two-vote majority in the United States Senate. In other words, had the Republicans somehow managed to capture that Senate seat from Texas, both parties would have counted forty-eight votes, and Republican Vice President Richard Nixon would have been in a position to cast any tie-breaking votes, including those to reorganize the Senate, from critical committee chairmanships all the way up to the post of majority leader. So, ironically, Yarborough's vote was critical to LBJ and to the Democratic leadership in their efforts to maintain a tenuous hold on power in the Senate.

From his first day in Washington, Yarborough realized that Johnson was trying to teach him a lesson in the exercise of power. The majority leader held seats on two of the most influential committees in the Senate — Appropriations and Armed Services. Yarborough did not even bother to express his preference for those assignments, for according to Senate custom and rules, two senators from the same state could not serve on the same standing committee. Then Johnson delayed swearing Yarborough into office. For nearly a month the freshman senator waited, and so did

Fig. 8.2. Following his special-election victory in 1957, Ralph Yarborough took the oath of office for the U.S. Senate from Vice President Richard Nixon as Democratic Senate majority leader Lyndon Johnson looked on. Yarborough (Ralph Webster) Papers, Center for American History, UT-Austin (CN 11082).

members of his staff. When Yarborough inquired, he was simply told that he could not legally take his place in the Senate chamber until the election results were certified. It would not be the last time that LBJ would deliberately thwart him. As Yarborough put it bluntly, "Lyndon wanted you under his thumb." Yarborough requested the assistance of Speaker Rayburn, who subsequently promised he would speak to Johnson. In short order, Yarborough's inauguration date was set.[35]

After being sworn into office by Vice President Nixon on April 29, 1957, Yarborough wasted no time in addressing the business of the people. He assumed his seat on the Committee on Labor and Public Welfare, alongside such giants as Everett Dirksen, the sagacious Republican senator from Illinois, Senator Barry Goldwater of Arizona, an articulate though sometimes abrasive spokesman for the conservative wing of the Republican Party, and the youthful and charismatic John F. Kennedy, Democratic senator from Massachusetts. Quickly the Texan established himself as one of the most hardworking, determined, and informed members of the Senate, and he earned the respect of his colleagues on Capitol Hill.

No sooner had Yarborough settled into his duties than he was approached about a Senate resolution officially entitled a Declaration of Constitutional Principles, otherwise known as the "Southern Manifesto." The measure strongly denounced the desegregation decision of the Supreme Court in the celebrated *Brown* case and called for resistance to forced federal integration of public schools: already nineteen of twenty-two senators from states of the former Confederacy had signed it. But the combative Yarborough refused, thus breaking ranks with his fellow southern Democrats. The adroit Johnson had avoided the controversial resolution, claiming that as Senate majority leader he should remain above the battle. Already, the first-term senator from Texas found himself in the center of a great political storm that was only beginning to sweep the nation. The *Dallas Morning News* proclaimed that Yarborough's test for acceptance by the southern fraternity in the Senate would be "his willingness to participate in a filibuster against civil rights legislation." [36]

The Little Rock crisis of 1957, which began when Governor Orval Faubus of Arkansas called out the National Guard to prevent black students from entering Central High School, led directly to the passage of the Civil Rights Act of 1957. The watered-down measure—the first civil rights law passed by Congress since Reconstruction—established a six-member Commission on Civil Rights, created a Civil Rights Division in the Department of Justice, and empowered the attorney general to employ federal court injunctions whenever an individual's voting rights were being violated. Although the compromise bill had been diluted by southern hard-liners, Yarborough recognized it as an important step forward, and he supported it. He was one of only four southerners in the Senate to do so. [37]

Yarborough was cautioned that his support for the civil rights measure could seriously hurt his chances for reelection in 1958. Conservative, white Texans would react negatively to his vote, he was warned. But the people of Texas had elected him to lead, not to follow. Moreover, he had come to Washington to legislate—and legislate he did. He drafted a bill to create the Padre Island National Seashore and worked tirelessly for its passage during the next four years. He wrote what is known as the Cold War GI Bill, which proposed to extend educational, job training, and housing benefits to veterans of the Korean War era. Unfortunately the bill failed to pass in 1958, despite Yarborough's relentless efforts to muster support; eight years later, however, it would be enacted as part of a flurry of federal measures to open the doors of higher education to millions of Americans.

"It was the longest, hardest fight of my senatorial career," Yarborough recollected. He enjoyed more immediate success when he coauthored and sponsored a companion measure, the National Defense Education Act of 1958, which established a loan fund of $295 million for students seeking a college education, many of whom would go on to become mathematicians, engineers, scientists, and linguists. The legislation likewise included $280 million to fund public school science laboratories and textbooks, as well as an additional $142 million in fellowships and federal matching grants for the states. Initially, Yarborough and other sponsors of the bill had difficulty garnering enough votes to ensure its passage. But one year after the Soviet launching of the world's first satellite, *Sputnik,* and the initiation of the "space race," a Congress conscious of national security now seemed eager to promote the sciences and technology. At the suggestion of Committee Chairman Lister Hill (D-Ala.), who predicted billions of dollars would appear, Yarborough and his allies had added the word "Defense" to the title of the proposed legislation, a brilliant tactic that apparently cleared the way for the enactment of this landmark measure.[38]

Yarborough pushed for the passage of the National Aeronautics and Space Act of 1958, which created NASA and committed the nation to the exploration of the high frontiers of space. He fought unsuccessfully to increase the personal income-tax exemption from $600 to $800 per dependent. He worked to liberalize Social Security benefits, to increase the salaries of postal service employees, and to boost career incentive pay raises for members of the armed forces. He championed legislation to bring flood relief and drought relief to farmers in Texas and across the nation. To combat the corrosive effects of economic recession, in 1958 he coauthored the National Highway Act and the National Housing Act. In 1958 he filed his first proposal to create the Padre Island National Seashore, a 130-mile pristine barrier island along the South Texas Gulf Coast.[39]

Yarborough's labors were soon rewarded as he triumphed easily over his opponent, Bill Blakley, in the 1958 Democratic primary, in spite of Blakley's backing by former governor Shivers and many conservative Democrats. During the campaign, Yarborough first used a theme that would forever be associated with his name: "Put the jam on the lower shelf so the little man can reach it." The following November he crushed a little-known Republican challenger, carrying 76 percent of the vote. When the Eighty-sixth Congress convened in January 1959, the junior senator from Texas became the third-ranking member of the Labor and Public Welfare Committee, and he rose to the chair of the Veterans Affairs Subcommittee, as well as continuing as a member of the Education and Health subcommittees. He was, therefore, positioned well to affect the course of virtually all legislative matters relating directly to working Americans.[40]

As the 1960 presidential campaign approached, the potential Democratic contenders included Yarborough's colleague and fellow progressive, Senator Hubert H. Humphrey of Minnesota, Senator Stuart Symington of Missouri, and the ever-present Adlai Stevenson of Illinois. Yarborough knew full well that Lyndon Johnson coveted the office of president and that the Senate majority leader privately hoped that the party would draft him. But Yarborough was equally convinced that the man to lead the country toward a better future was not his fellow Texan but his friend from Massachusetts, Jack Kennedy, whom he considered to be a man of vision and of extraordinary intellectual powers. In public statements, Yarborough stated that six qualified Democratic senators wanted the nomination. Privately, he chafed at the treatment he received from Lyndon Johnson during his first years in the Senate. Yarborough and Johnson's voting records were similar. Both men supported legislation that set the Texas senators apart from their southern counterparts; for example, they co-sponsored a constitutional amendment in 1959 to abolish the poll tax.[41]

However, Yarborough refused to support Johnson's presidential bid. He joined other Senate liberals in a challenge to Johnson in the Democratic caucus, a move that further alienated both Johnson and Rayburn. In a rare public criticism, Rayburn said, "I couldn't be more disappointed in a man than I was in what he did." The Johnson forces prevented Yarborough's selection as an at-large delegate to the Democratic National Convention in Los Angeles in July. Yarborough must have harbored mixed emotions when Kennedy offered the vice presidential spot to Johnson. But Yarborough of course campaigned enthusiastically for the Kennedy-Johnson ticket, encouraging his supporters to turn out the vote in what promised to be a close election in Texas. Unknown to Yarborough at the time, Kennedy had promised LBJ that he would be allowed to approve all federal appointments in the Lone Star State, typically the prerogative of the state's senior senator, which now would be Yarborough. As Johnson later understated the case, "Senator Yarborough resented this. If I had been in his position I . . . [would] have resented it too." So, following Kennedy's victory over Vice President Nixon in November 1960, Yarborough found himself in a peculiar position—gratified to be a trusted confidant of the president of the United States, yet understandably irritated that his old nemesis Johnson had undermined him again, this time by seizing Yarborough's senatorial privilege of patronage. In a confrontation before Attorney General Robert Kennedy, the two Texas antagonists reached a compromise that finally allowed for judicial appointments to be made.

The results likely satisfied neither Johnson nor Yarborough. But the episode created a solid bond between Robert Kennedy and Yarborough that proved beneficial in the near future.[42]

Yarborough was eager to play the role of partner with the Kennedy administration. He emerged as a loyal and dependable supporter of the New Frontier. He helped press for the passage of the new president's bold and idealistic innovations: the Peace Corps, which challenged young Americans to contribute their skills and their goodwill by volunteering to live and work in the underdeveloped nations of the "Third World"; the Alliance for Progress, which committed the United States to promoting a higher standard of living for the peoples of Latin America, millions of whom experienced the daily reality of grinding poverty, hunger, and disease; the Nuclear Test Ban Treaty, which banned the atmospheric testing of atomic weapons; and Kennedy's Olympian goal of a manned mission to the moon.

Yarborough continued to fight for increased federal funding for public and higher education and for an expanded national commitment to provide quality health care for the aged and the indigent. Each day he concerned himself with the problems of his constituents back in Texas, and he always took time from his busy schedule to answer the avalanche of mail that poured into his office. In September 1961, as President Kennedy noted, when Hurricane Carla struck the Texas coast with a fury, "before the winds died down . . . [Yarborough] was walking in the debris of the battered cities and towns on the Gulf Coast . . . asking, 'What can I do to help?'"[43]

Much, perhaps too much, has been said and written about President Kennedy's fateful trip to Dallas in November 1963. Then, as now, many observers speculated that JFK had traveled to Texas to mend the rift between the conservative wing of the state Democratic Party, headed by longtime Johnson protégé Governor John Connally, and the liberal wing of the party, led by Senator Yarborough. Connally said after the assassination there was a "public impression that the President went to Texas to settle a feud." But, as Johnson later remembered, "these political differences had nothing to do with his coming to Texas. . . . The trip was presidential politics, pure and simple." Indeed, President Kennedy came to Texas to solidify his support and to raise money for the 1964 reelection bid. He also wanted to dispel any rumors that Lyndon Johnson would be dumped from the ticket.[44]

The tragic events of that fateful Friday in Dallas have been told and retold. There is, therefore, no need to recount them here. In future months and years the grief-stricken Yarborough provided only a handful of interviews on the assassination. Although he rode two cars behind the president's vehicle, he stated that the Secret Service car that trailed the limousine partially blocked his view. Later, in a letter to Chief Justice Earl Warren, Yarborough, who had grown up with firearms, said that after the second shot he could smell gunpowder from overhead "very strongly and the rancid smell . . . stayed in our nostrils for minutes as we raced toward Parkland Hospital." [45]

Yarborough's opponents allowed him little time to grieve and mourn the slain president. A tough reelection campaign lay ahead in 1964. Governor Connally, recuperating from his near-fatal wounds, directed his conservative allies to find a candidate capable of unseating the progressive Yarborough. Much to Connally's chagrin, President Johnson distanced himself from any such effort, apparently fearing that a bitter primary battle might help the Republicans capture the seat in the general election. After all, the Republicans already held the other Senate seat from Texas. Conservative John Tower had replaced LBJ in 1961, and the prospect of a further embarrassing setback in his home state was too bitter for Johnson to accept. Besides, the president faced his own election fight and was grimly determined to carry Texas in a big way. To him, party harmony in the Lone Star State was not only a practical concern; it was a matter of pride. So when ultraconservative Dallas radio executive Gordon McLendon announced his challenge to Yarborough in the Democratic primary, Johnson made a point of endorsing the senator. During the course of the campaign, McLendon, known as "the Scotsman," leveled outrageous charges against Yarborough, falsely accusing him of accepting a bribe from the scandal-tainted West Texas promoter Billie Sol Estes. Yarborough requested Attorney General Robert Kennedy's assistance. When the FBI launched an investigation, key witnesses recanted their charges. Although he was cleared of any misdeeds, the Estes story would haunt Yarborough for years. Despite the fact that McLendon had a heavy campaign war chest and influential friends such as actor John Wayne, who flew to Texas to campaign for the millionaire broadcaster, the senator handily won the party's renomination. [46]

The general election fight was just as acrimonious. The Republican candidate, a Houston oilman and political upstart named George Bush, tried to depict the senator as a "liberal" who was "out of step" with Texans. Bush's television ads depicted Yarborough as an "extremist" and a "left-wing demagogue." The challenger also gained behind-the-scenes help from Governor Connally and the state Democratic Party hierarchy. Bush ran a well-financed but awkward campaign; as it turned out, he was the one who was out of step. Yarborough effectively characterized his opponent as a "Carpetbagger," a Yankee who had come to Texas to make his fortune in the oil business. The fact that Bush's father, former senator Prescott Bush of Connecticut, came to Texas to campaign for George only reinforced this perception. Bush's endorsement by the right-wing John Birch Society and his identification with Republican presidential nominee Barry Goldwater added fuel to Yarborough's claim that *his* opponent was an "extremist." In November, Yarborough's two-fisted style—and LBJ's landslide victory—sent Bush down to defeat.[47]

Perhaps the supreme irony of Yarborough's career remains the fact that, while he stood tall as one of the most productive members of Congress between 1963 and 1970, it is President Johnson who has received the acclaim for most of his efforts. By 1964 the two men had apparently made their peace—or at least an uneasy truce. "Once he got to be president," Yarborough observed of LBJ, "he finally got too busy to . . . [bother] with me. . . . He was better than having a reactionary president who wouldn't sign progressive legislation."[48]

Of all the progressive legislation passed by the Eighty-eighth Congress, none was more significant than the Civil Rights Act of 1964. Sweeping and even revolutionary in scope, the historic measure prohibited racial discrimination in employment, education, public accommodations, and voter registration. The omnibus law also authorized the attorney general of the United States to initiate suits on behalf of victims of racial discrimination. Fittingly, on June 19, 1964, on the ninety-ninth anniversary of the emancipation of the slaves in Texas, only one senator from the South rose to vote in favor of the bill. He was a Texan, a grandson of Confederate soldiers. His name was Ralph Yarborough.[49]

Oddly enough, President Johnson, ever the consummate politician, came to realize that one of his most dependable votes in the Senate was the fellow Texan whom he had once considered an adversary rather than an ally. During the next four years, Yarborough was not only present to vote for every initiative of Johnson's Great Society program, he emerged as one of its major architects in the Senate. He championed the Voting Rights Act of 1965, which empowered the attorney general to appoint federal examiners to supervise voter registration in states where such methods as literacy tests were still employed to exclude minorities. In so doing, he was one of only three southerners in the Senate to support this watershed measure. As a ranking member of both the Labor and Public Welfare Committee and the Commerce Committee, he helped frame and shepherd through the Congress what is generally known as the War on Poverty: the Job Corps, a manpower retraining initiative; VISTA (Volunteers in Service to America), a "domestic peace corps" to assist the poor; the Head

Start program for disadvantaged preschoolers, a bill Yarborough coauthored and sponsored; the Housing and Urban Development Act of 1965, which created HUD (the Department of Housing and Urban Development), and other urban renewal programs such as the so-called Model Cities Act of 1966, which appropriated $1.2 billion to be spent in slum areas to improve the quality of life in the inner cities; the creation of the Office of Economic Opportunity; an increase in the minimum wage standard, and an expansion of existing minimum wage legislation to include more than 8 million additional workers, most of them employees in restaurants, hotels, hospitals, laundries, and retail stores.[50]

But it was in the areas of education and health care that Yarborough made his greatest contributions. He sponsored the landmark Elementary and Secondary Education Act of 1965, which appropriated over $1 billion for textbooks, library materials, and other learning resources. After an eight-year struggle, he passed his Cold War GI Bill, to provide benefits for more than 8 million veterans of the Korean, Vietnam, and Cold War eras. He helped to draft and pass the Higher Education Act of 1965, which expanded federal student loans and scholarships to those in need. No one in Congress did more to lay the foundation for federal aid to both public and higher education. Yarborough authored and was the moving force behind the Bilingual Education Act, which provided funds for millions of non-English-speaking children to increase their fluency in English. Not surprisingly, therefore, one of Yarborough's Senate colleagues once labeled him "Mr. Education."[51]

Yarborough might also have earned the title "Mr. Health Care." He avidly supported the legislation creating Medicare for the aged and Medicaid for the indigent. And he helped press these monumental medical assistance programs to passage in the Senate in 1965. Clearly, though, his greatest personal triumph came with the passage of his last major act as a legislator—the watershed National Cancer Act, introduced by Senator Yarborough in December 1970 and signed into law one year later. In short, the program mobilized the medical science community in the United States for a war on cancer. No one, not even the bill's author, could even begin to estimate how many lives would be saved as a result of the research made possible by this historic commitment.[52]

Yarborough also helped draft and sponsor the legislation known as the Occupational Safety and Health Act of 1970, which created the federal regulatory agency known as OSHA. The measure was a landmark in the long struggle for better and safer working conditions in America. By any measure Yarborough must also be remembered as one of the leading environmentalist legislators of his generation. His vision of creating a national Youth Conservation Corps, modeled after the Civilian Conservation Corps of the 1930s, never became a reality. But he succeeded in creating three natural sanctuaries, all in his native Texas: the Padre Island National Seashore (1962), the 77,000-acre Guadalupe Mountains National Park (1966), and the 85,000-acre Big Thicket National Preserve (1971). He labored long for the enactment of clean air and clean water legislation. He coauthored and sponsored the Endangered Species Act of 1969, which was designed to halt the market for rare and exotic animals and to provide for greater protection of wildlife threatened with extinction.[53]

By 1970, liberal leaders like Yarborough were themselves becoming an endangered species. With the election of the Republican Richard Nixon as president in 1968, Cold War liberalism was in decline. The reforms of the 1960s had run their course. Both in Texas and across the country, opposition arose to proposed gun-control legislation, to court-ordered school busing, and to the controversial court ban on school prayer—all boding ill for progressives who had preferred to wage war on poverty, hunger, disease, and ignorance.

Ever since August 1964, when Congress approved the Gulf of Tonkin Resolution, giving LBJ a blank check to escalate America's commitment to the Southeast Asian conflict, Yarborough had expressed grave doubts about his country's policies in Vietnam but withheld public criticism during the Johnson administration. His quiet opposition to the war continued to grow as Vietnam replaced the Great Society as the administration's number one priority. In March 1968 Yarborough joined forces with those who were demanding an end to it—when President Johnson announced he would not seek reelection. It was this courageous stand, alongside such "doves" as Senator Eugene McCarthy of Minnesota and Senator George McGovern of South Dakota, that made Yarborough increasingly more unpopular with "hawks" back home in the Lone Star State. Yarborough supported Robert Kennedy for the Democratic presidential nomination until he was assassinated on June 5, 1968. He then backed McCarthy and finally united behind Hubert Humphrey after the tumultuous 1968 Democratic convention in Chicago. Yarborough and Congressman Jim Wright cochaired Humphrey's Texas campaign as many conservative Texas Democrats joined Allan Shivers in a Democrats-for-Nixon movement. Humphrey narrowly edged Nixon in Texas as third-party candidate George Wallace drew a sizable popular vote.[54]

Conservatives in the Texas Democratic Party were now more convinced than ever that Yarborough could be beaten. Once again former governor Connally encouraged a strong primary challenge to Yarborough's hold on the Senate seat. This time the challenger would be Houston entrepreneur and longtime Johnson and Connally ally Lloyd M. Bentsen Jr. Bentsen waged a brutally effective campaign against the incumbent. The 1970 Democratic primary was the toughest battle of Yarborough's career and the most disappointing defeat of all. Yarborough's opposition to the Vietnam War and his "anti-southern" votes on civil rights were exploited to damage his image with conservative Texans. Furthermore, many of his old campaign supporters either had passed away or were distracted by other races as many considered the "real campaign" to be in the fall in the anticipated rematch with George Bush.[55]

But that is another story. Perhaps the greatest compliment ever paid to Ralph Yarborough came from a longtime critic who observed that when the senator returned to private life in 1971, he went home to his modest Austin residence without a personal fortune. "He's got to be the dumbest guy we ever sent to Washington," an Austin banker once snarled. "He spent thirteen years up there and didn't make a dime." After all that time of serving the people, he must have had "holes in his pockets," another opponent joked.[56]

It is true. Ralph Yarborough never made much money while in the service of the people. What he made was a difference in the lives of millions of Americans. That is his legacy. Maybe his friend, the famed folklorist J. Frank Dobie, said it best when he maintained that "the only gain he has ever sought . . . has been public gain. He does not try to milk the public for private profit. I salute him for his civilized values, for his sense of justice, for his enlightened intellect, for his decency as a human being, and for his integrity." In the final analysis, therefore, what friends and foes alike remembered most about Ralph Yarborough were his abiding honesty, his unflinching faith in his principles, and his guiding sense of humanity.[57]

As for his longtime feud with Lyndon Johnson, Yarborough acknowledged that the rivalry shall always remain the stuff of Texas legends. In an interview, he summarized his feelings toward LBJ: "I was never a part of his team, and didn't want to be. Even after he became president, Johnson tried to take credit for my work. . . . He was a horse trader, the shrewdest politician I've ever seen operate." Then the senator confessed, "I didn't hate him, but I sure had reservations." Johnson admitted that "Senator Yarborough and I had our differences. But they were differences between two rather strong-minded men." Yet, as Yarborough looked back, he concluded that "it's not the personalities that matter, but what we did and didn't do in our moment on life's stage." Surely, at times it almost seemed as if Texas was not big enough for both Ralph and Lyndon. But thankfully the arena of American politics was.[58]

While millions of Americans remember the Great Society programs of the 1960s as a monument to LBJ (although conservatives consider it a crumbling monument), few realize that the shock troops of the War on Poverty and the fight for civil rights were the many members of Congress who drafted and supported and passed the watershed legislation of those years, and that a Texan named Ralph Yarborough stood on the front lines of those battles for social justice and equal economic opportunity. "My programs were eighty percent of his Great Society," Yarborough recollected. "[Johnson] admitted that to me once."[59]

Yarborough has continued to remain in the long shadow of Lyndon Johnson, but then so have other leaders of his generation. Even today most Texans remember Yarborough simply as Texas's other senator. All too quickly they have forgotten his towering accomplishments, forgotten that he was fighting to improve this "Great Society" before President Johnson even spoke in those terms. Perhaps in this age of cynicism when Americans perceive that too many politicians spend their entire careers trying merely to hold on to office, doing little more than extending their personal influence, exercising patronage, and passing pork-barrel legislation, they should remember that public service is a noble calling. Ralph Yarborough's life and works attest to that. For the only power that he ever really cared about was the power of the people.

After leaving the Senate the restive and indefatigable Yarborough devoted the remaining years of his life to public issues that were his passion: protecting the environment, defending civil rights, and promoting economic justice for the poor and powerless. He died on January 27, 1996, at the age of ninety-two. Fittingly, he is buried in the State Cemetery in Austin.

But his legacy as the "People's Senator" lives on. To this day liberals in the Lone Star State still lament the senator's bitter defeat in 1970. They remember well that, not so long ago, there was a Texan in the United States Senate who was a man of the people. And they long for the day when they, or maybe their children, might look upon his like again.

BARBARA JORDAN

Fig. 9.1. Barbara Jordan became the first African American woman elected to Congress from a former Confederate state. She gained national prominence as a member of the House Judiciary Committee during the Watergate hearings. Prints and Photographs Collection, Center for American History, UT-Austin (CN 02268).

BARBARA JORDAN

BY VISTA MCCROSKEY

On July 25, 1974, Representative Barbara Jordan (D-Tex.) addressed the House Judiciary Committee. Before a room filled with reporters and colleagues, she extolled the ideals of a democratic government and examined the impeachment process in a historical context. Enthusiastically, she asserted that President Richard M. Nixon should be impeached; however, such action would not—and could not—destroy all that Americans held dear. One document existed to prevent such a tragedy. "My faith in the Constitution is whole. It is complete. It is total," she declared in clear, mellifluous tones. And others agreed. With this oration, hastily completed but confidently delivered, the young congresswoman earned the respect of a nation. The moment had been long in coming.[1]

Barbara Charline Jordan was born in Houston, Texas, on February 26, 1936, the third child and youngest daughter of Ben and Arlyne Patten Jordan. Although poor in material goods, the Jordans were rich in loving spirit. The brick home in the city's Fifth Ward housed a seven-member family that included paternal grandfather Charles Jordan and his second wife, step-grandmother Alice, or "Gar." Everyone managed fairly well, though Barbara remembered that, because of crowding, "things got a little sticky" sometimes. All residents shared one bathroom, and the children slept together on a foldout bed until Ben Jordan added a third bedroom. While her husband was sometimes inordinately frugal, Arlyne Jordan worked hard to ensure her daughters a proper image in manner and dress, scrimping and saving to coordinate outfits for her children. Even during difficult times, their home was always filled with the smells of simple foods—greens, cornbread, cobblers, pies—and the sound of gospel music.[2]

Indeed, all things religious were an integral part of life as a Jordan. Grandfather Charles served as chairman of the board of trustees at Good Hope Missionary Baptist Church and was thus responsible for opening each Sunday meeting with a fifteen-minute prayer. Barbara's maternal grandmother, Martha Patten, was a lifelong member of the congregation, and her parents had met there. As youngsters, all three Jordan sisters— Rose Mary, Bennie, and Barbara—joined Good Hope and belonged to the Baptist Young People's Union. In 1947, after their father announced that

"God had called him" to preach, the family briefly worshiped at his first church, Greater Pleasant Hill (in Houston), before returning to Good Hope when he became an itinerant minister.[3]

While maternal grandfather John Ed Patten did not attend church, he too was a deeply religious man. Once a preacher himself, he had left the church for reasons unknown to his descendants. But on Sunday evenings he assumed the role of teacher, reading and interpreting his favorite sayings from the Bible for young Barbara. In her autobiography, *Barbara Jordan: A Self-Portrait,* she noted that "Grandfather Patten" taught her more about "Jesus and God [than did other ministers and teachers] . . . because he communicated in a language I could understand."[4]

John Ed Patten also imparted a legacy of hardship and struggle. A white man had killed his grandfather, and a brother, Steve, had died from wounds received in a skirmish over a horse. Patten's father had moved to Washington, D.C., where he fulfilled his dream of becoming a lawyer. Afterward, his mother had remarried and moved her sons from their native Evergreen into Houston's Fourth Ward, the "Negro district." There young John Ed married Martha Ellen Fletcher and fathered two daughters, Arlyne and Johnnie, and a son, Ed. To support his wife and young children, he became a small businessman, opening a candy store.[5]

But in the summer of 1918, unforeseen events once again shattered Patten's world. In pursuit of an after-hours thief, he clashed with a white law-enforcement officer who was unidentifiable in the darkness. In the resulting chaos, he mistakenly fired at the policeman, who, in turn, shot him—a "nigger" with a gun—through the hand. Accused of assault with intent to murder, Patten sat through the formality of a trial in which he was railroaded by incompetent counsel and an all-white jury. While serving ten years in prison at Huntsville, he hired a new lawyer who tried every possible appeal, all for naught. Finally, in 1925, Governor Miriam A. "Ma" Ferguson pardoned him, along with many others, because of prison overcrowding. He went home, where his baby son had died, and started a junk business, but he no longer felt "respectable." Realizing that he had lost his chance to escape the restrictions of ghetto life, he pinned all hope first on Arlyne, who, to his disgust, chose marriage, and later on his favorite granddaughter, Barbara.[6]

Jordan's childhood was much like that of other children in the Fifth Ward, though she admitted that a sense of individuality and independence had manifested within her at an early age. Her grandfather Patten played a large role in such development, fulfilling her every wish almost from the very beginning. At one time she had three bicycles and a pair of diamond earrings—all gifts from him. Such riches certainly distinguished her from both playmates and siblings. More important, Patten gave young Barbara a sense of self-worth, urging that she choose an exciting career over endless hours of housework. "You don't have to be like those others," he would say. "You just trot your own horse and don't get into the same rut as everyone else." Such advice also led to a minor rebellion against her overly strict father—occasional back talk and general "high-handedness." And while she indeed wished to be different, her sheltered family existence provided little or no exposure to alternative role models.[7]

So young Barbara, somewhat awkward and unsophisticated, struggled to fit in with her peers, especially at Phillis Wheatley High School. She and sister Bennie were particularly close during these years, belonging to the same social crowd. Together they threw slumber parties, attended football games, sang in the All Girls' Choir, and secretly spent occasional Friday nights at the Hester House canteen. They even sang gospel music—first with Rose Mary—as the Jordan Sisters. Both girls, along with some classmates, dreamed of their college days ahead, inspired by Rose Mary's success at Prairie View.[8]

At Phillis Wheatley High, Barbara also discovered a gift for oratory. Her speaking abilities should have come as no surprise; training had begun early in a family that greatly valued education. John Ed Patten had passed along stories of his father, the Washington lawyer, and a cousin who had become the first black woman physician in Houston. During their Sunday lessons, he also read to Barbara from a pronouncing dictionary, just as he had encouraged his daughter to polish her considerable vocal talents. Arlyne Jordan had been a popular orator at the Good Hope Church; in fact, one member noted that when she addressed the congregation "you knew you were well taken care of." Ben Jordan not only was an eloquent minister, as was his father; he also had attended Tuskegee Institute and stressed the importance of a good education to his daughters. Memorization came easily to Barbara because she had recited verses and hymns in church and at home. Even in singing lessons, her aunt, Mamie Reed Lee, had stressed diction.[9]

So, while still in high school, young Barbara Jordan found that her voice and sense of independence could serve her well. As a sophomore she became particularly involved in such organizations as the debate club and the honor society. In 1952, after Edith Sampson, a black female attorney and later judge, visited the school, Barbara declared her intention to become a lawyer, even though most of her friends planned to be teachers or housewives. Because of her activities, a national black sorority chose Jordan as "Girl of the Year." That same year, she also began to win state elocution competitions. Her greatest victory was the Ushers Oratorical Contest. She won first prize at Waco with her speech on the importance of higher education, then proceeded to the national meeting at Chicago. Finally, aboard a train headed north, this sheltered girl had a glimpse of what lay beyond the Fifth Ward. The experience was thrilling. Once again, she carried home the top honor, declaring in her yearbook that the trip had been "Wonderful, Enjoyable, Exciting, Adventurous, Adorable, Unforgettable, Rapturous—it was just the best doggone trip I have ever had."[10]

Even with the successes and the recognition that she was "outstanding or different," life within the segregated high school environment proved frustrating. Jordan began to realize that some of her teachers were "colorstruck," favoring the lighter-skinned students over others. These "half-white kids" more easily obtained certain positions. Young Barbara, well aware of this discrimination, accepted that certain avenues would be closed because she was, indeed, very dark. When a dean requested that she compete for attendant to "Miss Wheatley," a student symbolizing the spirit of the institution, she replied, "Miss Cunningham, I am not the right light color." Instead she turned to areas, such as debate, where brown schoolmates did not necessarily have the advantage over black ones. But Jordan would not forget; she carried the memory of that early prejudice with her into college and beyond.[11]

In the spring of 1952 Jordan graduated with honors from Phillis Wheatley. She had chosen Texas Southern University over Prairie View in order to remain in Houston—"I didn't want that view of the prairie." Although the segregated school was, in many ways, a reassuring extension of the black high school world, Jordan's shortcomings as a student soon became apparent. Sister Bennie, already accustomed to campus life, introduced her younger sibling to its many joys, but library visits and study groups were not on their agenda. Despite their father's protests, the two devoted the majority of their time to socializing with sorority sisters (Delta Sigma Theta), drinking beer at the Groovy Grill, and driving around with friends. Jordan attempted to become involved in student government—as president, no less—only to find that first-year students were ineligible. She turned again, and with some confidence, to debate, but found herself in a new, subordinate role. The coach, Dr. Tom Freeman, was impressed with her ability to project, but noted that "she was not good at thinking"; therefore, he "put her on . . . presentation, letting the boys do the refutation until she got the hang of it."[12]

And get "the hang of it" Jordan did, striving to earn acceptance as the first woman on the debate team. Because Coach Freeman had instigated a policy of never taking females along on trips to contests, she strove to become less feminine. Her style became more businesslike, wearing sensible jackets, tightly buttoned blouses, and flat-heeled shoes. Twenty additional pounds on an already large frame aided in her goal, as did much hard work. As a childhood friend recalled, "She was not the most attractive one [of us], but we always respected her ability." A woman who seemed less frivolous could be considered "one of the boys," and Jordan joined Freeman and his troupe on the road.[13]

Traveling in Texas and neighboring states, Barbara, for the first time, faced the societal prejudices of a white world. Only black hotels would provide lodging for the young people. The "Colored" facilities at any establishment usually consisted of a single outhouse in back. A lack of available eateries dictated that they pack their own meals. Only in such places as Chicago, New York, and Boston were there brief respites from segregation. Even after the U.S. Supreme Court decision in *Brown* v. *Board of Education of Topeka* (1954), nothing changed. Noting that her own hometown was determined to ignore the ruling, Jordan awoke to the realization that "some black people could make it in this white man's world, and that those who could had to" in order to "push integration along in a private way."[14]

As a college student, Jordan had become aware of the role to which society might relegate her and deemed it unacceptable. Instead, she would be one of the lucky few who "could make it." More determined than ever, she excelled in her debates, leading Texas Southern University to victory at the Southern Forensic Conference in its first integrated meet. She and her colleagues also proved themselves against Northwestern University and the University of Australia. But the most memorable event, and the one that would change her life forever, was a visit from the Harvard team. Freeman's star pupils managed a tie with their Ivy League challengers, and Barbara came to the conclusion that to be the best lawyer required the finest education—the type found, she believed, only in Boston. Discouraged from applying to Harvard because Texas Southern lacked prestige, she instead tried Boston University, planning to get into Harvard for postgraduate work. She graduated magna cum laude from Texas Southern in 1956, with a B.A. in political science and history, and left for Massachusetts, knowing that her father could not afford to pay her fare home for any holidays.[15]

The next three years would be a continuous learning process. Jordan found that going to school north of the Mason-Dixon line brought little shelter from racism and sexism. Of six hundred freshmen entering Boston University Law School, she and Issie Shelton, also from Houston, were the only black women. While the white students were cordial, certain taboos still existed. In this new, integrated environment, Barbara socialized along accepted lines, inviting potential friends for coffee ("I learned that white people love to stop doing whatever they're doing and go have a cup of coffee") and acquiring the cultural literacy necessary to make herself "interesting." But, mindful of her image, she was careful not to interfere with their activities uninvited, to admit that she had less money than most, or to complain that Louise Bailey, "my very good friend" who lived in Hartford, did not ask her to visit over the Christmas holiday. Never encouraged to participate in other study groups, Jordan and several black classmates organized their own. She also managed to accept that professors would urge her to speak in class only on "Ladies Day." In the legal profession, as in many others, women "were just tolerated," she later recalled, not "considered really top drawer." [16]

Most disconcerting, however, was her lack of a strong academic background. Jordan became aware that a segregated educational system had done little to prepare her for the rigors of law school. No longer able to manage by simply "spouting off [or] . . . speechifying," she concluded that her "deprivation had been stark . . . I was doing sixteen years of remedial work in thinking." No one had challenged her words before; now, it seemed, everyone did. The information itself was not enough; professors expected her to apply that knowledge, to prove her points. While she worked hard to compensate, self-doubt brought a brief crisis at semester's end. Terrified that she might have failed an exam, Jordan fled to the comfort of a darkened movie theater, agonizing over how to tell her family of this embarrassment. But she passed, and the Jordans could be proud of her performance in Boston. [17]

Indeed, her victory at law school was the result of a joint effort. Ben Jordan paid his daughter's tuition and each summer sent a plane ticket so that she could spend her vacation at home. Rose Mary and Bennie supplied books and money for other expenses. They also shared her excitement when she graduated in 1959. Her father, famous for his frugality, purchased a new car "as long as a city block" and drove the family to Boston to see the ceremony. In so many ways, she truly had left home to go "farther away than anybody in my family had ever been." [18]

From 1959 to 1962 Barbara Jordan was in a transitional phase. Despite passing the Massachusetts bar, she abandoned plans to remain in Boston and returned to Houston, telling herself that "it makes more sense to go home where people will be interested in helping you." Back in her parents' home, she worked hard to master the Texas bar exam and then distributed cards at church: "BARBARA JORDAN—ATTORNEY AT LAW." But when clients did not pour into the family living room—her "office"—she needed something to fill her "free time." Politics could certainly do that.

So Jordan volunteered at Harris County Democratic headquarters and became active in the 1960 Kennedy-Johnson presidential campaign.[19]

In the political realm, Jordan soon became a remarkable success. In 1960 her role as a blockworker in Houston's forty predominantly black precincts helped inspire an unprecedented 80 percent voter turnout. On one occasion, she substituted for an absent speaker, thus revealing great oratorical talent, which in turn inspired supervisors to exploit that ability. She spoke before many groups, and speaking-engagement requests continued to come in even after the election. As a result, her name became increasingly familiar to black Houstonians.[20]

In 1961 Jordan opened a new office on Lyons Avenue and taught summer courses at Tuskegee. Still, nothing seemed as exciting as politics, so when friends insisted that she run in 1962 for state representative, place ten, she was enthusiastic, if not realistic, about her chances. At her first public appearance, when county Democrats presented all twelve candidates, she received a standing ovation for an address that supported welfare and a budget cleanup, "the textbook type of concerns." The only woman—and the only black—she nevertheless appeared to provide some competition for her conservative Democratic primary opponent, Willis Whatley. But when election results came in, they revealed that Jordan had not done well. Though eager, she was a novice; she needed white votes as well as continued support from the black community to accomplish her goals.[21]

A second attempt for the seat in the Texas House against Whatley in 1964 also failed. Despite receiving more votes than before, Jordan was now a "two-time loser" in the midst of a new personal crisis. She therefore had to determine if a possible future in politics was worth the present frustration. Friends and family urged her to marry, believing that a future in government was becoming increasingly less possible—too many things worked against her. Society remained firmly entrenched in the double standard, expecting a woman to value a husband and home life above all else. But Jordan chose politics; it "was the most important thing to me . . . I did not want anything to take away from the singleness of my focus at that time."[22]

For the next two years, she attempted to remain active in local government while simultaneously building a law practice on Lyons Avenue. She spent the days working as County Judge Bill Elliott's administrative assistant (the first black woman to hold that position) and the evenings at her own office. But this routine would change, as would the city. In 1965, as a result of President Johnson's civil rights legislation, Harris County went through a reapportionment process. The Eleventh State Senatorial District was created, comprising the Fifth Ward and the majority of Jordan's supporters. While 36 percent of the constituents were white, 48 percent were black and 16 percent were Hispanic. Jordan therefore resigned her position and declared her candidacy in the 1966 Democratic primary. Her concerns were those of the people—industrial safety, welfare programs, insurance rates, vocational education, low wages, and voter registration. Working out of her headquarters on Lyons Avenue, she labored harder and more diligently than she had on any previous campaign.[23]

Her opponent, too, was determined. Charlie Whitfield, who had already served four terms as a representative, fought for the Democratic Party endorsement and, when unsuccessful in receiving the support of the Harris County Democratic Executive Committee, attacked his competitor with a vengeance. He charged that Jordan was little more than a token "to satisfy a few." Unhappy with party leaders, he accused them of succumbing to pressure from the Harris County Council of Organizations, which had, he asserted, demanded that a candidate from the Eleventh Senatorial District be "a member of the Negro race." One flyer asked, "Shall we have a seat for a member of the NEGRO race or shall we consider other factors such as qualifications and experience?"[24]

Jordan presented herself as a native and pointed out that Whitfield was a "Carpetbagger," having moved into the area in order to seek the position. She declared to supporters, "Our time has come!" Indeed it had. The final count was 15,710 to 8,654—she defeated Whitfield by winning 64.5 percent of the vote. At the age of thirty, Jordan became the first black woman to serve in the Texas legislature and, along with Curtis M. Graves, one of the first blacks elected in the state since 1882. To the press she remarked, "It feels good to know that the people of the 11th senatorial District recognize a qualified candidate when one is presented to them." A telegram from Whitfield read, "Congratulations. You showed surprising strength in your race. At least it surprised me."[25]

In Austin, the Sixtieth Legislature (1967–1968) convened on January 10, 1967. Believing that voters appreciated her not making race or gender an issue, Jordan operated in much the same manner as she had on Dr. Freeman's debate team. She managed to fit in with the "good ol' boys." Gaining their trust was important; therefore, she decided to work within "the system," to be approachable and flexible. And she considered this time her "apprenticeship." Consequently, Jordan alienated no one, learning as much as possible, even from conservative opponents. She attended social functions, allowing colleagues to "see [her] first-hand" rather than be intimidated by "this great thing that had happened in Houston." A studied lack of femininity—she even seemed to approve of their "salty language," although she did not use such colorful terminology herself—made her seem "safe" in the white male–dominated Texas Legislature. Jordan later remembered: "I just wanted them to be comfortable and not to keep saying: 'Excuse me,' 'Pardon me.'" Final acceptance was assured when she became the first woman invited on Senator Charles Wilson's (D-Lufkin) yearly quail hunt.[26]

Her caution was confusing to some supporters, but she believed that such tactics were quietly opening doors—a partial victory was surely better than none at all. Indeed, her accomplishments did attract some attention. In February 1967, when President Johnson invited civil rights leaders to Washington to confer on fair-housing legislation, Jordan was among those summoned. Surprised, and a bit perplexed by her inclusion, she contributed little to the proceedings but received national exposure. Back in Austin, she had requested assignment to the Labor and Management Relations and State Affairs Committees. Lieutenant Governor Preston Smith eagerly agreed; he even made her vice chairman of Labor Relations and a member of the Legislative Council, which was responsible for drafting and researching bills.[27]

Her first speech on the floor of the State Senate was in opposition to a one-cent local-option city sales tax, a fight she took to the newspapers to no avail. She also introduced several pieces of legislation designed to aid her working-class constituents, doing battle for them in the legislature and through the media. Particularly important was a bill to fight discrimination in employment, S.B. 79, which Jordan labored mightily to see pass 30 to 1 in the Senate. As the Fair Employment Practices Act, it created the Fair Employment Practices Commission to prevent unfairness in employment "on account of race, color, religion, national origin, sex, or age of the individual." To reporters, and anyone else who would listen, Jordan championed the poor, condemning the lack of state support for the Aid to Families with Dependent Children program and charging that the system failed to "reach the really needy." With other liberals, she blocked a restrictive voter registration plan and cast her vote against Governor John Connally in budget debates. In addition, she continued to demand legislative action for civil rights in her still numerous speaking engagements.[28]

Other state senators praised her poise, decorum, and professionalism. "She got along from the start," noted one. Whether conservative or liberal, they trusted her judgment. No doubt, she was not what they had expected in the turbulent 1960s—neither radical nor angry. President Johnson later praised her by noting that "she goes out of her way to represent all racial groups." Lieutenant Governor Smith demonstrated his respect late in March 1967, when, in an unprecedented and symbolic gesture, he yielded his gavel (as president of the Texas Senate) to Jordan, allowing her to preside over debate. Although she served as "Madame President" for only twenty minutes, no other black woman in American history had been accorded such an honor. The legislative body also passed a resolution "praising her . . . conduct as a freshman senator, her speaking ability and her concern for others."[29]

In 1968, after one term, Jordan was thoroughly addicted to this new way of life and sought reelection. Her platform stressed familiar issues and programs. Still a reformer in spirit, she promised to work for better workers' compensation, industrial safety legislation, and air pollution regulations. In addition, she hoped to create a new state junior college on the north side of Harris County that would allow constituents easier access to a higher education. As always, she demonstrated major concern for the poverty-stricken, now demanding a state agency for human resources and development; such a body, she asserted, "would concentrate on moving people out of welfare and relief and into productivity."[30]

As an incumbent who understood the needs of her supporters, Jordan was again victorious, this time with a term of four years instead of two. As a consequence, she became even more outspoken—but never strident— "a big woman with a soft voice and firm opinions." John Connally definitely drew out the most severely negative response from the young senator. At the 1968 Democratic National Convention in Chicago, Jordan had refused to support him as a favorite-son candidate, angrily commenting, "Why, that son-of-a-bitch. How does he think he can be anyone's favorite anything?" Besides believing that he cared little for the poor or minorities, she would never forgive his reaction to the assassination of Dr. Martin Luther King Jr.: "Those who live by the sword die by the sword." She also candidly announced that at the national convention "there was definitely a need for the police to be present." During a speech to one women's organization, Jordan urged that its members "[d]emand action . . . now" to end poverty and discrimination. The men who were currently in charge, she asserted, were too concerned with possible Soviet activities to address the most important issues at home. Openly admitting to higher ambitions, she told reporters that, given the opportunity, she would seek national office.[31]

Her legislative actions for the 1969–1973 term also reflected a new determination. While she still worked well with colleagues, the "apprenticeship" was definitely over. Preston Smith had now moved into the governorship; former Speaker Ben Barnes had been elected lieutenant governor. Jordan respected both men and was happy to work with a chief executive who was "a friend and ally." Barnes greatly increased her responsibilities, handing down appointments to the Jurisprudence, Education, Finance, Environmental Matters, State Affairs, and Youth Affairs committees, along with six others. He also assigned her to serve as chair of the Labor and Management Relations Committee and vice chair of three others—Congressional, Judicial, and Legislative. Through these positions, she battled to meet her goals, including a minimum wage law for Texas (S.B. 121 would pass, establishing the first such wage in Texas at $1.25 an hour), permanent voter registration, improved workers' compensation, and urban improvements.[32]

As chair of Labor and Management Relations, Jordan was particularly effective in passing legislation to protect workers from loss of revenue due to injury or illness. In the Sixty-first Legislature (1969–1971), she introduced seven bills that contained the phrase "Workmen's Compensation." Of these, S.B. 64 was a major reform law, designed to raise weekly payments from $35 to $49, the first increase in twelve years. It also stipulated that survivors of those killed in work-related accidents would receive 360 weeks of support. Other pieces of legislation also revised existing regulations.[33]

Jordan was equally active in the Sixty-second Legislature (1971–1973). In her capacity as chair of the interim Urban Affairs Committee, she had spent much of the previous year traveling through the state, hearing citizens' complaints concerning mass transit, unemployment rates, and public housing. When the Senate convened again in January 1971, she utilized much of this information to introduce thirty-three bills and cosponsor three with Chet Brooks (D-Pasadena). In March she presented an extensive package of urban reforms, which included provisions to extend state "technical assistance to local governments in regulating the physical development of unincorporated areas," allow counties "to regulate subdivision development and construction standards in unincorporated areas," and create both a regulatory Urban Assistance Board and the Texas Housing Finance Corporation (THFC). Jordan fought hard to pass these measures, which she argued would "save money by avoiding duplications of many costly services but still allow local policy setting control." In addition, Texas would finally have an agency (THFC) "to spur housing development" and urban regions would receive long-overdue recognition.[34]

State Senator Jordan also became increasingly active in the fight for civil rights. In 1970 she had balked at Governor Smith's plan to appoint the current Railroad Commission chair and former lieutenant governor Ben Ramsey as head of the state Democratic Party convention. Without hesitation, Jordan guaranteed that she would resign as temporary secretary of the convention because of Ramsey's conservative record. Whether for this reason or others, Smith withdrew the proposal. During the 1971 session, as in the previous one, she had sponsored antidiscrimination legislation. S.B. 81 required that "contracting agencies of the State and county, city or other political subdivision . . . include nondiscrimination provisions in all directly or indirectly funded contracts." She also worked with the National Association for the Advancement of Colored People, thereby augmenting her reputation with African Americans throughout the country.[35]

This increasing participation in the fight for civil rights did not dampen the enthusiasm of Jordan's supporters; Jordan remained one of the most admired, trusted, and respected solons in Austin. On June 10, 1972, her colleagues, in order to illustrate their affection and high regard, made Jordan "Governor for a Day." Once again, she was a "first"—no other black in American history had served in such a capacity. The process for this recognition began on March 28, during a special session of the legislature, when Senate members unanimously elected her president pro tem of the Senate, another original honor for a black and a woman. Traditionally, the governor and lieutenant governor have left the state at the same time for twenty-four hours to allow the president pro tem to serve as the state's chief executive; both Smith and Barnes would do so eagerly. All agreed that June 10 should be the date, and the young senator proceeded to invite every citizen of the Eleventh District to the state capitol because, she later recalled, "I wanted it as a celebration for all of my friends." That morning, Judge Andrew Jefferson of Houston administered the oath of office. On the platform with the family stood the Good Hope Missionary Baptist Church minister, who delivered the invocation. Throughout the day, the Texas Southern University choir sang, and bands from Phillis Wheatley and Jack Yates High Schools performed. In her temporary office, the new governor accepted congratulations and signed proclamations in which she declared September " sickle-cell anemia control month" for the state, praised the city of Austin, and recognized the work of the Texas Commission for the Blind.[36]

The day, however, was touched by tragedy. After the ceremony on the chamber floor, an ambulance rushed her stricken father to an emergency room. The Reverend Benjamin M. Jordan died on June 11. The previous morning he had told reporters that he had traveled to Austin despite a heart problem because "I wanted to see THIS DAY." Even in the hospital, Barbara Jordan recalled, his face had beamed with "just the most wonderful smile imaginable." He had watched as his youngest child, "a poor black girl from Houston's poverty-bound Fifth Ward, made her way into the history books."[37]

But even before serving as governor for a day, Jordan was campaigning to excel further politically. The population growth reflected in the 1970 census had led to redistricting and a new congressional seat for downtown Houston. She therefore had decided to run for national office. Such an ambition, however, brought controversy and criticism. Aware of her plan, Lieutenant Governor Barnes had appointed her vice chair of the Redistricting Committee—and therein the problem developed. In the process of reapportionment, committee members removed some black communities from the Eleventh Senatorial District, destroying the black majority there. Many saw this action as disloyal, especially Representative Curtis Graves (D-Houston), who had hoped to replace Jordan. "She has sold us out," he declared, and some agreed. Others charged that "redneck" legislators had simply used the changes as an excuse to rid themselves of as much minority representation as possible. Either way, Graves was determined to become a state senator, and he held Jordan personally responsible for the controversial plan. Vociferous in his complaints, he went to the media, the Harris County Democrats, and finally the Texas Supreme Court, insisting that the changes be nullified. In testimony, Jordan denied collusion but acknowledged the difficulties of a minority candidate in the reconstructed Eleventh District.[38]

Early in 1972, after the Texas Supreme Court denied his suit, Graves declared for the new congressional office, but to little avail. The Harris County Democratic Party endorsed both Jordan and him, with the general belief that the senatorial district was a minor sacrifice for a U.S. representative. And while some liberals charged that Jordan had become a member of "the Establishment" when they had "expected more," nothing seemed to diminish her popularity. She swept through the primary with 80 percent of the vote. An important part of her support came from labor unions, which contributed generously, as well as blacks of her generation and older. Before the general election in November, she gained an endorsement from the *Houston Chronicle* and continued to attract generous campaign contributions. Increasing recognition from the party also aided her cause; election as a vice president on the state Democratic Executive Committee automatically guaranteed her a role in the party's national convention.[39]

The final coup, however, came in October 1972, during a fund-raiser at the Rice Hotel when former president Lyndon Johnson made a "surprise appearance" (Jordan had invited him). Having long admired Johnson—"my President"—for his stand on civil rights legislation and aid to the poor, she believed that he was "the one man who did more than any other person to get us started down the road for putting race behind us as a problem." Without his lead, she might never have been able to represent an Eleventh Senatorial District. Johnson now publicly declared that he supported her as a "woman of keen intellect and unusual legislative ability." Summarizing the feelings of his audience, he declared, "She is . . . a symbol proving that We Can Overcome. Wherever she goes she is going to be at the top. Wherever she goes all of us are going to be behind her." Texas newspapers and *The New York Times* printed a photograph of the two embracing, laughing—one white, one black. The nexus was established. In November she easily defeated Republican Paul Merritt with 80.6 percent of the vote and then moved on to Washington as Johnson's "protégé." [40]

As a novice representative of the Eighteenth Congressional District, Jordan was first concerned with securing the appropriate committee assignments. She had expressed a desire to be on the House Judiciary Committee or, as an alternative, the Committee on Government Operations. The Black Congressional Caucus urged that she request Armed Services. But Jordan believed that the black movement was undergoing a transformation, that the focus was moving from the streets into the stateroom. This change would mean that she could accomplish more for minorities if she could get a seat on the Judiciary Committee, which also dealt with civil rights legislation. To ensure this position, she once again turned to Johnson, explaining her ambitions in a letter to the former president. He then placed phone calls to a few well-connected individuals, including Wilber Mills, chairman of Ways and Means. "I've already acted on it," he reported to Jordan. "What you want is Judiciary. If you get the Judiciary Committee and one day someone beats hell out of you, you can be a judge." The assignment, of course, was hers. [41]

Next, Jordan worked assiduously to establish a good rapport with other members of the House of Representatives and was especially determined, she later commented, "to get in good with . . . colleagues from Texas." As the first black woman in Congress, she wanted—and needed—their support. Once again, her self-confidence, hard work, and friendly humor put others at ease. On January 6, 1973, she insisted that the Texas delegation stand with her at the swearing-in ceremony, and in her inaugural speech requested that the audience say "Hi, Mother," to Arlyne Jordan. That same day, she was late to a reception because a House Rules Committee meeting had delayed her arrival. In order to "work comfortably" and as an equal with the men, she became the first woman to attend the Texas Democratic delegation luncheon, which traditionally met each Wednesday. The Johnson connection was also an advantage. When he died early in 1973, she delivered a moving tribute on the floor of the House, declaring that "old men straightened their stooped backs because Lyndon Johnson lived; little children dared look forward to intellectual achievement[;] . . . black Americans became excited about a future of opportunity, hope, justice, and dignity." Her sincerity was evident when she concluded, "Lyndon Johnson was my political mentor and my friend. I loved him and I shall miss him." With these words, she established herself as heir to his ideology.[42]

During her first term, Jordan's position on the Judiciary Committee indeed proved to be most influential. In 1974 she and other members dealt with confirming Gerald Ford to replace Spiro Agnew as Nixon's vice president. But the investigation of the illegal actions perpetrated by the Nixon administration that became known as the Watergate scandal was their top priority. That same year, the House charged the Judiciary Committee with the awesome task of determining whether Nixon himself could be charged with "high crimes and misdemeanors." From her first days in Congress, Jordan had openly opposed the president (as she had once railed against Connally) for refusing to accept the legislative branch as a "co-equal." Now she was faced with the daunting duty of reviewing all evidence in the case against the president—"what had been said and . . . done in terms of specific acts and whether they constituted a violation of the law." For weeks the committee met in closed sessions, which was the usual procedure in dealing with matters of personal character. Once the members had perused all pertinent materials, Chairman Peter Rodino granted each of the thirty-five members fifteen minutes for opening remarks. Wary of partisanship charges, Jordan was reluctant to "go public" but confident in her opinion, having studied "everything . . . ever . . . written, said, or uttered about impeachment." Finally, on July 25, 1974, with only three hours before her presentation, she prepared her statement.[43]

The moments that followed brought the young congresswoman a hail of praise and more national recognition than ever before. The best of her intellectual and oratorical abilities came together. Her presence was impressive, her voice precise, her countenance grave and dignified. "'We the people'—it is a very eloquent beginning," she intoned. "But when the Constitution of the United States was completed . . . I was not included." She then shared with the audience her understanding of the Constitution, often through the words of James Madison or Woodrow Wilson. Impeachment would not destroy that great document, but the criminal acts of a president might. She refused to witness "the diminution, subversion and destruction" of the governmental compact that had, through its flexibility, brought her to this point in history. In this brief discourse on constitutional history, she truly affected people, influencing, representing, and reassuring them. Overwhelming approval poured into her office. The next day, billboards in Houston read: "THANK YOU, BARBARA JORDAN, FOR EXPLAINING THE CONSTITUTION TO US." Americans had a new champion. She had expressed their feelings in words few could muster.[44]

Jordan would continue to attract attention, even from the new administration. Almost immediately after Nixon resigned on August 8, 1974, President Ford invited her to accompany a congressional delegation to China. Whether recognizing a new political force or merely patronizing a potential enemy, he also included her in meetings with the congressional caucus and ceremonies honoring Woman's Equality Day. In December, after an easy reelection campaign, she became a member of the influential Policy and Steering Committee of the Democratic caucus, joining fellow Texans Jim Wright and Wright Patman. And in February 1975 Lieutenant Governor Bill Hobby of Texas presided over a ceremony that placed her portrait in the State Senate chamber.[45]

Amid the flurry of activities, Jordan continued her battles in Congress. Her first piece of legislation, in 1973, had been the "Jordan Amendment" to the Omnibus Crime Control and Safe Streets Act, denying funds to any law-enforcement agency that practiced discrimination. She also supported equal rights and declared herself prochoice on the abortion issue. In the Ninety-fourth Congress (1975–1977), she continued on the Judiciary Committee and also served on Government Operations and Steering and Policy.[46]

During this session, two goals became primary. In 1975 Jordan sponsored and helped enact into law H.R. 2384, which revoked the Miller-Tydings Act (1937) and the McGuire Act (1952). The older laws had allowed manufacturers to engage in "price-fixing" and thereby avoid competition. The new measure would save consumers approximately $2 billion a year. Next Jordan was determined to bring Texas fully under the jurisdiction of President Johnson's civil rights legislation. The 1965 Voting Rights Act significantly increased minority participation in elections throughout Texas and the rest of the nation. Resistance remained among many state and local governments that continued to restrict minority voting through gerrymandering, at-large districts, and other procedures that prevented newly registered black voters from effectively using the ballot. In 1973 the U.S. Supreme Court held certain legislative multimember districts unconstitutional, ruling that they systematically diluted the voting strength of minority citizens in Bexar County, Texas. In addition, Congress heard extensive testimony about voting discrimination that had been suffered by Hispanic American, Asian American, and Native American citizens. The 1975 amendments to the Voting Rights Act added protections from voting discrimination for minority-language citizens.

Jordan immediately encountered stiff opposition, especially from Mark White, the Texas secretary of state. Legislators had eagerly accepted her proposal for bilingual ballots, but the state sought protection through the federal court system. White and others argued that Texas did not meet a particular requirement—that 5 percent of voting-age citizens belong to a "single-language minority"—because the majority of the Hispanics in the state were illegal aliens denied the franchise. The U.S. Supreme Court disagreed with this assessment, and in August 1975 President Ford signed H.R. 3247, extending the provisions of the Voting Rights Act.[47]

That same year Jordan made a controversial decision involving her old nemesis John Connally. Most recently U.S. secretary of the treasury, Connally had been accused of involvement in the Nixon administration's crimes, under bribery charges in the "milk fund scandal." When Robert Strauss, chairman of the Democratic National Committee, approached Jordan about testifying as a Connally character witness, the response was understandably negative. But upon reflection, Jordan decided that her reaction had been too hasty.

Asking herself, "has [he] lied to you or been dishonest with you?" she could remember no such instance. Because he had ignored, maybe even avoided, her in the Texas Senate, she owed him nothing. Yet, in the end she concluded: "There was really no good reason why I shouldn't do it." After the testimony, Connally called her with personal thanks, and she reassured him by saying, "I wouldn't have done it if I didn't feel it was the right thing to do." But the action would haunt her. Once again critics charged that she valued "establishment" approval over any principled political ideology.[48]

On July 12, 1976, Jordan silenced detractors for the moment with an impressive appearance as a keynote speaker at the Democratic National Convention. This opportunity also came at Robert Strauss's behest, but she would share the limelight with another politician: John Glenn gave the first address. Then Jordan came to the podium. "The response was startling," she remembered, and, once again, her style and delivery mesmerized Americans. She reminded them that her participation in this event was "one additional bit of evidence that the American Dream need not forever be deferred." After expounding on the ideals of the Democratic Party, she closed with the words of Abraham Lincoln: "As I would not be a slave, so I would not be a master. This expresses my idea of democracy. Whatever differs from this . . . is no democracy." The crowd reaction was incredible, the applause deafening.[49]

As in 1974, Jordan seemed to have secured her future with a single speech. On numerous occasions during the next few days, she stated that she would not accept a vice presidential nomination: "It is not my turn." The offer did not come, but she had not expected it. Presidential candidate Jimmy Carter requested her endorsement, and she went on the campaign trail for him. In November 1976, after she easily won reelection over her Republican opponent, Sam Wright, supporters predicted for her a cabinet position, a judiciary appointment, or even a future speakership. Rumors abounded that Carter would place her on his cabinet. And opinion polls declared Barbara Jordan "the one woman in America who stands out as a national leader."[50]

When President-elect Carter summoned her to a private meeting, Jordan stated her convictions about a possible place in his administration. As a "national figure" and a lawyer, she wanted "to be head" of something directly involving jurisprudence—that, of course, meant attorney general. But he suggested solicitor general or a post with the United Nations, and when she refused to compromise, the situation became clear. She would stay in Congress, at least for the time being.[51]

Jordan returned to the House for what would be a final, busy term. She chose to focus primarily on the nation's economic problems; in public she received an honorary doctoral degree from Harvard University and delivered that institution's spring 1977 commencement address; privately she dealt with health problems—chronic knee pain because of damaged cartilage—and a new question of conscience. While preparing the Harvard address, she had begun to question her own effectiveness. Because she had become so well known and could obtain a forum through speaking engagements, politics no longer seemed the most effective tool for change. She began to feel that Congress was actually entangled in the "minutiae" of daily business. And for some time she had been aware that many colleagues were Hamiltonians who felt that their constituents were not fit to be involved in the political process. She thus decided to leave government—to the surprise of many—to pursue "the country's needs" at her own pace and in her own manner.[52]

After announcing this decision, Jordan returned to her home in Austin, where she accepted the LBJ Centennial Chair in National Policy at the University of Texas LBJ School of Public Affairs. In that capacity she shaped many young minds and effectively prepared her students for political careers. The effects of deteriorating health, compounded by a swimming accident in July 1988, led her to reduce speaking appearances (outside the classroom) to a bare minimum, but she continued to be influential. In 1991 Governor Ann Richards appointed her to a newly cre-

Fig. 9.2. Barbara Jordan enjoys a laugh with her friend, Texas insurance executive and University of Texas regent Bernard Rapoport. Rapoport (Bernard) Papers, Center for American History, UT-Austin (CN 10496).

ated ethics commission, and in 1994 Jordan served as chair of the United States Commission on Immigration Reform. That same year, President Clinton awarded her the Presidential Medal of Freedom, the highest civilian award in the country.[53]

Because of her accomplishments and ideals, she was showered with honors during her lifetime. Magazine readers have declared her "Woman of the Year in Politics," and one of the "Women Who Could Be President." The Women's National Democratic Club named her "Democratic Woman of the Year." In 1984 she received the Distinguished Alumnus Award of the American Association of State Colleges and Universities. That same year, the International Platform Association chose Jordan "Best Living Orator," and she became an original member of the Texas Women's Hall of Fame. Four years later, she won the National Conference of Christians and Jews' Charles Evans Hughes Gold Medal, and in 1989 became the first recipient of the Barbara Jordan Award, which the Hollywood Women's Political Committee established. She became a member of the National Women's Hall of Fame in 1990. The main post office in Houston and several schools throughout Texas bear her name, and she has been a *Time* magazine "Woman of the Year." In addition to these awards, she received more than twenty honorary doctoral degrees.

On December 30, 1995, Barbara Jordan accepted the Honorary Chair of Hope for Families, Inc., a business/ministry of the Good Hope Baptist Church. Hope for Families is dedicated to rebuilding the community by rebuilding families through innovative and creative programs designed to address the needs of the people of the greater Houston area. She was, however, too ill to actually serve. On January 17, 1996, she died of a combination of ailments—pneumonia, multiple sclerosis, and leukemia.[54]

Barbara Jordan is still remembered as the first lady of Texas politics. She fearlessly opened doors—for blacks and for women—allowing Texans and other Americans to hope for a more harmonious future. As a teacher, she continued to urge that all citizens work assiduously to ensure that no dream is denied, no ambition stifled, because of poverty or discrimination. Many listened. There could be no greater legacy.

JOHN TOWER

Fig. 10.1. John Tower, elected to the U.S. Senate in a special election in 1961, became the first Republican to hold a statewide position in Texas since Reconstruction. Prints and Photographs Collection, Center for American History, UT-Austin (CN 04043).

JOHN TOWER

BY GEORGE N. GREEN AND JOHN J. KUSHMA

*"When you're 5 feet 5, a preacher's kid and a Republican in
Texas, you can't take anything for granted."*

JOHN TOWER

John Tower often joked about his stature, introducing himself to campaign
audiences early in his political career with the stock greeting, "My name's
Tower, but I don't." In a state that has traditionally prided itself on big-
ness, especially among its political leaders, the diminutive John Tower
presented an improbable physical image, one that was only enhanced by
his slicked-back hair and Savile Row suits and English cigarettes that gave
him the look of a London dandy. His political career was as remarkable as
his appearance. John Tower was the first Republican U.S. senator since
Reconstruction to be elected from a former Confederate state. He was
among the architects of the Republican "Southern Strategy" in the 1960s,
which, while leading to that party's electoral success, turned the nation's
attention away from the problems and challenges of racial injustice. As
chairman of the Senate Armed Services Committee, John Tower provided
the ideological rationale for and then presided over the huge defense
spending increases of the first Reagan administration, which shaped both
foreign and domestic policies during the 1980s. Following his retirement
from the Senate, he was subsequently tapped by President Ronald Reagan
to serve as a negotiator at the Strategic Arms Reduction Talks and as chairman of the President's Special Review Board that investigated the Iran-
contra scandal. John Tower's political conservatism was not remarkable.
Many of the Texans who preceded him in Washington were conservatives,
albeit Democrats. Tower's amorous affairs with women, the bottle, and defense contractors were also unremarkable. When they were widely publicized during the Senate hearings on his nomination to become secretary
of defense, one of his supporters summed them up by simply concluding:
"He's a Texan, make no mistake, and he's no angel."[1] Personal indiscre-
tions had never stood in the way of Texans' political success, nor had they
been sufficient grounds to disqualify previous cabinet nominees. What
was remarkable was that questions about his character resulted in John

Tower becoming the first cabinet nominee of an incoming president to be rejected by the Senate.

John Goodwin Tower was born in Houston on September 25, 1925, the son and grandson of Methodist ministers. Growing up during the depression of the 1930s, he spent his childhood in various towns in East Texas in which his father preached. He enlisted in the navy and, after washing out of the aviation cadet program, spent three years as a self-described "deck ape" on an amphibious gunboat in the Pacific. Following his wartime service, he enrolled in Southwestern University in Georgetown, from which he graduated in 1948 with a B.A. in political science. He worked for a short time as a radio announcer and then sold insurance in Dallas before securing, with his father's intervention, a position on the political science faculty at Midwestern University in Wichita Falls in 1951. Tower continued his studies in political science, spending the 1952–1953 school year at the London School of Economics. The focus of Tower's attention was the British Conservative Party, whose study he viewed "as an opportunity to pursue my own academic and practical interest in the mechanics of building a broad-based political movement." [2] He subsequently made this subject the topic of his master's essay at Southern Methodist University, where he was awarded a master's in political science in 1953.

John Tower began not only to teach but also to practice politics in Wichita Falls. Although he began his political life at the age of thirteen as a Democrat, distributing handbills for Ralph Yarborough's race for attorney general, John Tower abandoned the Democratic Party between 1948 and 1951 and joined the Republicans.[3] He maintained that as a political scientist he believed in a two-party system with ideologically distinct parties. As a conservative, he found the Republican Party a more appropriate vehicle for his beliefs. His marriage in 1952 to Lou Bullington cemented his ties to the Republican Party. Orville Bullington, Lou's cousin, was a highly influential Wichita Falls Republican and former Republican gubernatorial candidate who served as the party's state chairman. He sponsored Tower's participation in party activities, and under his tutelage the young professor spent a decade working his way up the organizational ladder to a position of power in the state GOP. Although trounced in an election for a seat in the state legislature in 1954, Tower managed the Eisenhower campaign in his state senatorial district in 1956. Winning a place on the state Republican Executive Committee in 1956, Tower made important contacts and friends as he journeyed through Texas with state GOP chairman Thad Hutcheson. Tower subsequently chaired the party committee on education and research, and his smooth, articulate, and stylish rhetoric made him a featured party speaker.[4]

The Texas Republican Party that John Tower joined was a moribund organization that had offered no competition for the dominant state Democratic Party throughout the twentieth century. For example, in the six gubernatorial elections between 1940 and 1950, the Republican Party's candidate for governor averaged less than 10 percent of the popular vote. Lacking the ability to contest statewide offices and with only a few isolated pockets of voting strength, the party had degenerated into little more than a patronage machine. But winds of change that fanned the fires of racism would soon shake the structure of the dominant Democratic coalition. The strong civil rights platform adopted by the Democrats in 1948 led some Texas conservative Democrats to bolt to "Dixiecrat" presidential candidate Strom Thurmond. Others voted for Thomas E. Dewey, resulting in the state's highest Republican vote in a presidential election since 1928. Although the Democratic Party's hegemonic control of the state was not immediately threatened, race would ultimately become the issue that would lead to the resurgence of the Republican Party in Texas.

John Tower's conversion to Republican activist thus coincided with the emergence of race as an important political question in Texas. Although he claimed to have thrown off "deep-seated prejudices," Tower did admit to being profoundly influenced by his paternal grandfather, an "unreconstructed rebel." He was never known as a race-baiter, but by the 1950s all but the crudest segregationists had learned to substitute code words like states' rights, local control, and constitutional government. When Tower proclaimed at a state party gathering in 1952 that "We have got to remove the shadow of Thaddeus Stevens and Charles Sumner from the Republican Party. We have got to convince Texas people that the Democratic Party no longer serves their interests," it is unlikely that he was referring solely to the historical antisouthern animus of the Republican Party. His reference to the two most zealous antislavery senators of the party of Abraham Lincoln was purposeful and predictable.[5]

The Eisenhower movement also energized Texas Republicans. Eisenhower carried the state in both 1952 and 1956, the first Republican victories in presidential elections since 1928, when an antiwet and anti-Catholic backlash placed the state in Herbert Hoover's column. The "presidential Republicanism" that had its origins in discontent with the liberal New Deal and Fair Deal policies of the Roosevelt and Truman administrations did little initially for the state Republican organization. Conservative Democrats like Governor Allan Shivers, who endorsed Eisenhower's candidacy, operated independent organizations. The national Republican Party, cognizant of the need to secure Democratic votes, did little to help the state party. A majority of Eisenhower voters simply returned to their Democratic moorings in state and local contests. In the three gubernatorial elections from 1954 to 1958, the Republican candidate averaged only slightly more than 12 percent.

It was not surprising, then, that Thad Hutcheson and other party leaders declined to make a hopeless race against Lyndon Johnson in his re-election bid to the Senate in 1960. John Tower offered himself as the party's sacrificial lamb. The party's leadership agreed to endorse him, provided he "lost" his panama hat, giant cigar, and Vandyke goatee. When a news conference was held to announce the party's nominee, as old party hand Norman Newton recalled, "There was nobody there." Despite his inauspicious beginning, Tower campaigned tirelessly and effectively. He was able to tap the public resentment at how Johnson had contrived to change the state election laws to provide himself a safe return to the Senate in case the voters spurned the Kennedy-Johnson national ticket. Johnson was elected vice president and senator, but Tower captured over 41 percent of the ballots in the Senate race, losing to Johnson 1,307,000 to 927,000. It was a startling performance by a poorly funded, unknown college professor. The success of his initial race carried him through to the special election held the next year.[6]

Governor Price Daniel named Dallas millionaire Bill Blakley to fill Johnson's vacant Senate seat for the five months until a special election would be held. Blakley had briefly served in the Senate before, but he had proven to be a hapless campaigner in the 1958 Democratic primary. There were consequently plenty of challengers for the Senate seat, particularly when former governor Allan Shivers, who would have been favored to win, decided not to run. Texas law mandated that candidates in special elections for the U.S. Senate run together in a primary without party affiliation. If no candidate received a majority of the vote, the top two contenders would face each other in a runoff. This law had been passed by conservative Democrats who were anxious to prevent a repeat of the 1957 special election, when Ralph Yarborough was elected to the Senate with a plurality over divided conservative opposition. Lacking a mechanism to secure a single party nominee, literally scores of Democrats appeared on the primary ballot. In addition to Blakley there were four nonfrivolous candidates: Fort Worth congressman Jim Wright, San Antonio lawyer Maury Maverick Jr., San Antonio state senator Henry Gonzalez, and Attorney General Will Wilson. Wright and Wilson split the moderate vote while Maverick and Gonzalez divided the liberal vote. This allowed the conservative Bill Blakley, with 18.3 percent of the vote, to slip into second place behind Tower, with 31.5 percent of the vote, in the first primary. The five Democrats had made a shambles of their party's unity, which had been shaky for over a decade anyway. Even so, had the parties nominated candidates in the usual manner, with a party runoff, and had the respective winners then been identified by party affiliation on the special election ballot, it is doubtful that Tower could have beaten any of the likely winners: Wright, Wilson, or Maverick.[7]

In the face of the bitter Democratic division, all Tower needed to do was to avoid making any stupid mistakes. He campaigned around the clock, frequently accompanied by fellow conservative Arizona senator Barry Goldwater, who had stumped the state for Tower in 1960. Tower also covered his left flank and appealed to moderates by enlisting Connecticut senator Prescott Bush to campaign on his behalf. Bush's appearances and a warm endorsement from former president Eisenhower undermined the allegation that Tower was a right-wing kook who would be ineffective in the Senate. Tower desperately needed this backing, for only fourteen out of the approximately five hundred newspapers in the state supported him.[8]

The May 1961 runoff resulted in a remarkable 10,000-vote victory by Tower. He carried only seventy-one counties, but ran well among white-collar Anglo voters in the state's burgeoning metropolitan areas and especially among newcomers to the state. He was aided by a small turnout: only 886,000 Texans voted in the runoff, a decline of 40 percent from the previous November. While running strongly in traditional Republican areas, he ultimately owed his victory to Democrats who had split their votes for liberal and moderate Democrats in the primary.[9] In the absence of polling data, ecological regression provides an estimation of the behavior in the runoff election of those Democrats who had previously supported Gonzalez, Maverick, Wilson, and Wright.

Liberal and moderate Democrats had no incentive to vote for Blakley, who was every bit as conservative as Tower. Many were consequently willing to help defeat Blakley in order to drive conservative Democrats into the Republican Party and thus bring about a more responsible two-party system in Texas. They assumed Tower would be merely a one-term oddity who would be easily defeated in 1966. Therefore, an initial Tower victory would demonstrate to autocratic and high-handed conservative Democrats that the days of co-optation were over. A significant proportion of moderate and liberal Democrats either voted for Tower in the runoff or, in the vernacular of the day, "went fishing" on election day. Blakley might have staved off these defections and dropouts had he moved slightly to the left, but instead he pulled such stunts as using a dinner in Waco, in the Central Texas farm belt, as a platform to attack the relatively popular Democratic farm program.[10]

ESTIMATES OF VOTING BEHAVIOR OF LIBERAL AND MODERATE
DEMOCRATS IN THE 1961 SENATE RUNOFF ELECTION [11]

Candidate Supported in the First Primary Election	Vote in Runoff Election		
	% Voting for Tower	% Voting for Blakley	% Not Voting
Gonzalez	04	46	50
Maverick	22	70	08
Wilson	−06	79	27
Wright	08	62	30

Arriving in Washington as the new junior senator from Texas, Tower basked in his newfound celebrity status as the first Republican to be elected from the South in nearly ninety years. Although conventional wisdom recognized Tower's victory as a fluke (Richard Nixon labeled it a "pure accident"), conservative Republicans proclaimed his triumph as the initial breakthrough that would allow them to challenge the Democrats' dominance not only in the South but throughout the nation. Tower was feted at many party functions, and he spent more time being toasted and appearing on behalf of other Republican candidates than he did attending to his Senate duties. He soon acquired a reputation of being lazy and indifferent in the chamber and a playboy outside of it. It was not until March 1, 1962, that he introduced a series of bills and resolutions that identified his policy objectives. They represented little more than a statement of conservative Republican verities: the purpose of U.S. foreign policy was victory over communism; the budget should always be balanced, except in the case of war; farm price-supports should be abolished; state laws should be superior to federal laws on the same subject; all taxes should be reduced; the government should cease competing with private enterprise; and a labor antitrust law should be adopted. None of his proposals stood any chance of getting out of committee. His economic philosophy was classically conservative as well. "A market-regulated economy," he maintained, "preserves the democracy of the market place in which people, by the manner in which they spend their dollars, in effect determine what goods and services will be produced." Anticommunism and the free-market system were the twin pillars of his political philosophy. Tower fleshed out his political ideology in a short book published that year entitled *A Program for Conservatives*. Goldwater provided its introduction and many of its ideas. Tower's book reads like a high-brow version of Goldwater's more popular *Conscience of a Conservative*. Roger

Olien, historian of the Republican Party in modern Texas, concludes that the "two volumes seem more like two drafts of the same manuscript than like two separate works." [12]

From the time he entered the Senate, Tower was more interested in foreign policy than domestic issues. He was an unabashed and unapologetic cold warrior who viewed victory over communism as the principal goal of U.S. foreign policy. His zealous anticommunism often led him to make public statements that lacked the nuances and qualifications one would have expected from a professor of political science. In a 1961 interview he stated, "I don't know what price we would have to pay to initiate a nuclear preventive war. We could have cleaned the matter up nicely in 1948 and '49 when the Russians didn't have the bomb." In 1962 he denounced President Kennedy's Soviet policy as appeasement and dismissed discussion of disarmament as naive. A year later he opposed the bipartisan Nuclear Test Ban Treaty and branded it "a cruel deception." The next year, on a television broadcast sponsored by the White Citizens' Council of Jackson, Mississippi, Tower advocated a blockade and invasion of Cuba. When asked if these actions could touch off World War III, Tower replied, "I don't think so. I don't think that [the Soviet Union] would initiate the thermonuclear war that they know they cannot win over Cuba. . . . Of course [thermonuclear war] would be highly destructive to us, but ultimately we would rebuild; but we would be victors, and communism would have disappeared from the world." Victory over communism, he asserted throughout his political career, should be the United States' primary objective, and the expenditure of funds necessary to secure this victory took precedence over his commitment to balanced budgets. [13]

Very early in his Senate career Tower revealed himself as an implacable foe of communism. In the fall of 1961 Texas members of the extremist John Birch Society and other hyperconservatives learned that a handful of Yugoslav pilots were being trained by U.S. Air Force instructors at Perrin Field in Sherman, Texas. The National Indignation Convention was quickly formed in Dallas, and it sponsored fiery meetings that denounced the training of Communist pilots whom Americans would one day doubtless have to fight. Tower introduced a resolution in 1962 to prohibit all military aid to Communist countries and to impeach any government official found guilty of violating the resolution's provisions. The latter item did not survive, but the military prohibition passed and the pilot training abruptly ceased. Tower quickly joined Senators Goldwater and Thurmond as a champion of the far right, whose banner he was initially happy to carry. Tower's affiliation with extremist groups and neglect of his Senate duties suggested to many observers that he too had come to regard his

victory as a fluke and saw no realistic chance for his reelection. Ken Tow-
ery, who joined Tower's staff in 1963, convinced him that he had a chance
for a second term, and he helped to steer the senator away from parties and
toward committee meetings.[14]

Tower had indeed had good reason to question his chances for reelection. The incredible series of events that led to his victory in 1961—a low-
turnout special election with a nonpartisan ballot, a highly factionalized
Democratic opposition, and unlikely help from liberal and moderate Democrats—would not be repeated, so he would be running for reelection as
a Republican in a state that was still overwhelmingly Democratic. Moreover, his victory had jolted Texas Democrats into action, particularly Lyndon Johnson, whose control of the state had been threatened not only by
the surging Republicans but also by the restive liberal Democrats. Conservative Democrats recognized that they needed a strong gubernatorial
candidate in 1962, and they tapped heretofore unknown John Connally, a
Johnson protégé. The handsome and charismatic Connally triumphed
easily in the gubernatorial election, but not nearly as easily as previous
Democratic candidates.

Although the state was still safely Democratic, Texas Republicans had
reason for optimism. Tower's Senate victory had broken a psychological
barrier that had discouraged conservatives from joining the Republicans
if they wished to win political office in Texas. A spate of conservative
activists now found a congenial home in the GOP, and they carried their
enthusiasm to the grass roots. More important, the racial issue had once
again emerged as a lever for Republicans to use in order to pry conservative Democrats away from their traditional partisan roots. In 1962 white
backlash over the Kennedy administration's civil rights initiatives helped
the Republicans win two congressional seats in Texas and significantly increase their strength throughout the state. The source of the Republicans'
newfound votes was revealed in "resignation rallies," at which crowds of
white, conservative Democrats announced their conversion to the Republican cause. Democratic Party strength (a composite average of the popular vote for governor, U.S. senator, and U.S. representative) plummeted
from 82 percent in 1958 to 55 percent in 1962. Three special elections for
seats in the Texas House went to Republicans in 1963, bringing the GOP
total to 10 in that 150-member body. Tower's 1961 U.S. Senate victory and
the subsequent increase in Republicans' voting strength in Texas provided
the raw materials out of which the "Southern Strategy" began to develop.
The right wing of the Republican Party under the leadership of Tower's
mentor, Goldwater, would employ this strategy in 1964. The political
amorality of manipulating racial antagonisms for partisan advantage that

underlay the divisive "Southern Strategy" would provoke a bitter debate within the national GOP ranks, but there was no denying that the strategy had worked. The only recent Republican gains had come in the South, and it appeared that the Democrats' commitment to civil rights would make them vulnerable there in 1964. Texas became the heart of the Goldwater-for-president movement, and John Tower became the first Republican senator to endorse Goldwater's candidacy.[15]

President Kennedy's assassination on Texas soil and Lyndon Johnson's elevation to the presidency temporarily deflated Texas Republicans. All of the incumbent Republicans save one were defeated in 1964, the same year that Lyndon Johnson called for the passage of a basic civil rights law as a monument to the slain President Kennedy. Johnson was returned to the presidential office in an overwhelming victory over Goldwater. But the "Southern Strategy" did partially succeed. Five southern states deserted the "solid South" and awarded their electoral votes to Goldwater. The issue of race would continue to be the Republican Party's trump card in building up electoral strength in the southern states.[16]

John Tower's only mention of civil rights in his memoirs is a brief concession that he joined the filibuster and voted against the 1964 civil rights bill because he believed the provision guaranteeing equal access to public accommodations to be unconstitutional. He apologized for this vote in hindsight. However, he was much too modest about his civil rights record and the importance of racial issues in the growth of the Republican Party in Texas. Tower had long opposed integration. At the 1958 state Republican convention, Tower read to the assembly a party platform that denounced federal enforcement of desegregation laws and urged that a gradual solution in Texas be left to Texans themselves. As political scientist Chandler Davidson writes, "Given the popular mood in Texas at the time, such a policy would have been tantamount to the perpetuation of segregation indefinitely." Tower supported the Texas poll tax that disfranchised poor and minority voters until it was struck down by Congress and the Supreme Court. As a Nixon delegate to the 1960 Republican National Convention, Tower led a group of Texans and southerners who threatened to bolt to Goldwater after Nixon acceded to Nelson Rockefeller's progressive civil rights planks. Tower was subsequently credited with preventing the platform committee from writing all of Rockefeller's proposals into the platform. In 1961 he opposed making the Civil Rights Commission a permanent agency. Tower was the only Republican to join the southern Democrats' filibuster against the 1964 civil rights bill, which, he claimed in an eighty-seven page speech, could not be enforced without the establishment of a police state. Once again he was in the forefront of the 1964 platform battle to restore the "lily-white" GOP. The unabashed hostility of Goldwater's supporters toward civil rights shocked many moderate Republicans, who showed their displeasure by supporting the victorious Lyndon Johnson that year. Tower and Strom Thurmond of South Carolina were the only Republicans who tried to block the Voting Rights Act of 1965, and Tower subsequently opposed civil rights legislation in 1968 as well.[17]

A few days after the Republican election debacle of 1964, Tower stunned a private gathering of state party leaders by offering not to seek reelection in 1966 if they felt that another GOP candidate (presumably George Bush, who had just lost a Senate race to incumbent Ralph Yarborough) would have a better chance of holding the seat. The group declined Tower's offer and resolved to enhance his reelection chances by focusing the party's attention and resources on his senatorial campaign. The party leaders agreed to discourage other statewide candidates and to ignore local Republican candidates except those in winnable districts. This all-or-nothing strategy represented the abandonment of constructive party building, but the leaders believed it was better to hazard all on the retention of a Senate seat. Republican prospects did not look particularly bright, however, when the John Kraft organization, hired by Tower to conduct a poll of Texas voters in the summer of 1965, reported that only a third of Texans were conservative and that Tower's political ideology was viewed as controversial.[18]

Chastened by the poll's findings and recognizing the need to moderate his reactionary stands, Tower did attempt to position himself somewhat closer to mainstream Republican conservatism. He broke with the extremist John Birch Society, labeling it a liability to the conservative cause, and his supporters discouraged ultraconservatives from volunteering their services at party headquarters. Before the 1964 election, Tower would fly anywhere in the country in order to assail Lyndon Johnson, but afterward he never mentioned the president except to praise his staunch leadership against the Communists in Vietnam. In 1965 he voted for the Johnson administration's omnibus farm bill, his first affirmative vote on farm legislation. He suddenly saw fit to support federal aid to higher education and even voted for the administration's omnibus housing bill that contained a controversial rent-supplement section. Tower joined Ralph Yarborough in introducing a GI Bill for Vietnam veterans that would entitle them to educational and loan benefits similar to those that had been made available to veterans of previous wars. His gestures toward political moderation increased during the election year of 1966. Tower voted more money than President Johnson had asked to fund the school lunch program. Even more important to his reelection campaign than his suddenly more moderate voting record was Tower's 1965 assignment to the powerful Armed Services Committee. It was a traditional Texas bailiwick where Tower could find great merit in multibillion-dollar military procurement programs in which Texas had a sizable stake. Texas voters understood well the importance of the pork barrel. By 1966 Tower had positioned himself well within the mainstream of conservatism, and if he could disassociate himself from the reactionary label that had brought down the 1964 Republican presidential ticket, he had a fair shot at reelection. Asked early in 1966 if he would invite Barry Goldwater to campaign with him, Tower replied with a smile, "Barry who?" [19]

Most political pundits agreed that a strong moderate-to-conservative Democrat would be clearly favored against Tower in the 1966 Senate race. The state remained predominantly Democratic, and the expected higher voter turnout than in the 1961 special election would bring that Democratic majority to the polls. Governor John Connally would have had an easy race against Tower, but the Senate did not interest Connally. Had Congressman Jim Wright been able to sustain President Johnson's interest in his candidacy, which would have guaranteed him sufficient funding, he, too, probably could have defeated Tower. With Connally and Wright on the sidelines, the Democratic senatorial nomination fell to State Attorney General Waggoner Carr. Connally and Johnson quickly lined up almost all of the state Democratic leaders behind Carr, an impressive demonstration of party unity that did not bode well for Tower's chances. [20]

Carr, however, had no experience in the federal government, and he quickly proved himself an ineffective campaigner. He was no match for the eloquent Tower as a public speaker, and he was unable to state his positions clearly and concisely. Nevertheless, Tower recognized the need to expand his base of support beyond the normal Republican ranks in order to stand a chance of winning. He departed from traditional Republican campaign practices by organizing an outreach program to court the vote of Mexican Americans, especially in those areas in which they were employed on military installations. Tower campaigned actively in Hispanic areas traditionally ignored by Republicans and introduced a resolution to enlarge the Equal Employment Opportunity Commission by adding a Hispanic member. [21]

The liberal and labor voters had to be courted again. They regarded Carr as a reactionary, antilabor creature of the conservative Texas establishment and the segregationists, but even for the sake of a two-party Texas, it was difficult for them to support Tower with his right-wing voting record. They told themselves that Tower had little real influence in Washington, which was true at the time. The senator did not help himself with liberals with his "ceaseless warmongering" or on the occasion when, in opposition to a state minimum wage proposal of $1.25 per hour, he announced that, "eighty-five cents an hour is better than nothing." But a greater turning point for the labor-liberal-Hispanic defector vote came when Governor John Connally and Attorney General Carr intercepted the striking Valley Farm Workers' march on Austin. Demanding the proposed minimum wage and more equitable treatment, the largely Hispanic force was wearily plodding along near New Braunfels when Connally, Carr, and their entourage materialized in a cavalcade of Lincoln Continentals. The governor informed the marchers that no top officials would greet them in Austin on Labor Day, even if they were in town. Connally warned them that marches could get out of hand, and he adamantly rejected their plea that he call a special session of the legislature to pass a minimum wage law. Outrage toward this callousness dragged down Carr's minority, labor, and liberal support. Tower was also lucky that somehow the media allowed him, with his staunch segregationist record, to get away with attacking Carr for having attended a segregationist rally in 1957. Moreover, Carr—despite a slight gesture toward the war on poverty—was unwilling to select an issue or two that might convince liberals to vote for him. It was thus not surprising that Larry L. King, writing in the liberal *Texas Observer*, lambasted Carr as the candidate of the conservative Texas establishment and encouraged liberals to join him in proclaiming "Long Live (Ugh! Choke! Sigh!) John Tower." [22]

Tower trounced Carr 843,000 to 642,000, while half the electorate stayed at home. White-collar, urban voters were again the bulk of Tower's support: he captured all the urban counties with 10,000 or more votes except McLennan (Waco). Nearly half of Tower's votes came from Democrats and Independents. The liberal-labor backlash was particularly evident in Jefferson and Travis Counties, and Tower did very well with the Mexican American vote in El Paso and Bexar Counties. From the twenty-eight counties that were at least 40 percent Hispanic, Tower received 49 percent of the aggregate vote. While the labor-liberal-minority vote was crucial, so, of course, was Tower's ability to undercut Carr's appeal to conservatives. Tower came out forcefully against repeal of the right-to-work provision of Taft-Hartley and continued his hawkish position on the Vietnam War. Tower also benefited from a growing dissatisfaction with the Johnson administration over such issues as civil rights and inflation. And finally, since Connally was not being seriously challenged by the GOP gubernatorial candidate, a number of the governor's supporters were willing to vote Republican for the U.S. Senate. The party leaders' decision to gamble all on Tower proved to be a winning one. [23]

Safely reelected, Tower flew to California in December 1966 to share with Governor-elect Ronald Reagan his belief that Republican conservatives should preserve their faction's bargaining position through favorite-son candidacies until the party's presidential situation was clarified. Reagan concurred. A "Tower for President Committee" was organized in June 1967, though, as historian Jonathan Kolkey argues, Tower's "uninspiring personality" prevented it from being anything more than a convention tactic. While the loose coalition leaned philosophically toward Richard Nixon rather than Republican moderates, Tower was well aware that he would be a logical running mate for more moderate Republicans like Governor George Romney of Michigan or Senator Charles Percy of Illinois. As Nixon gained ground in the mid-1960s and the moderates faded away, Tower, Goldwater, Thurmond, and many hyperconservatives supported the conservative Nixon rather than one of their own, the charismatic Governor Reagan. They feared that Reagan would be as out of step with national opinion as Goldwater had been in 1964.[24]

The next phase of the GOP's "Southern Strategy" was hammered out at the Marriott Motor Hotel in Atlanta, Georgia, on May 31, 1968. Richard Nixon reached an understanding with Tower, Thurmond, and thirteen southern and border-state Republican Party chairmen. In return for their support on the first ballot at the upcoming Republican National Convention, Nixon promised to slow down the desegregation of the public schools, select a conservative as his running mate, continue hefty defense expenditures, and provide considerable patronage and appointments for southern Republicans and other conservatives. Tower's release of the Texas delegates pledged to him should have immediately put Nixon over the top for the nomination, but the strategy nearly failed because at the convention the southern delegates almost stampeded for Reagan. Tower, Goldwater, and Thurmond cajoled the southerners—including their largest single bloc, the Texans—into voting against Reagan.[25]

Tower had worked on behalf of Nixon's candidacy for years and had played a major role in devising the strategy that had led to his nomination, but Tower was all but ignored once Nixon was in the White House. During Richard Nixon's first few months as president, Tower, Thurmond, and a very few others bluntly told the president that he was going too far in the enforcement of the U.S. Supreme Court decision that ordered American schools to desegregate "with all deliberate speed." They "complained bitterly," Nixon remembered, and demanded the firing of Jerris Leonard, the assistant attorney general for civil rights. But Nixon retained Leonard and desegregation continued.[26] On another occasion the White House assured Tower that John Connally would not receive a major appointment. Nixon's surprise selection of Connally as secretary of the treasury in 1970,

Fig. 10.2. *John Tower and George Bush, shown during a 1970 campaign stop with President Richard Nixon and Paul Eggers (left), helped establish the modern Republican Party in Texas. Prints and Photographs Collection, Center for American History, UT-Austin (CN 08689).*

concealed from Tower until the last moment, shattered Tower's image as Nixon's favorite Texan and virtually reduced him to a "supernumerary." Tower apparently was not invited to either of Nixon's famous 1972 visits to Connally's ranch, and Tower even had trouble getting his photograph taken with the president in that campaign year.[27]

Tower was also stunned by Nixon's dramatic 1971 visit to China and the corresponding revolution in U.S. foreign policy. In a rare departure from Republican unity, Tower proclaimed that "[r]approchement with Red China at the expense of the Republic of China will be counterproductive. It may well predestine the Nixon Doctrine to utter failure . . . and force a withdrawal of our security line back to the West Coast."[28] Besides ignoring the strategic benefits of playing the "China card" during the Cold War with the Soviet Union, Tower's grasp of global strategy apparently could not comprehend a "two China" policy or the continued presence of American bases in the Pacific as part of U.S. security forces. Perhaps strategy had less to do with Tower's stance than his rumored dalliance with Anna Chennault, the brains behind the China Lobby. She was widely reported to be one of the "infidelities" to which Tower later confessed in his memoirs. His opposition to Nixon's China policy did not keep him from exercising his deft floor leadership skills as he artfully guided the administration's antiballistic missile package through the Democratic-controlled Senate in 1970 by votes of 50 to 50 (with Agnew casting the tie-breaking vote) and 51 to 49.[29]

Tower continued in the vanguard of the "white man's front" in the 1970s and 1980s. In 1972 the Senate passed a compromise bill strengthening federal laws banning racial and other discrimination in employment. Tower voted against it and against the National Voter Registration Act that same year. He also rejected the seven-year extension of the Voting Rights Act in 1975, which brought Texas under the law. The Texas GOP, which he controlled, persistently badgered minority voters in the days before an election by saturating minority neighborhoods with pamphlets or radio ads containing dire warnings of punishments for anyone committing voter fraud. Their "ballot security" funds offered hundreds of thousands of dollars in rewards for anyone exposing voting irregularities. Texas Republicans went on record in endorsing English as the official language and continually intimated that crime, poverty, and welfare programs were exclusively minority problems.[30]

John Connally's appointment as secretary of the treasury had been made essentially for the purpose of allowing the former governor to organize a "Democrats for Nixon" drive in 1972 that would permit the president to carry Texas. Nixon, having failed to carry Texas in 1968, was under no illusion that the state had become Republican territory. For the organization to be credible, it had to support all Democrats except their presidential candidate. Connally, while stumping for Nixon, was thus publicly committed to voting for Tower's Democratic Senate opponent. For the public record, Tower embraced Connally's appointment to the cabinet, but privately, as Ben Barnes concludes, Tower wanted "to see John Connally dropped off a bridge." Nixon was so obsessed with winning big and so fearful of losing the "presidential Republican" vote that he kept at arm's length from Tower, who, despite his two previous victories, was not considered a sure winner. Tower was eventually reduced to using bootleg film to provide a picture of himself in the company of the president during his 1972 Senate race.[31]

By the 1970s Tower had gravitated away from the Goldwaters and Thurmonds, the purist outsiders, and toward the Texas corporate and country-club elite. The Texas "country-club wing" of the Republican Party, primarily Dallas-based and decidedly pro-Nixon, wanted to avoid diverting money and effort away from Nixon's and Tower's reelection efforts. Their prospective gubernatorial candidate, Albert Fay, had agreed to wage a low-key campaign in 1972. This was the same top-of-the-ticket strategy that had worked for Tower six years earlier. But grassroots Republicans were no longer willing to write off their chances elsewhere on the ballot. Fay was upended in the Republican primary by Houston Reaganite Hank Grover, who came from the obstreperous, right-wing "Lions Club" of the party that was beginning to flex its muscles. Tower, resenting the challenge to his control of the party, did nothing to help Grover in his race and all but ignored him during the election campaign.[32]

In 1972 Tower was once again confronted with the results of a secret poll that showed him to be vulnerable. He was also faced with an able Democratic opponent in Dallas attorney Barefoot Sanders, a former state legislator who had served as an assistant attorney general and White House aide during the Johnson administration. Sanders was gravely handicapped by the absence of name identification and a lack of money. He had never run for statewide office in Texas, and his campaign war chest was less than half the size of Tower's. But Sanders was hurt most of all by the Democrats' presidential nominee, anti–Vietnam War liberal, George McGovern. Although Sanders endeavored to distance himself from McGovern, Tower's campaign continually linked the two. Sanders slashed at Tower's absenteeism and hyperconservative voting record, including his opposition to civil rights legislation and Medicare. Openly derisive toward Tower's claim to have sponsored nearly one thousand pieces of legislation, Sanders noted that Tower had shepherded nine minor bills through the Senate in his second term while simply adding his name as cosponsor to others. Sanders also castigated Tower for accepting speaking fees from banking interests while the Senate Banking Committee, on which Tower served, debated banking legislation. Accusing Sanders of distorting his record, Tower ignored Sanders's charges and instead focused his attacks on McGovern's radicalism, his opponent's friendship with the controversial former attorney general Ramsey Clark, and the volatile busing issue. Sanders opposed busing and differed with the national ticket on other questions of public policy, but Tower was able to tie Sanders to McGovern, who was decidedly unpopular in the state. One historian has argued that "George McGovern cost the Texas Democrats a United States Senate seat" in 1972. Money was a crucial factor in Tower's success; he reported spending over $2.5 million, making his the most expensive nonpresidential campaign in the nation that year. Tower defeated Sanders rather easily by a popular vote of 1,823,000 to 1,512,000, but he ran a half million votes behind Richard Nixon in Texas. Tower received 54 percent of the vote in Texas's 27 most populous counties, and for the first time carried the countryside. The state's 175 rural counties gave Tower a bare majority of 51 percent. Although Texas Republicans had carried Nixon and Tower to victory, their candidate-centered campaigns probably cost Grover the governor's race. Grover's campaign was continually strapped for money, a problem he attributed to Tower and Nixon having milked all of the party's cash cows themselves. Tower and Grover had clashed at the state convention, and by the end of the campaign they were openly feuding. The growth of the state party was temporarily halted by this lack of unity. The subsequent revelations of the Watergate scandal also stymied the Republican Party's development in Texas as elsewhere.[33]

During the Nixon and Ford presidencies Tower moved into leadership roles in the national Republican Party and in the Senate. In 1970 he chaired the Senate GOP Campaign Committee, which distributed funds to senators facing reelection fights. (The maverick Republican senator Charles Goodell of New York was not provided any financial assistance by the committee.) Tower assumed the chairmanship of the Senate Republican Policy Committee in 1973, an office that required him to downplay his personal ideology in favor of party loyalty. So dogged was the formerly outspoken Tower in toeing the White House line that in the eyes of many he came "perilously close to being a presidential errand boy."[34]

Tower rallied to Nixon's side during the congressional investigation into Watergate, and he was among the last Republican offficeholders to withdraw his support. In March 1974, he argued that a resignation, forced or voluntary, would do "great damage and violence to the institution of the presidency." He maintained this position until the bipartisan impeachment votes in the House Judiciary Committee on August 1. Tower's support, along with that of other bitter-end defenders, quickly waned in early August, but he did not publicly break with the president until the "smoking gun" recording was disclosed on August 5 and Nixon was on the verge of resignation.[35]

Tower loyally backed incumbent Gerald Ford over Ronald Reagan for the Republican presidential nomination in 1976. Although there were few substantive ideological differences between Tower and Reagan, Tower's country-club wing still feared that Reagan might drag the party into an election debacle just as Barry Goldwater had done in 1964. In his television ads on behalf of Ford during the Republican primary campaign, Tower called Reagan "shallow, misinformed, and . . . a careless saber rattler." His failure to support Reagan's candidacy in 1976 earned Tower the enduring animosity of some of Reagan's most vehement supporters. But country-club Republican fears about Reagan were unfounded. Texas was Reagan country, and the California governor smashed Ford (and Tower) in the state's primary. It was a resounding vote of no-confidence in Tower's party leadership, and the victorious Reaganites went so far as to deny the senator a seat in the Texas delegation to the national convention. Although stung by this personal affront, Tower continued to work for Ford's nomination. He was among the handful of top Republicans who were invited to advise Ford on the selection of a running mate, but his suggestion that the post go to John Connally was summarily rejected. Tower's weakened position in the state party became even more apparent when he surrendered the chairmanship of Ford's presidential campaign in Texas to Connally.[36]

Nevertheless, Tower was well positioned for his own reelection campaign. Although the Reagan-Grover faction was still rankled, Tower faced no serious Republican opposition. As usual, money was no problem for the three-term incumbent; his war chest was stuffed with contributions from the medical profession and business interests. By the time he formally announced his candidacy in January 1978, his popularity in Texas had only increased because of his vehement opposition to the Labor Reform Act and the Panama Canal Treaty. His seat on the Senate Armed Services Committee continued to provide him with a valuable asset that many Texans viewed as vital to the state's economy. But a change in John Tower's personal life greatly complicated his reelection campaign. Tower and his wife of twenty-four years, Lou, had divorced in the fall of 1976. The next year he married real estate agent Lilla Cummings. Lilla, unlike Lou, was opinionated and abrasive, and although she lacked political sophistication she repeatedly asserted herself where she had no expertise. She alienated many valuable members of Tower's staff, and eventually even Tower's three daughters came to dislike her. Had he not been able to call upon loyal campaign leaders who were able to grit their teeth and work with or around Lilla, Tower could have been defeated in 1978. As it was, the race was closer than anyone expected.[37]

Tower's opponent was a two-term Democratic congressman, Robert Krueger, who had garnered considerable publicity in Texas through his ardent but unsuccessful attempts to deregulate the price of natural gas. A tireless and effective campaigner, Krueger's television spots portrayed him as an energetic, small-town Texas boy—in contrast to the divorced, high-living, and effete Tower. The Krueger campaigners sought to make effective use of the persistent rumors about Tower's life in the fast lane by circulating a column written by right-winger Tom Anderson that purportedly documented the vague charges. This tactic backfired spectacularly since the column was of dubious credibility, and it gave Tower the pretext for canceling four joint television appearances, which the lesser-known Krueger greatly needed to overcome Tower's advantage in name recognition. The campaign quickly degenerated into personal invective. When Krueger demanded that Lilla Tower disclose her financial holdings, Tower retorted that Krueger, a bachelor at the time, "knows little about marriage." Another incident that probably worked for Tower's benefit was his refusal to shake hands with his opponent at a Houston gathering. At first it looked like poor sportsmanship on Tower's part, but Tower's strategists were able to turn this perception around. They had Tower explain, through extensive advertising, that he had been raised to believe that a handshake was a symbol of friendship and respect, and since his unworthy opponent had slurred his wife and daughters, "my kind of Texan doesn't shake the hand of that kind of man." The Senate contest in Texas soon earned the title of "the dirtiest campaign in the nation."[38]

Issues occasionally emerged from behind the shower of mud. One effective Krueger television spot noted that in seventeen long years in the Senate, Tower had failed to author one piece of major legislation. Tower had no effective rebuttal. Tower's camp argued that their man was unable to author legislation since the Republicans had been the minority party in the Senate during Tower's years of service. That was a lame excuse since there were plenty of examples of senators from the minority party who had stamped their names on major pieces of legislation. Krueger also condemned Tower's customary racially divisive approach to issues, citing his vote opposing Senate representation for the District of Columbia. Tower easily gained the upper hand and deflected the racial angle by linking Krueger to the capital's liberal federal bureaucrats.[39]

Tower outspent Krueger by a more than two-to-one margin ($5.1 million to $2.3 million) during the campaign, but managed only a razor-thin victory, 1,151,000 to 1,139,000. His margin of 12,000 votes was less than one-half of 1 percent. Tower led Krueger by 71,000 in the aggregate of the twenty-five most populous counties, but did not run nearly so well in rural Texas as he had six years earlier. Indeed, it was oilman Bill Clements's stunning but narrow upset of Democrat John Hill in the governor's race that probably pulled Tower through, especially in the rural areas. Minority and traditional Democratic turnout was low, and the Republicans did a much better job in turning out their voters. Tower once again courted Hispanic voters, claiming to be "un amigo sincero," but he fell far short of the 35 percent he sought, securing only about 20 percent of the Mexican American vote in the election.[40]

Following the election, East Texas congressman Charles Wilson pointed out the improbable character of Tower's election victories: "Tower would never have made it without Clements. . . . He got elected on a fluke to start with. Then the next time he had a Democrat more conservative than he was, and all the liberals voted for him. Then the next time he got to run when his opponent was strapped with McGovern. He's just lucky."[41] Lucky or not, John Tower returned to the Senate, where his seniority ensured him a starring role in the legislative wars.

The Armed Services Committee in the 1970s and 1980s was the site of a continuing battle between Republicans favoring the Pentagon and Democrats trying to scale down military expenditures in the wake of the Vietnam War. Tower articulately defended all the big weapons systems, opposed the two SALT treaties, and argued adamantly that the United States was losing ground militarily to the Soviet Union. In 1979 he predicted that by 1982 the United States would rank second militarily to the Soviet Union. But Ronald Reagan's stunning victory over President Jimmy Carter in 1980 provided John Tower with the opportunity to ensure that his prediction would not be borne out. As Sidney Blumenthal puts it, "Ronald Reagan swept into the capital with long coattails and a Republican Senate. John Tower of Texas became the chairman of Armed Services. He was extremely partisan, knowledgeable, and disagreeable." Tower was also powerful. To the delight of the White House, he quickly encroached on the domain of the Foreign Relations Committee, chaired by moderate Republican Charles Percy. Under Tower's adroit leadership, the Senate Armed Services Committee quickly increased arms sales and escalated the arms race. Tower served notice that U.S. arms sales would no longer be hindered by a customer nation's failure to safeguard human rights. He supported production of the mobile MX missile system by arguing that it was only because America's intercontinental ballistic missiles could survive an attack that the Soviets "haven't launched a first strike to begin with." The senior senator from Texas also vainly attempted to repeal the War Powers Act and other 1970s legislation that set modest limits on the powers of the president to unilaterally set U.S. foreign policy.[42]

Tower was widely rumored to be in line to become secretary of defense and his desire for this position was well known, but President Reagan told him he would be more useful to his administration in the now Republican-controlled Senate. The new secretary of defense, Caspar Weinberger, was not knowledgeable about defense issues and deferred to Tower in formulating the administration's initial $33 billion increase in the Pentagon's budget. When public pressure to cut the swollen defense budget began to grow in the fall of 1981, the Reagan administration responded with a trifling $13 billion cut in defense spending over a three-year period. Although this modest reduction was widely regarded as a victory for the Pentagon, Tower still denounced it because he claimed that the military would now receive "less in the way of defense capability than even Jimmy Carter projected." *Time* magazine said of the Texas senator's statement, "That was clearly not true."[43]

Tower stunned Texans in August 1983 when he announced his intention to retire from the Senate at the end of his fourth term. He cited burnout as his reason for declining to seek reelection. Republican leaders privately predicted that Tower would have faced another difficult reelection campaign, but Tower had never shied away from tough challenges. His successor, Republican Phil Gramm, was elected easily with 59 percent of the vote. Tower professed to find the Senate a less congenial place to work, lacking the courtesy and collegiality that had characterized the chamber when he first entered it. He also experienced the frustration of having continually to defend the defense budget from attacks. His valedictory remarks to fellow legislators included his recommendation for continued high defense expenditures to ensure U.S. military superiority." [44]

Early in his career, John Tower wrote that he approved of "such measures as anti-trust laws and other legislation designed to protect the general citizenry against the unscrupulous and the greedy — laws that create a climate of opportunity for all the people, regardless of station or origin." [45] But he found remarkably few governmental programs that accorded with this philosophy. He invariably opposed any extension of the American welfare state. Because he remained a doctrinaire conservative who favored a reduced role for the federal government in American life, the absence of his name from important domestic legislation is not surprising. While defending the defense budget from proposed reductions in his last year in the Senate, when the public had begun to manifest concern about the federal budget deficit, he reiterated the philosophy that reconciled his advocacy of limiting domestic programs while not constraining defense expenditures: "Defense is mandated by the Constitution," he observed. "Other spending is not. Social Security's not in the Constitution. Higher education's not. [Nor the] arts and humanities. Defense isn't creating the deficit. Defense is the primary and sole responsibility of national government. These other things are not. Cut things the government's not mandated to do." [46] His lifelong commitment to the free market and limited government is apparent in his voting record in the Senate. His response to programs seeking to expand the federal role in the U.S. economy was a simple "No." He opposed training programs for unemployed workers in 1961, the War on Poverty in 1965, a federal day care system in 1971, nutrition for the elderly and health planning programs in 1974, and food stamps in 1981. He detested government regulations that stood in the way of the operation of the free market, a stance that led him to suggest the abolition of the Environmental Protection Agency, the Occupational Safety and Health Administration, the Legal Services Corporation for the poor, and, predictably, the Equal Employment Opportunity Commission. He was so willing to defend an unfettered American capitalism that in the mid-1970s he even went so far as to defend corporations' selling of carcinogenic products to the public. Of course, no American politician can survive as a pure, free-market ultraconservative when state concerns are at issue. Tower labored vigorously for the oil depletion allowance, oil import quotas, all military pork bills, and against a $20,000 cap on farm payments.[47]

Through his career Tower was among the Senate's most conservative members. The annual interest group scores assigned to all members of Congress by the conservative Americans for Constitutional Action (ACA), the liberal Americans for Democratic Action (ADA), and the AFL-CIO's Committee on Political Education (COPE) displayed in the figures on pages 217 and 218 demonstrate that John Tower consistently adopted more conservative positions than his fellow Republicans.[48] That Tower was initially viewed as an extremist and ended up his Senate career by being considered within the Republican mainstream testifies to the profound shift in public attitudes and policy from the Kennedy-Johnson to the Reagan-Bush administrations.

Two weeks after leaving the Senate, Tower was appointed to head the U.S. delegation at the Strategic Arms Reduction Talks (START) in Geneva. He held the post for fourteen months before resigning. Although he was commended for his work at the time, subsequent allegations after he was nominated for secretary of defense in 1988 suggested that, although his professional behavior at the conference had been beyond reproach, he had tolerated departures from accepted security practices and personal decorum. Former arms control chief Kenneth Adelman later remarked

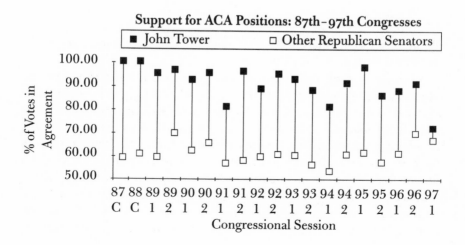

Support for ACA Positions: 87th-97th Congresses

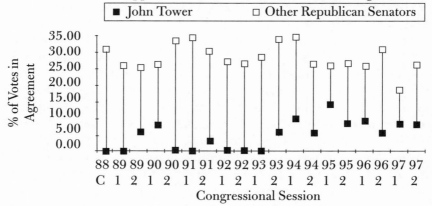

Support for ADA Positions: 88th–97th Congresses

■ John Tower   □ Other Republican Senators

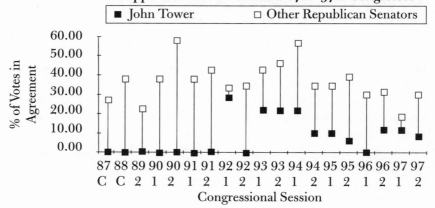

Support for COPE Positions: 87th–97th Congresses

■ John Tower   □ Other Republican Senators

about Tower's personal conduct in Geneva, "His lack of discretion proved troublesome then, as before and since."[49]

John Tower returned to public service in 1986 in the wake of revelations that funds received from secret arms sales to Iran had been secretly diverted to the contra rebels in Nicaragua by National Security Council (NSC) personnel. President Reagan attempted to fix the blame for the Iran-contra scandal by dismissing Lieutenant Colonel Oliver North from the NSC and accepting the resignation of National Security Advisor John Poindexter. Attorney General Edwin Meese's report that the illegal activities had been carried out without the president's knowledge was met with widespread public skepticism. Reagan acted quickly to head off criticism of his administration and to respond to his plummeting popularity by naming a special review board to investigate the operations of the National Security Council. John Tower was named to chair the board, which was quickly dubbed the Tower Commission. The board included former secretary of state Edmund S. Muskie and former national security advisor Lieutenant General (Ret.) Brent Scowcroft. The Tower Commission was hampered by the lack of power of subpoena and power to take sworn testimony, and it worked under severe time constraints. Nevertheless, it produced a report that was generally commended by the media. The report concluded that President Reagan's "detached" management style had created the opportunity for Oliver North and others to violate administration policy by selling arms to Iran and diverting the profits to the contras. The commission did not find any evidence that President Reagan knew about the illegal diversion of funds to the contras, and it concluded that Vice President George Bush was not involved, a conclusion that liberal critics predictably challenged. The report instead blamed the scandal on disarray within the White House, particularly the lack of control over White House personnel by Chief of Staff Donald Regan (who considered himself the scapegoat of the report) and National Security Advisor John Poindexter. Tower's memoir, *Consequences,* goes beyond the version outlined in the commission report to suggest a planned effort to conceal White House involvement. The report had noted that the president had shifted his story from admission to denial of approving the missile sales, but Tower's book marked the first time a principal figure had professed shock at Reagan's manner of recanting documented testimony. Tower's memoir seemed to suggest that the change in the president's story was part of an orchestrated cover-up, but when excerpts from the book were first released Tower told the press that he did not think that the president was deliberately participating in an effort at concealment.[50]

The Tower Commission took as an epigraph a quotation from the Roman satirist Juvenal, "Quis custodiet ipsos custodes?" ("Who will guard the guardians themselves?") The perspective that the members of the commission took in addressing this question was a decidedly narrow one. They chose to view the Iran-contra scandal as an aberration rather than the latest in a series of attempts by American presidents to further concentrate power in the White House and to make foreign policy independently of Congress. The National Security Act of 1947 had created the basic elements of the national security system—the Central Intelligence Agency (CIA), the National Security Council, and the Cold War machinery of secrecy (the classification system)—without a formal definition of "national security." Since World War II the system has been characterized by a continuing process of centralization of decision making in the executive branch, particularly with regard to foreign policy. Critics of this system have argued that it has limited the Congress's role in the making of foreign policy, institutionalized irresponsibility in the executive branch, and resulted in a series of disastrous foreign policy failures and illegal activities. John Tower never accepted this view. When he served on the Senate Select Intelligence Committee in the 1970s, he continually opposed its attempt to establish tighter reins on the national security and intelligence communities. He was the only member of the committee who did not vote in favor of releasing its interim report that documented CIA involvement in illegal assassination attempts against foreign leaders, and he formally dissociated himself from its publication. Along with Senator Goldwater, Tower refused to sign the final report and called its recommendations "potentially dangerous" to the nation's security. He argued that Congress was institutionally "ill-suited" to manage the intelligence community and warned that increased congressional oversight would make the community "fit for employment only in an ideal world." Tower was also, of course, an inveterate foe of the War Powers Act. The Tower Commission report bears the imprint of Tower's ideas about the national security system. It places blame on the individuals involved while concluding that "the system works." Its only recommendation for changing the structure of the system is one that the CIA and its conservative supporters had advocated for years, merging the House and Senate Intelligence Committees into a joint panel with a small staff: a change that liberals insisted would further reduce the extent of congressional oversight of the intelligence agencies. Whether John Tower's unquestioning acceptance of the structure of the national security system played a role in his selection to chair the president's review board cannot be determined. What is known, however, is that when it became apparent that Robert Gates could not be confirmed as director of the CIA as a result of his role in the Iran-contra affair, President Reagan twice approached John Tower to become director of the agency.[51]

In 1961 U.S. Senator Prescott Bush from Connecticut had helped the then-unknown college professor John Tower in his campaign for the Senate from Texas. In 1988 Senator Bush's son George was elected president, and he gave John Tower the opportunity to achieve his long-sought goal of becoming secretary of defense, thereby allowing him, as Tower put it, to close my "career in public service by bringing it full circle."[52] But it was not to be. The rejection of his nomination by the Armed Services Committee and subsequently by the full Senate brought John Tower's public life to an inglorious end. Ironically, Tower's public life had little to do with the Senate's decision.

Tower had been widely rumored to be in line for the post of defense secretary in the new Bush administration. But it was not until mid-December 1988 that the president-elect formally nominated Tower, a month after initial contact between the two men and thus long enough for rumors to circulate that Bush's advisers were divided over Tower's appointment. Critics of Tower's nomination initially argued that his tenacious opposition to Pentagon reform and to fiscal restraints on defense expenditures as chairman of the Armed Forces Committee made him the wrong man to preside over the Department of Defense. They pointed out that Tower had blocked legislation that sought changes in Pentagon procurement that were strongly advocated by a White House panel chaired by industrialist David Packard and subsequently mandated by the Goldwater-Nichols Act of 1986. Tower assured President-elect Bush in a November meeting that he would be willing to accept a strong manager as his deputy in the Department of Defense, but as the Tower FBI background investigation dragged on, the focus of Tower's critics shifted quickly from his political views to his consulting fees and personal life.[53]

When Tower announced his retirement from the Senate in 1983, he had stated that he would not work with defense-related companies, but in 1987 he established a consulting firm whose clients were defense contractors. The press release announcing the formation of John Tower and Associates stated, "In this most uncertain political and economic climate, we intend to serve our clients by drawing upon our many years of varied experience in analyzing the issues, developing a responsive strategic plan, and bringing it to a successful conclusion." When questioned by the Armed Services Committee about his consulting work, Tower claimed he provided clients with information and analysis and that everything he told them about strategic arms was "already in the public domain." He said his advice was "intangible," yet he earned $763,777 in less than two years. Tower maintained that he did no lobbying, and he did not officially register as a lobbyist until February 2, 1988. When pressed by Armed Services chairman Sam Nunn during his confirmation hearings to explain various contacts his firm had with congressional and Pentagon officials before he registered as a lobbyist, Tower professed not to know whether those contacts could be construed as lobbying. "There's a great difficulty in trying to define just precisely what lobbying is," he told the committee. Tower also hurt himself when he said he could not recall having done any work for British Aerospace, whereupon the committee discovered that two years earlier Tower had advised the company about the sale of military systems to the Pentagon.[54]

Tower's political ideology and ethics were ultimately not the subjects of the debate that soon broke over his nomination. Senate Democrats could not legitimately challenge George Bush's discretion in his choice of a fellow conservative, nor were they well positioned to question Tower's business dealings when former Democratic officeholders were busy plying their knowledge and political contacts for obscene profits. What Tower's critics ultimately fastened on was his personal life and character. Ironically, it was conservative activist Paul Weyrich who first publicly raised the issues of Tower's womanizing and drinking before the Senate Armed Services Committee. Weyrich claimed to have "grave doubts" about Tower's suitability to serve as secretary of defense and testified that "[o]ver the course of many years, I have encountered the nominee in a condition — a lack of sobriety — as well as with women to whom he was not married." Weyrich's testimony unleashed a debate that was without precedent in personal bitterness.[55]

Democratic senators could not reject Tower for his ideology or business practices, but the charges of moral weakness allowed them to conjure up their negative memories of their former colleague, based on his arrogant, hardball politics in the chamber. The sting of those memories made it easier for the Senate to apply to Tower relatively new standards of private behavior for public officials that had been ushered in by presidential candidate Gary Hart's celebrated extramarital affairs and rejected Supreme Court nominee Douglas Ginsburg's admission of having used marijuana. Tower's old reputation as a hard drinker and womanizer was the primary reason for his rejection. The rumors had been circulating for years, and they were enhanced by the charges of his second wife, Lilla, who publicly accused him of conducting a number of extramarital affairs during their bitter divorce proceedings. The White House did not try to refute the charges of Tower's womanizing: "everybody knows that's true," a senior Bush adviser said. Georgia's Democratic senator Sam Nunn in particular had never liked Tower, and he came to regard him as debauched and unworthy as accounts of Tower's drinking and womanizing piled up during the confirmation hearings.[56]

Tower appears to have been a steadfast drinker, at least through the late 1970s when Lilla confronted him with a choice — her or Johnny Walker Black. He maintained that he then limited his consumption of alcoholic beverages to wine. His former aide, Congressman Larry Combest of Lubbock, testified to the Armed Services Committee that Tower had overcome his former drinking problems. But by relating that Tower sometimes drank so heavily on campaign trips years ago that he and other aides had to help the senator to bed, Combest only lent credence to allegations about more recent incidents. The FBI investigated all of the allegations made to the committee, but since their reports were secret and could not be publicly discussed by the committee, rumors were given free rein, and Tower was neither informed of nor provided the opportunity to reply to the allegations. Washington buzzed with stories about Tower's drinking, such as the "occasion on which he passed out in the chili at his annual Texas Independence Day party." Sadly ironic was an editorial supporting Tower's nomination written by a friend from his undergraduate years at Southwestern. Published before the controversy over Tower's drinking broke, the warmly personal editorial recounted how its author and Tower while students "quaffed a little beer (he consumed his share from a kid's porcelain potty, usually singing country-western songs like 'I Saw Blood on the Highway, But I Didn't Hear No Body Pray' and 'Atomic Power,' most effectively screamed "ah-TOMMMM-ic POWWWW-er!!!!)" As Elizabeth Drew recognized, "The most deadly thing that can happen to a public figure befell Tower; he became a national joke."[57]

There were never any charges that Tower's personal conduct had affected his handling of official business in Geneva at the START talks or that his heavy drinking over the years ever interfered with his work in the Senate. But the controversy was no longer about Tower's professional life; it was about his character and personal behavior. Tower seemed not to realize the damage that was being done to his chances of confirmation until it was too late. When he then pledged to abstain from alcohol while serving as secretary of defense, his action only served to convince many that his drinking habits remained cause for concern. His claim that "I've never broken a pledge in my life" led to a tragicomic incident at the National Press Club in which a reporter asked him whether his claim included his wedding vows. Tower responded, "As a matter of fact, I have broken wedding vows. I think I'm probably not alone in that connection."[58]

The stories about Tower's personal life upset many social conservatives and members of the religious right, who comprised an important segment of the Republicans' winning 1988 electoral coalition. They deluged senators with letters opposing Tower's nomination. The Reverend Pat Robertson openly opposed Tower and said, on his Christian Broadcasting Network, "In my estimation George Bush is running down his tremendous moral fund and he should ask for Tower to withdraw." Almost 90 percent of Robertson's viewers opposed Tower because of his moral character.[59]

Tower did not withdraw, even when his nomination was voted down in the Armed Services Committee by a party-line vote of 11 to 9. President Bush stubbornly took the acrid fight to the floor of the Senate. Tower's nomination was defeated there on another party-line vote, 53 to 47, with all but one of the opposing votes being Democrats. Tower felt himself to have been the victim of a political mugging by opponents who relied on unsubstantiated rumor and innuendo, and he bitterly resented the fact that his former Senate colleagues had done him in. He subsequently compared Capitol Hill unfavorably with Beirut. "They're pretty straightforward what they do in Beirut. They hurl a grenade at someone or shoot a machine gun. Up here it's a little more subtle, but just as ruthless, just as brutal. They kill you in a different way." [60]

Tower was a legitimate trend-setter on Capitol Hill in hiring women for influential staff jobs. Moreover, he invariably had one of the best staffs in Congress, and there are dozens of people in federal agencies, Congress, and the executive branch who got into politics because of John Tower. They will serve for years to come. [61] His role as the senator who cracked the "solid South" gives him a place in history, as does his key work on behalf of the Republicans' "Southern Strategy." Conservatives hail him as one of the architects of the hard-line, Cold War policy that allegedly bankrupted the Soviet Union and drove it into oblivion. And even though the debate over whether the Soviet Union would have collapsed anyway from internal decay will continue, most historians will record Tower as a conventional cold warrior who never met a weapons system he did not like. America's undisciplined defense spending, for which John Tower was the "principal backer in the Senate," [62] contributed to unprecedented federal budget deficits. Had Tower been confirmed as secretary of defense, he would have been delighted to preside over Operation Desert Storm, which he would have ably done, but his bellicose mind-set would have been ill-equipped to slash defense budgets in the post–Cold War era.

John Tower, along with his daughter Marian, died in a fiery airplane crash on April 5, 1991, while traveling to promote his newly published memoir. In the epilogue he wrote about the painful end to his political career: "I don't so much resent my rejection by the Senate as the way it was done. Certainly, I am not happy with being held out as a bad example and being remembered by many only in the context of the publicity surrounding my confirmation struggle. Lost is the fact that I was once regarded as a competent leader, worthy of trust and capable of bearing the heavy responsibilities of sensitive and demanding assignments." As William F. Buckley Jr. noted in the *National Review*, John Tower "was able to manage everything except his domestic life, and the final challenge of his public life." [63]

JIM WRIGHT

Fig. 11.1. Jim Wright, U.S. congressman from Fort Worth, became the third Texan in the twentieth century to serve as Speaker of the House. Photo courtesy of Jim Wright.

JIM WRIGHT

BY BEN PROCTER

Speaker of the House Jim Wright, like many Americans, knew little about his ancestry. The Wright forebears, on his paternal side, supposedly came from County Tyrone, Ireland, where they belonged to the clan Dungannon. His grandfather, John Claude (or Calvin) Wright—the family is unsure about the middle name—arrived in Texas late in the 1880s either from Virginia, North Carolina, Tennessee, or Missouri. On his maternal side, grandfather Harry Haynington Lyster was born in Australia "of parents who traced their ancestries on both sides to Dungannon," also in County Tyrone. Consequently, Wright decided to tidy up this family enigma, this genealogist's nightmare, by saying, "Frankly, I claim kin to all the Wrights, though I suspect some of them may disavow the relationship." [1]

Jim Wright was surely proud of his heritage. That his ancestors were Irish may have had something to do with it. Or possibly, he liked the idea that the Irish usually have had an affinity for political life. But more important, he revered his mother and father—their character and humanity. Born on October 8, 1890, in the Shady Grove community west of Weatherford, Texas, Jim Wright's father, James Claude Wright Sr., was a self-made, self-taught individual, a voracious reader with an inquiring mind and a reverence for ideas. Despite a lack of formal schooling, he was, Jim Wright admiringly recalled, "one of the very best-educated men I have ever known." When only ten years old and in the fourth grade, he was forced to quit school because his father died and his mother, a victim of polio, was unable to walk. Wright Sr., therefore, had to help provide part of the family income, doing whatever work was available—chopping cotton, clerking at the local grocery store, doing manual labor in a brick factory. He grew into manhood, roughly handsome, just under six feet and well-muscled, possessing the graceful movements of a young athlete. In fact, he soon tried to escape poverty with his fists, boxing professionally as a middle-weight in Chicago, Detroit, and New York City—that is, until watching a friend and stable mate named Lemke suffer a fatal heart attack following a bout with a leading contender. He then opined somewhat pragmatically: "What the hell do I want to stay in this business for?" [2]

But an equally good reason for quitting the ring was a young woman named Marie Louella Lyster, whom he had met at a fair in Weatherford.

Born in New Mexico Territory on September 11, 1894, she had a some-what tenuous early life, which eventually became more settled and normal. When only eighteen months old, she lost her father, a civil engineer and a graduate of Heidelberg Union, who died of undulant fever while survey-ing a route for a railroad through New Mexico. Her mother then obtained a job managing the company commissary, until accepting an offer to help a great aunt and uncle operate a hotel in Weatherford. Thanks to a lov-ing and protective environment, Marie Lyster grew to be a pretty young woman, dark-haired with fair skin, somewhat winsome on a slender five-foot, six-inch frame. For early twentieth-century Texas, she received a good education and soon after graduation from high school taught "Ex-pression"—declamation, poetry reading, and extemporaneous speech—at a public school in Duncan, Oklahoma. Besides acquiring the usual skills expected of a teenage girl in rural America, such as cooking and sewing, she played the piano and reviewed books for literary societies. Then early in the 1910s at Weatherford she met Jim Wright Sr., who was at the time a captain and commander of the local Texas National Guard unit as well as the owner of a combination tailoring/cleaning and pressing establish-ment. In 1916, when his unit was ordered to the Big Bend to protect Tex-ans against possible raids by Pancho Villa, James and Marie decided to marry in Valentine, Texas. They even persuaded their Presbyterian min-ister, a Reverend Reeves, to travel the three hundred miles from Weather-ford to perform the ceremony. A year later, with the entry of the United States into World War I, Wright was shipped overseas to France, while Marie lived for a brief time with a fellow officer's wife and family at Far Rockaway on Long Island before returning to Weatherford.[3]

In 1919 Jim Wright Sr. came home from war to a different world and a changing society. Although depression seemed to be constant in Texas after the armistice, he had no difficulty as a provider. His son fondly re-membered him as "a super salesman" with a "hell of a personality. Dad was not so interested in products as ideas; in this capacity, he was quite gifted." Consequently, he became a distributor for the Pierce Oil Com-pany before accepting a job with the United States Chamber of Com-merce. Specifically, he was division field manager in charge of circulation and sales for *Nation's Business*, the Chamber's magazine; therefore, he had to travel widely throughout the Southwest, both hiring and training mem-bers of the sales force.[4]

In this milieu Marie and James Wright Sr. began their family. On De-cember 22, 1922, James Claude Wright Jr. was born in Fort Worth, Texas, the only son and eldest of three children. From his earliest remembrances he understood the life of a transient. His father was continually on the move, his job taking him from one city to another, with longer residences at Hutchinson, Kansas; Camden, Arkansas; Alexandria, Louisiana; Oklahoma City, and San Antonio, the family virtually "living out of suit cases." In September 1929 young Jim first attended public school in Houston, but by Christmas he had transferred to William James Elementary in Fort Worth. Then in the summer of 1930 the Wrights were in Dallas, where Jim began the second grade at John H. Reagan Elementary. By the spring of 1931, however, Wright Sr. resigned his job with the U.S. Chamber of Commerce in order to found a company selling street signs to small-town America. The concept was terrific, the demand obvious, the only difficulty being, his son later noted, that 1931 (with the United States in the throes of the Great Depression) was "the world's worst year to start a new business." Hence, with expenses high and debts mounting, Wright Sr. decided to establish his company's new base of operations in Weatherford.[5]

For young Jim Wright, small-town life was a new experience, in many ways a rewarding and satisfying one. By his own admission he was, at age eight, a "city boy," who knew nothing about the wonders of agrarian America. His father therefore decided to educate him in "the lore of the land." How young Jim reveled in the long drives that the two undertook through the surrounding countryside, and how he delighted in listening to his father teach him about the mysteries of nature. On one occasion they spotted nests of squirrels in a grove of trees and a raccoon "washing a morsel of food" at a nearby creek; on another, they discovered a quail's nest with tiny brown eggs flecked with green. And always Wright Sr. was instructing his eagerly attentive, redheaded son in the harsh practicalities of life, in the unfairness that some endured from a regimented society. He continually imbued him with an egalitarian philosophy of inclusion. Then, in regard to discrimination, he effectively fashioned a rhetorical question by asking young Jim what his reaction would be if a sign over a drinking fountain read: "No redheads can drink here."[6]

To fit into the community, to achieve a sense of belonging, was also a high priority—and to that end young Jim Wright worked diligently. At a boyhood friend's home he churned butter for the boy's mother to ingratiate himself. Across town, after buying some bantam roosters, he took his two fiercest, named Jiggs and Gene Tunney, to combat any challengers, thereby providing entertainment and becoming "one of the gang." And he attracted a large group of acquaintances to his house with his personal library of Edgar Rice Burroughs classics about Tarzan as well as a fascinating book entitled *Jack Dempsey, Idol of Fistiana* by Nat Fleischer. But more than anything else, his forced attendance in summer school (1931) to complete the second grade—he had missed the last two weeks of school in Dallas because of chicken pox—widened his circle of companions. And even though describing summer school as "an institution invented by adults which is, of all afflictions visited upon the defenseless young, the most nearly insufferable and incontestably the most boring," Wright profited both from the instruction and the intimacy of class camaraderie. In fact, because of his progress, especially in math and history, he was allowed to skip the third grade.[7]

Wright treasured his stay in Weatherford for its stabilizing influence and cherished memories. He later reflected upon the "brilliantly colored sunsets" marking the end of "velvety" days, upon evenings spent chasing fireflies with boyhood friends. He also fondly remembered playing in his first football game and his coach, who assumed heroic proportions, stressing "team work" as a key to victory. And since Weatherford was the Parker County seat, he and his family enjoyed its amenities—evening band concerts at the courthouse square, county fairs exhibiting the prize livestock of the area, and accompanying amusements with "a ferris wheel, calliope music, and a few side-shows."[8]

But alongside these pleasant memories evolved the harsh realities of the times. In the fall of 1931 the Wrights, like most families in Weatherford, were suffering from the continuing depression. The family had to move to a smaller house; his father began "rolling his own cigarettes," and he was forced into "long absences" from home in an effort to save his fledgling business. Soon young Jim realized that the family car was gone, that his weekly allowance of twenty-five cents was eliminated, and that their piano, which his mother dearly loved to play after evening meals, had vanished. Summing up their plight another way, he later wrote: "This was the year we ate the piano."[9]

The Great Depression left an indelible stamp on Jim Wright. Hoboes often visited the back door of the family home, seeking to perform some task in exchange for a meal; his mother never allowed anyone to go away hungry. Gradually he became aware of the local "Hooverville"—a group of crude lean-tos near the railroad tracks—and of the pitiful situation that many Americans were enduring. Then the greatest shock of all occurred: in the summer of 1932 he had to leave Weatherford. His maternal grandfather, who had worked in Fort Worth for a nationwide business firm for twenty-three years and lacked just two more for a retirement pension, was arbitrarily terminated, specifically because the company wanted to avoid the payment of promised retirement annuities. Hence, the family decided to move in with his grandparents and pay rent, thereby helping with household expenses and mortgage payments. At the same time, Jim Wright Sr. abandoned his own business venture and hired on as a salesman with a Fort Worth company. Young Jim Wright was thus beginning to realize what the term "child of the depression" meant—and he would strive during his career to prevent such conditions from ever occurring again in the United States.[10]

In Fort Worth the Wrights, like most Texans, were in a transitional stage, struggling to survive the depression. As did many of their neighbors, the "extended family" managed a small garden, raised chickens for meat and eggs, and planted peach trees. Most people had lost their cars; hence, transportation to town was a five-cent bus ride or a three-mile walk. With work almost impossible to find, nine-year-old Jim Wright decided to apply himself in school, at least in English and math, although slacking in the sciences and geography. He also participated in 75-pound sandlot football (until at season's end when he was disqualified for being three pounds too heavy), played boyhood games with his companions, and went to nearby Sycamore Park for free movies that the city provided on Thursday nights. But more than anything else, he developed a passion for boxing, both to spend time with his father and to win his approval. For birthday and Christmas presents in 1932 he received a regular-sized punching bag and a skipping rope, both of which he became most skilled in using. And when informed by his father of another residence change, this time to Duncan, Oklahoma, he was surely disappointed in leaving friends but accepted such uprooting as one of the hazards of the depression.[11]

In the fall of 1933 Jim Wright thus considered going to the so-called Indian Territory an "adventure"—and in many ways it was. The first order of business had to do with school; at Duncan he was allowed again to skip a grade (to the seventh). And therein lay a continuing problem for him. He always felt intellectually compatible and physically comfortable with older groups, but that forced an occasional concealment and, at times, an "innocent deception" about his own age. In turn, he was sometimes at a disadvantage because of size and maturity. In such school subjects as science, geography, and civics his performance was mediocre, while in English, history, and math, he excelled. In athletics he tried out for quarterback on the football team because weight was not a deciding factor, while in boxing he fought in the 112–pound category.

But what Wright "luxuriated in" most of all was the chance to be with his father, who had accepted a position as the chamber of commerce secretary at Duncan. A primary requisite of Wright Sr.'s job was to promote trade and commerce. Consequently, he initiated "goodwill tours" to nearby towns; more specifically, he provided a variety show of "hometown entertainment," the result being to encourage potential customers to visit Duncan merchants. By the fall of 1934, he was so successful that the chamber of commerce at Seminole, an oil boom town in southeastern Oklahoma, hired him away at a higher salary. And even though disappointed in having to move once again, young Jim Wright soon enjoyed his new surroundings. During the next eighteen months he became a part of the "good will" programs, at times accompanying singers or dancers with a harmonica as well as entertaining crowds with a two-round boxing exhibition. In fact, he would harbor many pleasant memories of his stay at Seminole—being captain and quarterback of the junior high football team, having three different girl friends, qualifying as a summer lifeguard, and participating in a regional AAU boxing tournament at nearby Ada (claiming to be sixteen years old even though barely thirteen).[12]

Then in 1935 Wright Sr. began experimenting with an idea that once again changed his family's life. To attract customers into Seminole he initiated an "Appreciation Day," whereby local merchants contributed two dollars weekly to a "community chest." Every Wednesday evening, after each customer had bought something for sale and received a numbered coupon—with the stub placed in a cage called the "Treasure Chest"—Seminole merchants held a drawing: the winner would receive a cash award, usually anywhere from 5 to 20 percent of the amount in the "Chest"—but never more than 50 percent of the total. Consequently, the "Treasure Chest" grew from week to week until it finally reached $1,000. "On that Wednesday," Wright recollected, "the town was so crowded that cars could barely drive in the broad main street." However, within two years Wright Sr. decided once again to begin his own business, but this time with a workable idea (patented and copyrighted) in depression-ridden America. By the summer of 1935 he had resigned his job with the Seminole chamber and become a "one-man national field force selling his plan." Within fifty-two weeks he had organized an equal number of towns, with participating merchants paying him a franchise fee of $7.50 and 25 cents weekly. In the summer of 1936 he even employed this system to boost attendance at the games of the Oklahoma City Chieftains baseball team. As a result, young Jim earned $5 a week for collecting both money and coupons from the local merchants for another "Treasure Chest" drawing.[13]

For this new business venture Wright Sr. needed a home base of operations; therefore, he chose Dallas, which necessitated a family move—and young Jim Wright "loved it." For the next three years he attended Adamson High School, where "every day," he fondly recalled, was better "than the day before." During his sophomore and junior years he played halfback on the football team—that is, until a knee injury ended his gridiron career. As a consequence, his coach urged him "to represent our school in debate." And with the encouragement of his mother and father as well as world history teacher Robert B. Harris, he became the leader of the high school debate team. Wright also captained the Oak Cliff YMCA boxing squad, organized a political party named the Progressives, and was elected president of the 1939 Adamson High senior class.[14]

The decision to debate, however, proved to be monumental in his life. Because his parents were "bibliophiles," Wright had always been encouraged to read. His ability to memorize and recall instantaneously helped immeasurably in arguments and discussions with opponents. Hungering for an awareness of the world, "I studied like a fiend," he asserted, and "became hooked on history." With Europe on the brink of war—Benito Mussolini conquering Ethiopia and Adolf Hitler invading the Rhineland as well as Czechoslovakia and Austria—Wright became more and more "obsessed with the idea that Woodrow Wilson was right, that the United States should have joined the League of Nations." He believed that his "generation most likely was going to have to fight again to win the war that my father and his generation thought they had won." And what did Wright decide to do about the forthcoming catastrophic fight against the Axis Powers? "My ambition from that time on," he asserted candidly, was "to go to Congress and do what I could for world peace. . . . I never wavered from it."[15]

As world war loomed after Germany invaded Poland on September 1, 1939, Wright was intent on pursuing a college education. Since his father decided to move company operations to Weatherford, he enrolled at the local two-year college. He soon began writing for the school's weekly newspaper, the *Weatherford College Coyote,* then was elected its editor. In this capacity he devoted tremendous energy to each eight-page edition, planning the layout, writing editorials, even setting type and running the linotype machine. Yet Wright still found time to represent Weatherford College in debate, join a school honor society in forensics, and become a member—and then president—of the International Relations Club, attending two annual conferences at Fayetteville, Arkansas, and New Orleans sponsored by the Carnegie Institute, and being elected a national vice president. And even with such a full schedule, he continued to box on Saturdays and write local sports stories for the *Fort Worth Star-Telegram.* Not surprisingly, he was elected president of the 1941 graduating class at Weatherford College.[16]

The remainder of 1941 was, Jim Wright later recalled, fast-moving and at times "a blur." During the summer he campaigned all over the state (using a sound truck) for Attorney General Gerald Mann of Dallas, who unsuccessfully ran for the United States Senate upon the death of four-term

Democrat Morris Sheppard. In September Wright entered the University of Texas at Austin, taking fifteen hours toward a double major in government and economics. He continued to be active, representing the university on the men's debate squad (with Edgar Shelton), while working part-time at the A.G.'s office for $30 a month. Continually he wavered between the thought of going to law school and pursuing a graduate degree in journalism. Then on December 7 all plans changed, at least for the moment. Within two weeks after Pearl Harbor, Wright volunteered for the Army Air Corps — of course, with his parents' blessing — and on the evening of December 31, 1941, he was inducted at Dallas with "some fifty to sixty recruits." [17]

Nineteen-year-old Jim Wright wanted to serve his country: it was not merely a matter of patriotism but one of obligation as an American citizen. Impatiently he sought combat but soon learned that the military had its own timetable. As a consequence he waited and fretted, first in Texas at Camp Wolters (near Mineral Wells), then at Sheppard Air Force Base (Wichita Falls), before proceeding to March Field in Southern California. After three weeks he shipped out to Hamilton Field (north of San Francisco), was assigned to the Group Intelligence section, and earned his corporal's stripes — but he was still no closer to flight training, nor seemingly the hope of it. [18]

Wright therefore resolved to expedite his military career. One afternoon in the spring of 1941 he impetuously called the base personnel office and, impersonating the "clipped accent" of his commanding officer, ordered that "the application of Corporal Wright for aviation cadet training" be processed immediately. Within four days he was on his way to cadet instruction at the Santa Anna Training Base, then for further preparation at Williams Field (near Chandler, Arizona). And on December 12, 1942, just prior to his twentieth birthday, Wright received his wings and commission as a navigator. [19]

Wright could not directly affect his military destiny further; otherwise, he might have chosen a different theater of war. But, overall, he appreciated his time in the service. In Tucson, on Christmas Day 1942, he married college sweetheart Mary Ethelyn "Mab" Lemmons, who then became an air corps wife, following her husband from El Paso to Denver to Topeka. In March 1943, as a member of the 380th Heavy Bombardment Group, flying B-24s, he received orders to go to Hickam Field in Hawaii. From there he went to the Fiji Islands en route to Australia. After a three-week stay at Brisbane, his squadron left for a remote outpost known as Fenton Field, approximately one hundred miles south of Darwin. For the next year he flew over three hundred hours of combat missions. His squadron's most notable accomplishments were the bombing of the Japanese oil refinery depot at Balikpapan in Borneo in August 1943 (a seventeen-hour, round-trip flight covering 2,700 miles), a similar raid on refineries at Surabaja in Java, and the destruction of Japanese gun emplacements during the first amphibious landings of American troops along the eastern New Guinea coast on January 1, 1944. As a consequence, the air corps rotated Wright "back to the States." He arrived at San Francisco on March 17, 1944. After a six-weeks "rest leave" at Weatherford and Miami, Florida, he went to the Lincoln Army Air Base in Nebraska, his assignment that of indoctrinating crews for overseas combat. Then on May 30, 1945, with the war in Europe over, First Lieutenant Jim Wright received his honorable discharge papers at Fort Sam Houston near San Antonio, having served his country for almost three and a half years.[20]

Wright easily adjusted to civilian life. While at Lincoln he agreed to be a regional representative in Texas for the National Federation of Small Business, a corporation headquartered in San Mateo, California. Immediately after his discharge he returned to Weatherford, rented a house, and began "earning a living" as well as paving the way for what was still his ultimate ambition—going to Congress. Because of his towering impatience for public service he accepted, or volunteered for, "every free job in town." He therefore helped recruit one hundred new members into the local American Legion post, taught a Sunday School class at the Presbyterian church, became a scout master, coached the Golden Gloves team, and spoke to such service organizations as the Rotary and Lions Clubs, especially in behalf of the academic-freedom controversy that then involved President Homer P. Rainey at the University of Texas. And with the guidance of Margaret and Jack Carter of Fort Worth, he helped reorganize the defunct Young Democrats of Texas and addressed a state meeting in Fort Worth of fifty-one clubs on December 6-7, 1945.[21]

But equally important, Wright began to evolve a philosophy that he would hold to throughout his political career. He surely accepted the term *populism* as a fighting faith. He was ready to do battle against "all prejudice—economic, racial, or social"; he wanted "justice" and, therefore, reform for the average American against the power and wealth of big business; and he believed that, through the legislative branch of government, all things were possible, that "a creative, vital, dynamic kind of capitalism based on expanding the purchasing power of workers" could bring equality as well as opportunity to the people. He soon became aware, however, that such ideas and concepts produced critics, if not enemies. His father therefore offered this sage advice—and a "challenge"—which Wright "doggedly" accepted: to make "friends" with your enemies, or at least "convince them that you're a solid citizen and a man to be trusted." And then his father added: "You cannot expect them to like you unless you can learn to like them." [22]

In January 1946, Wright became disenchanted with his job because his employer, the National Federation of Small Business, no longer seemed to be truly focusing on the interests of small businesspeople. He decided to announce for state representative from Parker County. And although assured of victory—no one filed against him—Wright "broke most of the conventional rules," he later confessed, "for anyone wanting to serve in the Texas legislature." Or as one of his friends put it: "If there was a mistake you didn't make, it was only because you didn't think of it." How true! With the arrogance and impatience of youth, he articulated, at times persuasively, to conservative-minded Texans a number of reforms that could only be considered "radical" at the time: more money for public education, better pay for teachers, an improved public welfare program, paved farm-to-market roads, and a statewide water plan, all of which would be paid for by levying severance taxes on the oil and gas and sulfur companies—the "sacred cows" of the Texas economy. To reform state government he advocated year-round salaries for lawmakers, a stringent lobby-registration law, and "a new and modern state constitution." He also spoke across the state in behalf of other legislative candidates, his most grievous mistake that of campaigning against the next Speaker of the House W. O. Reed of Dallas. To culminate this summer and fall of political mistakes, Wright campaigned for Homer P. Rainey against the next governor of Texas, Beauford Jester. [23]

But in January 1947 Wright arrived in Austin to participate in the Fiftieth Legislature, or, as he described it, "the carnival" under the capitol's "granite dome." What a revealing and educational and challenging experience it was! As one of the 95 first-term members (of a total of 181 legislators), he learned of the awesome, "simply overpowering" influence of the lobby known as the "Third House." He caused a "mild furor" by proposing a constitutional amendment for annual legislative salaries and a bill to place stiff controls on lobbyists, both of which were soon buried in house subcommittees. He also soon realized the necessity to understand procedures and rules and the importance of building alliances and friendships. Although a relative unknown, he was able to persuade his colleagues to pass a Hoover Commission bill, designed to streamline and consolidate over 125 state boards and agencies (which died in the senate) and a bill granting "modest" state funds for local soil and water conservation districts (which did become law). But what truly heightened Wright's profile was his proposal, along with five cosponsors, to fund education, roads, and old-age pensions more fully by taxing the state's most prominent natural resources—oil, natural gas, and sulfur. Although losing this battle, he noted: "I'd finished stronger than I began." And "no longer" could opponents "ignore" him.[24]

In June 1947, after the adjournment of the Fiftieth Legislature, Wright was extremely optimistic about his political future. After being persuaded to buy into his father's company and to take a prominent role in its management, he was in good shape financially. He had also emerged from the legislative session so well that he "felt politically invincible." But in the ensuing months, events both strange and bizarre proved him wrong. In the spring of 1948 a postcard arrived in Weatherford, addressed to "Jim Wright, c/o The Town Marshall," the contents of which praised him for endorsing communism and racial intermarriage at a recent speech in San Antonio. In small-town, post–World War II Texas such ideas were anathema—and, of course, Wright had never made such statements. But since the local law officer, Constable Bill Bledsoe, had received the postcard— and obviously had read it, as had others—certain "nagging suspicions" began to circulate. Soon thereafter, Wright became involved in a local labor dispute in which he was the only person in Weatherford who had copies of a recent state statute concerning strikes. In trying to be impartial, he alienated a number of rabid antagonists on both sides. As a result, he became labeled increasingly as a "liberal," which, to some, meant just a step away from being a Communist. Late that spring, Wright thus had two opponents for his seat in the legislature: Eugene Miller, a former state senator who had a reputation for political "mud-slinging," and Floyd Bradshaw, a teacher in the small country town of Dennis, who was generally unknown, hence inoffensive. In the ensuing campaign, featuring scheduled debates among the adversaries, Wright refused to be drawn into name-calling and "stuck to" discussing the issues. The people of Parker County obviously approved; local political pundits were predicting that he would win without a runoff—that is, until Miller was mysteriously shot and killed less than two weeks before the election. Wright, although quickly going to the Weatherford hospital to give blood and then offering a reward for information leading to Miller's assassin, could not combat last-minute negative campaigning. His opponent denounced him as a "liberal" representing prolabor forces and implied that he was either directly or indirectly responsible for the death of the Communist-baiting Eugene Miller. In July 1948 Jim Wright lost to Floyd Bradshaw by thirty-nine votes. Although Wright's wife wanted to move away from people who could be taken in by such insidious rumors and unfounded accusations, Wright was determined "to show them by the way we live that they were

*Fig. 11.2. Jim Wright (right), shown in a 1947 photo with Texas author
John Henry Faulk, rose through the congressional ranks to become
Speaker of the House. Other Texans to serve as House Speaker
included John Nance Garner and Sam Rayburn. Faulk
(John Henry) Papers, Center for American History,
UT-Austin (CN 05711).*

wrong." However, in his diary he sadly recorded that, at age twenty-five, "my political future is behind me."[25]

For the next sixteen months Wright devoted himself to private concerns, with politics relegated to a secondary status. "With a vengeance" he went to work with his father in their jointly owned company, the National Trade Day Association. He conducted searches constantly for ambitious young men who would serve in the field, then trained them in the techniques and methods perfected by his father. Periodically the Wrights held national meetings across the United States, where the sales force could give them the knowledge of field experiences as well as the valuable exchange of ideas so necessary in a successful business. Together father and son—the former with the "know-how" and the latter with excessive energy and competitive zeal—built an organization with annual net profits approaching an estimated $250,000. And Wright still had time for such community duties as a Boy Scout master and Sunday school teacher. Not too surprisingly, in the summer of 1948 he also volunteered to organize precincts and neighborhoods during the senatorial campaign of Lyndon Johnson (against former governor Coke Stevenson) and the presidential campaign of Harry Truman.[26]

Then in December 1949 the mayor of Weatherford resigned—and Wright once again realized an opportunity for public service. Although at first declining a draft movement by friends because of his father's opposition, he finally decided that "money was not my first love or ultimate ambition," but politics surely was. So with the help of American Legion and VFW veterans, members of the chamber of commerce, and former mayor Conrad Russell, who was his campaign manager, Wright ran for mayor and won easily. At age twenty-six, he was the youngest chief magistrate of any city in Texas.[27]

Time and again throughout his political career, Wright philosophized that he "never wanted any job just to hold the title." Performance and accomplishment were what counted. He therefore became an active, aggressive mayor, over the next four years achieving an impressive record of accomplishments for Weatherford. He and a three-man council immediately built three parks, replete with swimming pools and playground equipment for children. To provide better sanitary conditions, they bought closed, hydraulic compacting trucks for garbage disposal (instead of "old open ones") and created a sanitary landfill system southwest of town. They also incorporated—with overwhelming voter approval—small housing developments east toward Fort Worth and west toward Mineral Wells, extending streets as well as water and sewer lines to the residents. Then during the frigid winter of 1950–1951 he entered into negotiations with the

Brazos River Gas Company of Mineral Wells, determined to pressure the company into providing sufficient fuel to the residents of Weatherford's north side, who were literally freezing "in front of their heaters." Otherwise, he vehemently threatened, the city council would abandon the present contract for nonperformance and arrange one with Lone Star Gas Company. Once again Wright was successful.[28]

Even greater accomplishments were still to come. In keeping with his populist philosophy, Wright fought attempts by Southwestern Bell Telephone Company for a rate increase. After lengthy discussions with the company's "high-powered lawyers," he won a partial victory, keeping the cheapest rates—party lines—at the same level, while agreeing to "modest" increases in business and direct-line services. Wright thus became so popular as a "can-do" mayor that in 1953, during his second full term, the citizens of Weatherford voted bonds for a new, much needed sewage treatment plant by a nine-to-one margin (even as bond issues in surrounding communities were being defeated). Early that summer, during a terrible drought, he also negotiated to buy a small lake owned by the Texas and Pacific Railroad in the northwest quadrant of Weatherford, thus preparing the way for a more permanent water supply: Lake Weatherford.

But, more than any other achievement, Wright was proudest of his stance on education. In 1953 the Weatherford public schools afforded only minimal education for African Americans, providing teaching for grades one through eight in one isolated building. Wright therefore persuaded the city council to bus black students to I. M. Terrell High School in Fort Worth at the city's expense. And in small-town Texas, prior to *Brown* v. *Board of Education of Topeka,* such an undertaking was quite remarkable. Nor did all these accomplishments go unnoticed. In 1953–1954 Wright was elected president of the Texas Municipal League, which represented all the cities in the state.[29]

Wright thus believed that the time was right, the political climate propitious, to carry out his boyhood dream; in March 1954, he announced for Congress. Although his opponent was four-term incumbent Wingate Lucas, the personal choice of multimillionaire newspaper publisher Amon G. Carter of Fort Worth, Wright reflected, "Everything in this campaign went right." Almost everyone in Weatherford was eager to help; volunteers began writing letters of endorsement to their friends in Fort Worth (Tarrant County) as well as in the four other counties in his district—Parker, Somervell, Johnson, and Hood. Then, early in April, Wright officially opened his campaign with a dollar-a-plate barbecue in Fort Worth, which twelve hundred people attended. But the next day the *Star-Telegram* made no mention of, what Wright called, "the largest political event in the town's recollection." He therefore decided to reach his constituency through the relatively new medium of television, which in 1954 was economically affordable. In programs "at prime time," ranging anywhere from five to thirty minutes, Wright "looked straight into the camera and talked directly to people in their living rooms." And it worked. He began "picking up steam" even in Grapevine, Lucas's hometown. When the *Star-Telegram* tried to stem his momentum by a front-page endorsement of Lucas on July 22, 1954, two days before the election, Wright administered the coup de grace by writing "an open letter to Amon G. Carter," which was printed in the next day's edition of the *Star-Telegram*. In essence, this "almost" full-page ad (costing $974.40) "told Mr. Carter" that Wright "would be his congressman as well as everybody's, but not his personal private congressman." As a result, Jim Wright won by a 60 percent majority. At age thirty-one, he was on his way to Congress.[30]

His first years in Congress were, Wright fondly reflected, "halcyon" days. With President Dwight D. Eisenhower at the helm, Washington "was the center of world power." And with the United States prosperous and at peace (the Korean armistice came in 1953), the legislative branch worked "with almost machine-like precision" under the leadership of Speaker Sam Rayburn and Senate Majority Leader Lyndon Johnson. During these first years Wright also began "learning the ropes" by understanding the rules of the House, forming friendships and alliances, and working closely with the leadership.[31]

Since a new House member had relatively little power and influence, Wright struggled, as he put it, "to break out of the cocoon of anonymity"—but with only limited success. He decided that a seat on the prestigious Foreign Affairs Committee would go far in advancing his goal, but at the "suggestion" of Rayburn, he instead chose the Public Works Committee; Wright would never regret this decision. Besides helping determine some outstanding accomplishments of the Eisenhower years—the interstate highway system along with the establishment of the Highway Trust Fund, a clean water program, and the Pan-American Highway—he was able to contribute invaluably to his own constituency. In 1957, with a seven-year Texas drought finally ending after torrential downpours, Fort Worth and the surrounding areas suffered terribly from flooding. Wright thus guided resolutions through the Public Works Committee that instructed the Army Corps of Engineers to check the overflow of rampaging Big Fossil Creek as well as to complete the Fort Worth floodway. At the same time Wright also obtained government funds for a new post office in Arlington and a federal building in Fort Worth, while influencing the Defense Department to purchase B-58 bombers and TFX fighter planes from General Dynamics of Fort Worth.[32]

Wright, however, could not avoid the most volatile issue concerning his constituency—integration of public schools. And, in this regard, he demonstrated unusual courage for a Texas politician during the 1950s. Wright was one of the few southern congressmen and senators who would not sign the "Southern Manifesto," which specifically denounced the Supreme Court for abrogating the "separate but equal" clause in *Plessy* v. *Ferguson* (1896). Nor did he sidestep this volatile problem. For instance, at a Parent-Teacher Association meeting in the small southeastern Tarrant County community of Mansfield in 1957, a woman in the front row pointedly asked him: "What are you going to do about these niggers in our schools?" To which he candidly replied: "This is a nation of laws. Civilized society must abide by laws. Ours is a government of law, not a government of men. That's why it has lasted for 200 years. . . . The court has ruled, and I think we must comply with its ruling." After a long, deathlike silence, someone posed another question, totally unrelated. With Wright's answer, the crowd laughed and clapped. He was still their popularly elected congressman.[33]

In January 1961, after John F. Kennedy won the presidential election with Lyndon Johnson as his running mate, Wright opted for a "larger stage"—but not a change in career. He immediately announced for Johnson's vacated Senate seat, thereby hoping to discourage others from filing. How wrong he was in his judgment of this campaign. Within the next few weeks seventy others "followed suit." Although vowing to "travel more miles, shake more hands, make more speeches than anyone else," he soon realized that a state campaign in Texas was not only terribly expensive but also extremely exhausting. Or, as Wright later concluded: "I might as well have been trying to siphon off the Gulf of Mexico with an eyedropper." Money was surely a factor; he raised $260,000 but had to borrow $80,000 more for a last-minute media blitz in the Houston area. But the fates, Wright opined, were against him. Halfway into a thirty-minute speech, in which he was appealing directly to Gulf Coast voters on prime-time television, a power shortage occurred for a number of minutes, thus negating this final plea for support. The race was close; Wright placed third and missed the runoff. Three weeks later he was even more chagrined when the lone Republican, John Tower of Wichita Falls, won over Bill Blakley of Dallas.[34]

Upon returning to Congress in May 1961, Wright experienced events that made his feelings range from exhilaration and inspiration to pathos and despair. President Kennedy "sparked" his imagination and idealism. Idealistic Kennedy administration goals such as founding the Peace Corps, preparing to land a man on the moon, and creating a hemispheric brotherhood with Latin American countries—Alliance for Progress—encouraged him to believe that all things were possible. Yet a burden of personal debt from the Senate race and his wife's growing disenchantment with politics worsened family relationships. To pay off campaign obligations, Wright sold some of his properties, including a cherished ranch, while borrowing money from a Weatherford bank to cover the rest. Because of this financial onus, which would take sixteen years to remove, he "felt locked in a jail," author John Barry observed. "The House seat meant little to him." And on November 22, 1963, with John Kennedy's assassination in Dallas, he—like so many in the nation—was even more grieved and despondent.[35]

But within the next few months Wright would be forced to dispel his sorrow. Lyndon Johnson would see to that; the president would designate him as one of his chief congressional lieutenants. Wright was therefore "up to his ears" in legislation for what was called the Great Society. In rapid-fire succession he would help push through Congress measures endorsed by the late John F. Kennedy "but with the LBJ stamp." As a consequence, Wright "thrilled," he later reflected, in helping bring about "sweeping educational reforms, the war on poverty, the experiments in affordable housing. . . . [and a] voting rights bill."[36]

At the same time Wright began to receive recognition from his colleagues, to slip the cloak of anonymity, or, as he put it, "to make a broader mark in the legislative arena." In January 1965, after the Appalachian Regional Development bill had been approved by the Public Works Committee, he was appointed chairman of a task force to round up votes for passage. By stressing the theme "Not a handout but a hand" (one that he would often use during his congressional career), Wright was well pleased with a 257 to 165 victory in the House. Then he became a floor leader for Lady Bird Johnson's favorite project, the Highway Beautification bill, and for expanding the nation's clean water program. When successful in both efforts, Wright decided to push for a massive federal development of the Trinity River, which would enable barge traffic from the Gulf of Mexico to reach as far north as Dallas and Fort Worth. Although opposed by the Johnson administration, he persevered; the President signed the bill in the fall of 1965.[37]

Wright was simultaneously bolstering his newfound importance in other ways. Besides being recognized as a Johnson favorite—a frequent visitor at the White House—he established himself as a representative knowledgeable in the workings of the House and of its rules. In 1965 he published *You and Your Congressman,* which displayed his admiration of the legislative branch as "probably the most fascinating human institution in the world." Two years later he wrote *The Coming Water Famine,* which confirmed him as a congressional authority on the nation's water problems. And since he was a six-termer who, by his "workaholic" attitude, was seeking more responsibility, House Speaker Carl Albert rewarded Wright by appointing him a deputy whip.[38]

In the summer of 1968, however, with President Johnson having decided not to run for reelection, Wright momentarily submerged all personal ambition. And the reason: Democratic nominee Hubert H. Humphrey was in a tightly contested race for the presidency against Republican Richard M. Nixon. Wright thus agreed to cochair, along with Will Davis of Austin, the state campaign for Humphrey. He did so with abandon. For six weeks he labored in the state headquarters in Austin, organizing an effective political workforce. Because of his friendship with state leaders, he successfully effected a détente between the warring John Connally and Ralph Yarborough factions of the state Democratic Party, bringing the two leaders together at a Humphrey luncheon in Fort Worth for the first time since the Kennedy assassination. Then, in conjunction with liberal Billie Carr of Houston, Wright helped assemble one of the largest political crowds in state history: on the Sunday just prior to the election, Democrats filled the Houston Astrodome to overflowing, with both Humphrey and Johnson in attendance. While Wright did not seek recognition for such strenuous efforts, his reward came on election day; Humphrey carried Texas by fifty thousand votes, although narrowly losing the presidency to Nixon.[39]

Back in Washington in 1969, Wright surprisingly maintained a high profile during the Nixon years. He and the president had an unusual rapport. On foreign policy Wright maintained—and he did so consistently throughout his career—that the executive and legislative branches should present a unified front as often as possible. He therefore proposed a bipartisan resolution, having one hundred cosponsors, that was designed to help "negotiate a peace" for the Vietnam War. Nixon agreed, specifically endorsing the Wright proposal before a special session of the House in December 1969. Again the next year Wright received presidential support to deter the dumping of "crop destructive salt" into the Colorado River, the results of which were polluting Mexican streams and land. And again during the early 1970s Wright worked successfully on the House Public Works Committee with Don Claussen (R-Calif.), a Nixon lieutenant, to preserve the California redwoods, which lumber companies threatened to ravage. And even though opposing the president on many domestic matters—especially any attempt to "usurp" congressional powers—Wright maintained a friendship with Nixon. On a number of occasions he was invited to the White House to consult with the president; at times the two

went to Washington Redskins games together, and on many Sunday morn-
ings Jim Wright and his new wife, Betty—he and Mab agreed to a "no
fault" divorce in 1970—attended worship services in the East Room of the
White House.[40]

Nor did his power diminish with the resignation of Nixon on August 8,
1974; on the contrary, Wright continued to be an aggressive member of the
House leadership team during the Ford administration. Speaker Albert,
besides keeping Wright on as one of four deputy whips, asked him to head
up a bipartisan task force that would specifically address the serious energy problems facing the United States after the Arab oil embargo of 1973.
The Senate Democratic leadership soon asked to be allowed to participate; therefore, Wright worked successfully with Senator John Pastore
(D-R.I.) to effect a comprehensive plan, which future congresses used as a
starting point. Equally important, Wright was becoming a dominant force
on the House Public Works Committee. Because of a downturn in the national economy in 1975–1976, this committee orchestrated through Congress a massive $2 billion matching public works program for urban and
rural infrastructure, including funds for sewer line extensions, water projects, street and bridge maintenance, and the erection or upkeep of public
buildings. And when President Ford vetoed this measure, both the House
and Senate garnered the necessary two-thirds majority to override the
veto and enact it. At the same time, the House Public Works Committee
became even more powerful, extending its jurisdiction to all manner of
transportation, including airlines. And in 1976, when Committee Chairman Bob Jones (D-Ala.) announced plans to retire, Wright (as the ranking
Democrat) was the obvious successor.[41]

But with Speaker of the House Carl Albert also deciding to retire,
contests for House leadership posts forced a career-making decision
upon Wright, yet one that he had aspired to since high school. Majority
Leader Thomas "Tip" O'Neill (D-Mass.) was the uncontested candidate
for Speaker. The race for majority leader, however, seemed to evolve into
a three-way contest between John McFall (D-Calif.), who, as the majority
whip, was the third leading member of the Democratic leadership team,
affable and well liked, but lacking the "push" and "fire" so necessary
for the job; Richard Bolling (D-Mo.), brilliant, but sometimes caustic in
tongue and abrasive in manner, who "had served as the intellectual beacon
of the House for over a decade"; and Phil Burton (D-Calif.), an aggressive
and at times vindictive liberal, who had served as chairman of the House
Democratic Caucus. During the summer of 1976 all three campaigned vigorously for the job, each in his own way attempting to lock up a majority
commitment from the members—but seemingly to no avail.[42]

Because Democrats were unhappy with their several choices, Wright emerged as a fourth candidate late in August. His strategy was easy to understand. The Texas delegation and Public Works Committee members were his basic strengths, along with southerners and a number of moderate and conservative Democrats. Thus the contest "boiled down" to "counting noses." Wright's late entry meant that he would have to build his strategy on second- and third-round pledges; if no candidate received a majority, the man with the fewest votes would be dropped from the next round. Believing that McFall would be eliminated first, Wright worked to pick up a majority of those commitments. Then he hoped to eke out Burton or Bolling in the second round and "lay everything on the line and roll the dice" on the final ballot. That is exactly what happened. At the Democratic Caucus in December 1976, after Tip O'Neill was elected Speaker, the 295 assembled representatives voted for majority leader on the opening ballot: Burton, 106; Bolling, 81; Wright 77; McFall 31. Soon thereafter came the second ballot: Burton, 107; Wright 95; Bolling 93. Then, dramatically, the Members cast the third and final ballot: Wright, 148; Burton, 147. Jim "Landslide" Wright was the new majority leader of the House of Representatives.[43]

Although having made no specific preparations to assume this formidable position of leadership, Wright soon flourished in his new job. As he later reflected, "I really came into my own" during the Carter years. Time and again he worked closely with the new president, often as point man in Congress for administration proposals. For example, he was the key legislative figure in President Carter's efforts to develop a comprehensive energy program "to make this nation energy-independent by 1990." Hence, Congress established a number of monetary incentives for American business from 1977 to 1980, such as for exploratory drilling, for efforts to maximize recovery from every well, and for development of alternate fuels. At the same time, energy-conservation measures—the 55 mph speed limit, financial aid for home insulation, and government oil storage—were also necessary ingredients in the Carter program.[44]

In foreign affairs Wright became equally well involved. During the fall and spring of 1977–1978 he helped steer "implementing legislation" through the House that had to do with the controversial Panama Canal Treaties. "It was a hard sell," he later reflected, "but it was right." He also assisted Carter in Latin American relations. At the president's request he made several trips to Panama, El Salvador, and Nicaragua, meeting with those nations' leaders, conveying to them the position and policies of the United States, and then, upon his return, giving Carter a personal evaluation. In addition, Wright worked closely with President Anwar Sadat of

Egypt and Prime Minister Menachem Begin of Israel, on several occasions hosting their appearances before congressional audiences. Continually the president asked Wright to evaluate the two leaders, especially their reactions to peace initiatives, the outcome of which eventually resulted in the historic Camp David Accords of March 26, 1979. As a consequence, Wright developed an effective working relationship with, as well as a genuine fondness for, Jimmy Carter. In turn, he achieved what he considered to be the "ultimate" praise for his efforts. On January 14, 1980, a poll by *U.S. News and World Report* showed that colleagues had selected him as "the most respected" member of Congress as well as "the most persuasive in debate."[45]

With the election of Ronald Reagan, however, Wright would experience an entirely different kind of participation in government—that of the loyal opposition, whose counsel was ignored and whose legislative contribution was unwelcome. Although Wright had hoped to "build the same kind of relationship that had existed between President Eisenhower and Speaker Rayburn and Senate Leader Lyndon Johnson," Reagan wanted nothing to do with the House leadership. In fact, confrontation with O'Neill and Wright seemed to be the first item on the Republican agenda.[46]

And the new president, riding a wave of popularity, especially after his recovery from an assassination attempt, rode roughshod over the House leadership. Time and again, as Wright reflected, they "tasted the bitter dregs of defeat." In 1981 the two Gramm-Latta Amendments to the budgetary process assaulted many New Deal, Fair Deal, and Great Society programs, ripping "gaping holes," Wright lamented, "in the safety net which protected the least fortunate members of society." Again that same year, despite vigorous Democratic opposition, the Hance-Connable Tax Amendment (known as the National Economic Recovery Act), also "sailed" through Congress, drastically reducing taxes for upper-income Americans while adding billions of dollars to federal deficits. Then in 1986 the Reagan administration, with the help of Treasury Secretary James Baker and Chairman of the House Ways and Means Committee Dan Rostenkowski (D-Ill.), engineered through Congress an "uncomplicated, streamlined" tax bill that further aided the wealthiest Americans. No matter that Wright denounced all such legislation as attacks on Social Security, housing, job creation, and education programs; no matter that he repeatedly pointed out the destructive effects that such huge deficits would have upon the American economy and future generations of Americans—the public continued to support their "Teflon president," who aggressively continued his partisan course of action.[47]

Ever so gradually, however, the House leadership of O'Neill and Wright began making headway and realizing some success. Despite administration assurances that the Central Intelligence Agency was not involved in an attempt to overthrow the Nicaraguan government, evidence soon appeared to the contrary. Consequently, in 1985, Congress passed the Boland Amendment, which specifically forbade the use of covert funds to invade or overthrow a foreign government. In turn, Wright helped generate monetary aid for President José Napoleón Duarte of El Salvador, who was attempting to establish a democratic government in his country; in so doing he saved the Reagan administration from a bruising defeat in the House. Then in November 1986, the breaking Iran-Contra scandal brought embarrassment to the president, thereby weakening his prestige and influence. And one other event was equally devastating to Reagan. On January 7, 1987, the House leadership changed hands: Tip O'Neill retired and Jim Wright was elected Speaker.[48]

After thirty-two years in Congress as well as ten years as majority leader, Jim Wright was anxious to assume leadership, to have the legislative branch achieve its rightful position as a coequal in government with the executive branch. And he was in a hurry, not necessarily because of his age, but because he believed Congress needed to accomplish so many things for the nation. He therefore placed his rigorous stamp of leadership on the 100th Congress. Immediately he established control over major house committees — Steering and Policy, Rules, and Budget. He devised a plan to set the first twenty bills as specific leadership measures. As soon as possible he called together committee chairs and assigned them "particular blocks of time on the House floor for the consideration of the leadership bills." He also "gave early notice" to them that he expected such measures out of committee and before the House within the first four months (rather than rely on an elastic timetable that might stretch into September). And he expressed his determination to have all appropriations bills on the president's desk by October 1, which was the beginning of the new fiscal year.[49]

To facilitate this ambitious schedule, Wright initiated further reforms, both procedural and substantive. He informed organizations that had become accustomed to inviting House members to participate in Monday golf tournaments that House votes would not be postponed simply to accommodate them. But more important, he persuaded the members of the Rules Committee to help expedite legislative enactment by deterring "guerrilla tactics" by "extreme, rightwing Republicans," who had, in past years, "stalled legislation" through numerous, "frivolous" amendments. The Rules Committee thus streamlined debate by notifying members that amendments would "have to be on file the day prior to their being offered on the floor." [50]

And what were the results of such planning and leadership? The 100th Congress was the most productive and effective since the mid-1960s. Overriding four presidential vetoes, the House and Senate passed four measures of vital importance, specifically a Clean Water Act, a Highway Act, a Civil Rights Act, and a Trade Reform Act (the largest reform package since the 1960s). They also enacted a law providing shelters and emergency food for the growing number of homeless Americans; then, toward the closing days of the session, they passed a landmark antidrug initiative. And, following Wright's suggestions, the Budget Committee presented a $36 billion deficit-reduction proposal, divided evenly between spending cuts and tax increases. [51]

In order that the Congress be a coequal with the executive branch, Wright also expected the House to participate in foreign policy. At the Easter recess in 1987 he and a bipartisan House contingent visited the Soviet Union. While there he consulted with Premier Mikhail Gorbachev and top Kremlin leaders for two hours. Upon their invitation he addressed the Soviet people over television, the result of which was a deluge of three thousand letters. Then in the midsummer of 1987, through presidential mediator and former congressman Tom Loeffler (R-Tex.), he was invited by Reagan to sponsor an American bipartisan proposal for a viable Central American peace conference. Although most House leaders suspected an administrative trap, Wright was willing to "take the gamble," and he quickly accepted. As a consequence, five Central American presidents met at Esquipulas, Guatemala, just outside Guatemala City, in August 1987, where—to the surprise of the Reagan administration—they fashioned a joint agreement based on "cease fires, political amnesty, and reconciliation to honest and open elections." When Reagan showed signs of pulling back U.S. support for the accord, Wright doggedly continued to maintain his position, offering encouragement repeatedly to President Oscar Arias of Costa Rica as well as to the Nicaraguan Sandinista leaders. Thus, through such efforts and by taking hazardous political risks, Wright was, in large part, responsible for a Central American peace that has affected Nicaragua and El Salvador so consequentially. [52]

But such dynamic, forceful leadership was not without political peril, not without a heavy price to pay. The Republican minority in the House, long frustrated by thirty-four years of continuous Democratic rule, became increasingly desperate to change their situation. A vindictive representative Newt Gingrich (R-Ga.) was determined to gain power; therefore, he was willing to alter the makeup and damage the reputation of

Congress to achieve this objective. He knew of no better way than to attack the integrity of Jim Wright. In June 1987 Gingrich leveled six spurious charges of misconduct against the Speaker (he had unsuccessfully used the same ploy against Speaker O'Neill). After Gingrich exhorted Fred Wertheimer of Common Cause to ask for an investigation, the House Ethics Committee, under pressure, took up the matter.[53]

As a result, Jim Wright underwent, during the 101st Congress, an excruciating ordeal. During the 146 days of his second term as Speaker, forces—relentless, unforgiving, at times malevolent—were at work in Washington and soon throughout the nation. The House Ethics Committee members revealed the weaknesses of rules procedures by allowing Outside Counsel Richard J. Phelan, a politically ambitious Chicago trial attorney, to go on "an open-ended fishing expedition." He would go far beyond the six charges levied by Gingrich—of which Wright was acquitted—and investigate every aspect of Wright's forty-year political career. Phelan would thus persuade the Ethics Committee on April 17, 1987, by faulty logic and a distortion of the evidence, to charge the Speaker with sixty-nine violations of House rules on five separate counts. Then the news media administered the coup de grace, the "hole card" upon which Phelan was relying. In other words, he never expected a trial to take place, partly because of the expense to the Speaker (estimated at $1.5 million in defense fees) but mainly because of the political fallout. And he was correct in his analysis. Reporters, insatiable in their search for "the truth" and "the people's right to know," inspected every negative aspect of Wright's public and private life; they used the so-called Phelan Report—which many accepted as fact—as their point of reference. *The New York Times,* the *Washington Post,* the *Wall Street Journal,* the *Baltimore Sun,* the *Los Angeles Times,* and scores of other prominent newspapers praised the "courageous" work of the House Ethics Committee as well as the dedicated service of its appointed Outside Counsel. In fact, not one national journal assigned an investigative reporter to determine the accuracy of the Phelan Report.[54]

During the last ten days of May 1989, Wright realized that only one choice—in this awesome power struggle—remained to him. More and more he worried about the effects of this "furor" on his family, about the damaging attacks upon his reputation and "good name." By now he knew that the Ethics Committee was solidified against him, that an expensive and gut-wrenching trial in the House was in the offing, and that the news media were intent on his resignation. But of equal, if not greater, concern to him was that the legislative agenda in the House had ground to a standstill, that his troubles were inhibiting the Democratic leadership from being effective in behalf of the people. So on Wednesday, May 31, at 2:00 P.M., before a packed gallery, he strode to the well of the House, told his side of the story, and then resigned—in the hopes that such "mindless cannibalism" in the House would cease.[55]

What were the results of this brief, but dramatic, struggle for power in the House? In May 1990 Richard Phelan, after raising $2 million in campaign funds, was elected president of the Cook County Board of Commissioners (Chicago), considered the third most powerful public office in Illinois. At the beginning of the 102nd Congress the House reformed the Ethics Committee, enlarging its membership as well as bifurcating the investigatory and disciplinary phases of an inquiry. The news media, although "used" by Gingrich and Phelan, showed no signs of contrition or remorse for their biased reporting of the "news"; instead, the Fourth Estate, after abetting the downfall of a powerful Speaker who sought to demonstrate by his leadership in the 100th Congress that the legislative branch could be the coequal with the executive branch, has lamented continually the lack of leadership in Congress over the past thirteen years.

Jim Wright returned to his district in Fort Worth, where a poll of his constituents on June 25, 1989, showed that 81 percent believed that he had done an "outstanding" or "good" job. In the years that followed his retirement from public life, nothing has changed to dampen that approbation. Wright has maintained a busy speaking schedule nationwide; has completed his memoir, *Balance of Power: Presidents and Congress from the Era of McCarthy to the Age of Gingrich;* and has written a Sunday newspaper column for the *Fort Worth Star-Telegram.* He has also taught political science courses at Texas Christian University. Most importantly, he enjoys times of reflection with friends, and precious times with his loving wife, Betty, and their devoted family.

As for Newt Gingrich—who boasted to author John Barry, "This case was never about ethics; it was always about power"—he was first rewarded for his schemes by being selected Republican minority whip, then in 1995 Speaker of the House, the position that he coveted all along. It is fitting that in 1997, amid the Clinton scandals, Gingrich himself came under attack. After a series of charges that he had violated House ethics rules, several being the same rules that he had used earlier in his assault upon Jim Wright, Gingrich resigned in disgrace.[56]

Through it all, Jim Wright has accomplished something that has eluded Gingrich, something that transcends the fury of the political arena that the Texan mastered so well and for so long: He has risen above the rancor and bitterness that characterized his final years in Washington. As the former Speaker aptly reminisced: "My dad gave me, when I was fifteen, a framed copy of Kipling's poem 'If.' I gave it a special place on the wall of my room. Now I bribe my grandsons to memorize it. Well, maybe *bribe* isn't the right word. *I coax them with appropriate financial incentive,*" he admitted. "If any of them should go into politics—a prospect toward which I have highly mixed emotions—I want him to remember all the passages of that poem, and especially the one that says:

> Or, being lied about, don't deal in lies
> Or, being hated, don't give way to hating
> And yet don't look too good, nor talk too wise.[57]

LLOYD BENTSEN JR.

Fig. 12.1. Lloyd Bentsen, elected as U.S. senator in 1970, became the Democratic nominee for vice president in 1988 and later served as U.S. treasury secretary in the first Bill Clinton administration. Prints and Photographs Collection, Center for American History, UT-Austin (CN 10271).

LLOYD BENTSEN JR.

BY MICHAEL L. COLLINS

The white heat of the television lights seemed more intense than usual in Omaha, Nebraska, on the night of October 5, 1988. A capacity crowd filed into the civic auditorium as the major networks busily prepared to air a nationally televised debate between the Republican and Democratic parties' vice presidential candidates. For both participants and their campaigns, the event marked the emotional high point of a grueling marathon that had already turned out to be the most mean-spirited in memory. Despite Republican standard-bearer George Bush's assertions to the contrary, the contest had been anything but "kinder and gentler." Although debates between vice presidential aspirants were a recent invention in American politics—rarely had the American electorate expressed more than a passing interest in who occupied the second place on the national tickets—the atmosphere in Omaha seemed to be charged with electricity. Since the summer conventions the national media had reminded the public of the succession of "accidental presidents" in the Cold War era and of the real possibility that one of the two men facing the glare of the television cameras that evening might—in one sudden, terrible moment—become president of the United States. The familiar cliche was used by network broadcasters as the program went on the air: the outcome of the debate could determine who would soon stand "a heartbeat away" from the presidency.[1]

As moderator Judy Woodruff introduced the two candidates to the studio audience and to millions of viewers across the country, few could have expected that the next ninety minutes would be the most memorable of the entire 1988 presidential campaign. From the opening questions, the boyish-looking Republican senator Dan Quayle of Indiana was visibly nervous, uncomfortable, and too carefully scripted, while his Democratic opponent, the senior senator from Texas, sixty-seven-year-old Lloyd Millard Bentsen Jr., appeared relaxed, confident, and prepared. And soon it became apparent why. A calm and statesmanlike Bentsen articulated his grasp of the great domestic issues of the day—his concern over the national health care crisis, home mortgage and interest rates, the future of Social Security, the deteriorating national educational system, and America's growing dependence upon imported oil. He decried the economic policies of the Reagan-Bush administration and the excesses of the 1980s, specifically the dire consequences of mounting consumer indebtedness, the escalating international trade deficit, and the swelling national debt. In response to Quayle's assertion that President Ronald Reagan and Vice President George Bush had given the American people the longest period of uninterrupted economic growth since World War II, Bentsen retorted sardonically, "You know, if you let me write $200 billion worth of hot checks every year, I could give you the illusion of prosperity too."[2]

In contrast to the self-assured Bentsen, Quayle seemed able only to recite his résumé, to ramble about his devotion to family and flag, to make sneering references to the "liberal governor" of Massachusetts (the much demonized Democratic presidential nominee Michael Dukakis) and to deflect questions about his own qualifications for national leadership. At one point Quayle digressed from his rehearsed statements, boasting that he had read three books while on a recent vacation. Shortly thereafter, he even tried to impress the audience by claiming that British prime minister Margaret Thatcher and West German chancellor Helmut Kohl "know me." To most observers, Quayle's performance in the opening minutes of the debate appeared at best inept, at worst a babble of empty platitudes and grammatical errors. Twice he was pressed by panelists to explain what he would do if forced by fate to assume the presidency, and twice he refused the question, saying only that he would pray for the country. Then when asked for a third time by NBC anchor Tom Brokaw what would be his first act upon succeeding to the presidency, Quayle reminded viewers that he had as much experience to serve in the Oval Office as John F. Kennedy had had in 1960.[3]

It was the opening for which his opponent had hoped. Like a Texas game warden waiting to arrest a poacher, the angular, silver-haired Bentsen stared at Quayle, and silence fell over the auditorium. "Senator, I served with Jack Kennedy. I knew Jack Kennedy. Jack Kennedy was a friend of mine. Senator, you're no Jack Kennedy." "That remark was uncalled for, Senator," Quayle countered. "You're the one who was making the comparison," Bentsen bristled. "Frankly, I think you're so far apart in the objectives you choose for your country that I did not think the comparison was well taken." Bentsen had scored a direct hit.[4]

Only one day before the debate a *Newsweek* feature article previewing the vice presidential showdown had referred to Bentsen as the "invisible man of the campaign," the essay going so far as to assert that the "boring and pedantic" Texan was "clearly better suited to the cloakroom than the debate hall." Other political observers persisted in describing Bentsen as "bland," "unimaginative," "lacking passion." Humorist Mark Russell even jested that the Democrats, while at their Atlanta convention, should have asked broadcasting titan Ted Turner to "colorize" the Texan.[5]

But Bentsen's performance in Omaha had proved the pundits wrong again. No one was laughing at him now, least of all Dan Quayle. For the Bentsen family, and for friends and supporters across the Lone Star State and the nation, the vice presidential debate had been a moment of vindication. Those who knew the senator best were quick to point out that it was not the first time someone had made the mistake of underestimating Lloyd Bentsen.[6]

The story of Lloyd M. Bentsen Jr. began on February 11, 1921, in what is still the poorest region in the United States—the semiarid brush and mesquite country of the lower Rio Grande, long misnamed "the Valley." Born in a modest frame bungalow on a dirt road in Mission, Texas, the son of Lloyd and Edna Ruth "Dolly" Bentsen, young Lloyd grew to understand the importance of family and place. His grandfather Peter Bentsen, a Danish immigrant who had settled in a sod house in South Dakota in the 1880s, had escaped the harsh winters of the Northern Plains, moving his wife, Tena, and children to the warm summers and long growing seasons of South Texas in 1918. A successful nursery operator and citrus farmer, Peter had instilled in his sons a sense of self-reliance, and he taught them to understand the value of land—of buying land, owning land, working land, developing land, and selling land. The sons learned well that the South Texas plains demanded much of men, yet yielded little without hard work and the miracle of irrigation, the process that brought the life-giving water to the parched plains of the Valley. In time, Lloyd Bentsen Sr. taught his sons that they were themselves products of this barren border country, which had been transformed by an enterprising people into a semitropical oasis, a lush land of citrus orchards and green gardens and land promoters. It was a lesson they never forgot. On this modern-day frontier, it seemed that anything was possible, even reclaiming the sun-scorched earth from the stubborn forces of nature. Anything was possible, or so three generations of Bentsens came to believe.[7]

What began as Lloyd Sr. and brother Elmer Bentsen's profitable land-clearing operation that employed Mexican laborers in the post–World War I years soon turned into an expanding farming and ranching enterprise that sprawled far beyond Hidalgo County. From a single grocery store in the dusty village of McAllen, to controlling interest in at least eight South Texas banks, a family real estate and financial empire slowly emerged, an empire to which Lloyd Bentsen Jr. would one day be an heir.[8]

But the younger Bentsen was in a hurry to make his own mark upon the world. Graduating from Sharyland High School at the age of fifteen, Bentsen went on to the University of Texas, where he completed a law degree before his twenty-second birthday. While on the Austin campus, he had excelled academically, served as chapter president of the Sigma Nu fraternity, and made a number of lifelong friends, among them an ambitious and charismatic John Bowden Connally, the UT student body president who would soon find his way onto the staff of Congressman Lyndon Baines Johnson.[9]

Like others of his generation, Bentsen heeded his country's call to arms. Soon after his graduation in 1942, Bentsen enlisted in the United States Army as a private and, following basic training, was commissioned and assigned to Intelligence School. At twenty-three, Major Bentsen completed flight training before being shipped overseas to the European theater of the war, but not before marrying the young woman who had won his affections, a charming and attractive fashion model, Beryl Ann Longino of Lufkin, Texas, whom he had first met during their college days. In the final year of World War II, Bentsen commanded a bomber squadron of B-24 "Liberators" and flew some thirty-five missions over Germany and Italy. During one raid over Vienna, Bentsen's aircraft lost one of its four engines, then a second caught fire. Fast losing altitude over the rugged Alps, he eventually guided the crippled bomber and its eleven-man crew through the mountain peaks and over the Adriatic Sea, finally setting down safely on the secluded island of Viz, where he was greeted by Allied troops. As a result, by the age of twenty-four, Bentsen had earned a colonel's wings and was soon awarded the Distinguished Flying Cross.[10]

No sooner had the tall, angular Texan returned home to the Rio Grande Valley following the war than he opened a law practice. Then, almost immediately, he launched a political career that quickly led him into the corridors of power. His first campaign for public office ended with his election as Hidalgo County judge in 1946, giving him the distinction of being the youngest such official in the entire state. In 1948, after one term heading the county court, he announced his candidacy for the United States Congress. After incumbent congressman Milton West withdrew from the race because of failing health, young Bentsen ran in the Democratic primary with two effective slogans: "Beat the Machine," a reference to George Parr, the "Duke of Duval" County, and Mannie Raymond of Laredo, the same South Texas bosses who were supporting the candidacy of Lyndon B. Johnson for the United States Senate that year; and "The New Generation Offers a Leader," a phrase that Bentsen borrowed from the literature of another young war hero–candidate who also happened to be labeled a "rich kid" running against the odds and against the will of his local party bosses—John Fitzgerald Kennedy. He even borrowed another page out of Kennedy's 1946 successful campaign: the formation of women's groups throughout the district, made up mostly of mothers, sisters, and wives of former GIs, all eager to contribute to the campaign of a young candidate who understood veterans' concerns. Admittedly, in his campaign litera-ture he simply inserted "B-24 Liberator" in place of "P.T. 109." [11]

At the age of twenty-seven, the first-term representative from Texas was the youngest member of the Eighty-first Congress. Working quietly though diligently behind the scenes, the soft-spoken Bentsen followed the advice of fellow Texan Sam Rayburn, the seasoned and savvy Speaker of the House, who urged his young protégé to remain on the back bench of the legislative process, where he could listen and learn. Be patient, respectful of the seniority system, always open to compromise, willing to "go along in order to get along," Mr. Rayburn counseled, adding that Bentsen should remember that the most effective legislators are those who are workhorses, not show horses. Before long, Bentsen's intellect, prag-matism, and loyalty to party earned him a place in the inner sanctum of Speaker Rayburn. Although a freshman, a mere upstart, Bentsen began at-tending the so-called Board of Education, the closed-door bourbon-and-branch-water sessions held weekly in the Speaker's office where Rayburn, first-term senator Lyndon Johnson, and other insiders enjoyed laughs and libations while deciding the fate of bills before Congress. On Friday evenings, Bentsen even invited Rayburn, Johnson, Supreme Court Chief Justice Fred Vinson, and others to his home to play five-card stud poker. He learned well the lessons of legislative strategy and cloakroom diplo-macy that came from these informal gatherings—and well he should have. He could not have had a better mentor than "Mr. Sam." [12]

Rayburn saw in his young pupil a promising public servant who was mature beyond his years. On one occasion, when Bentsen and he sat chat-ting in the Speaker's office, an aide handed Rayburn a portrait that seemed to him unflattering. He looked over the photograph, which appeared to accentuate his bald head, then scowled, as if to mirror the expression and pose, and turned to throw it away. An amused Bentsen quickly re-trieved the photograph and asked if he could keep it, saying that it looked "Churchillian." Rayburn grinned and signed it, "To my friend Lloyd Bentsen, who likes ugly things." [13]

During his six-year career in the House of Representatives, Congress-man Bentsen enlisted in the crusade to contain communism both at home and abroad. He joined the growing chorus of concern on Capitol Hill about alleged sedition and espionage within the Departments of State and Defense, and he spoke openly of his determination to "ferret out the

Reds." At the outset of the Korean War in 1950, on the advice of Secretary of the Air Force Stuart Symington, he delivered a stunning speech on the House floor, urging President Harry Truman to issue an atomic ultimatum to the North Korean government: either withdraw beyond the 38th parallel within one week, or face nuclear destruction. Years later, a wiser and more prudent Bentsen would look back on this "nuke 'em" speech with some embarrassment, remembering the proposal as the youthful indiscretion of a former bomber pilot.[14]

While gaining the reputation as a spokesman for conservative causes — particularly on fiscal and national defense issues — the young Texan also served notice that he was faithful to neither faction nor philosophy. In 1949, much to the chagrin of many of his Anglo constituents, he was one of only two members of the Texas congressional delegation to bolt the southern Democratic block and vote against the poll tax as a requirement for participation in federal elections. Then in 1952 he resisted the entreaties of Governor Allan Shivers and other disgruntled conservative Texas Democrats who refused to support the party's presidential nominee, Governor Adlai Stevenson of Illinois, in part because of Stevenson's opposition to state control of Texas's "tidelands" offshore oil reserves. Rather than bolt Democratic ranks and endorse Republican nominee Dwight David Eisenhower — whom Bentsen had privately tried to persuade to run as a Democrat — Bentsen announced that he would reluctantly support Stevenson.[15]

By 1954, Bentsen had become bored with the tedious work of the House of Representatives, so he announced that he would step down and return to private life. Besides needing a new challenge, he found that the House's $12,500 annual salary was not enough to support his young family. To achieve the financial independence his father enjoyed, he would strike off into the competitive world of American business and not look back. Speaker Rayburn, distressed to learn that he would lose one of his favorite foot soldiers in the House, called Bentsen in and explained that it was foolish to give up his seat in a "safe district." In another twenty-five years you could be Speaker, Rayburn told him. "But I didn't have that much patience," Bentsen later recalled.[16]

Staked to a reported $7 million in capital by his father, "Big Lloyd," and Uncle Elmer, the thirty-three-year-old Bentsen moved to Houston and soon formed the Consolidated American Life Insurance Company (CALICO). Before long he acquired, through a leveraged buyout, the established firm of Lincoln Liberty Life Insurance Company of Omaha. By keeping that company's Nebraska charter, he was able to avoid restrictive Texas legislation that prohibited insurance companies from owning bank

Fig. 12.2. Congressman Lloyd Bentsen in 1950, early in his political career, at the Valley Livestock Yards in Donna, Texas. Bentsen (Lloyd M.) Papers, Center for American History, UT-Austin (CN 09805).

stocks. All his adult life, Bentsen had proved to be an exceptional poker player, so he was no stranger to risk taking. Only now the stakes were higher. He invested wisely—most of the time—and demonstrated the good judgment of a successful entrepreneur, taking advantage of every opportunity to expand and diversify his operations. Before he was finished, he had built a substantial insurance and banking conglomerate with few rivals in the Lone Star State and, in the process, had entered some of the most exclusive enclaves in the Texas corporate community, serving on the boards of directors of Lockheed Aircraft, Continental Oil, and Panhandle Eastern Pipeline Company.[17]

Still the political arena beckoned. In 1956 Bentsen made one of the toughest decisions of his public life when he joined forces with his old allies, Senate Majority Leader Lyndon Johnson and Speaker Sam Rayburn, both of whom were fighting to suppress another "Shivercrat" rebellion in the state Democratic Party. Still refusing to support the presidential aspirations of Adlai Stevenson, the rebellious Governor Shivers had again walked out on the party, calling for fellow conservative Democrats to defect with him to the Eisenhower-Nixon ticket. This time Bentsen openly declared his support for the LBJ-Rayburn faction, which narrowly carried a majority at the state Democratic convention and, therefore, controlled the Texas delegation to the national convention. Six years later, it was Bentsen who was among the first to urge his friend, John B. Connally, then secretary of the navy, to run for governor of Texas. When Connally wondered aloud where he would get his first campaign contribution, Bentsen purportedly pulled out his checkbook and began writing.[18]

During his sixteen years in the business world, Bentsen proved that he was good at making money, but by 1970 making money was no longer good enough for Bentsen. Encouraged by former President Johnson and by former governor Connally, he entered the race for the United States Senate seat held by Senator Ralph Yarborough, the populist folk hero from East Texas. Although he was armed with a full war chest and the legendary computerized mailing list of the Connally organization, the odds were clearly against Bentsen. One poll indicated that he had only a 2 percent name recognition across the state, and many respondents had confused him with Ezra Taft Benson, the controversial Mormon apostle and unpopular secretary of agriculture of the Eisenhower administration.[19]

Refusing to bow to the odds, Lloyd Bentsen wasted no time in launching a Democratic primary campaign, which soon turned into a brawling and bruising affair, even by Texas standards. His campaign managers, including former Connally crony and LBJ White House press secretary George Christian, recommended a television blitz across the state, using ads that labeled Yarborough a "liberal" and charging that he was a tool of eastern labor leaders and that his support for forced busing and gun control was inconsistent with the views of ordinary Texans. The TV spots, prepared by the Houston advertising firm of Rives, Dyke, and Company, also reminded voters of Yarborough's opposition to organized school prayer and the death penalty and of his support for the 1970 May Day war moratorium. One Bentsen ad even showed scenes of chaos during that demonstration, with long-haired, antiwar protesters burning the American flag; then the film stopped and a voice asked, "Did Ralph Yarborough represent your views?" Another Bentsen commercial asked Texans to recall Yarborough's support for Senator Eugene McCarthy of Minnesota at the 1968 Democratic National Convention in Chicago, then followed with images of the riots in Grant Park, of rock-hurling demonstrators taking to the streets, of tear gas canisters bursting amid the sounds of blaring police sirens.[20]

In turn, Yarborough attacked Bentsen as a patrician, a member of the monied aristocracy, an instrument of the big oil companies, a red-baiter, and a war hawk who was all too willing to press the thermonuclear button. Many of his campaign speeches even turned into diatribes directed against the elder Lloyd Bentsen, who was depicted as a patron whose fortune had been built upon Mexican "wetback" labor and land fraud. Understandably, supporters of both candidates feared that the winner of the fight might emerge so bloodied that the likely Republican nominee, Houston congressman George Bush, President Richard Nixon's hand-picked candidate, would be in a commanding position in the general election.[21]

Yarborough and his staff were caught off guard by Bentsen's strong challenge. All along they had planned a strategy that targeted Bush in the fall campaign, while Bush and his handlers had likewise assumed that they would be running against the incumbent Yarborough with his liberal voting record. But Bentsen blindsided them both. After upsetting Yarborough in the Democratic primary, 53 percent to 47 percent, Bentsen began the process of mending political fences, working to convince organized labor, farmers, and progressives to remain in the Democratic camp. His task was to assure these skeptical constituencies that he was not the right-wing ogre they had made him out to be. Compared to the brutal Democratic primary, the Bush-Bentsen battle proved to be a gentleman's contest, with both candidates saying much the same thing. By early October, Bentsen's own polls showed him trailing Bush by six percentage points, with Bush faring well in the Republican fortresses of Houston and Dallas as well as in West Texas; but Bentsen appeared to be holding on to comfortable leads in the traditional Democratic strongholds of Travis, Bexar, and Tarrant Counties and in his native South Texas. Perhaps it was in rural East Texas where the campaign turned in Bentsen's favor, especially when the abrasive Vice President Spiro Agnew intervened on Bush's behalf, an event that influenced many voters still seething over recent school desegregation suits brought by the Nixon administration.[22]

In the final weeks of the race the underdog Democrat defied the odds again, closing the gap by the November election with a late television saturation campaign and arguably the most effective get-out-the-vote organization the state had ever seen. As it turned out, Bentsen's come-from-behind victory determined not only his own political future but also that of Nixon protégé George Bush. Simply put, the outcome of that key race set both men on different yet parallel courses toward the pinnacle of power.[23]

Soon after being sworn into office in 1971, Senator Bentsen confided to colleague Gaylord Nelson of Wisconsin, "I'm not as conservative as you fellows think I am." Not long thereafter he explained to one reporter, "I am a moderate. But I dislike labels; I prefer to look at each issue." Indeed, as he had done in the House, the junior senator from Texas quickly established himself as an independent-minded and pragmatic spokesperson for his state and the nation, a man who was not afraid to admit mistakes and change course whenever circumstances dictated. During his first year in office he traveled to Southeast Asia and returned with the realization that Vietnam was a war America could not win, and one that the United States should never have entered. Back in Washington he shunned the suggestion by Vice President Agnew that his victory over Yarborough had been a triumph for Nixon's conservative agenda. "I'm coming here as part of the loyal opposition," Bentsen snapped, reminding reporters and the Republican administration of his Democratic credentials. Advancing the cause of former adversary Ralph Yarborough, he introduced legislation to set aside some 100,000 acres of East Texas timberlands for the establishment of the Big Thicket National Preserve, though he later had to settle for 86,000 acres to secure support for the bill's passage. Then he wasted little time in courting the favor of labor. Maybe he could not make them forgive or forget the brutal campaign that he had waged against Yarborough, but he began the slow process of winning the confidence of union organizations. So impressed was one labor lobbyist with the new senator from Texas that he admitted, "I feel good about the man . . . probably because I expected him to be so damned bad, and he turned out to be a reasonable man."[24]

Bentsen and organized labor soon found that they had something in common — a commitment to a pension reform bill sponsored by Senator Jacob Javits of New York. Bentsen was deeply touched and even moved to anger upon hearing that a fellow member of the River Oaks Baptist Church in Houston was suddenly fired by his employer within weeks of the date on which his pension was to be vested after thirty years of company service. Shortly thereafter the man died following a lengthy illness. Fighting for the bill that was designed to protect workers from such a circumstance thus became not only a just cause but one that Bentsen viewed more in personal than in political terms. Behind the scenes the quiet but methodical Texan used all of his persuasive powers to break the deadlock over the measure, which eventually passed in 1973.[25]

For those who expected Bentsen to live up to his "conservative" reputation, the senator's voting record seemed to belie the label and even defy political gravity. In all of the following — seeking to curb the investment powers of banks that controlled over $200 billion in pension assets; supporting tax reforms that proposed to limit the controversial oil depletion allowance; promoting welfare reform, the creation of temporary public service jobs for America's youths, and increased funding for research into alternative sources of energy — Bentsen followed his conscience first and party and ideology second.[26]

Nowhere was this more evident than on the issue of the Vietnam War. Time and again, Bentsen charged that President Nixon was not "leveling" with the American people about the expansion of the war into Laos and Cambodia. No longer the hawkish cold warrior, Bentsen supported a series of "end-the-war" amendments and also joined forces with those who sponsored the War Powers Act, designed to restrain the chief executive from committing United States forces to long-term hostilities without the consent of Congress.[27]

From the beginning of his senatorial career, Bentsen had understood the importance of cultivating alliances, and he quickly learned how to exercise power. He lobbied to land himself the committee assignments that would place him in a position to "make a difference." Befriended by the flinty Senate majority leader Mike Mansfield of Montana and by the seasoned Louisiana senator Russell Long, influential chairman of the Senate Finance Committee, the Texan ascended in stature, so rapidly in fact that some pundits began making the inevitable comparison between Bentsen and LBJ.

Irritated by press reports that he was nothing more than a Johnson clone—a "prettified version of Lyndon" as one commentator had called him—Bentsen was determined to prove that he stood in no man's shadow. Being a spokesman from the Lone Star State was anything but an advantage in those days. Not only would Bentsen suffer from comparisons with the unpopular former president, but he would discover that the political baggage carried by any Texan in the nation's capital included an association with "Lyndon's war," identification with the oil industry's windfall profits at a time when the public debated whether or not there really was an "energy crisis," envy over Texas's huge share of federal defense dollars and aerospace spending, and even haunting memories of President Kennedy's assassination in Dallas a decade earlier.[28]

Bentsen therefore tried to distance himself from his Texas ties as the 1976 presidential election approached. He set himself apart from most members of the Texas congressional delegation by supporting funding for an "Energy Bank" to develop solar, thermal, and nuclear energy as practical alternatives to burning fossil fuels. Early in 1975, as he "tested the waters" for a possible run at the White House, he took an even bigger step away from the powerful petrochemical industry in his home state when he proposed to limit the controversial oil depletion allowance for major oil companies yet retain the lucrative shelter for smaller independents. The forces of "Big Oil" were stunned. As a lobbyist for one of the "majors" put it: "with this bill Bentsen crossed the Rubicon. He damned well better win the Presidency, because he isn't going to get any more big oil support for the Senate."[29]

In the aftermath of the Watergate affair, the presidential impeachment crisis, and the subsequent resignation of Richard Nixon in August 1974, Democrats appeared to be positioned well to reclaim the White House. Already, in anticipation of unseating President Gerald R. Ford, many of the Democratic Party's faithful were beginning to talk about Bentsen as a possible contender to carry their standard in the 1976 campaign. In the corridors of Congress some began to speak openly of a Bentsen candidacy, while a few, including Senator Mansfield, even publicly mentioned the Texan as a front-runner for the nomination. Back home in Texas, the prospect of a Bentsen campaign generated considerable interest, not only in Austin political circles but also in corporate board rooms around the state. The fact that former Nixon administration secretary of the treasury John B. Connally might also run for the Republican nomination made the upcoming campaign all the more important in the Lone Star State.[30]

In February 1975, on a foggy Monday morning in Washington, D.C., and again later that same day in Houston, Bentsen formally announced his candidacy for the Democratic presidential nomination. Berating the Nixon and Ford administrations for the faltering economy, he vowed to "restore the meaning of America's two great promises: opportunity at home and moral leadership" abroad. He said little about the recent loss of public trust and confidence in the nation's elected leaders and the reigning cynicism about the Washington establishment. Such an omission was perhaps the first misjudgment of the ill-fated campaign.[31]

Crisscrossing the nation, delivering hundreds of speeches, "pressing the flesh," and raising money for his candidacy, Bentsen hurled himself into the minefields of presidential politics. Yet he had no constituency outside of Texas, little name identification "beyond the Beltway" of Washington, and he made the fatal mistake of bypassing early primary and caucus states like New Hampshire and Wisconsin in favor of concentrating his energies and resources on more populous states that would select large blocks of convention delegates later in the race. He probably relied too much on his financial supporters in Texas, especially considering the fact that the rumored candidacy of his old friend, Democrat-turned-Republican John B. Connally, threatened to tie up potential contributors, many of whom were awaiting to see what "Big John" would decide. Moreover, Bentsen failed to target effectively groups of likely Democratic contributors around the country. His lack of experience in international affairs did not help his chances. Neither did reports of disagreements between campaign manager Ben Palumbo, the tough-talking political strategist from New Jersey, and other members of Bentsen's "brain trust." This rift apparently led to Palumbo's abrupt and early departure from the campaign. Even more significant, Bentsen simply failed to master the medium of television. On camera he appeared stiff, too analytical, even dull.[32]

The rigors of a national campaign turned out to be even more exhausting than Bentsen had anticipated. As one journalist noted in November 1975, the grueling schedule had already "taken its toll." The candidate was weary, frustrated by the absence of momentum, by the small and oftentimes lethargic crowds, and "it showed in the deepening lines on his face, [and] in sluggish speeches."[33]

Then came the primary season and a series of early disappointments. Bentsen's hopes were dashed all too quickly with poor showings in the Oklahoma and Arkansas caucuses. Even before the critical New Hampshire primary, he was therefore labeled a loser. The networks were already anointing the smiling and telegenic Governor Jimmy Carter of Georgia as the man to beat. So on February 10, 1976, one year after launching his presidential bid, Bentsen withdrew from the race.[34]

Still there was much to be done: seeking reelection to the Senate over the Republican challenger, Congressman Alan Steelman of Dallas; handling bills before the tax-bill-writing Senate Finance Committee and the tax-revenue-spending Armed Services and Public Works Committees; working with the new Carter administration; and representing the interests of his constituents in the Lone Star State.

During the 1980s Senator Lloyd Bentsen had been all too simplistically characterized as a conservative. He was criticized by liberals as an agent of corporate interests, as "Pac Man," the recipient of large campaign contributions from political action committees, or PACs, and special interest groups representing American industry (most especially oil, natural gas, and defense industries). His critics on the left were quick to recall his earlier opposition to gun-control laws and to a comprehensive national health-care reform, his continuing support for the death penalty, his votes for Ronald Reagan's tax cuts of 1981, for increased Pentagon spending, including the Strategic Defense Initiative, otherwise known as "Star Wars," and for aid to the "Nicaraguan resistance," otherwise known as the "contras." Some liberals went so far as to label him "loophole Lloyd," in reference to the numerous tax shelters for the business community that he had supported for giant American corporations during his reign as the powerful chairman of the Senate Finance Committee. Then, when the Texan wanted to charge lobbyists $10,000 each to have breakfast with him in 1987, they pointed to the embarrassing "Eggs McBentsen" affair as evidence that he was nothing more than a "corporatist"—or worse, a Republican disguised as a Democrat.[35]

But, more often than not, Bentsen found himself at odds with those who proudly call themselves "conservative"—namely, Reagan's "New Right." Almost overlooked is the fact that while a number of conservative Texas Democrats were switching to the Republican Party, Bentsen not only remained within the Democratic fold, but he even worked to rebuild the fractious party in the most difficult of times. Time and again, he voted for civil rights legislation, for expansion of Medicare and Medicaid programs, for increased funding for prenatal and neonatal care, for laws to limit campaign contributions, and for workers' rights (such as the 1971 Pension Reform bill, the 1988 Plant Closing Notification bill, and long overdue increases in the minimum wage standard). During the Reagan-Bush era he opposed Republican plans to slash capital gains taxes for the wealthiest of Americans and even led one fight to offer tax relief to middle-income working families with children. Moreover, he consistently failed three important litmus tests that Reagan supporters administered to identify "real Conservatives," or true believers in their movement. He assumed a pro-choice position on abortion; he refused to join the "no new taxes" bandwagon, referring to George Bush's 1988 campaign pledge to veto new taxes as "pure Bushlips"; and he opposed the controversial Supreme Court nominations of ideological conservatives Robert Bork and Clarence Thomas.[36]

Bentsen's Republican opponents in the 1982 and 1988 reelection campaigns, the ultraconservative congressman Jim Collins of Dallas and Representative Beau Boulter of Amarillo, even tried to hang the liberal tag on Bentsen. But the truth is, as Bentsen gained stature and recognition as a leader of the national Democratic Party, he continued to defy broad and simplistic labels. As the senator put it succinctly, "I prefer to speak to each issue."[37]

Still, many persisted in making comparisons between Bentsen's career in the Senate and that of LBJ. Both were ambitious conservatives who were tugged to the left by the agenda of the national Democratic Party and by their own efforts to broaden their base of support beyond Texas. Both suffered unfairly from the burdens of Texas history—their associations with increasingly unpopular oil and defense industries so vital to their state, their unyielding Alamo mentality regarding foreign affairs, and their efforts to overcome the racial biases ingrained in Texas's past. Former Johnson press secretary George Christian said it best when he pointed out that Bentsen is "a lot like LBJ and most of our successful politicians in Texas. He doesn't want to pull anyone down, but to see to it that everyone gets a piece of the pie." Longtime Bentsen aide Lloyd Hackler went so far as to call his former boss "an LBJ with couth." Another observer pointed out that, while there were similarities between both men's careers, Bentsen would never "scratch or cuss in public."[38]

As Michael Dukakis prepared to claim the Democratic presidential nomination at the 1988 Atlanta convention and considered the matter of a running mate, he was mesmerized by the prospect of forming another Boston-Austin axis, as his idol John F. Kennedy had done twenty-eight years earlier. Despite much speculation that the rational and cautious Dukakis was blinded by the mystique of 1960, he chose Bentsen as the vice presidential candidate for another reason. It was logical. Dukakis staffers advised that the Texan's presence on the ticket would provide both geographic and ideological balance and also help unite and strengthen the party by appealing to more moderate and conservative voters, independents and "Reagan Democrats" alike, who might identify Dukakis as a social engineer and a "tax-and-spend" wastrel. Finally, they reminded him, no Democrat had ever won a presidential election without carrying Texas. No matter that party liberals might view the marriage as one of convenience, or that Jesse Jackson's "Rainbow Coalition" might threaten to sit out the campaign. Never mind that the press and Republican opponents would doubtless attack the partnership as a political "odd couple." Bentsen knew more about tax and trade policies than any member of Congress. Better yet, he had even defeated George Bush once before. Maybe he could "debunkport" Bush's Texas credentials once again, as he had in 1970. Most of the Massachusetts governor's inner circle therefore insisted that Bentsen was the right man. And Dukakis agreed.[39]

Lloyd Bentsen's greatest moment of triumph came at the 1988 Democratic National Convention in Atlanta. At last, the grandson of a Danish immigrant had arrived at the center stage of the American political arena as he stepped to the podium to accept his party's nomination for the vice presidency of the United States. Sounding again the theme of economic justice and opportunity for all, he spoke of the historic principles of his party and of his own hopes for a better America. He ridiculed the economic policies of the 1980s. "My friends, America has just passed through the ultimate epoch of illusion," he told a national television audience. "An eight-year coma in which slogans were confused with solutions and rhetoric passed for reality; a time when America tried to borrow its way to prosperity." He excoriated the Reagan-Bush administration for "turning the clock back" on civil rights. Then he reminisced about his own beginnings. Gazing up at the gallery, he smiled at his ninety-four-year-old father, a legend in his own right. Referring to the elder Bentsen as "a symbol of what people of courage and vision and daring can achieve," the senator motioned to his "dad" and concluded, "he has lived the American dream—the dream we want to come true for our children." [40]

That he should speak of his parents and grandparents in the most important address of his entire career should have come as no surprise. After all, as a boy Bentsen had learned from his family never to forget who he was and where he came from. As the campaign of 1988 droned on, the media continued to recall the campaign of 1960, and perhaps they should have. The analogies were striking: an incumbent Republican vice president struggling to establish his own political identity and succeed a popular two-term president, opposed by a "son of Massachusetts" and a veteran senator from the Lone Star State who, by virtue of what Texans call the LBJ law, could join the national ticket while, at the same time, running for reelection to the Senate. But as the coming campaign proved, Dukakis was no Jack Kennedy. [41]

For that matter, Lloyd Bentsen was no Lyndon Johnson. Uncomfortable with the hand-clasping, back-slapping politics for which LBJ was noted, Bentsen's style and temperament were strikingly different. He could never be the grasping, smothering figure who moved people by the sheer force of his personality. Still, the senior senator from Texas remained the last link with the Garner-Rayburn-Johnson dynasty.

To the surprise of many supporters, and despite rumors to the contrary, by late 1991 Bentsen had apparently opted against reentering what Theodore Roosevelt once called the "bear pit" of presidential politics. Bentsen continued to serve, however, as perhaps the most respected elder statesman in the much-beleaguered Congress. At the age of seventy-one, he still enjoyed the challenges of leadership and, more particularly, his role as President George Bush's "most effective Democratic tormentor," in the words of one observer. Whether it was insisting that the Bush administration was adrift without an effective national energy policy (Bentsen continued to preach the virtues of an oil import fee), or that the president had no plan for dealing with the growing international trade deficit, Bentsen often bedeviled and at times outfoxed his longtime adversary on such issues as capital gains, tax increases, and national health care. [42]

Maybe one Democrat was right about Bentsen when he noted the senator's dry sense of humor and lack of showmanship: "there ain't a lot of Elvis in Lloyd Bentsen." But perhaps, as Sam Rayburn might have put it, Bentsen was never cut out to be a show horse. Throughout his Senate career, though, he remained a workhorse, the kind of yeoman legislator who got the job done, albeit without much fanfare. [43]

This the newly elected Democratic president Bill Clinton understood and respected following his surprise victory in November, 1992. Even before Clinton was sworn into office on January 20, 1993, word leaked that he wanted Bentsen on his team, specifically in the important post of secretary of the treasury. No wonder the politically savvy Clinton looked to Bentsen as an invaluable asset. Leaders of both parties recognized the longtime chairman of the Senate Finance Committee as an elder sage, one of Capitol Hill's most seasoned authorities on economic, fiscal, and financial matters. Simply put, the tall, courtly Texan inspired confidence in the business community and in the world of high finance. And he could reassure markets as well as his old colleagues on the Hill. Moreover, liberals no longer labeled him "loophole Lloyd" for his probusiness posture on tax issues, while conservatives, who had largely forgiven him for eviscerating Dan Quayle on national television five years earlier, acknowledged that he was a "supply-sider" who had supported Reagan's economic policies. In sum, both camps generally viewed him, quite correctly, as a moderate, middle-of-the-road politician who could bring both experience and intelligence to the table.[44]

Clinton also recognized Bentsen's reputation as a cunning legislative negotiator and a hard-nosed realist with ties to corporate America. The president doubtless saw Bentsen as a valuable liaison with Congress. In the words of one journalist, the Texan would be the kind of secretary of the treasury "who kicks butt, takes names, and gets things done." In other words, investors, pundits, and politicians alike agreed that Bentsen was a tough but soft-spoken team player who knew "whose arm to twist and how to twist it."[45]

After all, Bentsen had studied all those years ago under masters like Rayburn and LBJ. And he had learned his lessons well. Besides, he could help the Clinton administration steer the Democratic Party and, more importantly, the nation back toward the political center. And that was precisely what Clinton, Al Gore, and their "New Democrats" wanted.

Although Bentsen served only two and a half years as treasury secretary, he should nevertheless be remembered as one of the principal architects of the longest sustained period of economic growth since World War II. A voice of reason and a symbol of fiscal responsibility, he fully supported Clinton's largely successful policies to reduce the deficit, balance the budget, slow down growth in the national debt (which had tripled during the Reagan-Bush era), open foreign markets, and expand the economy through investment incentives and rewards for productivity.[46]

As a cabinet member Bentsen became one of President Clinton's chief firefighters on Capitol Hill, taking the front line to lobby for such issues as the controversial North American Free Trade Agreement (NAFTA) and national health care reform. "I've never seen a Secretary of the Treasury doing as much lobbying as I do," the Texan confessed to a reporter in June 1993. Like a little-noticed administrative stealth weapon, the silver-haired secretary demonstrated time and again his quiet political acumen and skill in canvassing members of Congress, literally lining up votes with a combination of persuasion, promises, and the calling in of old debts.[47]

In 1995 seventy-four-year-old Lloyd Bentsen stepped down from his post at the Treasury Department. When he left Washington and returned home to Houston that year, it was not only the end of a long, distinguished career in public service, but also the end of the Lone Star Democratic dynasty that descended in line of succession from Jack Garner to Sam Rayburn to Lyndon Johnson, although the influence of Texans in the national and international arenas was surely not over.

After suffering a debilitating stroke in 1998, Bentsen convalesced for three months in a rehabilitation hospital in Galveston before at last returning to his Houston home. Perhaps it was altogether fitting. Although he stood for three decades as a fixture in the Texas and national political landscape, now in the twilight of his years the aging patriarch enjoys the solitude of private life and the support of a loving family.

Future generations of scholars will doubtless debate Bentsen's accomplishments and his legacy. Some may well view him as a transitional figure who helped lead the Democratic Party and the country away from old-style liberalism and toward the American political center. Others might argue that, as a former Rayburn and Johnson protégé, he was the heir of a rich Texas political tradition that contributed mightily to the twentieth century. But few can justly deny his contributions or his place in history, or as Bentsen would like to say, the fact that he made a difference for America.

GEORGE BUSH

Fig. 13.1. George Bush, shown campaigning for the Republican presidential nomination in New Hampshire in 1980, became vice president under Ronald Reagan and subsequently won election to the presidency in 1988. Halstead (Dirck) Photographic Archive, Center for American History, UT-Austin (CN 00396).

GEORGE BUSH

BY DOROTHY DEMOSS

In August 1989, *Time* magazine characterized George Bush as "Mr. Consensus, a careful, pragmatic politician [who] seeks opinions, relies on advisers and likes to split the difference on difficult choices." The article went on to summarize Bush's personal credo and ideology as being based on "hard work, country, public service, loyalty." These words accurately characterize the career of the second Texan to occupy the White House in the last third of the twentieth century.[1]

Born and raised in New England, Bush first became interested in politics and was elected to public office after his arrival in Texas. Serving effectively as Harris County Republican chairman, he was elected in 1966 to the U.S. House of Representatives from Houston's Seventh District. After his second term ended in 1971, he successively held an impressive number of diverse appointive positions including ambassador to the United Nations, chairman of the Republican National Committee, ambassador to China, and director of the Central Intelligence Agency. In 1980 he was elected vice president of the United States and in 1988 was elected president. Throughout the years and wherever in the world his career took him, Bush was careful to foster a close relationship with his adopted state and to maintain close ties with his many friends there.

George Herbert Walker Bush was born on June 12, 1924, at Milton, Massachusetts, the son of Prescott S. and Dorothy Walker Bush. His father was a successful businessman, a partner in the investment banking firm of Brown Brothers, Harriman and Company, and a leader in community affairs in Greenwich, Connecticut, where the family eventually settled. Prescott Bush served as U.S. senator from Connecticut from 1953 to 1963. The elder Bushes early instilled in their five children a strong belief in the Puritan work ethic, the importance of self-discipline, a strong sense of duty to others, and the significance of having religious faith. The family was a close and supportive group that enjoyed competitive sports, regularly attended the Episcopal Church, and spent summer vacations at the grandparents' home at Walker's Point in Kennebunkport, Maine.[2]

In 1936 young George entered the private Phillips Academy in Andover, Massachusetts, where he excelled in studies and sports and became a campus leader. During his senior year he met Barbara Pierce of Rye,

New York, daughter of Marvin Pierce, president of the McCall Company and publisher of *McCall's* and *Redbook* magazines. Their courtship was delayed, however, because of the United States' entry into World War II following the bombing of Pearl Harbor in December 1941. Shortly after his graduation from Phillips the following June, the eighteen-year-old Bush entered the U.S. Navy to become a pilot.[3]

Ensign Bush underwent flight training at Corpus Christi, Texas, and along the East Coast, and in the fall of 1943 he was assigned to VT-51, a Pacific squadron. There he flew the TBM Avenger, a single-engine torpedo bomber that carried a three-man crew, from the aircraft carrier *San Jacinto*. In September 1944, Bush's plane was shot down by enemy fire while attacking Chichi Jima, one of the Bonin Islands. Suffering from a head laceration and drifting alone in a raft, Bush was amazed when the submarine USS *Finback* surfaced near him and took him aboard. He spent a month on the vessel, a time of learning and reflection regarding the costs of war, especially the deaths of the two crewmen aboard his aircraft. Bush rejoined his squadron, was awarded the Distinguished Flying Cross, and was ordered home on leave in December 1944. Two weeks later, on January 6, 1945, he and Barbara were married. Bush was subsequently assigned to Oceana Naval Air Station in Virginia, where in August the newlyweds heard the news of the Japanese surrender and the end of the war.[4]

In the fall of 1945 Bush immediately entered Yale University, where he majored in economics. The couple's first child, George W. Bush, was born in New Haven. At that time the family lived in a sprawling home that had been divided into thirteen apartments to accommodate couples enduring the postwar housing shortage. The young father concentrated enough on his academic work to finish his course of study in three years and to earn election to the Phi Beta Kappa honor society. During those busy years he also joined the Delta Kappa Epsilon social fraternity, was chosen for the prestigious Skull and Bones Club, and played first base and served as captain of the Yale baseball team that won two NCAA Eastern Division championships.[5]

Wanting to strike out on his own in a new career in an entirely different part of the country following graduation, and desiring to break from the traditional family profession of investment banking, Bush sought the advice of A. Neil Mallon, an old friend and chief executive officer of Dresser Industries in Dallas. "What you need to do is head out to Texas and those oil fields," said Mallon.[6]

An extraordinary boom in the production of oil already was under way in the Permian Basin, a vast geological formation extending from western Texas to southeastern New Mexico. A broad range of business opportunities existed there for major oil companies, independent operators, drilling enterprises, and oil-well service companies. Bush secured a job from Mallon in Odessa, Texas, with Ideco, the International Derrick and Equipment Company, a subsidiary of Dresser. His job was to sell various field supplies, known as "soap, rope, and dope" products, that were used in the drilling process. The young family established their first home in Odessa, in a "shotgun" house on unpaved East 7th Street. Driving on sales trips throughout the region in the hot summer and fall of 1948, Bush thoroughly enjoyed meeting the friendly, colorful folks of the "oil patch," learning about the area's fanatical devotion to high school football, eating a delicious new food called "chicken-fried steak," and becoming a Texan in "heart and spirit." [7]

After a brief stint in California for Dresser, where a second child, Robin, was born, the Bushes moved back to Texas in 1949 and bought a home in Midland. The next year, at age twenty-six, Bush left the security of Dresser Industries and formed Bush-Overbey Oil Development Company with neighbor John Overbey. Bush received considerable funding for the venture from his maternal uncle, George Herbert Walker Jr., who headed a large investment banking firm. The next few years saw a frenzied increase in the number of independent and major oil companies doing business in Midland. Many of the new independents like Bush, who specialized in raising and placing capital from eastern and midwestern sources, were dubbed "Ivy Leaguers." By the end of 1950 the Permian Basin produced nearly one million barrels of oil a day and was the most active drilling area in the world. [8]

In 1953 Bush and Overbey joined forces with Hugh and Bill Liedtke, lawyers and oil developers from Tulsa, Oklahoma, to form Zapata Petroleum Company, named for the Mexican revolutionary, Emiliano Zapata. They participated heavily in the development of the West Jamieson Field in Coke County, Texas, which resulted in 127 productive wells for the company. In the midst of successful times, tragedy suddenly struck the Bushes when their four-year-old daughter, Robin, was diagnosed as having an advanced case of leukemia. Despite heroic efforts to save her at the Sloan Kettering Center at Memorial Hospital in New York City, she died in 1953 after six months of stress and heartache for her family. [9]

Perhaps to compensate for this loss, Bush soon developed a new business focus, the expansion of Zapata Off-Shore, a subsidiary company, which used three-legged platforms designed by R. G. LeTourneau to drill for oil in the deep waters of the Gulf of Mexico. Bush was eminently successful as a businessman and in 1956 was selected by the Texas Junior Chamber of Commerce as one of the five outstanding young men of

Texas. The offshore activity proved so interesting over the next few years that Bush negotiated a complex, but friendly, parting with the Liedtkes, whereby he gained controlling interest in Zapata Off-Shore in 1959 and moved his company and growing family, including four other children (Jeb, Neil, Marvin, and Dorothy), who were all born in the 1950s, to Houston.[10]

Working twelve-hour days as CEO, Bush thrived and prospered in the exciting new environment. He was active in civic affairs, chairing the Texas Heart Fund, and was a member and vestryman at St. Martin's Episcopal Church. He increasingly became interested in public service and political activity. Philosophically a Republican, he was aware that his party, so long a minority party in Texas, was undergoing divisive growing pains. In 1962 he successfully achieved the chairmanship of the Harris County Republican Party over the protest of members of the John Birch Society, an extremely conservative faction. In 1963, before the assassination of President John F. Kennedy, Republican state chairman Peter O'Donnell persuaded Bush to run the next year for the U.S. Senate seat from Texas against the incumbent liberal Democrat, Ralph Yarborough. Bush, whose background was that of the moderate, eastern wing of the national party, proclaimed himself a supporter of the Republican presidential candidate, "responsible" conservative Barry Goldwater.[11]

Bush entered the fray as an underdog lacking name identification but campaigned hard in the party primary and runoff campaigns. By October he was closing the gap but suffered when President Lyndon B. Johnson endorsed Yarborough, who had called Bush an "extremist," a "carpetbagger," and "the darling of the John Birch Society." Bush rebutted the charge of being an outsider by saying that since 1948 he had spent more time in Texas than LBJ! In the general election Bush polled 175,000 votes ahead of the Goldwater-Miller national ticket but was overwhelmed by the Johnson landslide.[12]

Bush considered his loss to Yarborough to be "a painful but temporary setback in a longer contest." His desire to see Texas become a two-party state and his growing political ambition motivated him in February 1966 to enter the race for the newly created Seventh District seat of the U.S. House of Representatives. More dramatically, he sold the Zapata Off-Shore Company for $1.1 million so he could concentrate all his energy on the campaign against his Democratic opponent, Frank Briscoe, Harris County district attorney and right-wing conservative. Bush told a Houston audience, "I want conservatism to be sensitive and dynamic, not scared and reactionary."[13] He repudiated the John Birch Society and sought support from blacks, who composed 15 percent of the congressional district located in affluent southwest Houston. Barbara Bush assisted in the hard-fought campaign by writing a persuasive letter to the 73,000 women voters of the district, urging them to vote for her husband. Bush, who won the victory with 57 percent of the vote, would soon find his life forever changed. Henceforth, he would build and effectively use a network of contacts in Washington, D.C.[14]

Congressman Bush arrived in the capital at a time when the nation increasingly was divided by the Vietnam War and by racial conflict in the inner cities. Bush was honored by being named to the House Ways and Means Committee, an unusually prominent appointment for a first-term representative. Chaired by Wilbur Mills of Arkansas, the committee provided Bush with a special opportunity to learn about tax legislation.[15]

The record that Bush compiled during four years of service in Congress can be interpreted as being either conservative or moderate, but above all, he was a pragmatist. On most occasions he voted in line with the conservative coalition of Republicans and southern Democrats. He introduced and cosponsored 167 bills, of which 22 were passed. Of these his most dedicated effort was to introduce an ethics bill that would require every member of Congress to make a full disclosure of assets and income, as he had done already. He also spoke out forcefully in favor of increased funding for bilingual education programs. He chaired the Republican Task Force on Earth Resources and Population and was a moderate on environmental matters dealing with pollution. Much of his time was spent solving small but important problems for constituents and making frequent trips home to his district.[16]

Bush's most controversial action as a member of Congress came in April 1968 when he voted in favor of the open-housing provision of the Civil Rights Act. Many conservatives in his home district feared increased government control of private property and confronted Bush in a hostile fashion at a rally held in Houston a week after the vote. Bush explained his belief that a representative must vote his conscience and told the audience, "I did what I thought was right." When he had finished speaking he had persuasively changed the minds of most in the group and recalled later, "Nothing I've experienced in public life, before or since, has measured up to the feeling I had when I went home that night." Bush was reelected in 1968 without opposition.[17]

As Bush returned to Washington in January 1969 to attend the inauguration of Richard M. Nixon, he made a special effort to go to Andrews Air Force Base to bid farewell to fellow Texan Lyndon B. Johnson. President Johnson thanked Bush, the only prominent Republican among the modest crowd, for his attendance, and the two men maintained a cordial relationship until Johnson's death in 1973. In 1970, motivated by his own ambition and encouraged by President Nixon, Bush decided once again to challenge Ralph Yarborough. He knowingly took the political risk of giving up a safe House seat to run for the Senate.[18]

Despite the able assistance of longtime friend and campaign manager James A. Baker III of Houston, Bush and all his carefully made plans were vastly disrupted when former congressman Lloyd Bentsen Jr. challenged and defeated Yarborough in the extremely divisive Democratic spring primary. In the general election campaign, Bentsen, a conservative insurance executive then living in Houston, again brought up the accusation that Bush was a "carpetbagger" from Connecticut. In late October voter interest was increased by a widespread campaign by forces for and against a controversial proposed state constitutional amendment endorsing the sale of "liquor by the drink." On election day 53.8 percent of the registered voters went to the polls, a heavy turnout for an off-year election. Rural Democrats, in particular, voted for Bentsen and against the liquor proposition. Bentsen defeated Bush by a margin of 150,000 votes, but Bush garnered more than a million votes statewide and carried the urban centers of Harris and Dallas Counties.[19]

In late 1970, at age forty-six, the lame-duck congressman, already labeled a "loser" by some newspapers, was startled to be summoned to the White House and nominated by President Richard Nixon to become the United States ambassador to the United Nations. Bush accepted his first major appointive position well aware that President Nixon, Henry Kissinger, head of the National Security Council, and Secretary of State William Rogers would be making all major decisions regarding America's role at the UN. It was Bush's job to carry out their orders. Bush studied intensively, worked hard, and concentrated much of his energy on cultivating personal relationships with delegates from many nations, and he and Barbara entertained often at the U.S. ambassador's official residence at the Waldorf Astoria Hotel.[20]

At UN sessions Bush made persuasive arguments but also was a good listener when dealing with complex issues facing the General Assembly and Security Council. Among the most frustrating matters were the treatment of American prisoners of war in Vietnam, the decolonization of Africa, the volatile relations between Israel, Syria, and Lebanon, and the election of the new UN secretary general, Kurt Waldheim. Bush fought hard for a "two China" policy and was dismayed at the ouster of the Taiwan Chinese and recognition of the People's Republic of China as the only legitimate Chinese government. In his two years at the UN, Bush was an effective instrument rather than an innovator of policy. But it was a good learning experience for him because he grew to understand the limits and possibilities of the UN. His personable style, conscientious hard work, intelligence, enthusiasm, and humor made him well liked by delegates from Europe, China, the Middle East, and other parts of the Third World.[21]

Amid the stresses of active engagement at the UN, Bush had faced the heartache of seeing his father, Prescott, suffer from lung cancer. The elder Bush died in October 1972. It was a great loss for all the family but especially for George, who considered his father to be his best friend.[22]

In January 1973 Bush was called to the White House to discuss a new assignment. While Nixon had roundly defeated George McGovern in the 1972 presidential contest, the Watergate scandal was gathering momentum. Nixon wanted Bush to become chairman of the Republican National Committee. Bush accepted the position, over the protest of his wife, but insisted on a free hand in running the committee and serving as a presidential adviser. Flying coach class on airline trips and driving small American-made rental cars, Bush crisscrossed the country to "wrap up party wounds" and to explain that it was the independent Committee to Reelect the President, not the official Republican National Committee, that had served as a base of operations to execute the illegal break-in at the Watergate Complex, which was being covered up. After the scandal had widened, Bush, who owed a great deal to Nixon, sent a letter to the president on August 7, 1974, urging him to resign.[23]

After Nixon's departure, President Gerald Ford appointed Bush to head the United States Liaison Office in China. Since there was not yet official diplomatic recognition between the United States and the People's Republic, Bush was to be referred to as envoy and head of the U.S. mission in Beijing, rather than ambassador. Bush believed that the United States should encourage Communist China to become a force for stability in East Asia. For thirteen months George and Barbara Bush wholeheartedly entered into their assignment in Beijing: riding bicycles with the Chinese people; attending diplomatic events; studying Chinese art and architecture; and trying to develop a relationship of mutual respect with Chairman Mao Zedong, whom they met only twice. Bush was greatly amazed at China's vigilance against the Soviet Union, which many Chinese considered to be their real enemy.[24]

In November 1975 President Ford made some major personnel changes and asked Bush to return to Washington to become director of the Central Intelligence Agency (CIA). The director serves as the nation's chief intelligence officer and principal adviser to the president on all foreign intelligence matters. Some analysts voiced criticism of Bush's appointment, saying he was "too political." Others answered that Bush would make decisions free of partisan considerations and help restore congressional and public confidence in the CIA, which had suffered following allegations that it had been involved in the overthrow of President Salvador Allende of Chile in 1973.[25]

Bush believed that there was a vital need for intelligence gathering in world affairs and greatly desired to boost the morale and defend the competence of professional intelligence officers. In the confirmation hearings before the Senate Armed Services Committee, Bush was sharply questioned by Senator Gary Hart of Colorado regarding Bush's desire to use the CIA position as a stepping-stone to the vice presidency in 1976. Bush answered: "I will not seek any office while I hold the job of CIA Director and . . . will put politics totally out of my sphere of activities." In answering questions regarding his view of America's role in the world, Bush asserted: "I think these three years in foreign affairs convinced me that we are the only hope of the free world. We must keep and strengthen our intelligence capability." The committee voted 12 to 4 to favorably report the nomination to the full Senate. Those opposing the nomination cited their concerns that the recent, rapid turnover of CIA directors indicated instability and that Bush's nomination set "a precedent of political appointments to a post that should be completely insulated from political considerations."[26]

Under Director Bush the CIA began to carry out reforms, suggested by the Rockefeller Commission in 1975, to remove the agency from the political arena. Bush appointed E. Henry Knoche to be deputy director and Admiral Daniel J. Murphy as his second deputy. As things developed, critics of Bush's appointment were correct, since Bush served only one year in the position before being replaced in January 1977 by Stansfield Turner, appointee of Jimmy Carter, the newly elected Democratic president.[27]

For the first time since leaving college Bush found himself jobless. He and Barbara returned to Houston and bought a home, smaller than their first one there, since all five of their children were grown and on their own. Over the next two years Bush was very busy in commercial ventures and civic activities. He served as a director or trustee on the boards of several Texas banks and colleges, taught as an adjunct professor at Rice University, served as chairman of the American Heart Fund, and was an active parishioner at St. Martin's Episcopal Church. While campaigning extensively for Republican candidates during the 1978 national elections, Bush came to the decision to run for president in 1980. He again asked James Baker, scion of the distinguished Houston family and undersecretary of commerce in the Ford administration, to serve as his campaign manager during the Republican primaries.[28]

Although his television skills were undeveloped and his speeches had little vitality, Bush campaigned doggedly against such high-profile opponents as Ronald Reagan, John Connally, and Senator Howard Baker of Tennessee. He focused especially on the early Iowa caucus, which he won by 2,000 votes. His much vaunted momentum was soon shattered, however, in a rancorous debate with his primary opponents in Nashua, New Hampshire, and Reagan easily won that state's primary. Bush's characterization of Reagan's supply-side proposals to reduce taxes without reducing spending as being "voodoo economics" lost Bush support from other Republicans. Even at home in Texas, Bush had no secure political base outside of the Seventh District in Houston. Most Texas Republicans regarded him as a good, pleasant man, but preferred Reagan. By late May the Bush campaign faced the reality that Reagan already had amassed nearly enough delegates to assure a first-ballot victory at the Republican National Convention in Detroit, Michigan, in July. Reluctantly, Bush called a press conference in Houston and withdrew from the presidential race.[29]

After being nominated at the convention, Ronald Reagan passed over the idea of a so-called dream ticket, with former president Ford as vice president; instead, Reagan dramatically chose his longtime rival, George Bush, to be a link to GOP moderates. Bush accepted and entered wholeheartedly into the grueling campaign against incumbent, Democrat opponents Jimmy Carter and Walter Mondale. The Reagan-Bush ticket, a marriage of convenience, did well in Texas, relying heavily on support from the growing suburban vote. Bush spoke out in favor of supply-side tax cuts, the need to create new jobs, and the importance of revitalizing America's cities. On election day Reagan and Bush won a landslide victory.[30]

George Bush as vice president was the quintessential government insider—the loyal, energetic, and effective servant to Ronald Reagan, himself a relative newcomer to Washington. From the start there was a sense of partnership and confidence between the two. Bush was assigned an office in the White House, was included in the decision-making process of cabinet and National Security Council meetings, and dined alone with Reagan every Thursday at lunchtime. Like many recent vice presidents, Bush represented the president overseas on numerous special missions, and he also fulfilled substantive domestic duties by heading up two task forces, one seeking to eliminate unnecessary federal regulations and the other to combat international drug smuggling.[31]

After only two months in office Bush faced the ultimate test of a vice president, the attempted assassination of President Reagan outside the Washington Hilton Hotel on March 30, 1981. Bush, who had gone home to Texas to deliver speeches in Fort Worth and Austin, quickly returned to the capital and carried out his temporary presidential duties with poise and restraint. After his recuperation, Reagan thanked Bush for his steadfast service and stated that he was "the best vice-president in our country's history." [32]

Early in his first term as vice president, Bush sold his home in Houston and used the payment to buy a vacation house at Kennebunkport, Maine, from his mother and aunt. His intention was, however, to maintain his Texas residence and return there after retirement from public service. He continued to own property in Houston, maintained a bank account there, continued his church membership, signed over his assets to a blind trust managed in the city, and kept current his Texas driver's license. [33]

A Texas-sized GOP national convention was held in Dallas in August 1984. Amid the speeches, festivities, and 100-degree temperatures, Reagan and Bush were renominated and projected an image of unity, enthusiasm, and success. The 1984 campaign was different, however, because Bush was pitted against Democrat Geraldine Ferraro, the first woman to be chosen by a national party to run for the vice presidency. Little wonder, therefore, that Bush and Ferraro's historic televised confrontation excited much interest by the media and the public. The Reagan-Bush campaign emphasized the "America Is Back" slogan and resulted in a smashing victory in which the incumbents carried forty-nine states. [34]

Barbara Bush always won praise for her performance as the nation's "second lady." Her warmth, candor, humor, and devotion to her husband, children, and grandchildren were well known and respected. Through the years she fulfilled such varied roles as Little League scorekeeper, "consummate good listener," and needlepointer during thousands of hours at political rallies; dedicated activist in the cause of expanding literacy in America; and adept writer and "editor" of two charming books by the Bush family dogs, "C. Fred" and "Millie." [35]

During his second term Bush continued to be a hardworking vice president, publicly supporting Reagan's policies without exception. Increasingly Bush was criticized for not speaking out or taking a separate stand on controversial policies. He was censured in the press as being a "wimp," a "lapdog," and a classic "yes-man" to Reagan. In regard to the Iran-contra scandal, Bush later maintained that he knew only vaguely of the effort by U.S. officials to reach out to one of the moderate Iranian factions that was planning a post-Khomeini Iran. These officials allegedly sold missiles to Iran and illegally channeled proceeds from the sale to the contras, guerrillas trying to overthrow the Sandinista regime in Nicaragua. [36]

Gradually Bush made it clear that he intended to run for the presidency in 1988, the first election in twenty years without an incumbent president in the race. He made several trips home to Texas to renew contacts and broaden his political base during the state's 1986 Sesquicentennial celebration. He likewise spoke out more forcefully, especially in a well-publicized confrontation about the Iran-contra affair with Dan Rather, CBS television anchor. During a Republican primary debate in Houston he defended his support of Reagan by saying, "In my family loyalty is not considered a character defect, it is considered a strength." Bush was surprised in the Iowa caucus, which he lost to Senator Robert Dole, but quickly worked to achieve victory in New Hampshire's primary. On "Super Tuesday," March 8, 1988, Bush swept all sixteen GOP primaries.[37]

From the moment of his arrival at the Republican National Convention in New Orleans in August, Bush was in charge. He asserted himself as the leader of the GOP and an energetic presidential candidate. Bush surprised the nation by announcing Senator J. Danforth Quayle of Indiana as his choice for a vice presidential running mate. Critics immediately characterized Bush's choice of Quayle as being an impulsive act done only to gain the vote of the conservative right. Quayle was portrayed as a young "immature lightweight" by many in the media. On the night of the presidential nomination all of the five Bush children spoke in favor of their father from their separate state delegations. George W. Bush, the eldest son, delivered the Texas delegation vote to put Bush over the top. The next evening Bush gave his acceptance speech, one of the finest performances of his career. In the address he strongly urged Americans to work together to achieve a sense of community, dignity, moral generosity, through "a thousand points of light," a phrase that would symbolize the network of volunteers whom he hoped would confront and meet needs at the local level.[38]

The 1988 presidential campaign was later criticized for its excessive length, its negative advertising, the brevity of discussion of real problems facing the country, and the intrusive nature of the media. The Bush campaign "came out swinging" to counteract statements made at the Democratic convention by U.S. Senator Edward Kennedy, who asked, "Where was George?" when the Iran-contra scam was planned and executed. He was taunted also by Texas State Treasurer Ann Richards, who stated that "Poor George . . . was born with a silver foot in his mouth," a reference to the gaffes Bush sometimes made when delivering speeches. The Bush effort focused on portraying the Democratic presidential nominee, Governor Michael Dukakis of Massachusetts, as being an extreme liberal severely lacking in the experience necessary to serve as president and manage America's global role. The Bush camp used petty campaign tactics to discredit Dukakis, particularly in regard to the "Willie Horton case," characterized by critics as a racist tactic, and the furor concerning the

Pledge of Allegiance. The Democratic vice presidential nominee, Senator Lloyd Bentsen of Texas, handily won the televised debate with Dan Quayle.[39]

Bush and Bentsen waged an especially rough and negative campaign to earn the electoral votes of their home state. On election day Texas voters gave Bush-Quayle 56 percent of their vote and the victory. Nationally, Bush garnered 54 percent to Dukakis's 46 percent. The Democrats maintained a majority in both houses of Congress. Bush, who had returned home to Houston to vote, celebrated his election by jogging in Memorial Park, telephoning and writing notes to friends, and attending a special service at his church.[40]

In his inaugural address on January 20, 1989, Bush called for "a kinder, gentler nation" and proffered his hand in cooperation to the Congress, especially to those of the "loyal opposition." In the parade that immediately followed, the bands from the University of Texas and Texas A&M University were prominently featured. At the Black Tie and Boots Ball, one of several inaugural celebrations held that evening, the requirement for securing entrance tickets was "You have to be a Texan, have been a Texan, or want to be a Texan." James Baker, Bush's longtime friend and counselor, was appointed to the prestigious position of secretary of state. Baker had served as Ronald Reagan's White House chief of staff and secretary of the treasury. Talented, highly organized, and hardworking, Baker began immediately to address complex foreign policy issues relating to the Soviet Union, Eastern Europe, and the Middle East.[41]

Bush enjoyed substantial popularity and faced few crises in his first months as president. He was pragmatic and less confrontational than Reagan had been in dealing with Congress. His style was predicated on dealing with problems immediately at hand and reacting to events, rather than anticipating them. This "active-reactive strategy," or "the art of the possible," seemed to be the type of leadership that many Americans had found compelling about Ronald Reagan and now seemed to want in George Bush.[42]

In mid-December 1989, Bush adopted a bolder and riskier foreign policy when he authorized the invasion of Panama. Believing that the lives of Americans were in danger, Bush ordered U.S. troops to attack Panama City, capture Panama's dictator, General Manuel Antonio Noriega, and help establish a democratic government. In Europe, where communism had collapsed, Bush and Soviet president Mikhail Gorbachev began negotiations regarding a future reduction in strategic arms and conventional weapons.[43]

There was a decided Texas accent placed on much of the Bush administration's activities, and the president's cabinet appointees included three Texans. Guided by the principle of helping Texas whenever possible without adversely affecting another state, Bush asserted: "I'm consciously not doing anything that will hurt the state of Texas and I'm not favoring Texas over any place else."[44]

World leaders, the international press corps, and thousands of visitors attended the Economic Summit in Houston during five hot and sultry days in July 1990. Bush had encouraged planners to hold the prestigious meeting in his adopted hometown. The rousing success of the occasion, which promoted international trade agreements, undoubtedly influenced Bush to give support to the decision by the Republican National Committee to hold the party's 1992 convention in Houston.[45]

The pleasant afterglow of the Economic Summit was abruptly shattered on August 2, 1990, when Saddam Hussein, president of Iraq, invaded and seized Kuwait, its oil-rich neighbor on the Persian Gulf. Bush was convinced that the ruthless Hussein had to be stopped before he committed further aggression in the region. Bush believed that the United States, as the sole remaining superpower, must lead a coalition of forces to repel Hussein. Using his knowledge of world leaders and politics acquired during years of service, he skillfully forged a historic international alliance that was closely aligned with the United Nations. Bush, as commander in chief of the U.S. armed forces, authorized the implementation of Operation Desert Shield, the largest overseas deployment of American troops and equipment since World War II. When Hussein vowed to keep thousands of Americans and other internationals in Iraq as hostages, the Bush administration urged the UN to use economic sanctions and diplomatic pressure to bring about their release. The UN also established a January 15, 1991, deadline for Saddam Hussein to withdraw his troops from Kuwait—or else face the coalition's military force.[46]

Despite strong support for his leadership in the Persian Gulf crisis, by October 1990 Bush began to receive widespread criticism of his handling of negotiations with the Congress to reduce the deficit of the national budget. Bush already had angered many fellow Republicans in June by abandoning his "no new taxes" pledge of the 1988 campaign. There were weeks of contentious wrangling during which it appeared as if neither the president nor the leaders of Congress were capable of leading. As anxiety mounted and the national economy weakened, the results of the midterm congressional elections gave Democrats added strength. Meanwhile, under the leadership of Secretary of Defense Dick Cheney, Chairman of the Joint Chiefs of Staff General Colin Powell, and Commander of Operation Desert Shield General Norman Schwarzkopf, the United States steadily moved unprecedented amounts of manpower and firepower into the Persian Gulf area. Secretary of State Baker sought support for Iraq's withdrawal from Kuwait by means of numerous diplomatic journeys to allied capitals.[47]

As 1990 drew to a close and George Bush's term as president neared the midpoint, it was clear that his major success lay in multilateral, personal diplomacy rather than in the domestic arena. Analysts agreed that Bush's foreign policy efforts had been brilliant, but on the domestic front, critics censured him as being a "do-nothing," caretaker president who had no vision or plan or real interest in solving such festering domestic problems as "drugs, homelessness, racial hostility, education and the environment." To underscore the existence of these two contradictory George Bushes, *Time* magazine named him as 1990's Men of the Year.[48]

The uneasy quiet and somber mood of the new year ended abruptly on January 16, 1991, with the commencement of Operation Desert Storm. Television viewers around the world were witness to pervasive coverage of allied air attacks and warship missile firings against Baghdad and other Iraqi targets. President Bush had made the decision that Kuwait could only be liberated by force. He had taken the biggest gamble of his presidency and, perhaps, defined his place in history.[49]

Following six weeks of allied air assaults and sporadic ground skirmishes, a major ground offensive to eject the Iraqi army from Kuwait and to occupy parts of southern Iraq began on February 24. Using unprecedented firepower from the land, air, and sea, troops of eleven nations stormed into enemy-held territory, inflicted devastating losses, took thousands of prisoners, and occupied vast areas. The fast and decisive ground war lasted only one hundred hours.[50]

Throughout the five and a half months of prewar uncertainty, President Bush remained resolute and unwavering in his leadership style. His speeches and State of the Union address were inspired rhetoric. Once fighting began and the success of the coalition cause became apparent, Bush's stature was enhanced even more. By March, Americans celebrated the decisive victory and welcomed home the first returning troops with an extraordinary sense of national pride and exaltation. It was clear, however, that there would be many ongoing problems in "winning the peace," providing security in the Persian Gulf, and dealing with Saddam Hussein, who remained in power in Iraq. Like most Americans, Bush was appalled by the subsequent massacre of thousands of Shiites and Kurds in a land whose internal strife had not been ended by Desert Storm.[51]

Euphoria over the dramatic military victory gradually began to ebb and Bush's approval rating declined as the American public continued to worry about economic issues. When the president developed a shortness of breath while jogging on May 4, 1991, the nation became concerned about the president's health. Medical tests revealed that his condition was caused by Graves' disease, a thyroid ailment that can be managed with medication and radiation treatment. By the summer of 1991 Bush again called for the establishment of a "new world order" in which the United States, the United Nations, and other international organizations would seek to solve crises and create stability through consensus building and compromise. He spoke in favor of the establishment of a free trade zone between the United States, Canada, Mexico, and Latin America. He traveled to London for the 1991 Economic Summit and planned special meetings with Soviet leader Gorbachev. Secretary Baker renewed his efforts to help solve the long and bitter conflict between the Israelis and the Palestinians and Arab nations in the Middle East.[52]

In August 1991 the world was stunned when Communist hard-line leaders in the Soviet Union attempted to overthrow Gorbachev. President Bush condemned the coup and supported the actions of Boris Yeltsin, head of the Russian republic, who rallied the people against the reactionary group and maintained that the country should become a confederation of independent republics. Bush maintained a cautious approach as the Soviet Union disintegrated, the Communist Party collapsed, and the Cold War ended.[53]

On the domestic front, Bush's record-high, postwar public approval rating declined sharply as the nation's economic woes worsened. Then a controversy arose regarding the president's appointment of Judge Clarence Thomas to the Supreme Court. Critics censured Bush for asserting that Thomas was the "best man for the job on the merits." Nationally televised hearings of the Senate Judiciary Committee regarding alleged sexual harassment by Thomas of Professor Anita Hill caused much national debate and charges of insensitivity to women's issues by the Bush administration.[54]

Supporters of Bush urged him to propose a coherent domestic agenda to solve economic problems and to take control of White House policy-making by replacing Chief of Staff John Sununu with Sam Skinner. In an effort to restore national confidence, Bush made trips to Texas to sign a multibillion-dollar national transportation bill and to survey severe flood damage. While there he touched base with the folks back home and hunted quail with friends near Beeville.[55]

The release of the last of the American hostages captured by Islamic radicals in Lebanon, the official dissolution of the Soviet Union, and continued Middle East peace talks captured international attention in late

1991. Stung by criticism that he devoted too much time to world affairs while ignoring economic troubles at home, Bush transformed a previously scheduled state visit to Australia and East Asian countries into a frenetic mission to secure jobs and trade concessions for American workers and businesses. Bush's sudden and unflattering attack of stomach flu in Japan and media questions regarding his trying to persuade the Japanese to buy more American cars and auto parts diminished any positive results that the administration had hoped would result from the fast-paced effort.[56]

As the New Hampshire primary neared, the president organized to overcome the unexpected challenge of conservative Republican Patrick Buchanan and sought to reap maximum political advantage from his State of the Union message, in which he called on the Democratic-controlled Congress to pass an array of modest tax cuts and investment incentives to spur economic recovery. In regard to domestic as well as foreign policy, many Americans hoped that the president would adopt a bolder approach and lead the nation toward meeting long-term needs as well as solving short-term crises.[57]

In August 1992 Bush was renominated by the Republican Party at its convention in Houston, Texas, and embarked on his last political campaign. His principal opponents were Democratic nominee William J. "Bill" Clinton, governor of Arkansas, and H. Ross Perot, an independent Texas billionaire. Bush was slow to get his campaign organized and from the beginning was kept on the defensive for breaking his "read my lips, no new taxes" pledge of 1988 and for the poor performance of the U.S. economy during his presidency. In three presidential debates with his opponents in October, Bush finally talked seriously about the economic, educational, and health care needs of the nation and focused his attacks primarily on Clinton's vulnerabilities: his lack of experience in foreign policy, his record as governor of Arkansas, and his military draft deferment during the Vietnam War. Clinton effectively counterpunched, emphasizing the need for change by new leadership, the disastrous results of Bush's "trickle-down economics," and the president's lack of candor concerning the Iran-contra and arms-for-hostages controversies. Despite weeks of furious campaigning, including a trip home to Texas to initial the North American Free Trade Agreement, Bush was unable to offset the early Clinton momentum and was overwhelmingly defeated on election day in the electoral college, though he did win the vote in Texas.[58]

George and Barbara Bush flew home to Houston following President Bill Clinton's inauguration on January 20, 1993, and settled into a "little rented house on West Post Oak." Barbara Bush recalled that "we were taken back into the community as if we had never left." In October they

moved into their permanent home in the Tanglewood area "that is everything anyone would dream of or want at our age." Bush's return to private
life after four frenzied years as president went smoothly. He immediately
opened an office with seven staffers in Houston, where he arrived by
7:00 A.M. daily, answered mail, returned phone calls, worked on speeches,
and made arrangements for an extensive public-speaking tour. The
Bushes continued to spend each summer and fall at their Kennebunkport,
Maine, home fishing, golfing, and entertaining family and friends.[59]

Early in his "retirement" the former president gave much time to mon-
itoring the planning and construction of the George Bush Presidential Library and Museum at Texas A&M University in College Station, Texas.
The groundbreaking ceremony was held November 30, 1994, and the facility was completed and opened to the public in 1997. The buildings
themselves were paid for with private funds, though the federal government provides the staff at the library through the National Archives and
Records Administration. The library is the archival depository for all of
George Bush's vice presidential and presidential records and memorabilia, as well as extensive personal papers dealing with his life before and
after his service in the White House. There is stack space for more than
38 million pages of documents. The library's scholarly programs have
been enhanced through cooperative programs with three academic com-
ponents at Texas A&M—the George Bush School of Government and
Public Service, the Center for Presidential Studies, and the Center for
Public Leadership Studies.[60]

The museum contains original artifacts, film, documents, music, sound
effects, and interactive video and computerization. It features a World
War II Avenger Torpedo Bomber, a 1947 Studebaker, a slab of the Berlin
Wall, and precise replicas of President Bush's Camp David and *Air Force
One* offices. "The overall theme of the museum is the nobility of public
service as exemplified by the lives of George and Barbara Bush."[61]

Contemporary with his efforts for the library Bush spent much time researching and writing a major book dealing with the dramatic international events of his presidency—especially the period 1989 to 1991. Along
with Brent Scowcroft, who had served as his national security advisor,
Bush wrote *A World Transformed,* a lengthy account of the end of the Cold
War, the collapse of the Soviet Empire, the upheaval in China, the unifi-
cation of Germany, the Gulf War (especially Operation Desert Storm),
and the "emergence of the United States as the preeminent power." Published in 1998, the volume was an important and detailed look at the conduct of American foreign policy and underscored Bush's strong belief that
"if the United States does not lead, there will be no leadership."[62]

By 1999 the former president and his wife were increasingly interested in the presidential aspirations of their oldest son, George W. Bush, governor of Texas and a baby-boomer who presented a more active program that differed from that of his father, a moderate, caretaker Republican. The younger Bush was nominated to be president at the 2000 Republican National Convention in Philadelphia amidst great support from the entire Bush family. During the hard-fought campaign between George W. Bush and Vice President Al Gore, George and Barbara Bush made numerous public appearances at political rallies for their son, but were reluctant to give him advice publicly. Long after the controversial thirty-six day delay and subsequent election of their son to be the forty-third president of the United States, the proud former president said, "I had my chance—he doesn't need me or his mother hovering over the scene."[63]

The elder Bush continued to keep up a hectic schedule giving several speeches a month on such subjects as the press, the American spirit, the importance of family and faith, and the confidence he had in his son's administration. Barbara Bush, likewise, had a busy speaking schedule, worked on a memoir about life after the White House, and devoted hours each week to charity, especially the Barbara Bush Foundation for Family Literacy, which helps teach and encourage parents and children to read together. In May 2002 George Bush gave the graduation address at the Lyndon B. Johnson School of Public Affairs at the University of Texas at Austin. As so often in the past, he spoke eloquently about the importance of volunteerism and public service by Americans: "I can think of no greater capstone for each of your lives, your careers, than to try to serve others. There can be no definition of a successful life that does not include service to others."[64] These words serve as a fitting summary of the life of George Bush.

HENRY B. GONZALEZ

Fig. 14.1. Henry B. Gonzalez, a strong voice for Mexican Americans in the state, served in the Texas Senate and became a long-term U.S. representative from San Antonio. Gonzalez also campaigned for the gubernatorial nomination in 1958 at the Texas Democratic State Convention. Lee (Russell) Photograph Collection, Center for American History, UT-Austin (CN 10748).

HENRY B. GONZALEZ

BY JULIE LEININGER PYCIOR

When Henry B. Gonzalez retired from Congress in 1998 after thirty-seven years of service, observers remarked on an amazing thing: in a political climate increasingly influenced by large financial contributions, the representative from San Antonio had lived modestly on his congressional salary for his entire career, even while serving as longtime chair of the influential House Banking Committee. "Henry B. told us how often PAC money turned our own representatives against us. He warned us about the concentration of power in ever-larger banks," journalist Molly Ivins recalled. Henry B. Gonzalez took the title "representative" literally. He was the representative of the voters.[1]

Henry Barbosa Gonzalez was born in San Antonio, Texas, in 1916. His parents were part of the mass influx from Mexico during the Mexican Revolution, but Leonidas Gonzalez and Genoveva Barbosa Prince de Gonzalez saw themselves as refugees rather than immigrants. They were part of the elite group of expatriates that hoped to return to the *madre patria.* The Gonzalez family had owned silver mines in Durango dating from the colonial era, and at the time that he fled his country, Leonidas was mayor of his hometown. Thus, as part of the established order, he was a natural target of revolutionaries. At the same time, his own father had served under the great liberal Indian leader Benito Juárez in the war against the French, and Leonidas as mayor had tried to serve all of his constituents. Indeed, family members would later recount how he received a last-minute reprieve in the face of a firing squad when a woman revolutionary spoke up for him, saying that the mayor had helped a friend of hers.[2]

The Gonzalezes came to a town the Spanish name of which reflects the Mexican-heritage residents who predated the Anglo Texans there. Nevertheless, Spanish-surnamed people in San Antonio and nearby counties were subject to widespread discrimination. Actually, the fact that Anglo Americans arrived after Mexicans sometimes worked to the latter's disadvantage, as they were often viewed as people somehow associated with an inferior, conquered enemy. The widespread prejudice no doubt reinforced the Gonzalez family's already strong tendency to focus their attention on Mexico and its affairs. Moreover, Leonidas became managing editor of *La Prensa,* which kept its readers informed of the latest events in

Mexico (even as it also reported on the activities in the Mexican colonias in the United States).[3]

The Gonzalezes expected their six children to apply themselves, and all became accomplished in the professions and/or the arts. Initially young Henry had difficulty in school, however, because he did not speak English, telling his biographer, "I couldn't even say mama." Nevertheless his love of reading stood him in good stead, and before long he was excelling at his studies. He loved to spend countless hours in the world of books, whether classic works of literature and philosophy in Spanish on the shelves at home, or the vast holdings in English at the San Antonio Public Library. Indeed, he turned to none other than Demosthenes as a model when public speaking proved daunting to him as a teen because of his Spanish accent. Like the legendary figure, the adolescent read aloud with marbles in his mouth until his father, exasperated at this strange behavior, made him stop.

The family lived in a respectable middle-class area, with both Mexican Texans and Anglo Texans for neighbors. When young Henry strayed even just a few blocks, however, he encountered bigotry. A revitalized Ku Klux Klan now threatened not only African Americans but Catholics and immigrants as well, holding in contempt the Catholic immigrants from Mexico for yet another factor: the mestizo heritage of many, which Klan members pointed out as a prime example of "racial mongrelization." (Not that such ideas originated with them; after all, the epithet "half-breed" had been in use for generations.) Anglo gangs targeted those they called "dirty Meskins," and public accommodations such as swimming pools were off limits. When harassed by thugs, however, young Henry fought back. Possessed of a feisty nature, and a good athlete, he also drew strength from his family's deep heritage and abiding faith. Years later he would recall as a kind of epiphany the moment that he read in his aunt's missal a "holy card" containing the famous maxim of Saint Teresa of Avila, which he said "gave me the courage that was essential to self-respect." It read:

> Let nothing disturb you
> Let nothing frighten you
> All things soon pass
> Patience prevails
> With God one lacks for nothing
> God alone suffices

"From then on, fear did not overwhelm me," he would recall more than fifty years later.[4]

After two years at San Antonio College, Gonzalez transferred to the University of Texas, where he roomed with his brother Joaquin. Although an able student, Henry found the experience a difficult one. He worked several jobs to make ends meet but could not find employment in any stores near campus because of the employers' preference for Anglos. Homesick, alienated from campus social life, he returned to San Antonio. While at St. Mary's University Law School he once again needed to cobble together a number of jobs, but this university proved more supportive, providing employment at the law library and contacts for a clerkship at a tax firm. Nonetheless, financial problems necessitated his receiving a blank paper at graduation rather than a diploma until he could finish paying his tuition bills. Problems also arose in connection with the bar exam. An eye boil prevented him from completing the test on the first try, and he never retook it, probably due to the fee involved and the fact that the following year Gonzalez was drafted, as the nation entered World War II. The military, recognizing his linguistic ability, assigned him to censor cables and radio transmissions. Upon discharge he applied for a position at the Federal Bureau of Investigation, but was rejected.

During these struggles the one bright spot was Gonzalez's marriage to Bertha Cuellar, "his *compañera* in all the battles of his life and the mother of his eight children," in Pete Hamill's words. Next he looked into local law-enforcement departments, applying to the juvenile division after being assured that there would be no unfair treatment of his application. Indeed, he was hired as assistant juvenile probation officer, and his diligence — devotion, even — led to rapid promotion. As he explained to journalist Ronnie Dugger, "You have to go to 'em . . . Lord Jesus Christ went among the sinners. He didn't sit on a swivel chair doing case work." Working long hours with the young people, the young probation officer gave speeches on the need to reform the juvenile justice system. Word of his ability continued to spread, and in 1946 he was named the chief juvenile probation officer, the first Hispanic person to hold that position. True to form, he seized the opportunity for reform, conducting a study that revealed that thousands of young people had been detained without specific charges. Gonzalez's study in turn led to improvements in the arrest procedure. He also resisted attempts by his superiors to segregate departmental employees by race.[5]

His budding campaign against bigotry was part of a larger movement by the World War II generation of Mexican Americans. With white supremacy discredited by Nazi atrocities, these veterans were particularly well qualified to combat "Wounds for which There Is No Purple Heart," as the League of United Latin American Citizens (LULAC) called them, and in

1946 a Mexican American and an African American became the first minority group persons elected as school board members in San Antonio. In addition to allying with African Americans, Mexican Americans worked with sympathetic Anglos, in particular fellow veterans, some of whom were asking the same questions about social and economic justice in postwar America. For example, a GI named Humphreys sold his house to a Mexican American, thereby violating a restrictive real estate covenant. Upon being sued for pursuing the sale, Humphreys explained, "I believe that a GI of Latin American descent has the same rights as any other American . . . I am convinced I am right in selling to Puente and I don't intend to back down." In fact, one of Puente's main advisers was Henry B. Gonzalez. Momentum was on their side, as the U.S. Supreme Court struck down restrictive covenants at the very time that the *Puente* case was in progress, prompting the local judge to rule in Puente's favor.[6]

The success of the 1947 *Puente* case bolstered Gonzalez's growing reputation, as did his leadership in organizations ranging from the Boy Scouts to the Bishop's Committee for the Spanish Speaking to the International Ladies Garment Worker's Union. As a result, many people were willing and eager to work on behalf of his 1950 campaign for the San Antonio city council. Political professionals, meanwhile, considered quixotic the candidacy of an inexperienced minority candidate, as none had ever been elected, and they were not surprised when Gonzalez went down to defeat. For his part the ambitious young Mexican American noted that he had mobilized thousands of new voters and had forced a close runoff election. Biding his time, he threw himself with his accustomed energy into a new position with the city housing authority. During his 1950–1953 tenure he relocated 455 families without causing a single eviction.[7]

With his growing knowledge of city operations, and based on his strong electoral showing in 1950, Gonzalez decided to run for the city council again in 1953. This time a split among the established factions worked to his advantage, with the group headed by former mayor Jack White even inviting him to join their ticket. A formidable campaigner in both English and Spanish, he was "a young man with a razor-sharp wit and a wide smile," according to the *San Antonio Light*. Moreover, Gonzalez had overcome his youthful public-speaking problems to such an extent that he was effective in the emerging media of radio and television.

Gonzalez was elected along with mayoral candidate White. Taking office in conservative Texas during the height of the McCarthy era did not prevent Gonzalez from opposing the effort to remove "communist-tinged" books from the public library, with the new council member charging that "the burning smells of Hitler tactics."[8] Gonzalez went on to criticize rate-hike proposals by the telephone and the water companies. In the latter case he suggested that the privately owned operation be replaced by a nonprofit public utility. He also reported that he had been offered a bribe as part of a municipal corruption scheme, and he received press coverage when the parks department of a nearby town refused him a picnic permit because of his ethnic background. Thus Gonzalez's reputation grew: to his supporters as a crusading reformer, to his critics as a publicity hound, even a radical. When a radio host raised the charge that he invited controversy, the councilman, citing French philosopher Charles Peguy, responded, "He who failed to bellow the truth when he knew the truth is an accomplice of liars and cheats." Gonzalez argued that as a public figure he should be held accountable, and that publicity, of whatever sort, brought the issues to the fore. For their part, reporters gave him high marks as one of the few city officials untainted by scandal, and in 1954 he received the endorsement of the *San Antonio Express and News.* Trouble was brewing, however. His populist stances prompted some of his business supporters to reconsider their financial assistance, talk surfaced of a recall campaign, and he began to experience harassment as his personal life came under attack. His professional qualifications were questioned, private investigators looked fruitlessly for evidence of sexual dalliances, and anonymous calls came in the middle of the night. Then one evening a gunman fired a shot at him. "I came home late one night, when all of a sudden I heard something rev up and a car spun by in the darkness of the alley. And I heard two shots, and they hit the door of [my] car." Characteristically undeterred, Gonzalez ran his usual energetic campaign, this time as an independent, emphasizing his record of championing the ordinary citizen and of rooting out corruption. He won comfortably, receiving for the first time more than a few votes from the predominantly Anglo North Side.[9]

As Gonzalez's biographer has noted, "As he approached his fortieth birthday he felt it time to move up or out of politics," and on his birthday itself he announced his candidacy for the Texas State Senate Democratic primary. Once again he faced daunting odds as a reform-minded Mexican American of modest means. No Hispanic had ever been elected to the State Senate, and his opponent, incumbent Owen Lattimer, had the support of entrenched conservatives with ties to the business community, the very people that dominated Texas politics. Moreover, the local legislative district was countywide; thus fully two-thirds of the voters were of Anglo background. Undaunted, the challenger stumped vigorously and eloquently throughout the district. By making significant inroads into Anglo precincts and carrying the minority ones overwhelmingly, Gonzalez was able to edge out Lattimer by 282 votes — enough for the *San Antonio News* to characterize it as a "staggering upset against long odds."

Then, on the heels of this exhausting campaign, the victor found that he was the only candidate for office in Bexar County facing a Republican candidate in the general election. Moreover, this new opponent, Jesse Oppenheimer, questioned his patriotism, was well financed, and had the additional advantage of running along with the nation's hero, President Dwight Eisenhower, who would end up carrying Texas by a wide margin. Virtually all of the leading Texas elected officials — Democrats to a man — either worked quietly on behalf of Ike or at least avoided associating themselves with their party's nominee, Governor Adlai Stevenson of Illinois. Gonzalez had the temerity to point this out, calling the most powerful figure in the state, Senate Majority Leader Lyndon Johnson, "Lyin' Down Lyndon," and refusing to retract the statement when approached by a top Johnson aide. Meanwhile Senator John F. Kennedy had come all the way from Massachusetts to campaign for Stevenson in Texas. At an event in San Antonio, Gonzalez reminded the senator that they had first met in 1951 at a housing conference in Washington. (The skinny young senator had impressed Gonzalez with his keen knowledge of the national housing problem.) Scrappy Gonzalez ended up trouncing his opponent, and this time votes from the West Side barrio spelled the difference.[10]

This was a period of mounting challenges to the racial status quo. The Supreme Court had ruled against discriminatory practices in 1954: most famously in *Brown* v. *Board of Education,* less famously in *Hernandez* v. *Texas.* Like *Brown* a unanimous ruling as well, the *Hernandez* decision stated that Mexican Americans had been unfairly excluded from juries as "a class apart." By 1956 the television news was broadcasting coverage of desegregation marches led by Dr. Martin Luther King Jr., while radios were blaring Elvis Presley's subversive mix of white country music and Afro-American rhythm and blues. For his part, Gonzalez was ready to make his mark in the civil rights movement. In addition to having personally experienced discrimination, he had long since established ties to the African American civil rights community, and in 1956 he successfully pushed through the city council measures abolishing all segregation ordinances.[11]

Gonzalez's tenure as a state senator turned out to be of momentous, even historic importance. As his biographer has noted,

> He became a symbol of the rewards that come to a politician who places principle above personal gain. He opened the minds of thousands of

Texans who impulsively believed in segregation. He helped give an articulate, intelligent, and witty voice to the liberal tradition of Texas. He gave effective voice to the "common citizen."

The legislator's finest hour came in his use of unlimited debate to stop proposals aimed at blocking implementation of the *Brown* v. *Board of Education* decision. The year was 1957, when black schoolchildren trying to attend Little Rock's Central High School were met with mob violence. "Once I had the floor I was determined to hold on to it," he recalled, adding, "They were determined to wait me out." For over twenty straight hours, Henry B. Gonzalez lectured his colleagues. Drawing on a lifetime of experience, he quoted with passionate conviction from his intellectual storehouse: Churchill, Lincoln, Horace, Herodotus. Having himself endured racial epithets and ejection from public accommodations, the legislator now cried, "Who speaks for the Negroes? What about them? . . . Is Texas liberty only for Anglo-Saxons?" He pointed out that the founders of the Republic of Texas had named one of their towns "Gonzales," that Tejanos and African Americans had died at the Alamo. In the *Texas Observer* Ronnie Dugger reported, "He started roaring, he roared on, and he closed roaring; never has his like been seen here before." Most San Antonio newspaper editors conceded the soundness of his arguments, while national newsmagazines gave the speeches extensive coverage, complete with lengthy quotes of his pithy phrases. Gonzalez and his filibuster partner, Senator Abraham Kazen, managed to engender so much controversy that only two of the ten bills became law. Meanwhile the San Antonio state senator also successfully sponsored legislation for his district, including a medical school and a measure for slum clearance. In later years critics would charge that urban renewal efforts of this type—focusing on the razing of dilapidated buildings—removed poor residents without providing adequate new housing. For his part, however, Gonzalez, the former housing administrator, did not see slum clearance as a panacea, and in fact would go on to sponsor major housing legislation as a member of Congress.[12]

The following year, 1958, Gonzalez ran for governor. Named "Man of the Year" by the National Association for the Advancement of Colored People, he was admired by the progressive Democrats of Texas (DOT), those Texas Democrats who had remained loyal Democratic campaigners for Adlai Stevenson in 1952 and 1956 and supported Ralph Yarborough in his unsuccessful gubernatorial efforts. At the DOT convention Gonzalez found himself carried into the hall on the shoulders of his enthusiastic supporters, then proceeded to galvanize the delegates with his ringing call for liberal activism. At the same time, his campaign had no organization and no state headquarters—just energy and idealism. Moreover, he refused to accept campaign contributions from vested interests. Crisscrossing the vast state of Texas alone in the old family station wagon, he offered an alternative to the standard state candidates, calling for controversial measures such as a tax on gas pipelines. Ronnie Dugger recalled, "Gandhi might as well have run for governor of South Africa before he returned to India." Meanwhile his opponent, Governor Price Daniel, had the support of the party mechanism and all the powerful Democratic leaders, including longtime ally Lyndon Johnson. For his part, Gonzalez had publicly criticized Johnson for not having campaigned on behalf of Adlai Stevenson. Nonetheless, neither LBJ nor Gonzalez wanted to burn their bridges. The Senate majority leader, with his eye on the 1960 presidential race, sought to broaden his Democratic base—particularly among those in the Party with ties to the northern/liberal wing—while Gonzalez realized that the other leading Texas elected officials were more conservative and hidebound than Johnson. In fact, the previous year he had shepherded through Congress the first civil rights bill since Reconstruction (albeit a weak one). Thus, at one point during Gonzalez's DOT convention speech the delegates sat in stunned silence as he praised Johnson's leadership. Moreover, the following year, when Robert Kennedy asked Gonzalez about the Texas prospects for a presidential bid by his brother, Gonzalez responded by asking Robert what he would think "if I go to Massachusetts and ask you, 'How do you think Lyndon Johnson will run in Massachusetts?'" Robert Kennedy replied, "I get it. Thank you very much." Thus, even though Gonzalez felt an affinity to John F. Kennedy in terms of religion and, especially, regarding issues ranging from civil rights to labor rights, in fact he supported Lyndon Johnson during the 1960 Democratic primary season, as a powerful figure with local ties who could deliver what he promised. Nonetheless the LBJ campaign operatives shunted Gonzalez aside, he said. When he complained to Johnson, the candidate refused to get involved, however, even as he replied that he was "honored" by the state senator's support. Then, once Kennedy became the Democratic Party's 1960 presidential candidate, Gonzalez threw himself into the Kennedy campaign, and when the newly anointed candidate asked for Gonzalez's assessment of the campaign's chances in Texas, he replied that a landslide for Kennedy in San Antonio would offset losses to Nixon in North Texas. As cochair of the "Viva Kennedy" effort, Gonzalez campaigned for the Kennedy-Johnson ticket in eleven states and of course in Texas, where he helped the Democrats win the Lone Star State, which proved crucial to their overall victory.[13]

Lyndon Johnson's election as vice president opened up his Senate seat.

In the 1961 special election, Gonzalez declared his candidacy, but so did fellow San Antonio liberal Maury Maverick Jr. As Eugene Rodriguez has written, "The two men knew that if they both ran the liberal vote would be split . . . [but] in developments that proved almost permanently disastrous to liberals, both Gonzalez and Maverick ran." Conservative Democrat William Blakley went on to win his feuding party's nomination, only to be defeated in the general election by Republican John Tower. Then, when San Antonio congressman Paul Kilday resigned to accept a Kennedy appointment, political observers were not surprised that Gonzalez announced that he would run for the seat; although he had only won 10 percent of the overall primary vote, he had carried the San Antonio area handily. (Kennedy had also offered an appointment to Gonzalez—in his case a Latin American ambassadorship—but as Pete Hamill put it, "he seemed to know in his bones what all the good ones learn the hard way: all politics is local.") This congressional race turned out to be the first one held during the Kennedy administration, so it attracted national coverage as a kind of referendum on the budding New Frontier. Consequently both parties sent important campaigners, with the Republicans dispatching none other than former president Eisenhower on behalf of their candidate, attorney and Republican Party County Chairman John Goode. Nonetheless Gonzalez, by now the leading political figure in San Antonio, won easily.[14]

The new congressman very much wanted a seat on the Armed Services Committee, given the many military bases in his district. Also, during the campaign he had pledged to follow in the steps of Congressman Kilday, who had served on the committee for over two decades. Instead Gonzalez was appointed to the Banking Committee. He complained to the vice president, but Johnson no longer wielded the power that he had exercised as a leader in Congress. For his part, Speaker of the House John W. McCormack advised the new congressman that any effort to wedge him into Armed Services would engender resentment among his more senior congressional colleagues. Perhaps most convincing was the advice of another Texan—one who, like Gonzalez, was known for defending the "little guy"—Representative Wright Patman. The veteran legislator, chair of the House Banking Committee, said, "Henry, you just stay on this Committee and quit making a wave about Armed Services, and you'll end up as chairman." So Gonzalez stayed, with Patman and Gonzalez often constituting the only two members who questioned conflicts-of-interest or hidden costs to small depositors. Such provisions often were drafted with the advice of bank lobbyists and then buried in the body of a bill, but Gonzalez and Patman would ferret them out and report them to the press. Moreover, when businesspeople even hinted at ways in which Gonzalez could cash in on his Banking Committee connections, the representative summarily ejected them from his office. From the beginning he also introduced important legislation unrelated to the Banking Committee, the first being an anti–poll tax measure, and he was one of only twenty members to vote in favor of abolishing the Un-American Activities Committee. When an El Paso Republican called the twenty dissenters "pinkos," Gonzalez punched him. The San Antonio representative soon established a reputation as a person of integrity, a liberal, something of a loner, but hardworking, outgoing, with a quick wit and, on occasion, a quick temper.[15]

On November 22, 1963, Congressman Gonzalez was riding in the Dallas presidential motorcade "when that immense hole was blown through America," in Pete Hamill's words. Hamill added, "He was in Parkland Hospital to light a cigarette for Jacqueline Kennedy while she sat in her bloodstained clothes. He signed for the belongings of Governor John Connally . . . he flew back to Washington with the presidential party on Air Force One . . . he wept without shame."[16] Then he, like the new president, got to work. Gonzalez supported virtually all of the new administration's proposals in 1964, more than any other member of the Texas delegation, and he served as cochair of the "Viva Johnson" organization during the President's 1964 campaign.[17]

Regarding the numerous Great Society bills emanating from the Johnson White House the following year, a Gonzalez aide recalled, "So much was happening so fast that it all, in retrospect, seems more like a hurly-burly than an organized effort." Johnson knew he could rely on his Texas cohort, remarking, "I don't have to worry about Henry—Henry's for the people." Indeed, LBJ's chief domestic adviser, Joe Califano, witnessed "genuine love" between the two men, and noted, "Gonzalez is the same kind of populist as LBJ was." Gonzalez took the lead in Congress on a number of Great Society bills, including those for housing and civil rights (as in his spearheading of the legislation to eliminate the poll tax). He regularly hitched rides back to Texas on *Air Force One,* where he would swap political intelligence with the president, and some afternoons LBJ, weary of listening to reports from bureaucrats, would invite his old Texas buddy over for a visit. Each had ancestors that included some distinguished figures, but both had endured hard times in their youth. Moreover, both had witnessed social wrongs as young men. Congressman Gonzalez never forgot watching his friend's mother go blind from having sewn baby clothes for piecework wages, and he knew that the President had been seared by his experience as a young teacher of poverty-stricken youngsters at a "Mexican" school in a segregated town. On the other hand,

Johnson had never experienced discrimination, and even had been known to utter a slur when in the company of powerful, reactionary supporters. Moreover, while Gonzalez had been a liberal from the start, Johnson had often opposed the Texas liberals in the 1950s, and his closest Texas ally was a conservative, Governor John Connally. Now, however, LBJ was showing himself to be a champion of civil rights and the poor, and his complicated relationship with this independent-minded congressman was indeed warm and affectionate, even if Gonzalez was never a White House insider. The president facilitated Gonzalez's district obtaining a large number of Great Society programs. If a project omitted San Antonio, Gonzalez would call Johnson, and soon the city would be added to the list. One Gonzalez aide recalled, "The big thing that Lyndon was able to help him on was the Hemisfair. That involved heavy federal appropriations." This international exhibition aimed to showcase San Antonio's bicultural heritage and help diversify the city's economic base (which relied on the military for 40 percent of its revenue).[18]

On the foreign affairs front Gonzalez also voted with the administration, but often with reluctance. He joined the unanimous vote in support of the 1964 Tonkin Gulf Resolution, authorizing the president to take any actions he deemed necessary against the North Vietnamese in defense of American forces. Within a year, however, Congressman Gonzalez was expressing regrets about this vote, as he later told his biographer. In private he also indicated misgivings about the 1965 bill authorizing supplemental funds for Vietnam, and he regarded the Dominican invasion that year a mistake. Gonzalez was LBJ's man in San Antonio, however, and was loath to break with his president, so he continued to vote with the administration, even as he tried to avoid making statements about these military actions. When pressed he toed the official line, however, as when he said that withdrawal from Vietnam "would mean the systematic fall of other Far Eastern nations. I doubt the Philippines could last a year."

By 1967 the Great Society's War on Poverty was being "strangled by the [Vietnam] War," in the words of the program's director Sargent Shriver, and Congressman Gonzalez made similar complaints. He also quietly began investigating the ethnic composition of the troops in Vietnam. "Every Thursday the casualty list would come in, so we would write these letters of condolence which seemed — then and now — to be hollow," said Gonzalez aide Kelsey Meeks. Moreover, when they analyzed the lists, they discovered that Spanish-surnamed men made up a markedly disproportionate percentage of the casualties. When this and similar discrepancies among African Americans and poor whites came to the attention of the president, he attempted to ameliorate the situation in part by eliminating graduate school draft deferments, knowing full well that this would fuel the growing campus discontent. Indeed, as Califano remembered, "All hell broke loose" as a result of this change in the selective service system.[19]

At this time the Chicano movement was on the rise. For his part Gonzalez had been called a radical and a rabble-rouser many times, and he fully supported new civil rights organizations such as the Mexican American Legal Defense and Education Fund, but MALDEF included Anglo attorneys; he had never joined groups made up solely of Hispanics, such as LULAC (League of United Latin American Citizens). More important, he considered the Chicano movement dangerous and racist. When *movimiento* activists accused the Federal Park Service of owning lands that belonged to individuals under the Treaty of Guadalupe Hidalgo (1848), Gonzalez shot back, "Now don't talk to me about land—you're all urban!" He advised Johnson that Chicano leaders should not be trusted. "They were really advocating violence," reflected the congressman, who pressured the Ford Foundation to cut back on its funding of Southwest Council of La Raza, which he cited for allowing some of its money to be used by "the militant Mexican-American Youth Organization . . . [which] regularly distributes literature that I can only describe as hate sheets." According to one of the founders of the Southwest Council, Notre Dame sociologist Julian Samora, Gonzalez also called the council's president a racist, which Professor Samora considered ridiculous. Highly charged disagreements over the Chicano movement and the Vietnam War turned ordinary battles for political turf into bitter disputes, as when Gonzalez accused Willie Velazquez—whom he had helped secure a State Department internship—of "consorting with my enemies," including San Antonio elected officials Joe J. Bernal and Albert Pena Jr. Moreover, by the election year of 1968 Lyndon Johnson himself had become a locus of controversy, and while Gonzalez remained loyal to the president, Bernal and Pena supported the candidacy of Robert Kennedy. After the assassination of Senator Robert Kennedy, all three Hispanics would support the Democratic nominee, Vice President Hubert Humphrey (although, predictably, only Gonzalez did so without needing the persuasion of Humphrey.)[20]

In the years that followed Gonzalez was instrumental in the establishment of congressional committees to investigate the assassinations of John F. Kennedy, Robert F. Kennedy, and Martin Luther King Jr. He also called for the investigation of what he considered the Reagan administration's misguided escalation of U.S. military involvement in Central America, even asking for the president's impeachment, for having countenanced the illegal arming of the Nicaraguan rebels.[21] For the most part, however, Gonzalez continued to focus on domestic problems, as in 1974 when he successfully modified the Safe Drinking Water Act to mandate federal protection of urban aquifers. In the words of Texas journalist Michael King, "The San Antonio chamber of commerce types and the media were livid at what they considered federal meddling in 'local affairs', but Gonzalez knew that municipalities would not protect public water resources against what he called 'unconscionable predators' poised to steal and pollute [the water]. Years later some 70 aquifers nationwide are under such federal protection."[22]

As chair of the House Banking Committee Gonzalez successfully pushed for a number of bills hailed by consumer groups, including improved credit measures for small businesses, reform of federal flood insurance, and increased accountability of the Federal Reserve System. "He demystified the Federal Reserve more than anybody in history," according to Congressman Barney Frank, who added, "He substantially changed the way the Fed operates, particularly in the way they release information to the public, in that he forced them to open minutes and elections." Moreover, throughout the 1980s the Banking Committee chair warned, almost alone, that deregulation of savings and loan institutions could lead to their collapse. After his prediction proved correct he found himself in charge of the bailout legislation, but only agreed to draft it on condition that the malfeasance of the bankers and their legislative supporters be brought to light. When it turned out that most of the guilty senators were Democrats, Gonzalez pursued the investigation with as much vigor as ever. For his trouble he found himself under pressure from a number of fellow Democrats to resign as committee chair, but he argued his case in Congress and the press, managing to keep his post in the end. As Pete Hamill noted, "More than any other Congressman, Gonzalez helped clean up the mess, forging the bailout of those people who had been hurt, and making clear that [major perpetrator] Charles Keating ended up in jail." In the wake of the crisis, moreover, Gonzalez led the effort to reform the Federal Deposit Insurance Corporation.[23]

In his capacity as Banking Committee chair Gonzalez also investigated loans from the U.S. government to Iraqi leader Saddam Hussein. The resulting report showed that President George Bush and his colleague James Baker had been involved in arranging over $3 billion in loans, supposedly for agricultural projects, but really for weapons development of various sorts, not excluding components for atomic application. The Bush administration responded by blocking the chairman's access to classified documents. Undeterred, Gonzalez went on to oppose the 1991 Gulf War conducted against that same country, Iraq, and he even called for Bush's impeachment. The Congressman charged, among other things, that President Bush "systematically eliminated every option for a peaceful resolution, rendering any substantive debate by Congress meaningless." Not surprisingly, his constituents—in the town of the Alamo, with military bases as the main employers—nearly all opposed this stand, and he even received some death threats. Some years later, when he voted against the impeachment of President Clinton—not convinced that this president's dalliances and courtroom testimony constituted "high crimes"—his critics accused Gonzalez of partisan politics in his selection of impeachment targets.[24]

As the only member of the House Banking Committee with experience in public housing, it was natural that Gonzalez would chair its Housing Subcommittee. There he vigorously opposed attempts by the Reagan and Bush administrations to slash housing funds. In these battles one of the congressman's main opponents was Samuel Pierce, the secretary of housing and urban development under President Reagan, and Gonzalez successfully demonstrated that Secretary Pierce had misused departmental funds. During that period Gonzalez even managed to obtain new programs, such as one bill that included housing for people with AIDS, and another that provided support for homeowners on the brink of foreclosure. In one of his last major proposals, the subcommittee chair successfully shepherded to passage the Homeownership and Equity Protection Act of 1994, which was "designed to curb creditors' practices of . . . targeting disadvantaged communities for credit on unfair terms," in the words of one longtime housing activist, who concluded, "We never needed to lobby him, because he was always on our side already."[25]

Upon retiring from Congress, Gonzalez was succeeded in office by his son Charles. Perhaps in a way this marks a bit of an ironic twist in the legacy of Henry B., the scrappy outsider who made it on his own, even as his son's victory certainly reflects the veteran congressman's devotion to his family and his success as a role model. Not long before his death, while accepting one of the many accolades of his later years, the old former representative summed up his philosophy thus: "In my time I have had the honor to be vilified for standing up against segregation. I have had the privilege of being a thorn in the side of unprincipled privilege, and the great joy of being demonized by entrenched special interests. . . . What I care about is . . . decency, justice, and an abhorrence for what is wrong and intolerance for mediocrity."

Henry B. Gonzalez died on November 29, 2000. The funeral was held in the same place that he had been baptized during the height of the Mexican Revolution, the Cathedral of San Fernando de Bexar, a building that had predated by so many years the first Anglo structures in town. "Tributes flowed in, from . . . President Bill Clinton to Governor George W. Bush," Pete Hamill wrote. "Ordinary people wept, lit candles, laid flowers in his name, and remembered a thousand small moments." They knew that Henry B. Gonzalez never forgot his mission. They knew—or would have guessed—that both in San Antonio and in Washington he had proudly displayed a plaque with the words "This office belongs to the people of the 20th Congressional District, Texas."[26]

NOTES

Abbreviations used in the notes:

CAH   Center for American History, University of Texas at Austin
CR   *Congressional Record*

PERIODICALS

AAS   *Austin American Statesman*
CD   *Congressional Digest*
CQWR   *Congressional Quarterly Weekly Report*
DMN   *Dallas Morning News*
DTH   *Dallas Times Herald*
FWST   *Fort Worth Star-Telegram*
HC   *Houston Chronicle*
HP   *Houston Post*
NR   *The New Republic*
NYT   *New York Times*
SWHQ   *Southwestern Historical Quarterly*
TO   *Texas Observer*
USNWR   *U.S. News and World Report*
WP   *Washington Post*

EDWARD M. HOUSE

1. House wrote two memoirs, "Reminiscences" in 1916 and "Memories" in 1929. Both are in the Papers of Edward M. House, Yale University Library. The quotation is from "Memories," 8. See also Charles M. Seymour, *The Intimate Papers of Colonel House,* 4 vols., Boston: Houghton Mifflin, 1926–28), 1:8–11; and Charles E. Neu, "In Search of Colonel Edward M. House: The Texas Years, 1858–1912," *SWHQ* XCIII, no. 1 (July 1989): 25–29.

2. The quotation is from "Reminiscences," 11. See also "Reminiscences," 8–10; "Memories," 6–8, 14–22; Neu, "In Search of Colonel House," 29–31; and Alexander L. George and Juliette L. George, *Woodrow Wilson and Colonel House: A Personality Study* (New York: John Day Co., 1956), 80–81.

3. The quotations are from "Memories," 23, 36. See also Rupert Norval Richard-

son, *Colonel Edward M. House: The Texas Years, 1858–1912* (Abilene, Tex.: Hardin Simmons University, 1964), 30–31; and Neu, "In Search of Colonel House," 31–33.

4. "Memories," 36; "Reminiscences," 12, 25; Lewis L. Gould, *Progressives and Prohibitionists: Texas Democrats in the Wilson Era* (Austin: University of Texas Press, 1973), 8–16; Richardson, *Colonel House,* 42–153; Neu, "In Search of Colonel House," 34–38; Seymour, *Intimate Papers,* 1:27–38; and George and George, *Wilson and House,* 82–84.

5. "Memories," 38; "Reminiscences," 13, 20–24; Gould, *Progressives and Prohibitionists,* 11–12, 15–16; Richardson, *Colonel House,* 60–153, 304–312; Evan Anders, *Boss Rule in South Texas: The Progressive Era* (Austin: University of Texas Press, 1982), 65–80; and Neu, "In Search of Colonel House," 34, 36.

6. The quotations are from Seymour, *Intimate Papers,* 1:38, 40. See also "Reminiscences," 27–31, 43–44; Neu, "In Search of Colonel House," 38–40; and George and George, *Wilson and House,* 86–88.

7. The quotation is from House to Sidney E. Mezes, November 25, 1911, House Papers, Yale University Library (hereafter cited as HP). See also Gould, *Progressives and Prohibitionists,* 70–77; and George and George, *Wilson and House,* 88–104.

8. "Memories," 9–10; Edwin A. Weinstein, *Woodrow Wilson: A Medical and Psychological Biography* (Princeton: Princeton University Press, 1981), 269–72; and Neu, "In Search of Colonel House," 38–39.

9. Weinstein, *Wilson,* 271; John Milton Cooper Jr., *The Warrior and the Priest: Woodrow Wilson and Theodore Roosevelt* (Cambridge: Harvard University Press, 1983), 241–245; Bert Edward Park, *The Impact of Illness on World Leaders* (Philadelphia: University of Pennsylvania Press, 1986), 3, 7, 331–342; and George and George, *Wilson and House,* 113–132.

10. Edward M. House, *Philip Dru, Administrator: A Story of Tomorrow, 1920–1933* (New York: B. W. Huebsch, 1912).

11. Ibid., 88–89.

12. Ibid., 42, 44–45, 154, 181–182, 225–230, 238–243, 272–273, 284–294.

13. House Diary, November 16, 18, December 6, 18, 19, 1912, February 8, 1913, HP; Seymour, *Intimate Papers,* 1:83–113, and Arthur S. Link, *Wilson,* 5 vols. (Princeton: Princeton University Press, 1947–1965), vol. 2: *The New Freedom,* 5–19.

14. The quotations are from House Diary, January 8, 1913, HP. See also Seymour, *Intimate Papers,* 1:100–101; Link, *Wilson,* 2:16; and House to Wilson, January 9, 1913, in Arthur S. Link, ed., *The Papers of Woodrow Wilson,* 62 vols. (Princeton: Princeton University Press, 1966–90; hereafter cited as Link, *PWW*), 27:26–27.

15. The quotations are from House Diary, January 22 and February 26, 1913, HP; and House, *Philip Dru,* 137. See also House Diary, February 13, 1913, HP; and Seymour, *Intimate Papers,* 1:156–158.

16. The quotations are from Seymour, *Intimate Papers,* 1:114. See also 1:115; Link, *Wilson,* 2:93–95; and Patrick Devlin, *Too Proud to Fight: Woodrow Wilson's Neutrality* (New York: Oxford University Press, 1975), 99–100.

17. Seymour, *Intimate Papers,* 1:158–167; and Link, *Wilson,* 2:199–237.

18. House Diary, January 22, March 20, April 15, May 9, 11, 1913, HP; House

to Wilson, April 23 and May 20, 1913, HP; and Walter Hines Page to House, July 8, 1913, HP.

19. The quotation is from House to Frances B. Denton, May 16, 1914, HP. See also House Diary, April 9, 28, May 11, 1914, HP; and Seymour, *Intimate Papers*, 1: 245–247.

20. The quotation is from House to Wilson, May 29, 1914, in Link, *PWW*, 30: 108–109. See also Seymour, *Intimate Papers*, 1:248–257; House Diary, May 27, June 1, 1914, HP; and Link, *Wilson*, 2:314–317.

21. The quotations are from House to Wilson, June 3, 1914, in Link, *PWW*, 30: 139–140; and House Diary, June 27, 1914, HP. See also Seymour, *Intimate Papers*, 1:257–275; and Link, *Wilson*, 2:317–318.

22. The quotations are from House to Wilson, August 1, 1914, in Link, *PWW*, 30:327; House to Wilson, August 5, 1914, in Link, *PWW*, 30:349; House to Wilson, August 7, 1914, in Link, *PWW*, 30:359. See also House Diary, August 30, 1914, HP.

23. The quotation is from House Diary, December 16, 1914, HP. See also Seymour, *Intimate Papers*, 1:209–210, 233–234; House Diary, December 17, 1914, January 13, 1915, HP, and Link, *Wilson*, 2:325–327.

24. The quotation is from House Diary, January 24, 1915, HP. See also House Diary, November 6–8, December 14, 16–20, 1914, HP.

25. The quotation is from Wilson to House, February 20, 1915, in Link, *PWW*, 32:265. See also House Diary, February 17, March 7, 1915, HP; Seymour, *Intimate Papers*, 1:359–411; Link, *Wilson*, 3:217–231; and Devlin, *Too Proud to Fight*, 264–282.

26. The quotation is from House to Wilson, February 9, 1915, HP. See also Wilson to House, April 19, 1915, in Link, *PWW*, 33:16–17; and Link, *Wilson*, 3:217–231.

27. House Diary, April 30, May 30, June 13, 16, 19, 24, 1915, HP; and House to Wilson, May 25, 1915, HP.

28. The quotation is from House to Wilson, July 15, 1915, HP. See also House Diary, July 10, 31, 1915, HP; and Devlin, *Too Proud to Fight*, 310–315.

29. The quotations are from House to Wilson, August 22, 1915, HP; and House Diary, August 22, 1915, HP. See also Wilson to House, August 21, 1915, in Link, *PWW*, 34:271–272; House Diary, September 12, 28, 1915, HP; House to Wilson, September 20, 1915, HP; and Link, *Wilson*, 3:567–587.

30. The quotation is from House Diary, June 24, 1915, HP. See also House Diary, July 31, 1915, HP; Tom Schactman, *Edith and Woodrow: A Presidential Romance* (New York: G. P. Putnam's Sons, 1981); Link, *Wilson*, 4:1–14; and Cooper, *The Warrior and the Priest*, 294–295.

31. House Diary, July 10, 31, October 8, 1915, HP; Link, *Wilson*, 4:101; Devlin, *Too Proud to Fight*, 376–378; and George and George, *Wilson and House*, 166–167.

32. The quotation is from House Diary, October 8, 1915, HP. See also Grey to House, August 10, 26, 1915, HP; and Link, *Wilson*, 4:102–103.

33. The quotation is from House Diary, October 14, 1915, HP. See also Grey to House, September 23, 1915, Wilson to House, October 18, 1915, and House to Grey, October 17, 1915, HP; and Link, *Wilson*, 4:104–105.

34. The quotation is from House Diary, November 25, 1918, HP. See also House Diary, January 6, 8, 10, 11, 14, 15, 19, 28, February 2, 3, 4, 7, 8, 9, 11, 14, 15, 16, 17, 21, 22, 1916, HP; and Link, *Wilson,* 4:106–136.

35. House-Grey Memorandum, February 22, 1916, HP; House Diary, February 10, 14, 17, 21, 1916, HP; House to Grey, March 8, 1916, HP; House to Wilson, February 10, 1916, in Link, *PWW,* 36:166–168; and Link, *Wilson,* 4:130–141.

36. The quotations are from House Diary, March 27, 30, 1916, HP. See also House to Wilson, April 3, 1916, in Link, *PWW,* 36:405; House to Wilson, May 5, 1916, in Link, *PWW,* 36:616–617; House to Wilson, May 6, 1916, in Link, *PWW,* 36:628–629; House Diary, April 2, 8, 21, 1916, HP; and Link, *Wilson,* 4:222–279.

37. The quotation is from House Diary, May 13, 1916, HP. See also Seymour, *Intimate Papers,* 2:277–290; and Link, *Wilson,* 5:17–38.

38. Wilson to House, June 10, 1916, HP, House Diary, June 17, 1916, Ibid., Seymour, *Intimate Papers,* 2:347–386; and Link, *Wilson,* 5:9–10.

39. House to Wilson, November 30, December 17, 1916, HP; Seymour, *Intimate Papers,* 2:347–386; and Link, *Wilson,* 5:9–10.

40. Bernstorff to House, January 31, 1917, HP; House Diary, February 1, 12, March 22, 27, 28, April 1, 1917, HP; Link, *Wilson,* 5:290–431.

41. House to Wilson, April 6, 1917, HP; House Diary, April 26, 29, 30, October 13, 14, 1917, HP; Wilson to the prime ministers of Great Britain, France, and Italy, October 14, 1917, HP; Seymour, *Intimate Papers,* 3:34–59, 184–209; and Inga Floto, *Colonel House in Paris: A Study of American Policy at the Paris Peace Conference 1919* (Princeton: Princeton University Press, 1980), 25–26.

42. The quotation is from House Diary, September 4, 1917, HP. See also House to Wilson, September 4, 1917, HP; Wilson to House, September 2, 1917, HP; Floto, *Colonel House in Paris,* 26–27; and Lawrence E. Gelfand, *The Inquiry: American Preparations for Peace, 1917* (New Haven: Yale University Press, 1963), 22–78.

43. The quotation is from House Diary, December 1, 1917, HP. See also House Report to Wilson, December 14, 1917, HP; House Diary, December 18, 1917, HP; and Seymour, *Intimate Papers,* 3:210–317.

44. The quotations are from Wilson to Whom It May Concern, October 14, 1918, HP; and House Diary, October 16, 1918, HP; See also Seymour, *Intimate Papers,* 4:74–88.

45. The quotations are from House to Wilson, November 5, 1918, HP. See also Seymour, *Intimate Papers,* 4:117–200; and Floto, *Colonel House in Paris,* 44–60.

46. House to Wilson, November 14, 1918, HP; Wilson to House, November 16, 1918, HP; House Diary, December 3, 1918, HP; Seymour, *Intimate Papers,* 4:201–249; Floto, *Colonel House in Paris,* 70, 86; and George and George, *Wilson and House,* 192–194, 203–204.

47. House Diary, January 1, 1919, HP; Floto, *Colonel House in Paris,* 98–101; and George and George, *Wilson and House,* 217–218.

48. House Diary, February 1, 13, 14, 1919, HP; and Seymour, *Intimate Papers,* 4:271–319.

49. The quotations are from House Diary, February 14, 1919, HP. See also Floto,

Colonel House in Paris, 120, 142–143; and George and George, *Wilson and House,* 228–230.

50. The quotation is from Wilson to House, February 23, 1919, in Link, *PWW,* 55:229–30. See also House to Wilson, February 19, 1919, HP; George and George, *Wilson and House,* 240–242; Floto, *Colonel House in Paris,* 120–163; and Seymour, *Intimate Papers,* 4:320–362.

51. The quotations are from House Diary, March 14, 1919, HP (emphasis added); and Edith Bolling Wilson, *My Memoir* (Indianapolis and New York: Bobbs-Merrill, 1939), 245–246. See also Link, *PWW,* 55:488, n. 2; Cary T. Grayson, "The Colonel's Folly and the President's Distress," *American Heritage* 15 (October 1964): 4–7, 94–101; and Floto, *Colonel House in Paris,* 164–170.

52. Sigmund Freud and William C. Bullitt, *Thomas Woodrow Wilson: A Personality Study* (Boston: Houghton Mifflin, 1966); Seymour, *Intimate Papers,* 4:363–376; and George and George, *Wilson and House,* 240–250.

53. From the Diary of Ray Stannard Baker, March 15, 1919, in Link, *PWW,* 55:531; House Diary, March 24, 1919, HP; Seymour, *Intimate Papers,* 4:385–487; and Floto, *Colonel House in Paris,* 171–327.

54. The quotation is from House to Seymour, April 20, 1928, in Seymour, *Intimate Papers,* 4:518. See also House to Wilson, November 14, 27, 1919, HP; George and George, *Wilson and House,* 304–306; and Charles Seymour, "Edward M. House," in *Dictionary of American Biography* (New York: Charles Scribner's Sons, 1958), Supplement 2:319–321.

MORRIS SHEPPARD

1. Scrapbook #4, 2, Sheppard Papers, CAH (hereafter cited as SP).

2. *Austin American,* December 12, 1930; *Dallas Dispatch Journal,* August 20, 1938.

3. Lucille Sheppard Keyes, "Morris Sheppard," typed MS in possession of Mrs. Lucille Sheppard Connally, Washington, D.C., 19–50, 53 (a copy with different pagination is available in the CAH—hereafter cited as Keyes, "Sheppard"); T. U. Taylor, *Fifty Years on Forty Acres* (Austin: Alec Book Company, 1938), 81–97; Nugent E. Brown, *B Hall, Texas* (San Antonio: Naylor Company, 1938), 1–58; George P. Garrison to Morris Sheppard, August 31, 1894, SP; *Dallas News,* October 14, 17, 1902; Scrapbook #1, 68, 72, Scrapbook #4, 5, SP; *WP,* December 14, 1902; *Texarkana (Tex.) Daily Courier,* October 25, 1902.

4. Scrapbook #4, 2, 25, Scrapbook #6, 92, 94, SP; Keyes, "Sheppard," 53, 61, 62; Joseph G. Cannon to William H. Moody, November 11, 1902, Moody Papers, in Library of Congress, Washington, D.C.; *CR,* 57th Cong., 2nd sess., 7657–7667; *Dallas News,* November 9, 1903; *HP,* December 23, 1902; Walter Wellman, "Spooner of Wisconsin," *American Monthly Review of Reviews* 26 (1902): 167; Claude G. Bowers, *Beveridge and the Progressive Era* (New York: Literary Guild, 1932), 184–187; Sam Hanna Acheson, *Joe Bailey, the Last Democrat* (New York: Macmillan, 1932), 155–

163; George E. Mowry, *The Era of Theodore Roosevelt and the Birth of Modern America* (New York: Harper and Row, 1958), 115–118, 238–239; Nathaniel W. Stephenson, *Nelson W. Aldrich, a Leader in American Politics* (Port Washington, N.Y.: Kennikut Press, 1930) 41, 136; *The Outlook* 75 (December 12, 1903): 865; Blaire Bolles, *Tyrant from Illinois: Uncle Joe Cannon's Experiment with Personal Power* (New York: W. W. Norton, 1951), 7; George E. Mowry, *Theodore Roosevelt and the Progressive Movement* (New York: Hill and Wang, 1946), 32, 40–44, 67–68; James Holt, *Congressional Insurgents and the Party System, 1909–1916* (Cambridge: Harvard University Press, 1967), 16–28.

5. *CR*, 58th Cong., 2nd sess., 2612–2614; *CR*, 59th Cong., 1st sess., 2784–2786; *CR*, 2nd sess., 1238–1244; *CR*, 61st Cong., 1st sess., 284–287; *CR*, 61st Cong., 2nd sess., 8144; *CR*, 62nd Cong., 3rd sess., 4050; *New York Evening Telegram*, June 15, 1910; *Dallas News*, March 2, 1904, February 28, 1906, and June 17, 1910; *WP*, April 19, 1911; Waldo Clifford Leland, "The National Archives Programme," *American Historical Review*, October 1912, 7; U.S. House, Hearings and Reports of the Committee on Public Buildings and Grounds (Washington, D.C.: GPO, 1911), iv; *HP*, March 2, 1904; *New York Press*, March 2, 1906; Keyes, "Sheppard," 64; Scrapbook #6, 56, 83, and Scrapbook #10, 36, 57, and Scrapbook #11, 39, SP; Mowry, *Theodore Roosevelt and Modern America*, 239.

6. Historians disagree regarding the exact nature of the Wilson-House relationship. Andrew Mellon, in a comment to Morris Sheppard's wife, offered a view that Wilson was the "Jack that House built" (interview with Lucille S. Connally, June 21, 1975, audiotape copy in possession of the author). Secretary of the Navy Josephus Daniels, however, stated in an undated memo in his papers that House was useful to Wilson and that the president controlled the relationship. (The memo appears to have been written around 1913; see Josephus Daniels Papers, in Library of Congress.) Woodrow Wilson to Albert Sidney Burleson, February 6, 1914; Burleson to Thomas H. Ball, July 23, 1911; House to Burleson, March 6, 1912; Thomas Watt Gregory to House, September 12, 1912, January 9, 1913; Gregory to Burleson, September 16, 1912; Burleson to House, November 9, 1912, in Albert Sidney Burleson Papers, in Library of Congress. Charles Seymour, *The Intimate Papers of Colonel House* (Boston: Houghton Mifflin, 1926–28), 1:44–82.

7. *CR*, 63rd Cong., 1st sess., 4211–4219, 4617; 63rd Cong., 2nd sess., 4533, 5091; *NYT*, July 30, 1913, September 10, 1913, October 4, 1913, May 13, 1914, May 5, 6, 1916, and July 18, 1916; *Austin Statesman*, February 27, 28, 1914; *Austin American*, October 30, 1915; *Dallas News*, March 11, 1914, October 30, 1915; Arthur S. Link, *Wilson: The New Freedom* (Princeton: Princeton University Press, 1956), 11, 193–195; "The American Commission on Co-operative Rural Credit," *The Survey* 30 (May 17, 1913): 239–240; U.S. Senate, *Agricultural Cooperation and Rural Credit in Europe*, Sen. Doc. 261, 63rd Cong., 2nd sess.; *Agricultural Credit*, Sen. Doc. 380, 63rd Cong., 2nd sess.; Sen. Doc. 21, 63rd Cong., 2nd sess., 3–4; David F. Houston to Wilson, December 23, 1913, and Wilson to D. U. Fletcher, January 9, 1914, in Wilson Papers, in Library of Congress. Carter Glass to Albert Sidney Burleson, May 12, 1914, Burleson Papers; Hollis to Wilson, December 11, 1914, Wilson Papers; Keyes, "Sheppard," 122–123; Morris Sheppard, "Rural Credits," speech delivered to the Texas Farmers'

Congress, College Station, Tex., August 3, 1915, SP; George P. Huckaby, "Oscar Branch Colquitt: A Political Biography" (Ph.D. diss., University of Texas, 1946); Sheppard to Ferguson, October 26, 1915, and Ferguson to Sheppard, October 26, 27, 1915, SP; Folder 2, "Campaigns," SP.

8. Scrapbook #15, 71, and Scrapbook #28, 5, SP; *Boston Globe,* December 26, 1915.

9. Bolles, *Tyrant from Illinois,* 112; James H. Timberlake, *Prohibition and the Progressive Movement* (Cambridge: Harvard University Press, 1963), 171–172; Herbert Asbury, *The Great Illusion* (Garden City, N.Y.: Doubleday, 1950), 126; *Dallas News,* August 14, 1918; *WP,* December 11, 1913, January 13, 14, 15, 19, 1915; *NYT,* March 29, 1926; *CR,* 63rd Cong., 2nd sess., 615–618, 3588, 8508, 9205–9206, 63rd Cong., 3rd sess., 495, 1357, 1383, 1395–1396, 1503, 1513, 1611, 1612, 1616–1619, 1621, 1623, 1628, 1683, 1688–1689, 1696–1697, 1736.

10. *CR,* 64th Cong., 1st sess., 90, 1665, 2564, 4195–4200, 4381–4391, 2nd sess., 142–145, 152, 366–374, 428, 469–471, 533, 547–555, 1049–1051, 1060; *CR,* 65th Cong., 1st sess., 198, 3871, 4017–4018, 4407–4408, 4748–4749, 4778–4811, 4997, 5379, 5522, 5548–5559, 5586–5587, 5595–5596, 5619–5626, 5636–5638, 5648–5663, 2nd sess., 337, 422; *CR,* 66th Cong., 1st sess., 1944, 7606; Scrapbook #18, 15, 34; *WP,* July 31, 1917; Robert D. Bowden, *Boies Penrose, Symbol of an Era* (New York: Greenburg Press, 1937), 249–250.

11. *NYT,* August 12, 1920; *Dallas Dispatch,* October 6, 1922.

12. *Austin Statesman,* January 20, 1919; *Austin American,* February 1, 1919; *San Antonio Evening News,* January 27, 1919; *WP,* July 20, 1919; *NYT,* May 28, 1920; J. B. Cranfill to Sheppard, January 17, 1918, in Scrapbook #18, 44, SP. J. B. Cranfill was a leader of the Anti-Saloon League in Texas. Wayne B. Wheeler to Sheppard, November 21, 1918, in Scrapbook #18, 36, SP; Scrapbook #19, 7, SP.

13. *CR,* 63rd Cong., 2nd sess., 5091; *CR,* 65th Cong., 2nd sess., 9206–9207, 3rd sess., 2946; *CR,* 66th Cong., 1st sess., 635, 1431–1435, 2nd sess., 4599; *CR,* 67th Cong., 1st sess., 6058, 4th sess., 1232; Woodrow Wilson to Sheppard, August 8, 1919, Wilson Papers; Folder 12, "Correspondence," SP; Scrapbook #23, 21, SP; Folder 2, "Campaigns," SP; *Dallas News,* January 7, 1915, January 10, 1918, May 29, 1919, October 6, 1921, February 27, 1923; *NYT,* January 4, 1923; *HP,* June 7, 1931; Keyes, "Sheppard," 172; Ida Husted Harper, ed., *The History of Woman Suffrage* (New York: J. J. Little and Ives Company, 1922), vol. 1, 571–572, 625, 638.

14. *CR,* 69th Cong., 1st sess., 6619; Scrapbook #19, 33, 35, 71, 73, 88, SP; Folder 10, "Personal and Political," SP; Folder 6, "Congressional Speeches, Resolutions and Bills, and Articles," SP; *NYT,* May 8, 1921; *CD,* February 1931, 42.

15. Judson C. Welliver, "The Agricultural Crisis and the Bloc," *Review of Reviews,* February 1922, 159–160, 165; Arthur Capper, "The Agricultural Bloc—What It Is and What It Isn't," *The Outlook* CXXX (February 1, 1922), 176–177; Scrapbook #23, 21, SP; Keyes, "Sheppard," 143; Mark Sullivan, "The Progressive Group in the Senate," *World's Work* 45 (February, 1923): 387, 392; *Literary Digest,* March 31, 1923, 8, March 10, 1923, 6; R. W. Childs, "Government by Blackmail," *Saturday Evening Post,* August 23, 1924, 4.

16. Scrapbook #22, 96, SP.

17. Scrapbook #23, 158, SP; *DTH,* May 24, 1924; *Dallas News,* January 16, 1924, December 19, 1925, March 13, 1926, April 15, 1926, June 28, 1926; Keyes, "Sheppard," 144-145.

18. *Dallas News,* May 21, 24, 25, 1928, August 25, 31, 1928, September 4, 1928, July 12, 1929; Keyes, "Sheppard," 163-164.

19. *HP,* February 22, 1929; *Dallas News,* February 12, 1929.

20. *Texarkana (Tex.) Press,* November 30, 1931; *Dallas News,* October 31, 1932; Folder 20, "Printed," SP.

21. U.S. Senate, Sen. Rpt., 73rd Cong., 2nd sess., No. 555, 1-2, 5-7; *CR,* 73rd Cong., 2nd sess., 7259, 8459; *Dallas News,* May 14, 1934, October 2, 1934; *St. Louis Post-Dispatch,* June 19, 1934; *Washington Evening Star,* November 13, 1937.

22. *Washington Post Magazine,* April 22, 1934; Ernest McCormack to Sheppard, May 27, 1935, Ernest L. Tutt to Sheppard, June 10, 1935, J. E. W. Thomas to Sheppard, October 23, 1935, and W. O. Cox to Sheppard, November 14, 1935, in Folder 14, "Correspondence," SP; *Dallas News,* November 11, 12, 1935, January 25, 1936.

23. *Schecter Poultry Corporation v United States,* 295 US 495 (1934); *United States v Butler,* 297 US 1 (1936).

24. Folder 3, "New Deal," SP; *United States v Butler,* 297 US 1 (1936).

25. Tom Connally, *My Name Is Tom Connally* (New York: Thomas Y. Crowell Company, 1954), 186-187, 190-192; *Dallas News,* February 6, 7, 10, 1937; *NYT,* February 10, 1937, May 19, 1937; Folder 3, "Reorganization of the Federal Judiciary," SP.

26. *US News,* August 15, 1938; *NYT,* June 18, 1938, July 24, 27, 28, 30, 1938, August 17, 1938, September 20, 21, 1938, January 4, 1939, April 14, 1939, March 4, 1940; *WP,* June 18, 30, 1938, August 4, 14, 1938, September 5, 1938; *New York World Telegram,* June 16, 1938; *Dallas Dispatch Journal,* August 20, 1938; *HP,* July 11, 1938; *Dallas News,* June 25, 29, 1938, August 30, 1938, September 12, 1938, August 3, 1939; *Washington Herald,* July 27, 1938, August 3, 1938; *Washington Daily News,* August 27, 1938; *Washington Star,* August 14, 1938; *Washington News,* October 27, 1938; *Daily Worker,* September 13, 1938; *Cleveland Plain Dealer,* January 4, 1939; *Philadelphia Bulletin,* August 18, 1938; U.S. Senate, Sen. Rpt., 76th Cong., 1st sess., No. 1, 3, 5, 9, 11-12, 18, 14-15, 30-31, 39-41, 43-47, 176; *CR,* 76th Cong., 1st sess., 8; Folder 3, "Federal Corrupt Practices Act," SP; Scrapbook #19, 99; *America,* January 14, 1939; *Time,* January 9, 1939.

27. Folder 1, "Campaigns," SP; Scrapbook #17, 198; Folder 10, "Personal," SP; Folder 19, "Correspondence 1937-1940," SP; *CR,* 74th Cong., 1st sess., 1536, 3397, 4657, 4683, 5076, 5194; Boston Transcript, April 23, 1935; *NYT,* August 11, 1935; Sheppard to H. B. Prother, January 3, 1937, in Folder 19, "Correspondence 1937 1940," SP; *Washington Times,* April 3, 1935.

28. Douglas MacArthur to Sheppard, September 4, 1935, September 12, 1936, in Folder 14, "Correspondence," SP.

29. Louis Johnson to Sheppard, April 7, 1938, in Scrapbook #19, 75, SP; *CR,* 76th Cong., 1st sess., 1737, 1915, 1920-1921, 2371.

30. Connally, *My Name Is Tom Connally,* 117; James MacGregor Burns, *Roosevelt: The Lion and the Fox* (New York: Harcourt, Brace and Company, 1956), 155; *NYT,*

September 14, 1939, November 5, 1939; Scrapbook #29, 154, SP; Folder 5, "Neutrality, Preparedness, Defense," SP; *CR*, 76th Cong., 2nd sess., 1014.

31. Scrapbook #17, 156, SP; Folder 10, "Personal and Political," SP; *NYT,* January 17, 1940, March 7, 1940, May 16, 1940; *CR*, 76th Cong., 3rd sess., 671; *Washington Times Herald*, July 8, 1940; *WP*, March 19, 1940.

32. *Dallas News*, August 4, 12, 1940; *Texarkana (Tex.) Gazette*, August 4, 1940; *CR*, 76th Cong., 3rd sess., 9837–9838, 10068, 10092–10093, 10096, 10102, 11142, 11144, 12156, 12227, *FWST,* August 10, 1940; *NYT,* September 17, 1940; Keyes, "Sheppard," 210.

33. Keyes, "Sheppard," 210–211; *CR*, 77th Cong., 1st sess., 87, 1493–1494; *Dallas News*, April 9, 1941.

34. *Dallas News*, April 10, 1941; *WP*, April 10, 1941; *NYT,* April 18, 1941; interviews with Lucille S. Connally, June 11, November 11, 1975, Washington, D.C. (audiotape, notes, and transcript in possession of the author).

JOHN NANCE GARNER

1. Bascom N. Timmons, *Garner of Texas: A Personal History* (New York: Harper and Brothers, 1948), 3–10.

2. *Uvalde Leader News*, December 5, 1991. The Garner Abstract and Land Company celebrated its centennial in 1991.

3. "John Nance Garner," *Handbook of Texas Online*, http://www.tsha.utexas.edu/handbook/online (accessed 5/29/02).

4. Mrs. John N. (Marietta) Garner, "30 Years of Dictation." *Good Housekeeping* 94 (May 1932): 28.

5. Evan Anders, *Boss Rule in South Texas* (Austin: University of Texas Press, 1982), 106; *USNWR*, November 21, 1958, 98.

6. Anders, *Boss Rule*, 107–109; *Seguin Enterprise*, September 19, 1902. Anders stated that Garner worked closely with Wells during his first four terms in Congress, then gradually developed his own political base in South Texas and Washington as he became more independent.

7. *San Antonio Light*, May 1, 1932.

8. Anders, *Boss Rule*, 121–123; *DMN*, November 1, 1915.

9. Lewis L. Gould, *Progressives and Prohibitionists: Texas Democrats in the Wilson Era* (Austin: University of Texas Press, 1973), 110–112; O. C. Fisher, *Cactus Jack* (Waco: Texian Press, 1978), 46.

10. *DMN*, August 21–28, 1913; Gould, *Progressives and Prohibitionists*, 112–113.

11. Anti-Saloon League, *Brewers and Texas Politics* (San Antonio: Passing Show Printing Co., 1916), 1472; Gould, *Progressives and Prohibitionists*, 48–52.

12. Fisher, *Cactus Jack*, 47–48; Gould, *Progressives and Prohibitionists*, 111; *NYT,* May 4, 1913.

13. Patrick L. Cox, "An Enemy Closer to Us Than Any European Power: The Impact of Mexico on Texan Public Opinion before World War I," *SWHQ* 105, no. 1

(July 2001): 63–64; Jim Wells to John Nance Garner, July 7, 1916, Wells Papers, CAH; *San Antonio Express*, February 26, 1913, August 14, 1915.

14. Cox, "Enemy Closer to Us," 50–53; Gould, *Progressives and Prohibitionists*, 283; Fisher, *Cactus Jack*, 49.

15. Garner to Wells, September 19, 1921, Wells Papers, CAH.

16. Norman Brown, *Hood, Bonnet, and Little Brown Jug* (College Station, Texas A&M University Press, 1984), 118; Timmons, *Garner*, 95.

17. Fisher, *Cactus Jack*, 58–59; *Collier's*, August 20, 1927, 29.

18. Timmons, *Garner of Texas*, 120–121; Fisher, *Cactus Jack*, 69.

19. Timmons, *Garner of Texas*, 125–126; Fisher, *Cactus Jack*, 70–71.

20. *NYT*, November 22, 1931; *HP*, December 8, 1931; Timmons, *Garner of Texas*, 134; Fisher, *Cactus Jack*, 77–78.

21. Norman Brown, "Garnering Votes for Cactus Jack," *SWHQ* 104, no. 2 (October 2000): 162–163.

22. Fisher, *Cactus Jack*, 84–85; *NYT*, March 29, 1932.

23. Brown, "Garnering Votes," 166–169; *San Antonio Express*, February 22, 1932.

24. Mark O. Hatfield, *Vice Presidents of the United States, 1789–1993* (Washington, D.C.: GPO, 1997), 387–388; Brown, "Garnering Votes," 186–187; Sam Rayburn to William Gibbs McAdoo, February 23, 1938, Sam Rayburn Papers, CAH.

25. "Speaker Garner's Letter of Acceptance," August 23, 1932, *CD*, August–September 1932, 224; Timmons, *Garner of Texas*, 168; Fisher, *Cactus Jack*, 92–93.

26. Hatfield, *Vice Presidents*, xix–xx, 24, 388; Fisher, *Cactus Jack*, 101–102.

27. *NYT*, December 30, 1934; *Literary Digest*, August 3, 1935; "John Nance Garner," *Handbook of Texas Online*, http://www.tsha.utexas.edu/handbook/online (accessed 5/29/02).

28. *Time*, June 3, 1935; Hatfield, *Vice Presidents*, 389; Timmons, *Garner of Texas*, 140, 202; Fisher, *Cactus Jack*, 110.

29. Ettie R. Garner to Jesse H. Jones, June 23, 1934, in John Nance Garner Press Clippings, 1932–1952, Box 10, Jesse H. Jones Papers, in Library of Congress (hereafter cited as JHJP).

30. Hatfield, *Vice Presidents*, 388–389; Fisher, *Cactus Jack*, 113–114.

31. Hatfield, *Vice Presidents*, 389, 393; Timmons, *Garner of Texas*, 208.

32. *DMN*, August 2, 1936; Hatfield, *Vice Presidents*, 389–390.

33. James Patterson, *Congressional Conservatism and the New Deal* (Lexington: University Press of Kentucky, 1967), 137; Fisher, *Cactus Jack*, 129–130.

34. Roger Biles, *The South and the New Deal* (Lexington: University Press of Kentucky, 1994), 142; Patterson, *Congressional Conservatism*, 97.

35. *NYT*, April 9, 1938; Biles, *South and the New Deal*, 144–145; Fisher, *Cactus Jack*, 132–134. After the revised court bill passed, Roosevelt appointed five of the nine Supreme Court justices within the next three years.

36. *USNWR*, November 21, 1958; Biles, *South and the New Deal*, 147.

37. James A. Farley, *Jim Farley's Story: The Roosevelt Years* (New York: McGraw-Hill, 1948), 152; Hatfield, *Vice Presidents*, 391–392; Fisher, *Cactus Jack*, 145–146. The leaders in the March 1939 Gallup poll were Garner, 45 percent; Cordell Hull, 10 percent; and James Farley, 8 percent.

38. *Austin American,* February 27, 1948.

39. *DMN,* July 27, November 17, 1939; Timmons, *Garner of Texas,* 262; Fisher, *Cactus Jack,* 143; *Time,* March 20, 1939, 12–13.

40. *New York Herald Tribune,* March 24, 1940, in Garner Clippings 328, JHJP.

41. Sam Rayburn to F. C. Allen, January 9, 1940, Sam Rayburn Papers, CAH.

42. Timmons, *Garner of Texas,* 272–276.

43. Jesse H. Jones to John Nance Garner, November 13, 1940, and Garner to Jones, November 19, 1940, in Garner Clippings, 1932–1952, Box 10, JHJP.

44. *WP,* January 21, 1941; *Washington Star,* January 21, 1941; Timmons, *Garner of Texas,* 278.

45. *DTH,* July 5, 1947, in Garner Clippings, CAH. Garner maintained that he burned his papers because of their sensitive nature.

46. *FWST,* November 27, 1945, August 8, 1948; *NYT,* August 18, 1948, November 8, 1967.

47. *NYT,* November 8, 1967; *DMN,* November 9, 1967; *San Antonio Express,* November 10, 1967.

48. Hatfield, *Vice Presidents,* 393.

JESSE JONES

1. George B. Tindall, *The Emergence of the New South, 1913–1945* (Baton Rouge: Louisiana State University Press, 1967), 453. For basic biographical information see Bascom N. Timmons, *Jesse H. Jones: The Man and the Statesman* (New York: Henry Holt, 1956); Walter L. Buenger, "Jesse H. Jones," in Larry Schwiekart, ed., *Encyclopedia of American Business History and Biography: Banking and Finance, 1913–1985* (Columbia, S.C.: Facts On File, 1990), 191–198. On Jones' role in the New Deal see Arthur M. Schlesinger Jr., *The Coming of the New Deal* (Boston: Houghton Mifflin, 1958), 425–433; James S. Olson, *Saving Capitalism: The Reconstruction Finance Corporation and the New Deal, 1933–1940* (Princeton: Princeton University Press, 1988). For a contemporary estimate of his power, see Samuel Lubell, "New Deal's J. P. Morgan," *Saturday Evening Post,* November 30, 1940, 9–10.

2. For a more detailed assessment of Jones's worldview before 1932, see Walter L. Buenger, "Between Community and Corporation: The Southern Roots of Jesse H. Jones and the Reconstruction Finance Corporation," *Journal of Southern History* 56 (August 1990): 481–510. On community and the South see Thomas Bender, *Community and Social Change in America* (New Brunswick: Rutgers University Press, 1978); George B. Tindall, *The Persistent Tradition in New South Politics* (Baton Rouge: Louisiana State University Press, 1975). Also revealing is Jesse H. Jones with Edward Angly, *Fifty Billion Dollars: My Thirteen Years with the RFC, 1932–1945* (New York: Macmillan, 1951).

3. For examples of those viewing Jones as a "new man," see Olson, *Saving Capitalism,* 48, 60; Tindall, *Emergence of the New South,* 458–459; Schlesinger, *Coming of the New Deal,* 433. On the movies and Texas see Don Graham, *Cowboys and Cadillacs: How Hollywood Looks at Texas* (Austin: Texas Monthly Press, 1983).

4. Timmons, *Jesse H. Jones*, 19. On Middle Tennessee at the time of Jones's birth and childhood, see Stephen V. Ash, *Middle Tennessee Society Transformed, 1860– 1870: War and Peace in the Upper South* (Baton Rouge: Louisiana State University Press, 1988); and relevant chapters in Don H. Doyle, *New Men, New Cities, New South: Atlanta, Nashville, Charleston, Mobile 1860–1910* (Chapel Hill: University of North Carolina Press, 1990).

5. Olson, *Saving Capitalism*, 60.

6. Jesse H. Jones to Mrs. Blanche Babcock, August 25, 1937, Jesse H. Jones Papers, in Library of Congress (cited as JHJP).

7. Timmons, *Jesse H. Jones*, 19–46; "Will of M. T. Jones," *HP,* July 1, 1898.

8. Buenger, "Between Community and Corporation," 486–489; Timmons, *Jesse H. Jones*, 23–24, 32, 33, 45, 50–54, 68–70.

9. Timmons, *Jesse H. Jones*, 15. Also see Jones to Babcock, August 25, 1937, JHJP; Timmons, *Jesse H. Jones*, 21–25.

10. Robert V. Haynes, *A Night of Violence: The Houston Riot of 1917* (Baton Rouge: Louisiana State University Press, 1976); Norman D. Brown, *Hood, Bonnet, and Little Brown Jug: Texas Politics, 1921–1928* (College Station: Texas A&M University Press, 1984), 62–63; Timmons, *Jesse H. Jones*, 120–123, 376–379.

11. For an interesting treatment of the triumph of corporate capitalism, see Martin J. Sklar, *The Corporate Reconstruction of American Capitalism, 1890–1916: The Market, the Law, and Politics* (Cambridge: Cambridge University Press, 1988). Also see Robert H. Wiebe, *The Search for Order, 1877–1920* (New York: Hill and Wang, 1967).

12. Buenger, "Between Community and Corporation," 486–490; Timmons, *Jesse H. Jones*, 49–96.

13. Jones to Babcock, August 25, 1937, JHJP.

14. The comment on Jones came from a relative of Benjamin A. Shepherd, who came to Houston in 1839 and was a banker in the early days. See W. A. Kirkland, "Memories of Jesse H. Jones" (undated typescript in possession of the author). Also see W. A. Kirkland, *Old Bank—New Bank: The First National Bank, Houston, 1866– 1976* (Houston: Pacesetter Press, 1971). The Jones quote is from Timmons, *Jesse H. Jones*, 119. For information on the Houston elite, see *Men of Affairs of Houston and Environs: A Newspaper Reference Work* (Houston: Houston Press Club, 1913); Jones is described on page 19. On Jones's sense of family, his drive to acquire money, and his need for control, see interview with J. Howard Creekmore by Walter L. Buenger, September 17, 1982, Texas Commerce Bank Archives, Houston, Tex. (hereafter cited as TCB Archives); interview with J. Howard Creekmore by Joseph A. Pratt, March 6, 1985, TCB Archives. Creekmore worked for Jones from 1926 until Jones died in 1956. He continued to work for the charitable trust organized by Jones through the 1980s and late in life still regarded Jones as a father figure. For the views of those more directly related to Jones, see interview with George A. Butler by Thomas Kreneck and Louis Marchiafava, November 18, 1982, Houston Metropolitan Research Center; interview with John T. Jones by Walter L. Buenger, August 21, 1982, TCB Archives. Also see Timmons, *Jesse H. Jones*, 115–123.

15. Timmons, *Jesse H. Jones,* 85–96; Marilyn McAdams Sibley, *The Port of Houston: A History* (Austin: University of Texas Press, 1968), 137–139.

16. Jones, *Fifty Billion Dollars,* 292; Buenger, "Between Community and Corporation," 491–493. Years later Jones's rise to political power was still linked to E. M. House. See *NYT,* January 13, 1928.

17. Herbert Hoover to Jesse Jones, March 6, 18, 1931, JHJP; Timmons, *Jesse H. Jones,* 109–110; Jesse H. Jones to George B. Case, c. 1923, Jesse Holman Jones Papers, CAH (hereafter cited as JP); Jesse H. Jones to F. J. Heyne, February 16, 1919, JP.

18. Jones to Heyne, February 16, 1919; Jesse H. Jones to N. E. Meador, February 18, 1919 (cable), JP. Also see Jesse H. Jones to Woodrow Wilson, February 28, 1919 (cable); Jesse H. Jones to E. M. House, February 27, 1919; Bernard Baruch to Jesse H. Jones, February 27, 1919, all in JP.

19. John W. Davis to Jesse H. Jones, November 1, 1924, JHJP. Also see Franklin D. Roosevelt to Jesse H. Jones, July 7, 1926; Jesse H. Jones to Franklin D. Roosevelt, July 14, 1926, JHJP.

20. Tom Connally, as told to Alfred Steinberg, *My Name Is Tom Connally* (New York: Thomas Y. Crowell, 1954), 131–132.

21. Quoted in Brown, *Hood, Bonnet, and Little Brown Jug,* 394. On Hogg see Walter Prescott Webb and H. Bailey Carroll, eds., *The Handbook of Texas* (Austin: Texas State Historical Association, 1952), 1:824.

22. *NYT,* January 13, 1928; *HC,* January 13, 14, 1928; *HP,* January 13, 14, 18, 1928.

23. National Bank of Commerce, *Directors' Minutes* 3 (November 10, 1931): 136, TCB Archives. Also see S. M. McAshan to James A. Baker, October 7, 1931, in South Texas Commercial National Bank, *Director's Minutes* 6 (October 29, 1931): 197.

24. Buenger, "Between Community and Corporation," 501–505; Henrietta Larson and Kenneth Porter, *History of Humble Oil and Refining Company: A Study in Industrial Growth* (New York: Harper and Row, 1959).

25. Jones, *Fifty Billion Dollars,* 23–24.

26. Jesse H. Jones to Cordell Hull, January 5, 1949, JHJP. Also see Jones, *Fifty Billion Dollars,* 290–293; Timmons, *Jesse H. Jones,* 187–188; David Sarasohn, *The Party of Reform: Democrats in the Progressive Era* (Jackson: University Press of Mississippi, 1989); Walter L. Buenger and Joseph A. Pratt, *But Also Good Business: Texas Commerce Banks and the Financing of Houston and Texas, 1886–1986* (College Station: Texas A&M University Press, 1986), 40–63.

27. Jones to Hull, January 5, 1949, JHJP. Also see Jones to Babcock, August 25, 1937, JHJP.

28. Timmons, *Jesse H. Jones,* 164; Jones, *Fifty Billion Dollars,* 32.

29. Schlesinger, *Coming of the New Deal,* 433; Olson, *Saving Capitalism,* 46–49. For examples of this resentment of Wall Street and its persistence into the 1970s see Buenger and Pratt, *But Also Good Business,* 170–172, 219–220.

30. Olson, *Saving Capitalism,* 31.

31. Speech by Jesse Jones to the American Bankers' Association, September 5, 1933, JHJP. Also quoted in Timmons, *Jesse H. Jones,* 200; Schlesinger, *Coming of the New Deal,* 428.

32. *WP,* January 26, 1932.

33. James Stuart Olson, *Herbert Hoover and the Reconstruction Finance Corporation, 1931–1933* (Ames: Iowa State University Press, 1977); Gerald D. Nash, "Herbert Hoover and the Origins of the Reconstruction Finance Corporation," *Mississippi Valley Historical Review* 46 (December 1959): 455–468; Ellis W. Hawley, *The Great War and the Search for a Modern Order: A History of the American People and Their Institutions, 1917–1933* (New York: St. Martin's Press, 1979; Susan Estabrook Kennedy, *The Banking Crisis of 1933* (Lexington: University Press of Kentucky, 1973), 22–54; Timmons, *Jesse H. Jones,* 162 165; Jones, *Fifty Billion Dollars,* 512–514.

34. Quoted in Timmons, *Jesse H. Jones,* 172. Also see Kennedy, *Banking Crisis of 1933,* 40–43; Bascom N. Timmons, *Portrait of an American: Charles G. Dawes* (New York: Henry Holt, 1953), 316–323; Olson, *Reconstruction Finance Corporation,* 58–61.

35. Jesse Jones to M. H. Gossett, March 17, 1932, JHJP; Olson, *Reconstruction Finance Corporation,* 47–75.

36. Jones, *Fifty Billion Dollars,* 521–523.

37. Olson, *Saving Capitalism,* 42–62.

38. Chester Morrill, Columbia University Oral History Research Office, 182–183; Jerome Frank, Columbia University Oral History Research Office, 50–51.

39. On Daniel Garrett see Webb and Carroll, *Handbook of Texas,* 1:672–673; *HP,* December 13, 1932; *HC,* December 13, 1932. On other members of the Texas delegation, see Lionel V. Patenaude, *Texans, Politics, and the New Deal* (New York: Garland, 1983).

40. Janet Louise Schmelzer, "The Early Life and Early Congressional Career of Wright Patman: 1894–1941" (Ph.D. diss., Texas Christian University, 1978); Wright Patman to *DMN,* March 22, 1940.

41. Nancy Beck Young, *Wright Patman: Populism, Liberalism, and the American Dream* (Dallas: Southern Methodist University Press, 2000), 29–104; Schlesinger, *Coming of the New Deal,* 430–432; Olson, *Saving Capitalism,* 60–61; Jones, *Fifty Billion Dollars,* 45 46, 277–287, 522–540.

42. Jones, *Fifty Billion Dollars,* 20.

43. For his summary of the first years of the RFC, see Jesse H. Jones, *Reconstruction Finance Corporation Seven-Year Report* (Washington, D.C.: Reconstruction Finance Corporation, 1939).

44. Olson, *Saving Capitalism,* 42–62; Jones, *Fifty Billion Dollars,* 512–546; Timmons, *Jesse H. Jones,* 274–275.

45. National Bank of Commerce, *Director's Minutes* 8 (October 9, 1956): 24–25.

46. Olson, *Saving Capitalism,* 111–277; Jones, *Fifty Billion Dollars,* 290–293, 485–510.

47. For a comparison of Jones and fellow Houstonian Hugh Roy Cullen, see Don E. Carlton, *Red Scare! Right-wing Hysteria, Fifties Fanaticism, and Their Legacy in Texas* (Austin: Texas Monthly Press, 1985), 65–74.

48. *NYT,* July 2, 1939.

49. Timmons, *Jesse H. Jones,* 376–390; Kirkland, "Memories of Jesse H. Jones."
50. Brown, *Hood, Bonnet, and Little Brown Jug,* 394 (quote).

TOM CONNALLY

1. "Tom Connally Is Dead; Served in Senate for 24 Years," *NYT,* October 9, 1963.
2. Tom Connally, as told to Alfred Steinberg, *My Name Is Tom Connally* (New York: Thomas Y. Crowell Company, 1954), 1, 9–10, 13–14, 16, 17; Frank H. Smyrl, "Tom Connally and the New Deal" (Ph.D. diss., University of Oklahoma, 1968), 1–6; David Leon Matheny, "A Comparison of Selected Foreign Policy Speeches of Senator Tom Connally" (Ph.D. diss., University of Oklahoma, 1965), 13–15, 22; Scrapbook 1915–1916, in Tom Connally Papers, in Library of Congress (hereafter cited as TCP); "Life in a Nutshell," *Houston Press,* April 19, 1934, TCP; Gerald Movius and Jack Beall, "Plush-Covered Cactus," *Saturday Evening Post,* April 4, 1942, 58, 61; "Tom Connally Is Dead," 35.
3. Connally, *Connally,* 19, 20, 23, 25; Scrapbook 1915–1916, TCP; Smyrl, "Connally and the New Deal," 6–8.
4. Connally, *Connally,* 26–28, 33, 36, 38, 40–41; Scrapbook 1915–1916, TCP; Smyrl, "Connally and the New Deal," 8, 11–14; "Tom Connally Is Dead," 35.
5. Connally, *Connally,* 41–45; Scrapbook 1915–1916, TCP; Smyrl, "Connally and the New Deal," 14–15; Matheny, "Speeches of Senator Tom Connally," 14.
6. Connally, *Connally,* 46–47, 49.
7. Ibid., 48–52; Scrapbook 1915–1916, TCP; Texas House, *Journal,* 27th Legis., reg. sess., 1901, 51, 79–80, 178, 837–841, 1297, 1352.
8. Connally, *Connally,* 47–48; Jesse Guy Smith, "The Bailey Controversy in Texas Politics" (master's thesis, University of Chicago, 1924), 25–27; Smyrl, "Connally and the New Deal," 18.
9. Texas House, *Journal,* 28th Legis., reg. sess., 1903, 5–6, 102, 479, 653, 941, 1154, 1199, 1281, 1283–1286, 1288–1290, 1292, 1295; HB 457, *General Laws of the State of Texas,* 28th Legis., reg. sess., 1903; Scrapbook 1915–1916, TCP; Connally, *Connally,* 51–52; Smyrl, "Connally and the New Deal," 19–21.
10. Connally, *Connally,* 52–53.
11. Ibid., 54, 61; Smyrl, "Connally and the New Deal," 22–23.
12. Connally, *Connally,* 66–67, 69, 71–72, 75; Scrapbook 1915–1916, TCP; Smyrl, "Connally and the New Deal," 25, 30.
13. Connally, *Connally,* 76–78; Scrapbook 1915–1916, TCP; Smyrl, "Connally and the New Deal," 31.
14. Connally, *Connally,* 78–81; "Tom Connally Is Dead," 35.
15. Connally, *Connally,* 83–84; *CR,* 65th Cong., 1st sess., 1557.
16. Connally, *Connally,* 84, 87–88, 90–91, 95; Scrapbook 1915–1916, TCP; *CR,* 65th Cong., 2nd sess., 10212–10216.

17. Connally, *Connally,* 95; Scrapbook 1915–1916, TCP; Movius and Beall, "Plush-Covered Cactus," 61; "Tom Connally Is Dead," 35; Smyrl, "Connally and the New Deal," 35–36.

18. Connally, *Connally,* 95–107; Scrapbook 1915–1916, TCP; "Tom Connally Is Dead," 35; "The Congress: The Senate and the Peace," *Time,* March 13, 1944, 14–16.

19. Connally, *Connally,* 108–109, 113; Scrapbook 1922, TCP; Scrapbook 1926, TCP; Connally to George B. Terrell, February 9, 1928, Legislation File, 1903–1929, TCP; Connally to Texas Farm Bureau Federation, February 23, 1928, Legislation File 1903–1929; "Address to State Convention American Legion at Waco, 1922," Speech File 1922, TCP; speech on the Revenue Act of 1921, Speech File 1923, TCP; *CR,* 69th Cong., 1st sess., 9472–9475.

20. Connally, *Connally,* 107–108, 111; Scrapbook 1922, TCP; speech on disarmament, Speech File 1921, TCP; Smyrl, "Connally and the New Deal," 39–40.

21. The final vote was 320,071 for Connally and 257,747 for Mayfield. Connally, *Connally,* 118–129; Smyrl, "Connally and the New Deal," 49–69; campaign speeches, Speech File 1928, TCP; "Connally Beats Mayfield in Race for U.S. Senate," *Austin Statesman,* August 26, 1928, 1; "Connally Wins an Easy Victory," *Austin Statesman,* August 26, 1928, 2; Norman Brown, *Hood, Bonnet, and Little Brown Jug: Texas Politics, 1921–1928* (College Station: Texas A&M University Press, 1984), 406–408; Seth S. McKay, *Texas Politics, 1906–1944 With Special Reference to the German Counties* (Lubbock: Texas Tech University Press, 1952), 164–177.

22. Connally, *Connally,* 134–135; Speech File 1929, 1930, 1932, TCP; Smyrl, "Connally and the New Deal," 72–83; Lionel V Patenaude, "The Texas Congressional Delegation," *Texana* 9 (1971): 9; *CR,* 71st Cong., 1st sess., 786.

23. Connally, *Connally,* 136; *CR,* 71st Cong., 2nd sess., 9722, 9876; 3rd sess., 3117, 6622–6623; Smyrl, "Connally and the New Deal," 88–92.

24. Connally, *Connally,* 134, 136; Smyrl, "Connally and the New Deal," 87.

25. Connally's actual role in the Roosevelt-Garner nomination is somewhat in dispute. See Connally, *Connally,* 139–146; nomination speech for Garner, Speech File 1932, TCP; Smyrl, "Connally and the New Deal," 96–102; Arthur F. Mullen, *Western Democrat* (New York: Wilfred Funk, Inc., 1940), 270–275; Elliott A. Rosen, *Hoover, Roosevelt, and the Brains Trust: From Depression to New Deal* (New York: Columbia University Press, 1977), 251–254, 262–264; Bascom N. Timmons, *Garner of Texas: A Personal History* (New York: Harper and Brothers, 1948), 156, 158–166; Lionel V. Patenaude, "The Garner Vote Switch to Roosevelt: 1932 Democratic Convention," *SWHQ* 79, no. 2 (October 1975): 189–204; Lionel V. Patenaude, "The New Deal and Texas" (Ph.D. diss., University of Texas, 1953), 17–25; Lionel V. Patenaude, *Texans, Politics, and the New Deal* (New York: Garland, 1983), 9, 17–18, 23; Alfred Steinberg, *Sam Johnson's Boy* (New York: Macmillan, 1968), 325; Arthur M. Schlesinger Jr., *The Age of Roosevelt,* vol. 1: *Crisis of the Old Order, 1919–1933* (Boston: Houghton Mifflin, 1957), 303, 306–311.

26. Connally, *Connally,* 150; Smyrl, "Connally and the New Deal," 108; Matheny, "Speeches of Senator Tom Connally," 22–31; "Tom Connally Is Dead," 35; Steinberg, *Sam Johnson's Boy,* 69, 155; Michael L. Collins, "The Influence of Texans

upon Roosevelt's Court-Packing Plan" (master's thesis, Texas Christian University, 1975), 35.

27. Connally, *Connally*, 150–155; Smyrl, "Connally and the New Deal," 109–114; Speech File 1933, 1937–1939, TCP.

28. Speech File 1934, 1937, TCP; "Press Release 1938," Speech File 1937–1939, TCP; Connally, *Connally*, 154, 162; Smyrl, "Connally and the New Deal," 122–131; Arthur Schlesinger Jr., *The Age of Roosevelt*, vol. 2: *The Coming of the New Deal* (Boston: Houghton Mifflin, 1959), 41.

29. "Hot oil" is "oil produced in violation of quotas or other laws enacted by the states." See Harold L. Ickes, *The Secret Diary of Harold L. Ickes*, vol. 1: *The First Thousand Days, 1933–1936* (New York: Simon and Schuster, 1953), 13, 47, 49–50. For the Supreme Court case see *Panama Refining Co. et al. v. Ryan et al.*, 293 US 388 (1935). See also Connally, *Connally*, 160–164; Smyrl, "Connally and the New Deal," 116–119; Steinberg, *Sam Johnson's Boy*, 155; Speech File 1934, TCP; Linda J. Lear, "Harold L. Ickes and the Oil Crisis of the First Hundred Days," *MidAmerica* 63, no. 1 (January 1981): 3–17; U.S. Senate, *Connally Hot Oil Act*, Sen. Rpt. 14, 74th Cong., 1st sess., Senate Foreign Relations Committee Files, National Archives, Washington, D.C.; James Presley, *A Saga of Wealth: The Rise of the Texas Oilmen* (New York: G. P. Putnam's Sons, 1978), 138–139, 147–149, 159, 176–178; David F. Prindle, *Petroleum Politics and the Texas Railroad Commission* (Austin: University of Texas Press, 1981), 37–38; Gerald D. Nash, *United States Oil Policy, 1890–1964* (Pittsburgh: University of Pittsburgh Press, 1968), 135, 136, 144–145.

30. Although set to expire in June 1936, the Connally "Hot Oil" Act became permanent in 1942. See Connally, *Connally*, 162–163; Richard Lowitt, *The New Deal and the West* (Bloomington: Indiana University Press, 1984), 102, 105, 108; Nash, *United States Oil Policy*, 146, 150; Smyrl, "Connally and the New Deal," 116–122; Samuel B. Pettengill, *Hot Oil: The Problem of Petroleum* (New York: Economic Forum, 1936), 207, 296–300; Ickes, *Secret Diary*, 1:418; Prindle, *Petroleum Politics*, 38–39; Presley, *Saga of Wealth*, 178–179; U.S. House, *Movement of Petroleum in Interstate Commerce, February 22, 1935*, H. Rpt. 215, 74th Cong., 1st sess., Senate Foreign Relations Committee Files, National Archives, Washington, D.C.; Harold L. Ickes to Pat Harrison, March 13, 1939, Senate Finance Committee Files, National Archives, Washington, D.C.

31. Connally, *Connally*, 178–179.

32. Ibid., 184–185, 187–188; George Norris Green, *The Establishment in Texas Politics: The Primitive Years, 1938–1957* (Westport, Conn.: Greenwood Press, 1979), 7; Patenaude, *Texans, Politics*, 67–68; "Tom Connally Quits Roosevelt for Foes of Court Revamping," *Austin Statesman*, March 3, 1937, 1, 2.

33. Connally, *Connally*, 185–191; Smyrl, "Connally and the New Deal," 167–178; Collins, "Influence of Texans," 37–41; Edward Weller Jr., "Senate Majority Leader Joseph Taylor Robinson: His Legislative Prowess" (master's thesis, Texas Christian University, 1986), 52–53; Ron Law, "Congressman Hatton W. Sumners of Dallas, Texas: His Life and Congressional Career, 1875–1937" (Ph.D. diss., Texas Christian University, 1990), 110ff.; Richard B. Henderson, *Maury Maverick: A Political Biog-*

raphy (Austin: University of Texas Press, 1970), 180; Arthur Schlesinger Jr., *The Age of Roosevelt*, vol. 3: *The Politics of Upheaval* (Boston: Houghton Mifflin, 1960), 485; Lionel V. Patenaude, "Garner, Sumners, and Connally: The Defeat of the Roosevelt Court Bill in 1937," *SWHQ* 74, no. 1 (July 1970): 36, 39, 43-46; Patenaude, "New Deal and Texas," 183-190; Patenaude, *Texans, Politics,* 122, 131-135; Ickes, *Secret Diary of Harold L. Ickes,* vol. 2: *The Inside Struggle, 1936-1939* (New York: Simon and Schuster, 1954), 105.

34. Connally, *Connally,* 191, 192; Weller, "Joseph Taylor Robinson," 61.

35. Connally, *Connally,* 194-195; Press Release, August 20, 1937, Speech File 1937, TCP; Political Files 1940-1952, TCP; Ickes, *Secret Diary,* 2:421; Patenaude, *Texans, Politics,* 68, 76, 135; Patenaude, "Garner, Sumners, and Connally," 47, 51; Patenaude, "The New Deal and Texas," 133, 135, 451; Collins, "Influence of Texans," 77-78; Smyrl, "Connally and the New Deal," 182-183, 189-191.

36. Connally, *Connally,* 211-212; Smyrl, "Connally and the New Deal," 208-209.

37. Connally, *Connally,* 220-221, 223-224, 227-228; Smyrl, "Connally and the New Deal," 210-215.

38. Connally, *Connally,* 228-231; "Effects of Embargo Repeal on Foreign Trade and Shipping," Speech File 1937-1939, TCP; Neutrality Act File, Pre-December 7, 1941, Senate Foreign Relations Committee Files, 77th Cong., National Archives, Washington, D.C.; Tindall, *Emergence of the New South,* 689-690; Steinberg, *Sam Johnson's Boy,* 155; Charles A. Beard, *American Foreign Policy in the Making, 1932-1940: A Study in Responsibilities* (New Haven: Yale University Press, 1946), 245; Smyrl, "Connally and the New Deal," 217-218; Matheny, "Speeches of Senator Tom Connally," 46-53.

39. Connally, *Connally,* 241-245.

40. Ibid., 246-247; Press Statement December 5, 1941, Speech File 1941, TCP.

41. Connally, *Connally,* 248-250; Harold Ickes, *Secret Diary of Harold L. Ickes,* vol. 3: *The Lowering Clouds, 1939-1941* (New York: Simon and Schuster, 1954), 661, 664; "Southwest Collection," *SWHQ* 86, no. 4 (April 1983): 546; Connally Press Release, December 8, 1941; Connally Press Release, December 11, 1941, Speech File 1940-1941, TCP.

42. Connally, *Connally,* 251-253; Press Release, December 7, 1941, Speech File 1940-1941, TCP; Press Statement May 11, 1944, Speech File 1944, TCP; Connally to National Association for the Advancement of Colored People Youth Council, May 13, 1944, Speech File 1944, TCP; Press Release from the National Labor Relations Board (on the Smith-Connally Act), July 31, 1943; War Labor Disputes Act Public Law 89; Sen. Doc. 75, War Labor Disputes Act—Veto Message, Judiciary Committee Files, 78th Cong., National Archives, Washington, D.C.

43. In 1942 Connally married Lucile Sanderson Sheppard, widow of Morris Sheppard. Connally, *Connally,* 254-264; Press Statement, January 21, 1942, Speech File 1942, TCP; Press Statement, June 2, 1942, Speech File 1942, TCP; Arthur H. Vandenberg Jr., ed., *The Private Papers of Senator Vandenberg* (Westport, Conn.: Greenwood Press, 1952), 25-26, 70-72; Cordell Hull, *The Memoirs of Cordell Hull* (New

York: Macmillan, 1948), 2:1635–1637; John C. Campbell, *The United States in World Affairs, 1947–1948* (New York: Harper and Brothers, 1948), 18; Ruth B. Russell, *A History of the United Nations Charter: The Role of the United States, 1940–1945* (Washington, D.C.: Brookings Institution, 1958), 70.

44. Connally, *Connally,* 263–267; 271–272; Matheny, "Speeches of Senator Tom Connally," 71–97, 102, 109; Vandenberg, *Private Papers,* 38–65, 90–107, 149–155; Press Statement, November 5, 1943, Speech File 1944, TCP; undated speech, Speech File 1945, TCP; Gwen Morgan, "Senate Treaty Control Upheld by Connally," April 21, 1944, Speech File 1944, TCP; Press Statement, October 9, 1944, Speech File 1944, TCP; "Highlights in the Development of the Bipartisan Foreign Policy," General Legislation File, TCP; U.S. Senate, Senate Foreign Relations Committee, *A Decade of American Foreign Policy: Basic Documents, 1941–1949,* Sen. Doc. 123, 81st Cong., 1st sess., 14; U.S. Department of State, *Charter of the United Nations: Report to the President on the Results of the San Francisco Conference . . . ,* Conference Series 71, June 26, 1945, 20–21, 23, 24–25; Hull, *Memoirs,* 2:1262–1263, 1657–1699; Connally to Hull, April 15, 1944; Hull to Connally, April 17, 1944, Microfilm, Reel 167; Hull to Connally, August 23, 1944, Microfilm, Reel 169, in Hull, *Memoirs;* "The Senate and the Peace," 14; L. K. Hyde, *The United States and the United Nations: Promoting the Public Welfare; Examples of American Cooperation, 1945–1955* (New York: Manhattan Publishing Company, 1960), 28–29; Russell, *United Nations Charter,* 126–127, 194, 196, 543.

45. Connally, *Connally,* 277–285; Vandenberg, *Private Papers,* 156–165, 172–216; Matheny, "Speeches of Senator Tom Connally," 109–111; Department of State, *Charter,* 27–31; "Texas Tom Fights for World Peace," *Look,* April 3, 1945, 23–27; Russell, *United Nations Charter,* 733, 735; radio interview with Connally by Roy Hoffheinz, April 9, 1945, TCP; Hull, *Memoirs,* 2:1660–1699; Harry S. Truman, *Memoirs,* vol. 1: *Year of Decisions* (Garden City, N.Y.: Doubleday, 1955), 272–289; Arthur M. Schlesinger Jr., ed., *The Dynamics of World Power: A Documentary History of United States Foreign Policy, 1945–1973,* vol. 5: *The United Nations,* ed. Richard C. Hottelet (New York: Chelsea House Publishers, 1973), 6–8; interview with Francis O. Wilcox by Donald A. Richie, February 1, 1984, Senate Historical Office, Washington, D.C., Oral History Interviews, in Library of Congress.

46. Connally, *Connally,* 285–286; Vandenberg, *Private Papers,* 216–219; Matheny, "Speeches of Senator Tom Connally," 111–130; Ruth B. Russell, *The United Nations and the United States Security Policy* (Washington, D.C.: Brookings Institution, 1968), 294–298; "Tom Connally Is Dead," 35; Russell, *United Nations Charter,* 935–943; "The Senate and the Peace," 15; Press Statement on the United Nations, Speech File 1945, TCP; Beard, *American Foreign Policy,* 3; Schlesinger, *Dynamics of World Power,* 5:6–7.

47. Connally, *Connally,* 287–289, 305–307; Vandenberg, *Private Papers,* 222–223, 252–261; Connally to L. C. Polk, June 4, 1947, TCP; Truman, *Memoirs,* 1:529.

48. Connally, *Connally,* 287–289, 305–307; Truman, *Memoirs,* 1:547–548; Lisle A. Rose, *After Yalta* (New York: Charles Scribner's Sons, 1973), 161; James F. Byrnes

to President Truman, March 1, 1946, Senate Foreign Relations Files, 78th Cong., National Archives, Washington, D.C.; "Our Prospects for World Peace," Speech File 1947, TCP.

49. Connally, *Connally,* 296–303; Vandenberg, *Private Papers,* 298–303; Sen. Rpt., July 19, 1946, Speech File 1946, TCP; "Highlights in the Development of the Bipartisan Foreign Policy," General Legislation File, TCP.

50. Wilcox interview, February 10, 1984; interview with Pat M. Holt by Donald A. Richie, September 18, 1980, Senate Historical Office, Oral History Interviews; Connally, *Connally,* 310–311; Vandenberg, *Private Papers,* 318–352; "Highlights in Bipartisan Foreign Policy"; Press Statement, March 12, 1947, Legislation File, 80th Cong., TCP; Merrill F. Pritchett, "The Texas Congressional Delegation and American Foreign Assistance, 1946–1952" (master's thesis, East Texas State University, Commerce, 1967), 20, 23; Donald R. McCoy, *The Presidency of Harry S. Truman* (Lawrence: University Press of Kansas, 1984), 122; Truman, *Memoirs,* vol. 2: *Years of Trial and Hope* (Garden City, N.Y.: Doubleday, 1956), 103–107; Arthur M. Schlesinger Jr., ed., *The Dynamics of World Power: A Documentary History of United States Foreign Policy, 1945–1973,* vol. 2: *Eastern Europe and the Soviet Union,* ed. Walter LaFeber (New York: Chelsea House Publishers, 1973), 304–310.

51. Connally, *Connally,* 328, 332–338; Matheny, "Speeches of Senator Tom Connally," 143–147, 152–156; Vandenberg, *Private Papers,* 26, 41; Speech on NATO; Press Statement on NATO; Press Statements, April 21, June 6, October 26, 1949; Senate speech, July 5, 1949, Speech File 1949, TCP.

52. Connally, *Connally,* 338–340; Matheny, "Speeches of Senator Tom Connally," 147–167; Vandenberg, *Private Papers,* 502–518, 548–553, 556; McCoy, *Truman,* 198–201.

53. Connally, *Connally,* 350–357; McCoy, *Presidency of Harry S. Truman,* 221–263; Vandenberg, *Private Papers,* 541–545; Schlesinger, *Dynamics of World Power,* 5:235–236; Truman, *Memoirs,* 2:338, 390–391, 414–417; Steinberg, *Sam Johnson's Boy,* 316–317, 320.

54. Connally, *Connally,* 358–361; Green, *Establishment in Texas Politics,* 142–149; Steinberg, *Sam Johnson's Boy,* 325, 329; David Murph, "Price Daniel: The Life of a Public Man, 1910–1956" (Ph.D. diss., Texas Christian University, 1975), 163–170, 192–220; Paul T. David et al., eds., *Presidential Nominating Politics in 1952,* vol. 3: *The South* (Baltimore: Johns Hopkins University Press, 1954), 315–351; Seth Shepard McKay, *Texas and the Fair Deal, 1945–1952* (San Antonio: Naylor Company, 1954), 376–377; Robert Engler, *The Politics of Oil: A Study of Private Power and Democratic Directions* (New York: Macmillan, 1961), 355–359, 373; interview with Carl M. Marcy by Donald Richie, November 16, 1963, Senate Historical Office, Oral History Interviews; Connally to Frank B. Potter, May 8, 1952, Personal Correspondence Miscellaneous 1920–1937; Scrapbook 1951; Scrapbook 1957; Memorandum on Selected Votes against Administration, Speech File 1951; Press Release, June 12, 1952, Speech File 1952, TCP.

55. "Tom Connally Is Dead," 1, 35.

SAM RAYBURN

1. First quote appears in H. G. Dulaney, Edward H. Phillips, and MacPhelan Reese, eds., *Speak, Mr. Speaker* (Bonham, Tex.: Sam Rayburn Foundation, 1978), 473; ibid., 474; ibid.; ibid., 473; ibid., 471.

2. Quote appears in D. B. Hardeman and Donald C. Bacon, *Rayburn: A Biography* (Austin: Texas Monthly Press, 1987), 2. Several biographies of Rayburn have been published, with the Hardeman and Bacon volume being the best known. Much of the material in this essay is taken from that book. See also Anthony Champagne, *Congressman Sam Rayburn* (New Brunswick: Rutgers University Press, 1984).

3. Alfred Steinberg, *Sam Rayburn: A Biography* (New York: Hawthorn Books, 1975), 18; interview with Price Daniel by Fred Garrett, February 25, 1967, Liberty, Tex., North Texas State University Oral History Project.

4. Hardeman and Bacon, *Rayburn,* 60.

5. Quote appears in ibid., 69.

6. Rayburn's marriage in 1927 to Metze Jones, or rather the reasons for their divorce, has been a subject of speculation since they parted. Probably the best account of the brief episode is set forth in Hardeman and Bacon, *Rayburn,* 121–131. Quote appears in ibid., 123.

7. For the most thorough account of the events, see Lionel V. Patenaude, *Texans, Politics, and the New Deal* (New York: Garland, 1983), 23–24. Patenaude believes that the "key man was Sam Rayburn."

8. Hardeman and Bacon, *Rayburn,* 150; ibid.

9. Ibid., 156.

10. Ibid., 198.

11. D. Clayton Brown, *Electricity for Rural America: The Fight for the REA* (Westport, Conn., Greenwood Press, 1980), 64.

12. Ibid.

13. This account comes from Hardeman and Bacon, *Rayburn,* 201–213.

14. Ibid., 264.

15. See ibid., 263–270, for a full account of Rayburn's part in the U.S. entry to the war.

16. The Board of Education met in a small room in the House building, where Rayburn invited a few persons to share drinks at the end of the day. Most considered it an honor to be invited.

17. Steinberg, *Sam Rayburn,* 350.

18. Hardeman and Bacon, *Rayburn,* 377.

19. Ibid., 413.

20. Ibid., 427.

21. Steinberg, *Sam Rayburn,* 349.

22. Ibid., 474; H. G. Dulaney to Clayton Brown, June 5, 1991, Bonham, Tex., letter in author's private papers.

LYNDON BAINES JOHNSON

1. Robert A. Caro, *The Years of Lyndon Johnson*, vol. 1: *The Path to Power* (New York: Alfred A. Knopf, 1982), 50–137; Doris Kearns, *Lyndon Johnson and the American Dream* (New York: Harper and Row, 1976), 19–44; Ronnie Dugger, *The Politician: The Life and Times of Lyndon Johnson; the Drive for Power, from the Frontier to Master of the Senate* (New York: W. W. Norton, 1982), 25–107; Paul K. Conkin, *Big Daddy from the Pedernales: Lyndon Baines Johnson* (Boston: Twayne, 1986), 1–36; Robert Dallek, *Lone Star Rising: Lyndon Johnson and His Times, 1908–1960* (New York: Oxford University Press, 1990), 1–61.

2. Caro, *Path to Power*, 141–214; Kearns, *Lyndon Johnson*, 46–71; Dugger, *The Politician*, 108–129; Conkin, *Big Daddy from the Pedernales*, 37–61; Dallek, *Lone Star Rising*, 62–92.

3. Caro, *Path to Power*, 217–314; Kearns, *Lyndon Johnson*, 46–71; Dugger, *The Politician*, 128–129, 175–181; Conkin, *Big Daddy from the Pedernales*, 62–86; Dallek, *Lone Star Rising*, 93–124.

4. Caro, *Path to Power*, 341–368; Dugger, *The Politician*, 184–190; 192–193; Kenneth E. Hendrickson Jr., "The National Youth Administration in Texas," *Midwestern State University Faculty Papers* (Series 2, vol. 8, 1981–1983), 63–75; Dallek, *Lone Star Rising*, 124–146.

5. Caro, *Path to Power*, 369–768; Conkin, *Big Daddy from the Pedernales*, 87–105; Dallek, *Lone Star Rising*, 159–224.

6. Robert A. Caro, *The Years of Lyndon Johnson*, vol. 2: *Means of Ascent* (New York: Alfred A. Knopf, 1990), 62–70; Dugger, *The Politician*, 239–250; Conkin, *Big Daddy from the Pedernales*, 106–108; Kearns, *Lyndon Johnson*, 94–95; Merle Miller, *Lyndon: An Oral Biography* (New York: Putnam, 1980), 93–100; Dallek, *Lone Star Rising*, 225–243.

7. Caro, *Means of Ascent*, 82–118; Dugger, *The Politician*, 266–273; Conkin, *Big Daddy from the Pedernales*, 110–112; Kearns, *Lyndon Johnson*, 98–100; Miller, *Lyndon*, 106–110; Dallek, *Lone Star Rising*, 245–267.

8. Caro, *Means of Ascent*, 312, 320; Dugger, *The Politician*, 309–341; Conkin, *Big Daddy from the Pedernales*, 115–118; Kearns, *Lyndon Johnson*, 100–101; Miller, *Lyndon*, 133–137; Dallek, *Lone Star Rising*, 298–348.

9. Conkin, *Big Daddy from the Pedernales*, 119–147; Kearns, *Lyndon Johnson*, 102–159; Roland Evans and Robert Novak, *Lyndon B. Johnson: The Exercise of Power* (New York: New American Library, 1966), 23–304 passim; Miller, *Lyndon*, 160–163, 192–200, 190–191, 204–212, 226–229. For a lengthy and highly critical account of Johnson's career in the Senate, see Robert A. Caro, *The Years of Lyndon Johnson*, vol. 3: *Master of the Senate* (New York: Alfred A. Knopf, 2002).

10. Evans and Novak, *Exercise of Power*, 289–304; Miller, *Lyndon*, 236–238, 262–272; Arthur M. Schlesinger Jr., *A Thousand Days: John F. Kennedy in the White House* (Boston: Houghton Mifflin, 1965), 39–57; Dallek, *Lone Star Rising*, 544–591.

11. Leonard Baker, *The Johnson Eclipse* (New York: Macmillan, 1966), Evans and Novak, *Exercise of Power*, 305–334; Miller, *Lyndon*, 235–325; Conkin, *Big Daddy*

from the Pedernales, 148–172; Robert Dallek, *Flawed Giant: Lyndon Johnson and His Times, 1961–1973* (New York: Oxford University Press, 1990), 3–44.

12. Kearns, *Lyndon Johnson,* 170–209; Eric Goldman, *The Tragedy of Lyndon Johnson* (New York: Alfred A. Knopf, 1969), 213–256.

13. Conkin, *Big Daddy from the Pedernales,* 173–208.

14. Kearns, *Lyndon Johnson,* 210–250; Steven F. Lawson, "Civil Rights"; Mark I. Gelfand, "The War on Poverty"; Hugh Davis Graham, "The Transformation of Federal Education Policy;" in Robert A. Divine, ed., *Exploring the Johnson Years* (Austin: University of Texas Press, 1981), 93–184. See also William H. Chafe, *The Unfinished Journey* (New York: Oxford University Press, 1986), 221–246; Dallek, *Flawed Giant,* 185–237, 293–339; Irving Bernstein, *Guns or Butter: The Presidency of Lyndon Johnson* (New York: Oxford University Press, 1996), 27–314 passim.

15. Conkin, *Big Daddy from the Pedernales,* 243–286; Kearns, *Lyndon Johnson,* 251–334. See also Stanley Karnow, *Vietnam: A History* (New York: Viking, 1983); Dallek, *Flawed Giant,* 340–390; Bernstein, *Guns or Butter,* 324–357.

16. Kearns, *Lyndon Johnson,* 335–352; Dallek, *Flawed Giant,* 569–600; Bernstein, *Guns or Butter,* 471–521.

17. Conkin, *Big Daddy from the Pedernales,* 287–296; Kearns, *Lyndon Johnson,* 353–356; Dallek, *Flawed Giant,* 601–623; For a more objective view see Dallek, *Lone Star Rising,* 351–543 passim.

RALPH YARBOROUGH

1. For a thorough, encyclopedic survey of Henderson County, Tex., see J. J. Faulk, *History of Henderson County Texas* (Athens, Tex.: Athens Printing Co., 1929).

2. William G. Phillips, *Yarborough of Texas* (Washington, D.C.: Acropolis Books, 1969), 5–6.

3. For a comprehensive summary of Yarborough's legislative accomplishments, see Patrick Cox, *Ralph W. Yarborough: The People's Senator* (Austin: University of Texas Press, 2001), 201–253, and Chandler Davidson, *Race and Class in Texas Politics* (Princeton: Princeton University Press, 1990), 29–34.

4. Mark Adams and Creekmore Fath, *Yarborough: Portrait of a Steadfast Democrat* (Austin: Chaparral Press, 1957), 3–6; interview with Ralph Yarborough by author Collins, March 19, 1992, Austin, Tex. (hereafter cited as Yarborough interview).

5. Yarborough interview.

6. Adams and Fath, *Yarborough,* 7; Yarborough interview.

7. Yarborough interview; Cox, *People's Senator,* 8–9.

8. Adams and Fath, *Yarborough,* 7–8.

9. Ibid.; Yarborough interview.

10. Adams and Fath, *Yarborough,* 7–8.

11. Ibid., 8.

12. Ibid.

13. Ibid.; Yarborough interview; Phillips, *Yarborough of Texas,* 18–21.

14. Cox, *People's Senator*, 16–17; Yarborough interview.

15. Cox, *People's Senator*, 26–29; Adams and Fath, *Yarborough*, 12–14. The Texas Supreme Court sustained the state's victory in the *Magnolia v. Walker* suit, which resulted in billions of dollars from oil and gas revenues to the Permanent School Fund.

16. Adams and Fath, *Yarborough*, 12–14.

17. Cox, *People's Senator*, 44–47; Yarborough interview.

18. Cox, *People's Senator*, 81–90; Phillips, *Yarborough of Texas*, 24; Yarborough interview.

19. Adams and Fath, *Yarborough*, 15–16; Yarborough interview; Phillips, *Yarborough of Texas*, 24–28.

20. Adams and Fath, *Yarborough*, 16–17; Phillips, *Yarborough of Texas*, 24–25.

21. Yarborough interview; Adams and Fath, *Yarborough*, 18–19; "Ralph Yarborough: Biographical Sketch," typescript, Center for American History, University of Texas.

22. Don Carleton, *A Breed So Rare* (Austin: Texas State Historical Association, 1998), 410–415; Yarborough interview; Cox, *People's Senator*, 99–100. The best accounts of Yarborough's challenge to the Shivers "machine" can be found in George N. Green, *The Establishment in Texas Politics: The Primitive Years, 1938–1957* (Norman: University of Oklahoma Press, 1984), 141–142, 145, and Cox, *People's Senator*, 96–121.

23. Cox, *People's Senator*, 102–105; Phillips, *Yarborough of Texas*, 34–35.

24. Cox, *People's Senator*, 102–105; See also Sam Kinch and Stuart Long, *Allan Shivers: The Pied Piper of Texas Politics* (Austin: Shoal Creek Publishers, 1973).

25. Cox, *People's Senator*, 105–110; Green, *Establishment in Texas Politics*, 174–177, 219–224, 227.

26. Cox, *People's Senator*, 105–110; Green, *Establishment in Texas Politics*, 174–177, 219–224, 227.

27. Cox, *People's Senator*, 105–110; Green, *Establishment in Texas Politics*, 174–177, 219–224, 227; Phillips, *Yarborough of Texas*, 38–42.

28. Cox, *People's Senator*, 115–120; Green, *Establishment in Texas Politics*, 159–165.

29. Green, *Establishment in Texas Politics*, 159–165. For a complete discussion of the *Brown* decision and southern massive resistance in the South, see Dewey W. Grantham, *The Life and Death of the Solid South* (Lexington: University Press of Kentucky, 1988).

30. Kenneth E. Hendrickson Jr., "Modern Texas: The Political Scene since 1945," in Ben Procter and Archie McDonald, eds., *The Texas Heritage*, 2nd ed. (Arlington Heights, Ill.: Harlan Davidson, 1992), 194–195; Cox, *People's Senator*, 122–124.

31. Yarborough interview; Cox, *People's Senator*, 134–137; Green, *Establishment in Texas Politics*, 174–177, 219–224, 227.

32. Cox, *People's Senator*, 139–142; Green, *Establishment in Texas Politics*, 174–177, 219–224, 227.

33. "After the Free-for-All," *Newsweek*, April 15, 1957, 35; Ronnie Dugger, "Texas' New Junior Senator," *NR*, April 22, 1957, 8; "Winner at Last," *USNWR*, April 12, 1957, 20–27; "The Ayes of Texas," *Time*, April 15, 1957, 33–34.

34. *AAS,* April 8, 1957; Phillips, *Yarborough of Texas,* 6.

35. Yarborough interview; Cox, *People's Senator,* 144–145.

36. *DMN,* April 7, 1957; Yarborough interview; Cox, *People's Senator,* 145–147.

37. Yarborough interview; Cox, *People's Senator,* 145–147.

38. Cox, *People's Senator,* 150–152; Davidson, *Race and Class,* 29–32.

39. "Statewide Texas Salute to Senator Ralph W. Yarborough," program, appreciation dinner in honor of Senator Ralph Yarborough, Austin, Tex., October 19, 1963, CAH; *CR,* 85th Cong., 2nd sess., August 22, 1958, 19085.

40. "The Story of Bill Blakley," campaign brochure, William Blakley vertical file, CAH; Cox, *People's Senator,* 152–157.

41. Ernest M. B. Obadele-Starks, "Ralph Yarborough of Texas and the Road to Civil Rights," *East Texas Historical Journal* 32, no. 1 (1994): 39–48; Cox, *People's Senator,* 163–165. In 1959 Johnson and Yarborough agreed on 86 percent of 215 record votes in U.S. Senate.

42. Yarborough interview; Cox, *People's Senator,* 166–169, 172–173; Lyndon Baines Johnson, *Vantage Point: Perspectives on the Presidency* (New York: Holt, Rinehart and Winston, 1971), 7. Harsh sentiments existed between Robert Kennedy and Lyndon Johnson, stemming from the 1960 Democratic presidential nomination campaign.

43. JFK's comment was broadcast live to an audience in Austin's Municipal Auditorium during the "Statewide Texas Salute" to the senator on October 19, 1963.

44. John Connally with Mickey Herskowitz, *In History's Shadow: An American Odyssey* (New York: Hyperion Books, 1993), 6–7; Cox, *People's Senator,* 192–199; Johnson, *Vantage Point,* 7.

45. RWY to Chief Justice Earl Warren, December 16, 1963, Kennedy, 2R515, Yarborough Papers, CAH; Cox, *People's Senator,* 192–195.

46. Cox, *People's Senator,* 202–209; James Reston Jr., *The Lone Star: The Life of John Connally* (New York: Harper and Row, 1989), 295–296.

47. George Bush, with Victor Gold, *Looking Backward: An Autobiography* (Garden City, N.Y.: Doubleday, 1987), 77–80; "Cactus Nasty Campaign," *Time,* October 16, 1964; Cox, *People's Senator,* 214–220.

48. Billy Porterfield, "Yarborough: Making the World a Better Place," *AAS,* March 13, 1991.

49. Yarborough interview.

50. *Committee on Labor and Public Welfare, United States Senate: 100th Anniversary, 1869–1969* (Washington, D.C.: GPO, 1970); of course, Yarborough's numerous speeches, extended remarks, and votes in the Senate can be found in the *CR.*

51. Cox, *People's Senator,* 229–234; Yarborough interview; Davidson, *Race and Class,* 29–32.

52. Yarborough interview; U.S. Senate, 92nd Cong., 1st sess., Sen. Doc. no. 92-9, National Program for the Conquest of Cancer: Report of the National Panel of Consultants on the Conquest of Cancer, Authorized by Sen. Res. 376, Prepared for the Committee on Labor and Public Welfare, U.S. Senate (Washington, D.C.: GPO, 1971); Phillips, *Yarborough of Texas,* 109–125.

53. Cox, *People's Senator,* 235–238; Phillips, *Yarborough of Texas,* 130–132, 138;

Mark W. Oberle, "Endangered Species: Congress Curbs International Trade in Rare Animals," *Science,* January 9, 1970, 152-154.

54. Lewis Gould, *1968: the Election that Changed America* (Chicago: Ivan R. Dee, 1993), 142-169; Cox, *People's Senator,* 239-249.

55. Cox, *People's Senator,* 254-264; *TO,* April 17, May 1, 15, 1970.

56. Porterfield, "Yarborough." See also Paul R. Wieck, "Whose Texas?" *NR,* November 9, 1968, 11-13; Ronnie Dugger, "Hot After Yarborough," *NR,* April 18, 1970, 11-12; Paul R. Wieck, "Defying the Bosses in Illinois and Texas," *NR,* February 27, 1971, 11-13; "Texas Democratic Primary G.O.P. Gain," *Time,* May 11, 1970, 37.

57. "Statewide Salute to Senator Ralph Yarborough," October 19, 1963; the quote was also included in Ralph Yarborough, *Frank Dobie: Man and Friend* (Washington, D.C.: Potomac Corral, the Westerners, 1967), i.

58. Porterfield, "Yarborough"; Johnson, *Vantage Point,* 7.

59. Porterfield, "Yarborough."

BARBARA JORDAN

1. Barbara Jordan and Shelby Hearon, *Barbara Jordan: A Self-Portrait* (Garden City, N.Y.: Doubleday, 1979), 185-187; Ira B. Bryant, *Barbara Charline Jordan: From the Ghetto to the Capitol* (Houston: D. Armstrong Co., 1977), 51; B. J. Phillips, "Recognizing the Gentleladies of the Judiciary Committee," *Ms.,* November 1974, 70-71; "Jordan Condemns Nixon in Forceful Panel Speech," *HC,* July 26, 1974, clipping in Barbara Jordan Scrapbooks, CAH (hereafter cited as BJ Scrapbooks), vol. 1; Seth Kantor, "Proof of American Dream: 'Jordan's Impact Began with Watergate Speech,'" *AAS,* July 31, 198l, clipping in "Barbara Jordan" vertical file, CAH (hereafter cited as BJ vert. file).

2. Jordan and Hearon, *Self-Portrait,* 22, 30, 34-37, 44-45; Ann Fears Crawford and Crystal Sasse Ragsdale, "Congresswoman from Texas: Barbara Jordan," *Women in Texas: Their Lives, Their Experiences, Their Accomplishments* (Austin: Eakin Press, 1982), 297; Molly Ivins, "A Profile of Barbara Jordan," *TO,* November 3, 1972; Bryant, *Ghetto to Capitol,* 2; Zarko Franks, "Sen. Jordan: Even as Little Girl She Was One of the Rare Ones," *HC,* November 30, 1969, clipping in BJ Scrapbooks, vol. 1; Ruthe Winegarten, *Texas Women: A Pictorial History from Indians to Astronauts* (Austin: Eakin Press, 1986), 138; Liz Carpenter, "A Conversation between Lady Bird Johnson and Barbara Jordan," *Family Circle,* February 1977, clipping in BJ Scrapbooks, vol. l.

3. Even while preaching, Ben Jordan kept his job as a warehouse clerk in order to support his family. Jordan and Hearon, *Self-Portrait,* 25, 27-29, 32, 39-40, 42; Franks, "Rare Ones"; Ivins, "A Profile," 11; Bryant, *Ghetto to Capitol,* 2; "Barbara Jordan, Senate President Pro Tem," *DMN,* March 29, 1972; June Bingham, "One Woman's Voice: Peek into Barbara's Life," *Wichita Falls Times,* December 12, 1976, clipping in BJ Scrapbooks, vol. 2.

4. Barbara Jordan and Shelby Hearon, "Barbara Jordan: Self-Portrait of a Retir-

ing Activist," *Washington Post Magazine,* January 7, 1979, 6; Jordan and Hearon, *Self-Portrait,* 9–11.

5. Jordan and Hearon, *Self-Portrait,* 11–13.

6. Ibid., 13, 19–22.

7. Ibid., 6–7, 22, 47–48; Gay Elliott McFarland, "Barbara Jordan's Houston," *HC,* February 5, 1979, clipping in BJ Scrapbooks, vol. 2; Ivins, "A Profile," 11.

8. Jordan and Hearon, *Self-Portrait,* 39–40, 46, 57–60; McFarland, "Barbara Jordan's Houston"; Ivins, "A Profile," 11.

9. Because of a lack of funds, Ben Jordan did not complete his final year at Tuskegee. Jordan and Hearon, *Self-Portrait,* 11, 23, 29–30, 35, 66; Bryant, *Ghetto to Capitol,* 5.

10. Franks, "Rare Ones"; Ivins, "A Profile," 11; Jordan and Hearon, *Self-Portrait,* 64, 66–72; Bryant, *Ghetto to Capitol,* 7–8; Donald Lambro, "Barbara Jordan's Meteoric Rise in the House," *HC,* February 14, 1976; Charlotte Phelan, "State Sen. Barbara Jordan . . . Wins Her Battles through 'the System,'" *HP,* May 14, 1970; Ernest Bailey, "Only Negro in Senate, Miss Jordan Sure She'll Be Accepted," *HP,* May 21, 1966; Crawford and Ragsdale, "Congresswoman from Texas," 298.

11. Jordan and Hearon, *Self-Portrait,* 64–65; Ivins, "A Profile," 11; Jordan and Hearon, "Barbara Jordan," 6.

12. Jordan and Hearon, *Self-Portrait,* 62, 75–77; "The Barbara Jordan Archives," pamphlet published by Texas Southern University, in BJ vert. file; Ivins, "A Profile," 11.

13. Lambro, "Jordan's Meteoric Rise"; Ivins, "A Profile," 11; Jordan and Hearon, *Self-Portrait,* 78.

14. Jordan and Hearon, "Barbara Jordan," 6–7; Jordan and Hearon, *Self-Portrait,* 79–81.

15. Lambro, "Jordan's Meteoric Rise"; Jordan and Hearon, *Self-Portrait,* 82–83; Bryant, *Ghetto to Capitol,* 10; Franks, "Rare Ones," BJ Scrapbooks, vol. 1; Saul Kohler, "The Barbara Jordan Question: Whatever Happened on Her Way to Carter's Cabinet?" *HC,* December 26, 1976, clipping in BJ vert. file; Phelan, "State Senator Barbara Jordan"; Phillips, "Recognizing the Gentleladies," 71.

16. Louise Bailey was the daughter of John Bailey, then chairman of the Democratic National Convention. Jordan and Hearon, *Self-Portrait,* 89–92; Phillips, "Recognizing the Gentleladies," 71.

17. Phelan, "State Senator Barbara Jordan"; Dave McNeely, "Jordan: Richards' Right Arm of the Law on Ethics," *AAS,* March 31, 1991, clipping in BJ vert. file; Jordan and Hearon, "Barbara Jordan," 7; Jordan and Hearon, *Self-Portrait,* 89, 91, 93.

18. At one point, Jordan, possessing a newfound appreciation for religion now that "the Reverend (her father) . . . and the Deacon (Grandfather Jordan)" were far away, thrilled Ben Jordan with the notion that she might leave her law studies for theology. Jordan and Hearon, *Self-Portrait,* 86, 94, 98; Franks, "Rare Ones"; Phelan, "State Senator Barbara Jordan."

19. Rose Mary Jordan had married John McGowan while her youngest sister was away. Bennie would wed Ben Creswell in 1961. Jordan and Hearon, *Self-Portrait,*

108–110; Phillips, "Recognizing the Gentleladies," 71; Phelan, "State Senator Barbara Jordan"; Franks, "Rare Ones"; Ivins, "A Profile," 11; Bryant, *Ghetto to Capitol,* 17.

20. At this time, Texas was still a one-party state. Jordan and Hearon, *Self-Portrait,* 110–111; Crawford and Ragsdale, "Congresswoman from Texas," 298.

21. Ivins, "A Profile," 11; Jordan and Hearon, *Self-Portrait,* 100–101, 112–115; Franks, "Rare Ones"; Phelan, "State Senator Barbara Jordan"; Bryant, *Ghetto to Capitol,* 11; "Negro Wins Seat in State Senate," *DTH,* May 8, 1966, clipping in BJ Scrapbooks, vol. 1.

22. Phillips, "Recognizing the Gentleladies," 71; Phelan, "State Senator Barbara Jordan"; Ivins, "A Profile," 11; "Negro Wins Seat"; Jordan and Hearon, *Self-Portrait,* 117–119.

23. Franks, "Rare Ones"; Phelan, "State Senator Barbara Jordan"; Jordan and Hearon, *Self-Portrait,* 129–130, 132–134; Bryant, *Ghetto to Capitol,* 18; "Republican, Negro Win in Harris," *AAS,* November 9, 1966; "State Senate to Honor Representative Jordan," *Daily Texan,* February 7, 1975, clipping in BJ Scrapbooks, vol. 2; Carolyn Barta, "Negro Senator-to-Be Seeks Equality," *DMN,* May 30, 1966, clipping in BJ Scrapbooks, vol. 1; Walter Mansell, "Barbara Has No Fears about Serving in State Senate," *HC,* May 22, 1966, clipping in BJ Scrapbooks, vol. 1; Ernest Bailey, "Only Negro in Senate," BJ Scrapbooks, vol. 1.

24. According to State Representative Bob Eckhardt (D-Houston), the executive committee of the Harris County Democratic Party supported Jordan over Whitfield because blacks in Houston needed "a leader of their own." Jordan and Hearon, *Self-Portrait,* 131–133; "Republican, Negro Win," 20; Phelan, "State Senator Barbara Jordan"; Barta, "Negro Senator-to-Be."

25. "Barbara Jordan Archives," pamphlet, BJ vert. file; Bailey, "Only Negro in Senate"; "Negro Wins Seat"; Phelan, "State Senator Barbara Jordan"; Jordan and Hearon, *Self-Portrait,* 134–136.

26. Bryant, *Ghetto to Capitol,* 18; Phelan, "State Senator Barbara Jordan"; Negro Wins Seat"; Mansell, "Barbara Has No Fears"; Jordan and Hearon, *Self-Portrait,* 138–140, 142, 149.

27. Franks, "Rare Ones"; Jordan and Hearon, *Self-Portrait,* 139, 145–50; Phelan, "State Senator Barbara Jordan"; Bryant, *Ghetto to Capitol,* 18, 20; Carolyn Barta, "Senator Says Texans Face Tax Problem," *DMN,* July 23, 1967; Ernestine Wheelock, "In Politics—Dream Comes True for Young Senator," *AAS,* January 22, 1967, clipping in BJ Scrapbooks, vol. 1; "His Presence Speaks for the Negro," *AAS,* June 16, 1968.

28. Jordan and Hearon, *Self-Portrait,* 148–152; Bryant, *Ghetto to Capitol,* 18, 20, 95; Barbara Fulenwider, "An Eye on Jordan: A Pioneer in Politics," *HP,* November 3, 1968; Saralee Tiede, *HC,* December 25, 1967, clipping in BJ Scrapbooks, vol. 1.

29. Jordan and Hearon, *Self-Portrait,* 139, 142; William H. Gardner, "Sen[.] Jordan Scores First by Presiding," *HP,* March 22, 1966, clipping in BJ Scrapbooks, vol. 1; Franks, "Rare Ones"; Bryant, *Ghetto to Capitol,* 21; Phelan, "State Senator Barbara Jordan."

30. Terms were staggered, and Jordan had drawn a two-year position in 1966, four

years in 1968. Jordan and Hearon, *Self-Portrait*, 152; Bryant, *Ghetto to Capitol*, 20; "Sen[.] Jordan Will Seek Reelection: Seeks Agency for Human Resources," *HP*, January 11, 1963.

31. Fulenwider, "An Eye on Jordan," 3; Judy Tritz, "Of Rats and Foul Air," *HP*, March 32, 1970; Phelan, "State Senator Barbara Jordan"; Jordan and Hearon, *Self-Portrait*, '52; Ivins, "A Profile," 13.

32. Jordan and Hearon, *Self-Portrait*, 153; Phelan, "State Senator Barbara Jordan"; Ivins, "A Profile," 13; William H. Gardner, "In Bill Offered by Sen[.] Jordan, Worker Compensation Hike Sought," *HP*, January 30, 1969; Henry Holcomb, "Sen[.] Jordan Tackles Selling of Urban Bill Package," *HP*, March 7, 1971; untitled article, *AAS*, April 18, 1971, clipping in BJ Scrapbooks, vol. 1.

33. Gardner, "Worker Compensation Hike Sought," sec. 1, 6; Ivins, "A Profile," 13; Bryant, *Ghetto to Capitol*, 22, 97–98; Phelan, "State Senator Barbara Jordan"; Julia Scott Reed, "Rep. Jordan Begins Work," *DMN*, January 14, 1973.

34. Bryant, *Ghetto to Capitol*, 95–96; Phelan, "State Senator Barbara Jordan"; Holcomb, "Selling of Urban Bill," sec. A, 5.

35. Phelan, "State Senator Barbara Jordan"; Bryant, *Ghetto to Capitol*, 95–97; "Sen. Jordan to Quit If Ramsey Chosen," *DMN*, September 15, 1970.

36. Ivins, "A Profile," 13; "Barbara Jordan Archives," pamphlet, BJ vert. file; Bryan, *Ghetto to Capitol*, 15; Jordan and Hearon, *Self-Portrait*, 160–168; "Sen. Jordan to Serve as Governor for Day," *HP*, June 9, 1971; "Jordan Due Oath: First Black Governor for Day," *DMN*, June 10, 1971; "Governor Jordan: History in One Day," *HC*, June 10, 1971, clipping in BJ Scrapbooks, vol. 1; "It Makes Sense," *DTH*, March 31, 1971, clipping in BJ Scrapbooks, vol. 1; "Proclamations Abound on Governor Barbara Jordan Day," *HC*, June 11, 1971, clipping in BJ Scrapbooks, vol. 1; Carolyn Bobo, "Governor for a Day: Sen[.] Jordan Adds Top State Chair to List of Victories," *AAS*, June 11, 1971; "Miss Jordan Serves as Governor," *DMN*, June 11, 1972; "Governor for a Day, Sen[.] Barbara Jordan Gives Texas an Historic 'First,'" *DTH*, June 11, 1971; Henry Holcomb, "Sen[.] Jordan Takes Oath: First Black in Governor's Chair," *HP*, June 11, 1972.

37. "Miss Jordan Serves as Governor," 43; Holcomb, "Sen[.] Jordan Takes Oath," 1–2; Jordan and Hearon, *Self-Portrait*, 166–170, 171–174; "Senator's Father Dies," *DMN*, June 11, 1971, clipping in BJ Scrapbooks, vol. 1.

38. Ivins, "A Profile," 13; Susan Kent Caudill, "Getting Things Done the Issue in Jordan-Graves Race," *HP*, May 5, 1971; Franks, "Rare Ones"; Jordan and Hearon, *Self-Portrait*, 154–157; Glen Castlebury, "Sen. Jordan's Chances for Congress Are Good," *AAS*, April 16, 1971.

39. Ivins, "A Profile," 13; Caudill, "Getting Things Done," 1; "Vote for Barbara Jordan," editorial in *HC*, October 26, 1971, clipping in BJ Scrapbooks, vol. 1; Darrell Hancock and Henry Holcomb, "Compromise Prevents Democratic Splinter," *HP*, September 10, 1971; Steward Davis, "Barbara Favored; 3 Incumbents Confident," *DMN*, October 13, 1971; Bill Lee, "Barbara Jordan's Contributions 5 to 1 over Graves," *HC*, April 16, 1971; Bryant, *Ghetto to Capitol*, 15; Jordan and Hearon, *Self-Portrait*, 157.

40. Jordan and Hearon, *Self-Portrait,* 157–160; Carpenter, "A Conversation"; Tom Curtis, "Johnson at Head of List Honoring Barbara Jordan," *HC,* October 22, 1972, clipping in BJ Scrapbooks, vol. 1; "New 'First' for Negro: House Seat," *DTH,* November 8, 1971, clipping in BJ Scrapbooks, vol. 1; Darrell Hancock, "Conservative Paul Merritt Challenging Barbara Jordan's Bid for Congress," *HP,* October 29, 1972; Bryant, *Ghetto to Capitol,* 27; Reed, "Rep. Jordan Begins Work," 10; "Democrats Won't Stay Buried under Landslide, Jordan Says," *HP,* November 11, 1972.

41. "Jordan Says Rights Movement Will Focus on Jobs and Money," *HC,* December 12, 1971, clipping in BJ Scrapbooks, vol. 1; "Rep. Jordan Looks to Judiciary Panel," *HC,* January 3, 1973; Fred Bonavita, "Miss Jordan, Charles Wilson Attend Caucus, Ready Offices," *HP,* January 3, 1973; Reed, "Rep. Jordan Begins Work," 10; Phillips, "Recognizing the Gentleladies," 72; Jordan and Hearon, *Self-Portrait,* 178–180.

42. Jordan and Hearon, *Self-Portrait,* 180–181; Reed, "Rep. Jordan Begins Work," 10; Norman Baxter, "Barbara Jordan, Late to Party, Was 'Working.'" *HC,* January 4, 1973, clipping in BJ Scrapbooks, vol. 1.

43. Jordan voted against Ford's confirmation as vice president. "Equality Still Off, Jordan Says," *WP,* March 25, 1975, clipping in BJ Scrapbooks, vol. 2; Phillips, "Recognizing the Gentleladies," 72; Bryant, *Ghetto to Capitol.*

44. "Jordan Condemns Nixon in Forceful Panel Speech," *HC,* July 26, 1974, clipping in BJ Scrapbooks, vol. 1; Bryant, *Ghetto to Capitol,* 43–49, 63–66; Jordan and Hearon, *Self-Portrait,* 186–193; Phillips, "Recognizing the Gentleladies," 70–71; Winegarten, *Texas Women,* 138.

45. After the televised Judiciary Committee speech, Jordan commanded $2,000 for each speaking engagement. Jordan and Hearon, *Self-Portrait,* 201–204; "Jordan to Visit Red China," *HP,* August 27, 1974; "Rep. Jordan Joins Caucus Policy Panel," *DTH,* December 5, 1974, clipping in BJ Scrapbooks, vol. 1; "State Senate to Honor Rep. Jordan," *Daily Texan,* February 7, 1975, clipping in BJ Scrapbooks, vol. 2; "Jordan Portrait Unveiled," *Daily Texan,* February 10, 1975, clipping, BJ Scrapbooks, vol. 2.

46. Jordan and Hearon, *Self-Portrait,* 204-212, 214; Cragg Hines, "Jordan Gets Both Her Wishes—Voting Act and Ford Cards," *HC,* August 7, 1975, clipping in BJ Scrapbooks, vol. 2; Bryant, *Ghetto to Capitol,* 79, 87, 100.

47. Jordan and Hearon, *Self-Portrait,* 223, 226.

48. Ibid., 223–226.

49. Ibid., 229–231; Bryant, *Ghetto to Capitol,* 22, 58; Zarko Franks, "It Was Pure Jordan, and That's What Turned on the Delegates," *HC,* clipping in BJ Scrapbooks, vol. 2; Norman Baxter, "Congresswoman Barbara Jordan: A Hero for All Times," *HC,* June 18, 1976, clipping in BJ Scrapbooks, vol. 2; Dave Montgomery, "Jordan's Address to Set Tenor for the Convention," *DTH,* July 12, 1976, clipping in BJ Scrapbooks, vol. 2; Mary Walsh and Barry Baxter, "Jordan First Black to Open Convention," *Daily Texan,* July 13, 1976, 1; "We Are a People in Search of Our Future," *DMN,* July 18, 1976, clipping in BJ Scrapbooks, vol. 2; Cragg Hines, "Rep. Jordan's Speech Lifts Convention Out of Lethargy," *HC,* July 13, 1976.

50. 'Bryant, *Ghetto to Capitol,* 58; Jordan and Hearon, *Self-Portrait,* 234, 236, 243–244; Kohler, "The Barbara Jordan Question," BJ vert. file; Jordan and Hearon, "Barbara Jordan," 6.

51. Kohler, "The Barbara Jordan Question"; Jordan and Hearon, *Self-Portrait,* 244–246; "Rep. Jordan's Ambition, Opponents May Quash Cabinet Hopes," *El Paso Times,* December 17, 1976, clipping in BJ Scrapbooks, vol. 2.

52. Jordan and Hearon, *Self-Portrait,* 229, 247–250.

53. "Jordan Serves Well, "*FWST,* December 18, 1977, clipping in BJ Scrapbooks, vol. 1; University of Texas at Austin press releases, June 9, 1978, October 17, 1979, January 8, 1980, December 13, 1984, February 9, 1987, in BJ vert. file; Winegarten, *Texas Women,* 144. Becky Knapp, "Barbara Jordan Named to National Women's Hall of Fame," *AAS,* March 3, 1990, clipping in BJ vert. file; Crawford and Ragsdale, "Congresswoman from Texas," 305.

54. "A Short Biography from the Good Hope Memorial Service," http://www .rice.edu/armadillo/ Texas/Jordan/goodhopebio.html.

JOHN TOWER

The data utilized in this study were made available in part by the Inter-university Consortium for Political and Social Research. The voting studies data for members of the United States Congress were originally collected by Congressional Quarterly, Inc. Neither the collector of the original data nor the Consortium bears any responsibility for the analyses or interpretation presented here.

1. John Tower, *Consequences: A Personal and Political Memoir* (Boston: Little, Brown, 1991), 92. Tower admitted that this was one of his favorite quotes from the confirmation period.

2. Transcript of interview with John Tower, Oral History Collection, Lyndon B. Johnson Library; Griffin Smith Jr., "Little Big Man," *Texas Monthly,* January 1977, 86; *HP,* May 21, 1961, August 24, 1983; Tower, *Consequences,* 78, 106 (quote).

3. There are conflicting accounts of when Tower joined the Republican Party.

4. Tower interview; Barry Schlachter, column in *FWST,* February 20, 1989; Jimmy Banks, *Money, Marbles, and Chalk* (Austin: Texas Publishing Company, 1971), 180; Tower, *Consequences,* 168.

5. Robert Sherrill, "Tower of Texas Is Small in the Saddle, But . . . ," *New York Times Magazine,* April 26, 1970, 114 (1st and 2nd quotes); Roger M. Olien, *From Token to Triumph: Texas Republicans since 1920* (Dallas: Southern Methodist University Press, 1982), 133 (3rd quote). See also Chandler Davidson, *Race and Class in Texas Politics* (Princeton: Princeton University Press, 1991), 224–225.

6. *HP,* August 24, 1983 (quote); *DMN,* April 6, 1991; Smith, "Little Big Man," 86–87; Robert Eubank, "Understanding Texas Republicans," in Wendell Bedicheck and Neal Tannahill, eds., *Public Policy in Texas* (Glenview, Ill.: Scott Foresman, 1982), 172–173; John Tower, *Consequences,* 14–17; Banks, *Money, Marbles, and Chalk,* 181.

7. John Knaggs, *Two-Party Texas* (Austin: Eakin Press, 1986), 7–10; Smith, "Little Big Man," 86; James Soukup, Clifton McKleskey, and Harry Holloway, *Party and Factional Division in Texas* (Austin: University of Texas Press, 1964), 15–16, 26. See also H. M. Baggarly, *The Texas Country Democrat* (San Angelo, Tex.: Anchor, 1970), 190-197.

8. Tower, *Consequences*, 23–25; Knaggs, *Two-Party Texas*, 12.

9. Knaggs, *Two-Party Texas*, 10–15; Olien, *From Token to Triumph*, 196–200; "Low in the Saddle," *Nation*, June 10, 1961, 491; Douglas Weeks, *Texas in the 1960 Presidential Election* (Austin: Institute of Public Affairs, University of Texas, 1961), 74–75.

10. Knaggs, *Two-Party Texas*, 10–15; Olien, *From Token to Triumph*, 74–5; Tower, *Consequences*, 23–5; Weeks, *1960 Presidential Election*, 74–75; "Low in the Saddle," 491; *USNWR*, May 22, 1961, 83; "Jack the Giant Killer," *Time*, June 9, 1961, 16.

11. The cell entries in this table are derived from a weighted, linear least-squares model using data from all 254 Texas counties. The total number of voters in each county was specified as the larger of the total vote cast in the primary or the runoff. Because this is an estimating procedure, a negative value, such as the one calculated for the percentage of Wilson voters who voted for Tower in the runoff, can occur when the actual value is near zero. The literature on ecological regression is extensive. A useful introduction can be found in Laura Irwin Langbein and Allan J. Lichtman, *Ecological Inference*, Sage University Paper Series on Quantitative Applications in the Social Sciences No. 07-010 (Beverly Hills, Calif.: Sage Publications, 1978).

12. Schlachter, in *FWST* (1st quote); Richard Dudman, *Men of the Far Right* (New York: Pyramid Books, 1962), 177; Smith, "Little Big Man," 130; Stephen Hess and David Broder, *The Republican Establishment* (New York: Harper and Row, 1967), 346–347; John Tower, column in *TO*, March 21, 1963 (2nd quote); John Tower, *A Program for Conservatives* (New York: McFadden-Bartell, 1962); Olien, *From Token to Triumph*, 188–189 (3rd quote).

13. Larry Lee, *TO*, January 21, 1966; Jonathan Kolkey, *The New Right, 1960–1968: with Epilogue, 1969–1980* (Washington, D.C.: University Press of America, 1983), 113–115, 117, 124; *CD*, June 1963, 175.

14. Donald Janson and Bernard Eismann, *The Far Right* (New York: McGraw-Hill, 1963), 108–115, 198–215; "John Tower," *Current Biography* (1962), 426–428; Sherrill, "Tower of Texas," 114.

15. Hess and Broder, *Republican Establishment*, 346–347; Charles Ashman, *Connally* (New Work: William Morrow, 1974), 99; Alexander Lamis, *The Two-Party South* (New York: Oxford University Press, 1984), 195–196; Olien, *From Token to Triumph*, 188; David Reinhard, *The Republican Right since 1945* (Lexington: University Press of Kentucky, 1983), 168–169; Knaggs, *Two-Party Texas*, 32–35.

16. Walter Dean Burnham, "American Voting Behavior and the 1964 Election," in Melvin Richter, ed., *Essays in Theory and History: An Approach to the Social Sciences* (Cambridge: Harvard University Press, 1970), 186–220; Bernard Cosman, *Five States for Goldwater: Continuity and Change in Southern Voting Patterns* (Tuscaloosa: University of Alabama Press, 1966; Joseph L. Bernd, "The 1964 Presidential

Election in Texas," in John M. Claunch, ed., *The 1964 Presidential Election in the Southwest* (Dallas: Arnold Foundation, Southern Methodist University, 1966), 7-32; Tower, *Consequences*, 167.

17. Tower, *Consequences*, 56, 167; Davidson, *Race and Class*, 224 (quote), 224-231; *HP*, August 24, 1983; Larry Lee, column in *TO*, January 21, 1966; Kaye Northcott, column in *TO*, October 20, 1972; "John Tower," *Current Biography*, 428.

18. Knaggs, *Two-Party Texas*, 56-61; Tower, *Consequences*, 170-171; Hess and Broder, *Republican Establishment*, 347; Reinhard, *Republican Right*, 217; Dan Nimmo, *The Political Persuaders* (Englewood Cliffs, N.J.: Prentice-Hall, 1970), 91.

19. Hess and Broder, *Republican Establishment*, 347-348 (quote); *TO*, December 10, 1965, September 16, 30, 1966; Larry Lee, *TO*, January 21, 1966; Eubank, "Understanding Texas Republicans," 175; *HP*, August 24, 1983; Knaggs, *Two-Party Texas*, 61, 71; Tower, *Consequences*, 171.

20. Richard Morehead, *50 Years in Texas Politics* (Austin: Eakin Press, 1982), 191; Andrew Kopkind, "Connally's Texas," *NR*, November 20, 1965, 11-12; Rowland Evans and Robert Novak, column in *St. Petersburg Times*, January 6, 1965; Ann Fears Crawford and Jack Keever, *John B. Connally* (Austin: Jenkins, 1973), 325; Knaggs, *Two-Party Texas*, 64-65, 74, 82-83; Olien, *From Token to Triumph*, 207-208.

21. Knaggs, *Two-Party Texas*, 65-66, 81; *TO*, June 24, 1966.

22. Knaggs, *Two-Party Texas*, 84-88, 96-97; Tower, *Consequences*, 176-177 (2nd quote); "Texas Liberal Democrats: The Question of Supporting Waggoner Carr for U.S. Senator," 1966 brochure in possession of authors; Olien, *From Token to Triumph*, 210-211; George N. Green, *A Liberal View of Texas Politics since the 1930s* (Boston: American Press, 1981), 34; *TO*, April 15 (3rd quote), and July 8, 22 (1st quote), 1966.

23. Knaggs, *Two-Party Texas*, 63, 103-104; Tower, *Consequences*, 176; Dick West, column in *DMN*, November 27, 1966; Dorothy Lillad, column in *DMN*, November 10, 1966; Robert Ford, column in *DMN*, November 13, 1966; Louis Seagull, *Southern Republicanism* (New York: Wiley, 1975), 137.

24. Hess and Broder, *Republican Establishment*, 348-349; Davidson, *Race and Class*, 202; Reinhard, *Republican Right*, 219; Kolkey, *New Right*, 255 (quote), 278-279.

25. Kolkey, *New Right*, 280, 281; Knaggs, *Two-Party Texas*, 127; *TO*, July 12, 1968; Richard Nixon, *The Memoirs of Richard Nixon* (New York: Grosset and Dunlap, 1978), 305-309; Theodore White, *The Making of the President, 1968* (New York: Atheneum, 1969), 160-161. Reagan, Goldwater, and Tower were being hailed at this time as the three leading Sunbelt conservatives. See Kevin Phillips, *The Emerging Republican Majority* (New Rochelle, N.Y.: Arlington House, 1969), 440.

26. White, *Making of the President*, 294; Sherrill, "Tower of Texas," 29, 113; Nixon, *Memoirs*, 442-443 (quote); Harry Dent, *The Prodigal South Returns to Power* (New York: Wiley, 1978), 187-188.

27. James Reston Jr., *The Lone Star: The Life of John Connally* (New York: Harper and Row, 1989), 380; Crawford and Keever, *John B. Connally*, 326 (quote), 327, 341.

28. *TO*, August 27, 1971.

29. Walter Scott, column in *Parade Magazine,* November 28, 1971; Tower, *Consequences,* 30; Cheryl Arvidson, column in *DTH,* February 13, 1991; Sherrill, "Tower of Texas," 18.

30. Davidson, *Race and Class,* 235–236, 243; *HP,* August 24, 1983; Northcott, *TO,* October 20, 1972, August 22, 1975.

31. Crawford and Keever, *John B. Connally,* 316–317, 328 (quote); Knaggs, *Two-Party Texas,* 170–171; Tower, *Consequences,* 207–208; Monroe Lee Billington, *The Political South in the Twentieth Century* (New York: Scribner, 1975), 158.

32. Olien, *From Token to Triumph,* 229–230; Smith, "Little Big Man," 132–136.

33. Olien, *From Token to Triumph,* 231–232 (quote), 233–234; Smith, "Little Big Man," 134–135; Knaggs, *Two-Party Texas,* 172–176; Neal Peirce, *The Great Plains States of America* (New York: W. W. Norton, 1973), 297, 309; Lamis, *Two-Party South,* 200; *TO,* October 20, 1972; "'Solid South': Makings of a New Senate Majority?" *CQWR* 30 (October 18, 1972): 2780–2781. Rural Texans shifted to the right in part because Lyndon Johnson was effectively removed from politics; the rest of the rural South had shifted some years earlier. See Michael Barone, Grant Ujifusa, and Douglas Matthews, *The Almanac of American Politics, 1974* (Boston: Gambit, 1973), 961.

34. *TO,* November 19, 1972; Smith, "Little Big Man," 131 (quote).

35. *HP,* August 24, 1983 (quote); Smith, "Little Big Man," 131; Bob Woodward and Carl Bernstein, *The Final Days* (New York: Avon Books, 1976), 347, 365.

36. Davidson, *Race and Class,* 202; Tower, *Consequences,* 53, 118–119; Smith, "Little Big Man," 84, 134; Carolyn Barta, column in *DMN,* July 9, 1990; Nicholas Lemann, "Underachiever," *New York Review of Books,* June 27, 1991, 44; Jules Witcover, *Marathon* (New York: Viking, 1977), 495, 506–507; *TO,* May 11, 1976 (quote).

37. Doug Harlan, column in *TO,* October 7, 1977; Tower, *Consequences,* 208–210; Knaggs, *Two-Party Texas,* 204–206, 209–210; Olien, *From Token to Triumph,* 245–246.

38. Smith, "Little Big Man," 87 (1st quote): Olien, *From Token to Triumph,* 247–249; Knaggs, *Two-Party Texas,* 214 (2nd quote), 221–225, 226 (3rd quote); Tower, *Consequences,* 208–212; John Geddie, column in *DMN,* November 10, 1978.

39. Knaggs, *Two-Party Texas,* 219.

40. Stewart Davis and Sam Kinch Jr., column in *DMN,* November 12, 1978; Stewart Davis, column in *DMN,* November 9, 1978; Peter Applebome, column in *DMN,* November 11, 1978; *DMN,* December 2, 1978; *TO,* December 29, 1978; Doug Harlan, column in *TO,* July 7, 1978; Knaggs, *Two-Party Texas,* 229–230; Carolyn Barta, column in *DMN,* November 9, 1978; Dave Montgomery, column in *DTH,* November 10, 1978; Bronson Havard, column in *DTH,* November 10, 1978; Bob Estrada, column in *DMN,* June 9, 1991. The Southwest Voter Registration Education Project, "Mexican American Voting in the 1978 Texas General Election," 3–8, disputes several of the above columnists who contend that Tower fared considerably better than Clements among Hispanic voters.

41. Lamis, *Two-Party South,* 204.

42. Lemann, "Underachiever," 45; "How the Superpowers Stand Now," *USNWR,*

January 10, 1983, 19-20; "Is the Hollings Proposal to Incorporate Future National Defense Budgets Sound?" *CD*, November 1979, 272; Sidney Blumenthal, "The Mystique of Sam Nunn," *NR*, March 4, 1991, 26 (1st quote); Pat Towell, "Senate Armed Services Panel Ready for Defense Buildup," January 6, 2003, *CQWR* 39 (March 14, 1981): 469-474; John Winston, "The Percy-Tower Turf War," *National Review*, October 30, 1981, 1256; *Aviation Week and Space Technology*, December 1, 1980, 21; John Tower, "Nothing Less than Military Inferiority," *USNWR*, February 16, 1981, 37 (2nd quote); John Tower, "Congress v. the President: The Formulation and Implementation of American Foreign Policy," *Foreign Affairs* 60 (winter 1980-81): 234-238, 246.

43. Lemann, "Underachiever," 45-46; *TO*, December 26, 1980, September 25, 1981 (quotes).

44. Tower, *Consequences*, 246-251; "A Towering GOP Loss," *Newsweek*, September 5, 1983, 19; *Aviation Week and Space Technology*, April 20, 1984, 54.

45. Tower, *TO*, March 21, 1963.

46. Lemann, "Underachiever," 46.

47. Larry Lee, *TO*, January 21, 1966; *TO*, December 31, 1971, February 14, September 19, October 3, 1975, October 1, 1976, June 26, 1981; "John Tower," *Current Biography*, 427; *DTH*, April 6, 1991; "National Council of Senior Citizens Voting Record," February 1975; John Tower, "The Invisible Hand of Government," *USA Today*, September 1980, 14-15; "Should Congress Significantly Reduce the Scope of the Legal Services Corporation?" *CD*, May 1981, 138; Sherrill, "Tower of Texas," 115.

48. Scores were compiled annually (or sometimes for combined congressional sessions) for all members of Congress by Congressional Quarterly, Inc. The averages have been calculated by the authors.

49. "Reagan Arms Team: A Balanced Ticket," *USNWR*, January 28, 1985, 16; Liz Galtney, "What Did the Swallows Learn in Geneva? A Party Atmosphere and Potential Security Risks Prompted a CIA Inquiry," *USNWR*, February 20, 1989, 27: Schlachter, *FWST*, February 20, 1989 (quote).

50. Tower, *Consequences*, 280-287; Donald Regan, *For the Record* (New York: St. Martin's Press, 1989), 89-91, 401-407; *The Tower Commission Report* (New York: New York Times and Bantam Books, 1987), 79-83, 138; "White House Outlaws," *NR*, March 23, 1987, 7-8; Christopher Hitchens, "Minority Report," *Nation*, March 27, 1989, 402; *DTH*, December 6, 1990; John Felton, "Tower Panel Lays Out Reagan Policy Failures," *CQWR* 45 (February 28, 1987): 339-342. In light of subsequent congressional investigations and criminal trials, a much fuller picture of the Iran-contra scandal has emerged. The best account is given by Theodore Draper, *A Very Thin Line: The Iran-Contra Affairs* (New York: Hill and Wang, 1991).

51. *Tower Commission Report*, 87-99; "CIA Role in Assassination Attempts Detailed," *CQWR* 33 (November 22, 1975): 2573; "Divided Intelligence Panel Issues Final Report," *CQWR* 34 (May 1, 1976): 1019-1025; Tower, *Consequences*, 148-149, 366-367; John Felton, "Gates' Nomination to Head CIA Withdrawn," *CQWR* 45 (March 7, 1987): 418.

52. *DMN*, April 6, 1991.

53. Pat Towell, "Tower Offers Assurances on Policies, Finances," *CQWR* 47 (January 28, 1989): 167–168; *NYT,* December 4, 1988; *WP,* December 9, 1988; Fred Barnes, "Tottering Tower," *NR,* December 19, 1980, 8–10.

54. "The Sleazeball Watch," *NR,* September 14, 21, 1987, 10 (1st quote); Lemann, "Underachiever," 46–47 (2nd quote); Pat Towell, "No Conflict . . . I Have No Interest," *CQWR* 47 (January 28, 1989): 168 (4th quote); Schlachter, *FWST,* February 20, 1989 (3rd quote); Susan Feeney and Robert Dodge, column in *DMN,* April 6, 1991; *NYT,* February 12, 1989.

55. Tower, *Consequences,* 119–121; Suzanne Garment, "The Tower Precedent," *Commentary* 87 (May 1989): 43 (quote).

56. Fred Bonavita, column in *HP,* August 24, 1983; Lemann, "Underachiever," 46–47; Barnes, "Tottering Tower," 8 (quote); Blumenthal, "Mystique of Sam Nunn," 26; Feeney and Dodge, *DMN,* April 6, 1991; *DMN,* April 6, 1991; Donna Cassata, column in *FWST,* December 26, 1990; Schlachter, *FWST,* February 20, 1989; Garment, "Tower Precedent," 47.

57. Tower, *Consequences,* 3–8, 123–128, 179–182, 309–312, 357; Molly Ivins, column in *DTH,* April 6, 1991 (1st quote); Charles M. Cooper, "Oil and Gas in Washington," *World Oil,* January 1989, 29 (2nd quote); Elizabeth Drew, "Letter from Washington," *New Yorker,* March 20, 1989, 98 (3rd quote).

58. Garment, "Tower Precedent," 44; Tower, *Consequences,* 329 (quote).

59. Drew, "Letter from Washington," 98–99 (quote); "Tower Tipples and Topples," *Economist,* March 4, 1989, 23.

60. Tower, *Consequences,* 3–8, 309–312, 357; *NYT,* March 10, 1989, April 6, 1991 (quote).

61. Richard Dunham, column in *DTH,* April 6, 1991; Carl Leubsdorf, column in *DMN,* April 6, 1991.

62. *NYT,* February 9, 1989 (quote).

63. Tower, *Consequences,* 359 (1st quote); William F. Buckley Jr., " John Tower, RIP," *National Review,* April 29, 1991, 16 (2nd quote).

JIM WRIGHT

1. The Royal Hibernian Society, during Wright's speakership, did find information about his ancestry on his maternal side. See also Jim Wright to cousin Robert G. Wright, June 9, 1990, in Jim Wright Collection, Texas Christian University, Fort Worth, Tex. (hereafter cited as JWC); John M. Barry, *The Ambition and the Power* (New York: Penguin Books, 1989), 380; telephone interview with Jim Wright by Ben Procter, January 16, 1992, Houston, Tex.; Jim Wright, "Streams of Hope, Rivers of Fear," chap. 1, 1–2, MS in possession of Jim Wright, Fort Worth, Tex.

2. Wright interview, January 16, 1992; Jim Wright, "To Make a Difference," MS, chap. 1, 24; telephone interview with Jim Wright by Ben Procter, January 18, 1992, Houston, Tex.; Barry, *The Ambition and the Power,* 42–43.

3. Wright interviews, January 16, 18, 1992; Wright, "To Make a Difference," chap. 1, 17–18, 24; Wright, "Streams of Hope," chap. 1, 2–3.

4. Wright interviews, January 16, 18, 1992; interview with Jim Wright by Ben Procter, January 23, 1992, Fort Worth, Tex.; Barry, *The Ambition and the Power,* 43.

5. Wright interviews, January 16, 18, 23, 1992; Wright, "To Make a Difference," chap. 1, 34; Barry, *The Ambition and the Power,* 43. Wright's two younger sisters are Mary Nelle and Betty Lee.

6. Wright, "To Make a Difference," chap. 1, 4, 5; Wright interviews, January 16, 18, 1992.

7. Wright, "To Make a Difference," chap. 1, 6, 7, 11–12, 21–23; Wright interview, January 16, 1992.

8. Wright, "To Make a Difference," chap. 2, 5–6, 21, 23, 24.

9. Ibid., 1–2, 4–5, 9–10; Wright interviews, January 16, 18, 1992.

10. Wright, "To Make a Difference," chap. 2, 15–20, 31–32; chap. 3, 3, 12.

11. Wright, "To Make a Difference," chap. 3, 4–6, 10, 15–16, 22–24; Wright interviews, January 16, 18, 1992.

12. Wright, "To Make a Difference," chap. 4, 1–2, 4, 6, 9, 13–14, 17–19, 21; telephone interview with Jim Wright by Ben Procter, February 5, 1992, Houston, Tex.

13. Wright interviews, January 18, February 5, 1992; Wright, "To Make a Difference," chap. 4, 19–20. See Barry, *The Ambition and the Power,* 43–44, for a different view of Wright's boyhood.

14. Wright interview, February 5, 1992; interview with Jim Wright by twelve members of the national press, June 1, 1989, Washington, D.C.

15. Wright interview, February 5, 1992; telephone interview with Jim Wright by Ben Procter, February 6, 1992, Houston, Tex.

16. Wright interview, February 5, 1992; telephone interview with Jim Wright by Ben Procter, February 6, 1992, Houston, Tex.

17. Wright interview, February 5, 1992; telephone interview with Jim Wright by Ben Procter, February 6, 1992, Houston, Tex.; Wright, "To Make a Difference," chap. 6, 2–3.

18. Wright, "To Make a Difference," chap. 6, 4–8; Wright interview, February 6, 1992.

19. Wright, "To Make a Difference," chap. 6, 12–13; Barry, *The Ambition and the Power,* 46.

20. Wright, "To Make a Difference," chap. 6, 22–51, chap. 7, 1; Wright interview, February 6, 1992; telephone interview with Jim Wright by Ben Procter, February 18, 1992, Houston, Tex.

21. Wright, "To Make a Difference," chap. 7, 1–4, 6, 9, 12, 18, 20–27; Wright interview, February 6, 18, 1992.

22. Wright, "To Make a Difference," chap. 7, 19–20; Barry, *The Ambition and the Power,* 46–48; telephone interview with Jim Wright by Ben Procter, February 20, 1992, Houston, Tex.

23. Wright, "To Make a Difference," chap. 8, 1–6, 11–13; Wright interview, February 18, 1992.

24. Wright, "To Make a Difference," chap. 9, 1–14, 17; chap. 10, 8–18.

25. Ibid., chap. 10, 1–27; Wright interview, February 20, 1992; Barry, *The Ambition and the Power,* 49–50.

26. Wright interview, February 20, 1992; Barry, *The Ambition and the Power,* 50.

27. Ibid.

28. Ibid., 50–51.

29. Wright interview, February 20, 1992. In *The Ambition and the Power,* 51, Barry gives a slightly different interpretation concerning Wright's mayorship.

30. Wright interview, February 20, 1992; Wright, "To Make a Difference," chap. outline, 12–15; interview with Jim Wright by Ben Procter, March 3, 1992, Fort Worth, Tex.; *FWST,* July 22, 1954; July 23, 1954; Kay Crites, "A Man of Peace," honors paper, Tarleton State University, 1991, in JWC; chap. 3; Barry, *The Ambition and the Power,* 51.

31. Wright, "To Make a Difference," chap. 16, 1–2; Jim Wright, "Learning the Ropes in the Eisenhower Years," MS in possession of Jim Wright, Fort Worth, Tex.

32. Wright, "To Make a Difference," chap. outline, 15–17; Barry, *The Ambition and the Power,* 52.

33. Wright interview, March 3, 1992; Jim Wright, "Ike and the World: Race, Rayburn, Recession," 1–6, MS in possession of Jim Wright, Fort Worth, Tex. For a slightly different interpretation, see Barry, *The Ambition and the Power,* 52.

34. Wright, "To Make a Difference," chap. outline, 18–19; Barry, *The Ambition and the Power,* 53; interview with Jim Wright by Ben Procter, March 3, 1992, Fort Worth, Tex.; Jim Wright, "John F. Kennedy," 16–18, MS in possession of Jim Wright, Fort Worth, Tex.

35. Wright, "To Make a Difference," chap. outline, 18–19; Wright, "John F. Kennedy," 1–31; interview with Jim Wright by Ben Procter, March 16, 1992, Fort Worth, Tex.; Barry, *The Ambition and the Power,* 53–55.

36. Wright, "To Make a Difference," chap. outline, 19–20; Jim Wright, "The Great Society," MS in possession of Jim Wright, Fort Worth, Tex.; Jim Wright, "Johnson Ascends," 15–16, 24–25, 31–33, MS in possession of Jim Wright, Fort Worth, Tex.

37. Wright, "To Make a Difference," chap. outline, 20–21; Wright, "Great Society," 1–32ff.; Wright, "Johnson Ascends," 25–28. In November 1973, Texans voted against funding the Trinity River Waterway; therefore, Wright let the matter rest.

38. Wright interview, March 16, 1992; Wright, "Great Society," 1–32ff.; Barry, *The Ambition and the Power,* 54–55. See Jim Wright, *You and Your Congressman* (New York: G. P. Putnam's Sons, 1965); and Jim Wright, *The Coming Water Famine* (New York: Coward-McCann, 1966).

39. Wright interview, March 16, 1992; Wright, "To Make a Difference," chap. outline, 21.

40. Wright interview, March 16, 1992; Wright, "To Make a Difference," chap. outline, 22. See Wright, *You and Your Congressman,* rev. ed. (New York: G. P. Putnam's Sons, 1976), 152–154, and Wright, "Great Society," 29–32, for background and spe-

cifics of the House Vietnam resolution. Because Mab Wright disliked politics so intensely, she divorced Jim Wright in August 1970. On November 12, 1972, Wright married Betty Hay of St. Louis, who had been a secretary for the House Public Works Committee since 1965. See Barry, *The Ambition and the Power,* 54–57ff.

41. Wright interview, March 16, 1992; interview with Jim Wright by Ben Procter, April 26, 1992, Fort Worth, Tex.

42. Wright interview, April 26, 1992; Barry, *The Ambition and the Power,* 14–15.

43. Wright interview, April 26, 1992; Barry, *The Ambition and the Power,* 15–29. See manuscripts on this election in JWC.

44. Jim Wright, "Thoughts on the Years as Majority Leader and Speaker," MS in JWC; interview with Jim Wright by Ben Procter, May 6, 1992, Fort Worth, Tex.; Jim Wright, "This Time, We Must Get the Job Done on Energy Policy," *DMN,* October 28, 1990, in JWC; Wright, "To Make a Difference," chap. outline, 24–25.

45. Wright, "Years as Majority Leader and Speaker"; Wright interview, May 6, 1992; *USNWR,* January 14, 1980, 39; Wright, "To Make a Difference," chap. outline, 25–27.

46. Wright, "Years as Majority Leader and Speaker"; Wright, "To Make a Difference," chap. outline, 27–28; Wright interview, May 6, 1992.

47. Wright, "Years as Majority Leader and Speaker"; Wright, "To Make a Difference," chap. outline, 28–29; Wright interview, May 6, 1992.

48. Wright, "Years as Majority Leader and Speaker"; Wright, "To Make a Difference," chap. outline, 29–32.

49. Wright, "Years as Majority Leader and Speaker"; Wright, "To Make a Difference," chap. outline, 31–33.

50. Wright, "Years as Majority Leader and Speaker"; Wright interview, May 6, 1992; Barbara Sinclair, "House Majority Party Leadership in the Late 1980s," in Lawrence C. Dodd and Bruce I. Oppenheimer, eds., *Congress Reconsidered,* 4th ed. (Washington, D.C.: CQ Press, 1990), 313–314, 316–320.

51. Wright, "Years as Majority Leader and Speaker"; Wright, "To Make a Difference," chap. outline, 32–34; Sinclair, "House Majority Party Leadership," 313–322ff.

52. Wright, "Years as Majority Leader and Speaker"; Wright, "To Make a Difference," chap. outline, 34–39; Barry, *The Ambition and the Power,* 207–211, 309–361.

53. Ben Procter, "Mindless Cannibalism: The Resignation of Speaker Jim Wright," paper delivered at the Southern Historical Association meeting in November 1991, is supported by multiple primary source materials. See also Barry, *The Ambition and the Power,* for the best coverage of Wright's Speakership as well as the activities of Gingrich, Phelan, and the House Ethics Committee. See also Wright, "To Make a Difference," chap. outline, 40–41.

54. Procter, "Mindless Cannibalism"; Barry, *The Ambition and the Power;* Wright, "To Make a Difference," chap. outline, 41–45.

55. Procter, "Mindless Cannibalism"; Barry, *The Ambition and the Power;* Wright, "To Make a Difference," chap. outline, 45–46.

56. Procter, "Mindless Cannibalism"; Barry, *The Ambition and the Power,* 757–

763; "Home Folks Favor Race by Wright," *FWST,* June 25, 1989; Jim Wright to Martin Frost, December 27, 1989; Wright Letter File, in JWC; John M. Barry, "Wright Legacy Brightens after Two Years," *Roll Call,* July 11, 1991, 1.

57. Jim Wright, *Balance of Power: Presidents and Congress from the Era of McCarthy to the Age of Gingrich* (Atlanta: Turner Publishing, 1996), 514.

LLOYD BENTSEN

1. "Ninety Long Minutes in Omaha," *Time,* October 17, 1988, 20–22; *NYT,* October 5, 1988.

2. "Ninety Long Minutes in Omaha," *Time,* October 17, 1988, 20–22; *NYT,* October 5, 1988; Eleanor Clift and Larry Martz, "In Search of a Message," *Newsweek,* October 17, 1988, 22–23.

3. "Ninety Long Minutes," 20-22.

4. Ibid.; Michael Kramer, "The Electronic Campaign: The Peacock's Head in the Sand," *USNWR,* October 17, 1988, 37.

5. Joseph Alter and Eleanor Clift, *Newsweek,* October 10, 1988, 40–41; Gloria Borger, "Now Ready for Prime Time?" *USNWR,* October 10, 1988, 22–23; Howard Fineman, "Atlanta's Odd Couple," *Newsweek,* July 25, 1988, 16 20; Fred Bames, "Bentsen and Hedges," *NR,* August 1, 1988, 18; Molly Ivins, "Corporation Man," *Nation,* July 30, 1988, 81, August 6, 1988, 81–82; "The Duke and the Baron," *NR,* August 1, 1988, 10; Richard Stengel, "An Indelicate Balance," *Time,* July 25, 1988, 20–21.

6. For more favorable portraits of Bentsen, see Douglas Harbrecht, "Why Bland Lloyd Bentsen Was Just the Ticket," *Business Week,* July 25, 1988, 30; "The Liberal's Conservative," *National Review,* November 7, 1988, 15; W. P. Hoar, "Eyes of Texas Are on Lloyd Bentsen," *Conservative Digest,* August 1988, 53–58.

7. Joseph C. Goulden, "Bentsen: Money Man from Texas," *Nation,* March 8, 1975, 267–269; Paul R. Wieck, "Lloyd Bentsen: Progressive Capitalist," *NR,* November 22, 1975, 15–16; Jan Jarboe, "Lord of the Valley," *Texas Monthly,* January 1986, 184; Mrs. James Watson, comp., *The Lower Rio Grande Valley of Texas and Its Builders* (Mission, Tex.: Lower Rio Grande Valley and Its Builders, Inc., 1931), 306.

8. Jarboe, "Lord of the Valley," 184–187; Kaye Northcott, "Lloyd Bentsen's Fortune," *TO,* December 29, 1989.

9. A. I. Reinert, "The Unveiling of Lloyd Bentsen," *Texas Monthly,* December 1974, 66–68; Wieck, "Progressive Capitalist," 16; William W. Hamilton, "Can a Rich Guy Lose in Texas?" *Nation,* September 28, 1970, 274–276; Goulden, "Money Man from Texas," 267–269.

10. Bruce Collins, interview with Lloyd Bentsen, "American Profile," C-Span Network, June 1991 (hereafter cited as Bentsen interview); Reinert, "Unveiling of Lloyd Bentsen," 66–68; Mark Nelson, "Quiet Contender," *Houston City Magazine,* July 1982, 34.

11. Bentsen interview; Wieck, "Progressive Capitalist," 15–16; the subject of South Texas machine politics in the earlier twentieth century has been surveyed credibly in Evan Anders, *Boss Rule in South Texas* (Austin: University of Texas Press, 1979).

12. For a discussion of Mr. Rayburn's "Board of Education" and its significance in plotting legislative strategy, see D. B. Hardeman and Donald Bacon, *Rayburn: A Biography* (Houston: Gulf Publishing Co., 1987), 303–308, 389–390.

13. Bentsen interview.

14. *CR*, 81st Cong., 2nd sess., 10534; Margaret Carlson, "Patrician Power Player," *Time*, July 25, 1988, 22–23.

15. Carlson, "Patrician Power Player," 22–23; Nelson, "Quiet Contender," 36–37.

16. Goulden, "Money Man from Texas," 267–269; Gerald Rosen, "A Democrat Businessmen Like," *Dun's Review,* March 1975, 67–69.

17. Hamilton, "Rich Guy Lose in Texas?" 275; Reinert, "Unveiling of Lloyd Bentsen," 74, 104; Nelson, "Quiet Contender," Morton Krondracke, "Is Bentsen a Democrat?" *NR,* September 26, 1988, 22; Goulden, "Money Man from Texas," 270.

18. Paul Burka, "Texas Primer: Bentsen vs. Bush," *Texas Monthly,* September 1988, 112.

19. James Reston Jr., *The Lone Star: The Life of John Connally* (New York: Harper and Row, 1989), 377–378; Ronnie Dugger, "Hot After Yarborough," *NR,* April 18, 1970, 11–12; Hamilton, "Rich Guy Lose in Texas," 274–275.

20. James Reston Jr., *The Lone Star: The Life of John Connally* (New York: Harper and Row, 1989), 377–378; Ronnie Dugger, "Hot After Yarborough," *NR,* April 18, 1970, 11–12; Hamilton, "Rich Guy Lose in Texas," 274–275; Wieck, "Progressive Capitalist," 15–17.

21. Goulden, "Bentsen: Money Man from Texas," 269–270; Reinert, "Unveiling of Lloyd Bentsen," 67–68; Dugger, "Hot After Yarborough," 12; Paul R. Wieck, "The Other Texan: Bentsen in '76?" *NR,* December 29, 1973, 8–10.

22. "Conservative v. Conservative," *Texas Business,* September 1982, 37; James Fallows, "Can Another Texan Apply?" *Atlantic,* December 1974, 86–90.

23. Burka, "Texas Primer," 112; Nelson, "Quiet Contender," 37; Goulden, "Money Man from Texas," 270.

24. Rosen, "Democrat Businessmen Like," 68; Wieck, "Progressive Capitalist," 16–17; *DMN,* May 21, 1991.

25. Krondracke, "Is Bentsen a Democrat?" 21–23.

26. Goulden, "Money Man from Texas," 267–268; "Bentsen Continues His Banking War," *Business Week,* February 2, 1974, 26; Krondracke, "Is Bentsen a Democrat?" 22–23.

27. Wieck, "The Other Texan," 8–10.

28. Ibid.; see also "Bentsen Continues Banking War."

29. Goulden, "Money Man from Texas," 267–270.

30. Wieck, "The Other Texan," 8–10; Fallows, "Can Another Texan Apply?" 86–90.

31. *NYT,* February 18, 1975.

32. Wieck, "The Other Texan," 8-10.

33. Wieck, "Progressive Capitalist," 15-17.

34. "Bentsen: No Chasing of Rainbows," *Time,* September 19, 1975, 31-32; Howard Gleckman and Douglas Harbrecht, "In Taxes and Trade, Lloyd Bentsen Is the Senator to See," *Business Week,* December 15, 1986, 39; "Guess Who's Not Coming to Brunch," *Newsweek,* February 16, 1987, 19; Jim Hightower, "Senate Series: Texas," *NR,* October 30, 1976, 13-14; Lloyd Bentsen, "American Foreign Policy," *Vital Speeches of the Day,* October 15, 1974, 25-28.

35. "Bentsen: No Chasing of Rainbows," *Time,* September 29, 1975, 31-32; Howard Gleckman and Douglas Harbrecht, "In Taxes and Trade, Lloyd Bentsen is the Senator to See," *Business Week,* December 15, 1986, 39; "Guess Who's Not Coming to Brunch," *Newsweek,* February 16, 1987, 19; Jim Hightower, "Senate Series: Texas," *NR,* October 30, 1976, 13-14; Lloyd Bentsen, "American Foreign Policy," *Vital Speeches of the Day,* October 15, 1974, 25-28.

36. The speeches Senator Bentsen delivered in the United States Senate, too numerous to list here, may be found in *CR,* along with extended remarks and votes cast.

37. Bentsen interview.

38. Bentsen interview; Krondracke, "Is Bentsen a Democrat?" 20-21; Rosen, "Democrat Businessmen Like," 67-69.

39. Peter Applebome, "The Battle for Texas," *New York Times Magazine,* October 30, 1988, 34-37, 66-69, 100-101.

40. Lloyd Bentsen, "Acceptance Speech," *Vital Speeches of the Day,* August 15, 1988, 645-646.

41. Applebome, "Battle for Texas," 34, 37, 66-69, 101; Stengel, "Indelicate Balance," 20-21; "How Blind a Trust," *Newsweek,* August 29, 1988, 29; "In Search of a Message," *Newsweek,* October 17, 1988, 22-23; Bentsen, "Acceptance Speech," 645-646; William Murchison, "How to Start a Landslide," *National Review,* November 7, 1988, 48; Marci McDonald, "A Presidential Misstep," *MacLean's,* July 25, 1988, 14-15; *WP,* July 13, 1988; Peter Ross Range and Gloria Borger, "The Bentsen Factor," *USNWR,* July 25, 1988, 22-23.

42. Douglas Harbrecht and Howard Gleckman, "Lloyd Bentsen Is Having a Ball Bashing George Bush," *Business Week,* October 23, 1989, 57.

43. Reinert, "Unveiling of Lloyd Bentsen," 66-68.

44. Richard Dunham, "Very Slow, Very Steady," *Business Week,* December 21, 1992, 26; Richard Dunham, "The Courtly, Cunning New Man at Treasury," *Business Week,* December 21, 1992, 28; Paul Craig Roberts, "Lloyd Bentsen Has the Soul of a Supply Sider," *Business Week,* January 25, 1993, 16.

45. Dunham, "Very Slow, Very Steady," 26; Dunham, "New Man at Treasury," 28; P. C. Roberts, "A Supply Sider at Treasury," *National Review,* February 1, 1993, 47.

46. "That Wasn't in the Job Description," *Business Week,* June 21, 1993, 36; Donald Brock, "Lloyds of Clinton," *American Spectator,* October 1994, 24-26.

47. "Wasn't in the Job Description," 36.

GEORGE BUSH

1. Michael Duffy, "Mr. Consensus," *Time,* August 21, 1989, 22.

2. George Bush with Victor Gold, *Looking Forward: An Autobiography* (Garden City, N.Y.: Doubleday, 1987), 23–39; Fitzhugh Green, *George Bush: An Intimate Portrait* (New York: Hippocrene Books, 1989), 1–18; Nicholas King, *George Bush: A Biography* (New York: Dodd, Mead, and Company, 1980), 1–16.

3. Harry Hurt III, "George Bush, Plucky Lad," *Texas Monthly,* June 1983, 142–143; Bush and Gold, *Looking Forward,* 29–32.

4. Bush and Gold, *Looking Forward,* 32–40; Joe Hyams, *Flight of the Avenger: George Bush at War* (San Diego: Harcourt Brace Jovanovich, 1991), 157–158; George Bush with Doug Wead, *Man of Integrity* (Eugene, Ore.: Harvest House Publishers, 1988), 1-2; Richard Ben Cramer, "George Bush: How He Got Here," *Esquire* 115 (June 1991): 75–82.

5. Bush and Gold, *Looking Forward,* 41–46; Hurt, "Plucky Lad," 192.

6. Bush and Gold, *Looking Forward,* 46; Darwin Payne, *Initiative in Energy: Dresser Industries, Inc., 1880–1978* (New York: Simon and Schuster, 1979), 232; Cramer, "How He Got Here," 82–88.

7. George Bush, "Texas 1948: Some Fond Memories," *American West* 23 (January–February 1986): 36–40; Roger M. Olien and Diana Davids Olien, *Wildcatters: Texas Independent Oilmen* (Austin: Texas Monthly Press, 1984), x, 89–92.

8. Olien and Olien, *Wildcatters,* 93; Hurt, "Plucky Lad," 193; Cramer, "How He Got Here," 128–134.

9. Hurt, "Plucky Lad," 193–194; Bush and Gold, *Looking Forward,* 67–69.

10. Green, *George Bush,* 66–68; Bush and Gold, *Looking Forward,* 70–73; Hearing Before the Committee on Armed Services, U.S. Senate, 94th Cong., 1st sess., Hearing on Nomination of George Bush to be Director of Central Intelligence, December 15, 16, 1975 (Washington, D.C.: GPO, 1975), 5.

11. Bush and Gold, *Looking Forward,* 84–85; Chandler Davidson, *Race and Class in Texas Politics* (Princeton: Princeton University Press, 1990), 137–138, 202; Ronnie Dugger, "The Substance of the Senate Campaign," *TO,* September 18, 1964.

12. Roger M. Olien, *From Token to Triumph: The Texas Republicans Since 1920* (Dallas: Southern Methodist University Press, 1982), 191–192; Paul D. Cassdorph, *A History of the Republican Party in Texas, 1865–1965* (Austin: Pemberton Press, 1965), 233–247.

13. Green, *George Bush,* 89.

14. *TO,* October 14, 1966; Olien, *From Token to Triumph,* 212; "Bush Bulletin" (campaign letter) No. 1, May 10, 1966, 1; "George Bush for Congress," *TO,* October 25, 1966.

15. Bush and Gold, *Looking Forward,* 95–96.

16. "Bush Responds to Bentsen's Charge," *DMN,* October 2, 1970; *TO,* 90th Cong., 1st sess., 4567 (February 27, 1967); *TO,* 90th Cong., 2nd sess., 8656 (April 2, 1968); *TO,* 90th Cong., 2nd sess., 18594 (June 25, 1968); Green, *George Bush,* 105;

President Bush: The Challenge Ahead (Washington, D.C.: Congressional Quarterly, 1989), 11–12.

17. Bush and Gold, *Looking Forward,* 92–93; Hurt, "Plucky Lad," 197.

18. Bush and Gold, *Looking Forward,* 98–99; *DMN,* April 29, 1990.

19. *DMN,* October 8, 1970; Olien, *From Token to Triumph,* 223; Bush and Gold, *Looking Forward,* 101–103.

20. Seymour Maxwell Finger, *American Ambassadors at the UN* (New York: Holmes and Meier, 1988), 195–222.

21. Ibid.; Bush and Gold, *Looking Forward,* 107–120; Green, *George Bush,* 126.

22. Bush and Gold, *Looking Forward,* 119; Hurt, "Plucky Lad," 200; Green, *George Bush,* 126.

23. Green, *George Bush,* 119; Bush and Gold, *Looking Forward,* 120.

24. Bush and Gold, *Looking Forward,* 129–149; Bruce W. Nelan, "Getting China Wrong," *Time,* June 10, 1991, 35–36.

25. Bush and Gold, *Looking Forward,* 153–158.

26. Ray S. Cline, *The CIA under Reagan, Bush, and Casey: The Evolution of the Agency from Roosevelt to Reagan* (Washington, D.C.: Acropolis Books, 1981), 19, 265–325; Hearing before the Committee on Armed Services, U.S. Senate, 94th Cong., 1st sess., on Nomination of George Bush, 9; U.S. Senate, Committee on Armed Services. Nomination of George Bush, Ex Rpt. 94-21, January 6, 1976 (Washington, D.C.: GPO, 1976), 1976 CIS Microfiche S204-1.

27. Cline, *CIA under Reagan, Bush,* 19, 226–269; Bush and Gold, *Looking Forward,* 162–179.

28. Green, *George Bush,* 165–174; Hurt, "Plucky Lad," 202; Tom Overton, "At Home: George and Barbara Bush," *TO,* May 5, 1979; Scott Bennett, "Connally vs. Bush: Who's Better for Business?" *Texas Business* 4 (September 1979): 24–64; Arthur E. Wiese, *George Bush: Interview on the Issues* (Washington, D.C.: Political Profiles, Inc., 1979), 3–28.

29. Michael Kramer, "George Bush: A Republican for All Factions," *New York* 13 (January 21, 1980): 43–47; Hurt, "Plucky Lad," 202–204; Roy Reed, "Bush on the Move," *New York Times Magazine,* February 10, 1980, 20–54; Roy Reed, "The Candidate," *Houston City Magazine,* April 1980, 29; Bush and Gold, *Looking Forward,* 183–213.

30. Bush and Gold, *Looking Forward,* 3–16; Joseph Kraft, "Heart of Texas Lies in Suburbs," *TO,* September 9, 1980; "The Vice President," *Washington Star,* January 20, 1981; Bill Peterson, "For Bush, a Potential for the Spotlight," *WP,* January 20, 1981.

31. Lance Morrow, "The Strange Destiny of a Vice President," *Time,* May 20, 1991, 23; Bush and Gold, *Looking Forward,* 226–239.

32. *We the People: An American Celebration, 1985 Presidential Inauguration* (Washington, D.C.: 1985 Presidential Inaugural Committee, 1985), 31.

33. Jane Ely, "OK Aggies, Now You Can Gloat," *HC,* May 1991.

34. Jack W. Germond and Jules Witcover, *Wake Us When It's Over: Presidential*

Politics of 1984 (New York: Macmillan, 1985), 510–512; Garry Wills, *Reagan's America* (New York: Penguin Books, 1988), 236; *We the People,* 47.

35. Hurt, "Plucky Lad," 206; *We the People,* 33–37; see *Millie's Book as Dictated to Barbara Bush* (New York: William Morrow, 1990).

36. Green, *George Bush,* 216–218; Gail Sheehy, *Character: America's Search for Leadership* (New York: William Morrow, 1988), 154–160; Marvin Kalb and Hendrik Hertzberg, *Candidates '88* (Dover, Mass.: Auburn House Publishing Company, 1989), 282.

37. Peter Applebome, "The Battle for Texas," *New York Times Magazine,* October 30, 1988, 34–37; Jack W. Germond and Jules Witcover, "Bush's Efforts to Broaden Base Could Hurt His Image," *TO,* February 7, 1986; Elizabeth Drew, *Election Journal: Political Events of 1987–1988* (New York: William Morrow, 1989), 47, 87; Peter Goldman, Tom Mathews et al., *The Quest for the Presidency, 1988* (New York: Simon and Schuster, 1989), 198–201.

38. Bert A. Rockman, "The Leadership Style of George Bush," in Colin Campbell and Bert A. Rockman, eds., *The Bush Presidency: First Appraisals* (Chatham, N.J.: Chatham House Publishers, 1991), 30; Peggy Noonan, *What I Saw at the Revolution: A Political Life in the Reagan Era* (New York: Random House, 1990) 298–317; Green, *George Bush,* 225; Goldman and Mathews, *Quest for the Presidency,* 328–329.

39. David R. Runkel, ed., *Campaign for President: The Managers Look at '88* (Dover, Mass.: Auburn House Publishing Company, 1989), ix; Green, *George Bush;* Goldman and Mathews, *Quest for the Presidency,* 226–240, 357–361.

40. Applebome, "Battle for Texas," 34–101; Green, *George Bush,* 242–244.

41. *President Bush: The Challenge Ahead* (Washington, D.C.: Congressional Quarterly, 1989), 107–118; Tony Kornheiser, "Cutting Chaff and Shooting Straight with Jim Baker," *WP,* January 18, 1981.

42. John Dillin, "Bush: Slow Start, Mixed Reviews," *Christian Science Monitor,* April 10, 1989, 1–2; "Chief Concerns," *DMN,* November 5, 1989; Rockman, "Leadership Style of George Bush," 31; Campbell and Rockman, "Conclusion," in *The Bush Presidency,* 293–294; for a critical appraisal see Charles Tiefer, *The Semi-Sovereign Presidency: The Bush Administration's Strategy for Governing without Congress* (Boulder, Colo.: Westview Press, 1994); see also David Mervin, *George Bush and the Guardianship Presidency* (New York: St. Martin's Press), 1996.

43. George J. Church, "Showing Muscle," *Time,* January 1, 1990, 20–31; Carl Leubsdorf, "President's First Year Ends on High Note," *DMN,* January 14, 1990, sec. A, 1; Alexander DeConde, *Presidential Machismo* (Boston: Northeastern University Press, 2000), 247.

44. Kevin Merida, "Patronage and the President," *DMN,* May 14, 1990; Kevin Merida and Susan Feeney, "Texan at the Top," *DMN,* May 3, 1990; Susan Feeney and Kevin Merida, "Lone Star Fever," *DMN,* May 15, 1990.

45. David Plesa, "Houston Gears for GOP," *TO,* July 15, 1990; Carl Leubsdorf, "New Global Order Tops Agenda," *DMN,* July 8, 1990.

46. Michael Kramer, "Read My Slips," *Time,* August 20, 1990, 18-22; Michael Kramer, "Must This Mean War?" *Time,* August 27, 1990, 14-30.

47. Dan Goodgame, "Two Faces of George Bush," *Time,* July 2, 1990, 23; Carl Leubsdorf, "Bush Losing Popularity over Budget," *DMN,* October 14, 1990; James Reston Jr., "Bush Fumbles the Little Things," *DMN,* October 22, 1990; John Greenwald, "All Shook Up," *Time,* October 15, 1990, 30-56; Otto Friedrich, "On the War Path," *Time,* November 12, 1990, 24-38; George J. Church, "Raising the Ante," *Time,* November 19, 1990, 46-51.

48. Carolyn Barta, "President Bush at Midterm," *DMN,* December 16, 1990; George J. Church, "A Tale of Two Bushes," *Time,* January 7, 1991, 3-31; Robert Kaufman, "Appeasement Can Only Hurt Bush," *Denton Record Chronicle,* November 19, 1990, sec. A, 8; Georgie Anne Geyer, "Year Closes with a Question Mark," *DMN,* January 1, 1991.

49. Michael Kramer, "The Moment of Truth," *Time,* January 21, 1991, 22-44; Strobe Talbot, "A Storm Erupts," *Time,* January 28, 1991, 16-71.

50. Lance Morrow, "The Fog of War," *Time,* February 4, 1991, 16-18; George J. Church, "Combat in the Sands," *Time,* February 11, 1991, 16-55; George J. Church, "Saddam's Endgame," *Time,* February 25, 1991, 16-55; Anne Reifenberg, "Ground War Begins," *DMN,* February 24, 1991; Anne Reifenberg and Ed Timms, "Allies Blitz Iraqi Positions," *DMN,* February 25, 1991; Carl Leubsdorf, "Bush Declares Victory," *DMN,* February 28, 1991; See Bob Woodward, *The Commanders* (New York: Simon and Schuster, 1991).

51. Lance Morrow, "Triumphant Return," *Time,* March 18, 1991, 18-58; Nancy Gibbs, "Making Sense of the Storm," *Time,* June 17, 1991, 23-26.

52. Richard Lacayo, "Back to Reality," *Time,* April 22, 1991, 28-29; Dan Goodgame, "Why Not the Best?" *Time,* May 20, 1991, 16; Richard Brookhiser, "Two Centuries of New World Order," *Time,* May 6, 1991, 76; Richard Rose, *The Postmodern President: George Bush Meets the World,* 2nd ed. (Chatham, N.J: Chatham House Publishers, 1991), 305-338; Strobe Talbot, "The Summit Goodfellas," *Time,* August 5, 1991, 20-24.

53. Michael Duffy, " Let's Stay in Touch," *Time,* September 2, 1991, 48; Lance Morrow, "The Russian Revolution," *Time,* September 2, 1991, 20-44; Stanley W. Cloud, "After the War," *Time,* September 9, 1991, 16-18.

54. Michael Kramer, "Shame on Them All," *Time,* October 21, 1991, 46.

55. Carl Leubsdorf, "President Set to Begin Fund-Raising," *DMN,* October 31, 1991; William McKenzie, "Can George Bush Move From Steward to Reformer?" *DMN,* October 31, 1991; Carl Leubsdorf, "Bush Shake-up Reassures Few," *DMN,* December 7, 1991; Jack E. White, "Clearing the Decks," *Time,* December 16, 1991, 33-34; Michael Duffy, "Loyal but Not So Arrogant," *Time,* December 16, 1991, 36.

56. Jill Smolowe, "Why Should Americans Care?" *Time,* November 11, 1991, 56; *DMN,* December 5, 1991; Strobe Talbot, "A State That Deserved to Die," *Time,* December 30, 1991, 28; Carl Leubsdorf, "Questions Raised About Health's Effect on Campaign," *DMN,* January 9, 1992.

57. "Bush Team Steps Up Efforts," *DMN,* January 19, 1992; Carl Leubsdorf,

"Americans Need Help Now," *DMN,* January 29, 1992; Peter Goldman, Thomas M. DeFrank et al., *The Quest for the Presidency, 1992* (College Station: Texas A&M University Press, 1994), 341, 367, 381–384.

58. Michael Duffy and Dan Goodgame, "Warrior for the Status Quo," *Time,* August 24, 1992, 32–45; Laurence I. Barret, "The Fat Lady Hasn't Quite Sung," *Time,* November 1, 1992, 24–27; Bob Woodward, "The Anatomy of a Decision, *WP,* October 12–18, 1992 (National Weekly edition); *DMN,* November 5, 1992; Goldman, DeFrank, *Quest for the Presidency,* 517, 605, 614.

59. Michael Kramer, "Playing Out the End Game," *Time,* October 26, 1992, 43; "Bringing It All Back Home," *Time,* July 29, 1991, 13; Carl Leubsdorf and Kathy Lewis, "Bush Picks A&M as Site for Library," *DMN,* May 4, 1991; Paul Burka, "The Revision Thing," *Texas Monthly,* November 1997, 136–140, 166–168, 170; Barbara Bush, *Barbara Bush: A Memoir* (New York: Charles Scribner's Sons, 1994), 516, 529–530; Herbert S. Parnet, *George Bush: The Life of a Lone Star Yankee* (New York: Scribner, 1997), 510–511.

60. David E. Alsobrook, "The Birth of the Tenth Presidential Library," http:/ bushlibrary.tamu.edu/museum/library/giq.html (accessed 5/21/2002); "Feature Exhibits," http:/bushlibrary.tamu.edu/museum/exhibits/41.html (accessed 5/21/2002); Burka, "Revision Thing," 168.

61. "Welcome to the George Bush Presidential Library and Museum," http:// bushlibrary.tamu.edu/home.html (accessed 5/21/2002); Rosemary Williams, "The Presidential Corridor," *Texas Highways,* March 2002, 14.

62. George Bush and Brent Scowcroft, *A World Transformed* (New York: Alfred A. Knopf, 1998), xi, 566.

63. Dana Milbank, *Smashmouth: Notes from the 2000 Campaign Trail* (New York: Basic Books, 2001), 79; Martha Brant and Weston Kosova, "The Queen Mother," *Newsweek,* May 13, 2002, 36; "Endgame," *USNWR,* November 27, 2000, 24–48; Roger Simon, *Divided We Stand* (New York: Crown Publishers, 2001), 67–69.

64. http://www.nationalgrocers.org/NewsReleases2002/NR2002-10.html (accessed 5/21/2002); Bush, *Barbara Bush,* 535; Connie Mabin, "Elder Bush's Address Includes Cynicism Concerns, Carvey Jokes," *DMN,* May 19, 2002 (Texas and Southwest News).

HENRY B. GONZALEZ

1. "PAC" refers to a political action committee. Molly Ivins, "Henry Gonzalez," *FWST,* November 30, 2000.

2. For more on the expatriate elite, see Richard García, chap. 8: "The Exiled Ricos," in *The Rise of the Mexican American Middle Class: San Antonio, 1929–1941* (College Station: Texas A&M University Press, 1991); Eugene Rodriguez Jr., *Henry B. Gonzalez: A Political Profile* (New York: Arno Press, 1976), 30–32; Pete Hamill, "Henry B. Gonzalez," in Caroline Kennedy, ed., *Profiles in Courage for Our Time* (New York: Hyperion Books, 2002), 91, 94.

3. García, *Mexican American Middle Class,* chap. 8.

4. The original Spanish of Saint Teresa is: "Nada te turbe/Nada te epante/Todo se pasa/La paciencia todo lo alcanza/Quien a Dios tiene la falta/Solo Dios basta (translation by JLP). Rodriguez, *Henry B. Gonzalez,* 32–39; Ronnie Dugger, "Henry Gonzalez: His Life and Times," *TO,* June 13, 1958; Hamill, "Henry B. Gonzalez," 94–95.

5. Rodriguez, *Henry B. Gonzalez,* 39–45; Ronnie Dugger, "Gonzalez of San Antonio," *TO,* May 7, 1957 (reprinted January 10, 1985); Hamill, "Henry B. Gonzalez," 97.

6. Julie Leininger Pycior, *LBJ and Mexican Americans: The Paradox of Power* (Austin: University of Texas Press, 1997), 55–56; Rodriguez, *Henry B. Gonzalez,* 47.

7. Rodriguez, *Henry B. Gonzalez,* 50–63; Hamill, "Henry B. Gonzalez," 98.

8. Rodriguez, *Henry B. Gonzalez,* 50–63; Hamill, "Henry B. Gonzalez," 98.

9. Hamill, "Henry B. Gonzalez," 98; Rodriguez, *Henry B. Gonzalez,* 65–71.

10. During the 1840s José Antonio Navarro had served in the State Senate as an appointee. Pycior, *LBJ and Mexican Americans,* 89; Rodriguez, *Henry B. Gonzalez,* 72–77, 110.

11. Mario T. García, *Mexican Americans: Leadership, Ideology, and Identity, 1930–1960* (New Haven: Yale University Press, 1989), 49–51; Pycior, *LBJ and Mexican Americans,* 93–95, 101; Robert Caro, *The Years of Lyndon Johnson: Master of the Senate* (New York: Alfred A. Knopf, 2002), 789–799.

12. Dugger, "Gonzalez of San Antonio"; Rodriguez, *Henry B. Gonzalez,* 80; Hamill, "Henry B. Gonzalez," 99–100; Pycior, *LBJ and Mexican Americans,* 103; Ivins, "Henry Gonzalez"; "Henry B. González," http://www.loc.gov/rr/hispanic/congress/gonzalez.html (hereafter cited as "González," loc.gov).

13. Pycior, *LBJ and Mexican Americans,* 104, 116, 118, 121; Hamill, "Henry B. Gonzalez," 101.

14. Rodriguez, *Henry B. Gonzalez,* 95–96, 112–116; Hamill, "Henry B. Gonzalez," 98; Pycior, *LBJ and Mexican Americans,* 124–147.

15. Pycior, *LBJ and Mexican Americans,* 127–128; Rodriguez, 119–120, 125–127; Chandler Davidson, *Race and Class in Texas Politics* (Princeton: Princeton University Press, 1990), 52–53; Hamill, "Henry B. Gonzalez," 103.

16. Hamill, "Henry B. Gonzalez," 101–102.

17. Pycior, *LBJ and Mexican Americans,* 143; Hamill, "Henry B. Gonzalez," 104.

18. Pycior, *LBJ and Mexican Americans,* 152–153; Rodriguez, *Henry B. Gonzalez,* 127; James E. Garcia, "Maverick Congressman Memorialized as 'A Voice for the Downtrodden,'" http://www.politicomagazine.com/henryb112900.html.

19. Rodriguez, *Henry B. Gonzalez,* 128–129, 136; Pycior, *LBJ and Mexican Americans,* 190–192, 195, 217–218.

20. Pycior, *LBJ and Mexican Americans,* 217, 227, 232; Henry B. Gonzalez, *CR,* 91st Cong., 1st sess., April 22, 1969.

21. Louis Dubose, "Naked City," *Austin Chronicle,* December 1, 2000; Michael King, "The Legacy of Henry B. Gonzalez," *Austin Chronicle,* December 8, 2000.

22. Hamill, "Henry B. Gonzalez," 104; King, "Legacy of Henry B. Gonzalez."

23. "González," loc.gov; "Profile in Courage," http://www.geocities.com/theaddictedtourist/gonzalez.html; Winton Pitcoff, "Congressman Henry Gonzalez," *Shelterforce Online* (National Housing Institute), http://www.nhi.org/online/issues/98/pitcoff.html.

24. Dubose, "Naked City"; King, "Legacy of Henry B. Gonzalez"; Hamill, "Henry B. Gonzalez," 104.

25. Pitcoff, "Congressman Henry Gonzalez"; Hamill, "Henry B. Gonzalez," 104–105; "González," loc.gov.

26. King, "Legacy of Henry B. Gonzalez"; Pitcoff, "Congressman Henry Gonzalez"; "González," loc.gov; Kennedy, *Profiles in Courage for Our Time*, 4–7; Hamill, "Henry B. Gonzalez," 106–107.

CONTRIBUTORS

RICHARD BAILEY is a professor of history and the vice president of instruction at San Jacinto College North. His doctoral dissertation remains the definitive study on the subject of Morris Sheppard.

D. CLAYTON BROWN, professor of history at Texas Christian University, is the author of *Electricity for Rural America* (1980). In 1975 he won the Texas State Historical Association's H. Bailey Carroll Award for "Sam Rayburn and the Development of Public Power in the Southwest," *Southwestern Historical Quarterly* (1974).

WALTER L. BUENGER, professor of history and interim department head at Texas A&M University, won the Texas State Historical Association's Tullis Award for his most recent book *Path to a Modern South: Northeast Texas Between Reconstruction and the Great Depression* (2001). He is also the author of *Texas Merchant: Marvin Leonard and Fort Worth* (1998), *But Also Good Business: Texas Commerce Banks and the Financing of Houston and Texas* (1986), and *Secession and the Union in Texas* (1984).

MICHAEL L. COLLINS, professor of history and dean of the College of Liberal Arts at Midwestern State University, is the author of *That Damned Cowboy: Theodore Roosevelt and the American West, 1883–1898* (1989) and is a coeditor of *Profiles in Power*.

PATRICK L. COX is an assistant director of the Center for American History at the University of Texas at Austin and is the author of *Ralph W. Yarborough: The People's Senator* (2001) and numerous articles on Texas and twentieth-century American history. He is a coeditor of *Profiles in Power*.

DOROTHY DEMOSS, professor of history at Texas Woman's University, is a specialist in women's history, the history of Texas, and twentieth-century American history.

GEORGE N. GREEN, professor of history at the University of Texas at Arlington, is the author of *The Establishment in Texas Politics: The Primitive Years, 1938–1957* (1979) and numerous articles on Texas and twentieth-century American history.

KENNETH E. HENDRICKSON JR., Hardin Distinguished Professor of American History and chair of the Department of History at Midwestern State University, is a former member of the executive council of the Texas State Historical Association and of the board of directors of the Texas Oral History Association. He is the president of the East Texas Historical Association and the immediate past president of Phi Alpha Theta. His major publications include *The Waters of the Brazos: A History of the Brazos River Authority* (1981), *Hard Times in Oklahoma* (1983), and *The Chief Executives of Texas from Stephen F. Austin to John B. Connally Jr.* He is a coeditor of *Profiles in Power.*

ROBERT C. HILDERBRAND, professor of history at the University of South Dakota, is the author of *Power and the People: Executive Management of Public Opinion in Foreign Affairs, 1897–1921* (1981) and *The Complete Press Conferences of Woodrow Wilson,* vol. 50 of *The Papers of Woodrow Wilson* (1985).

JOHN J. KUSHMA has taught history and political science at the University of Pennsylvania and the University of Texas at Arlington. He is a coeditor of *Essays on American Antebellum Politics, 1840–1860* (1982) and of *Essays on the Postbellum Southern Economy* (1985). He now works in the fields of mediation and labor relations.

VISTA MCCROSKEY, former assistant professor of history at the University of Texas at Tyler, is a former member of the staff of the Texas State Historical Association and is a specialist in women's history, Texas history and the Old South.

BEN PROCTER, professor emeritus of history at Texas Christian University, is a past president of the Texas State Historical Association and is the author of numerous books and articles on Texas history. Among his credits are *Not Without Honor: The Life of John H. Reagan* (1962), *Texas Under a Cloud* (1972), *Just One Riot: Episodes of Texas Rangers in the Twentieth Century* (1991), and *William Randolph Hearst: The Early Years, 1863–1910* (1998).

JULIE LEININGER PYCIOR, associate professor of history at Manhattan College, is the author of *LBJ and Mexican Americans: The Paradox of Power* (winner of the 1997 T. R. Fehrenbach Prize of the Texas Historical Commission), and of various articles in scholarly journals.

JANET SCHMELZER, professor of history at Tarleton State University, is the author of *Where the West Begins: Fort Worth and Tarrant County* (1984), coauthor of *Texas USA* (1997), and author of several articles and chapters on Texas history. She is the past president of the Southwestern Social Science Association.

INDEX

Page numbers in italics indicate photographs.